The Paradox of Freedom

The Paradox of Freedom

A Biographical Dialogue

David Scott
Orlando Patterson

polity

Pages 23–213 were originally published as "The Paradox of Freedom: An Interview with Orlando Patterson," in *Small Axe*, 17/1 (40), pp. 92–242. © 2013, Small Axe, Inc. All rights reserved. Republished by permission of the copyright holder, and the present publisher, Duke University Press, www.dukeupress.edu

Pages 1–22 and 214–241 © David Scott and Orlando Patterson 2023

The right of David Scott and Orlando Patterson to be identified as Authors of this Work has been asserted in accordance with the UK Copyright, Designs and Patents Act 1988.

First published in 2023 by Polity Press

About the cover image: This series was commissioned by *Small Axe* for a project entitled "The Visual Life of Catastrophic History" with funding provided by the Andy Warhol Foundation for the Visual Arts. The prints were published in *Small Axe* 40, March 2013.

Polity Press
65 Bridge Street
Cambridge CB2 1UR, UK

Polity Press
111 River Street
Hoboken, NJ 07030, USA

All rights reserved. Except for the quotation of short passages for the purpose of criticism and review, no part of this publication may be reproduced, stored in a retrieval system or transmitted, in any form or by any means, electronic, mechanical, photocopying, recording or otherwise, without the prior permission of the publisher.

ISBN-13: 978-1-5095-5116-3
ISBN-13: 978-1-5095-5117-0 (pb)

A catalogue record for this book is available from the British Library.

Library of Congress Control Number: 2022945713

Typeset in 10.5 on 12 pt Sabon
by Fakenham Prepress Solutions, Fakenham, Norfolk NR21 8NL
Printed and bound in Great Britain by TJ Books Ltd, Padstow, Cornwall

The publisher has used its best endeavours to ensure that the URLs for external websites referred to in this book are correct and active at the time of going to press. However, the publisher has no responsibility for the websites and can make no guarantee that a site will remain live or that the content is or will remain appropriate.

Every effort has been made to trace all copyright holders, but if any have been overlooked the publisher will be pleased to include any necessary credits in any subsequent reprint or edition.

For further information on Polity, visit our website:
politybooks.com

ACKNOWLEDGMENTS

The original interview on which this book is based was conducted over a number of sessions between June 2010 and December 2011 in Cambridge, Massachusetts. It was first published in *Small Axe*, no. 40 (March 2013): 96–242. For the Polity publication, the interview was expanded and, where necessary, re-edited, between late January and May 2022. As ever, I am grateful to Orlando Patterson for his generosity and patience through the several sessions that constituted our long conversation and his willingness to respond to the additional questions I put to him for the republication. What I have learned through this process is beyond measure. I once more thank Catherine Barnett for her careful transcription of the original interview, Liberty Martin for her work on the revised and updated version, and Juliet Ali for help with the images.

David Scott

INTRODUCTION: ORLANDO PATTERSON AND THE PARADOX OF FREEDOM'S BIRTH FROM SLAVERY

David Scott

The Paradox of Slavery and Freedom

What is the relationship between domination and freedom? This is undoubtedly an old and tenacious question that haunts at least the archive of Western culture, where freedom is presumed to be a sacred value. More specifically, though, what is the relationship between *enslavement*, arguably the most extreme form of domination, and freedom? I mean here not only freedom thought of as a *civic* and *political* value but *moral* and *existential* freedom as well. What is the relationship between slavery and the individual *experience* of personal freedom? What is it to aspire to freedom as a value from a condition in which it is non-existent, in which freedom is violently withheld? Or, to put this a little differently, in order to highlight the sheer *novelty* of freedom as a positive value: What does it mean to live in anticipation or hope of, or longing for, a value of *non*-enslavement? Might there be a relevant sense in which the experience of freedom as a novel and incomparable and inextinguishable value depends precisely upon the *background* experience of its radical *deprivation* and *suppression*, and especially its deprivation and suppression in the experience of heritable enslavement? Are freedom and slavery perhaps more closely (if you like, *dialectically*) connected than has typically been thought? The historical story of freedom in Western culture is often told as though this anointed value grew out of the heads of Western intellectuals, especially from the liberal Enlightenment onwards, as though it was the achievement of an act of consummate White European intelligence. But it might well be wondered whether this isn't really no more than a familiar self-serving story – that is, the celebrated autobiography of White

1

THE PARADOX OF FREEDOM

liberal freedom. Is it worth considering whether slavery and freedom are not simply contingently and randomly connected but *integrally* and *internally* fastened to each other such that their traces and their shadows intermingle? And, if it is true that freedom is deeply and fundamentally intertwined with slavery, what are the moral and political implications for how we think of this most revered and sanctified of values, both for the past and for the present, both for the ruled and for those who rule?

In my view, though he might not have posed them in quite this way, these are the sorts of questions that have motivated and animated a significant dimension of Orlando Patterson's thinking for more than five decades. They are the sorts of questions that not only constitute a recognizable thematic in the subject matter of his work but register also, at a deeper level, I believe, a broadly recurring pattern or *motif* of preoccupation. I want to suggest that in a certain respect they point to a *pre-critical* intuition concerning the paradoxical relation between freedom and slavery. Part of what Patterson came to understand, I believe, perhaps only dimly and incompletely at first, but gradually and with sharpening illumination and a broadening archive, is that, coming as he does from a certain form of life, an historical society that has been shaped – fundamentally, and maybe even persistently, chronically – by the powers of colonial plantation slavery, namely Jamaica, he could discern, almost as a form of implicit, embodied knowing, the ways in which these momentous universal questions about freedom's origins and standing had a humble and poignant and also immutable particularity. (Indeed, we will see that, across the length and breadth of his work, the *problem* of the relationship between the "general" and the "particular" has necessarily been a recursive issue in Patterson's thinking.) Already in the archive of the Jamaican slave experience, he had formed an awareness of the need to *defamiliarize* our assumptions about freedom's self-evidence. For Patterson, Jamaica has always been distinctive in the history of New World slavery (not only distinctive in its barbarity, but distinctive also for being long devoid of elementary social cohesion), and, as wide or as global as his scholarly lens has become, it remains a comparative point of reference – and return.[1] In his hermeneutic itinerary, Jamaica is simultaneously the concrete ground of historical particularity and an instance of moral universality.

Patterson makes the point about the densely paradoxical relationship between slavery and freedom with subtle insight and personal allusion in the preface to *Freedom in the Making of Western*

2

INTRODUCTION

Culture, to my mind his conceptually most ambitious book. He writes:

> Originally, the problem I had set out to explore was the sociohistorical significance of that taken-for-granted tradition of slavery in the West. Armed with the weapons of an historical sociologist, I had gone in search of a man-killing wolf called slavery; to my dismay I kept finding the tracks of a lamb called freedom. A lamb that stared back at me, on our first furtive encounters in the foothills of the Western past, with strange, uninnocent eyes. Was I to believe that slavery was a lamb in wolf's clothing? Not with my past. And so I changed my quarry. Finding the sociohistorical roots of freedom, understanding its nature in time and context, became my goal, and remained so for these past eight years.[2]

I think, in a sense, that something about the very ethos – and, even, cast of mind – of Patterson's life's work is evoked in this complex passage. Uncannily, in the relentless scholarly attempt to grasp the nature and meaning of slavery as a mode of domination, in the historical specificity of Jamaica as well as in world-comparative perspective, Patterson has the disconcerting experience of persistently finding himself in the presence of freedom. How odd is that? How puzzling? But this freedom that stands there in the path, mocking his understanding of slavery, is not a pure and innocent virtue, a wholly untainted value. Rather, it has about it the ambiguous odor of an unwholesome and degraded origin. It is not, Patterson suspects, that slavery was other than he thought it was all along, a power of absolute bondage; it is not that slavery was masquerading in borrowed clothing, playing at what it plainly is not. Certainly, the lamb and the wolf are not identical. But they are not unfamiliar with each other either. What Patterson recognizes is that freedom is both more *and* less than it has been presumed to be in Western history; freedom has a more intimate and therefore more complex relation to slavery than has usually been taken to be the case in the idealized and teleological histories that characterize the West's autobiography. Patterson recognizes that freedom is a paradoxical and tragic value: the good of freedom is inextricably tied to the evil of slavery.

It is a very curious but also very well-known (if not very well-advertised) fact that historically, at least in those worlds written into the authorized story of Western culture, it is precisely in the great slave-owning societies that freedom emerged as a deep and profound and cherished value – among slave-owners and their backers and

THE PARADOX OF FREEDOM

ideologues, that is. Think of Cicero, the Stoic statesman and philosopher of virtue, duty, and *libertas* in ancient Rome whose freed slave, Marcus Tullius Tiro, would publish his former master's speeches and letters. But, closer in time and influence, think of the Englishman John Locke, in the seventeenth century, and the American Thomas Jefferson, in the eighteenth. The modern value of liberty that Locke and Jefferson proclaimed, and that *we* have inherited, depended on an asymmetrical structure in which White slave-owning men enjoyed its possession while their enslaved Blacks suffered its radical dispossession.[3] But is there, perhaps, another story of freedom, not so hegemonic as this one, in which the value of freedom emerges not simply from the powerful but from the powerless, not from the enslaver's abstracted experience but from the "social death" of the enslaved? This would be a *counter-story* in which the great idea of freedom comes to us not from the rarefied minds of free intellectuals but from the social suffering of the enslaved and the lowly militancy of antislavery struggles. This is the story Patterson aims to tell.

In this introductory essay, I have a relatively limited aim. I do not offer a comprehensive introduction to Orlando Patterson's life and work. That is largely the purpose of the text that follows, the biographical interview. My hope, of course, is that the interview will help to complicate our sense of the trajectory of Patterson's life and work, invite us to better discern the continuities and discontinuities that mark its still unfolding path, the provocations and motivations that drive its concerns, the sensibilities and sensitivities that animate its preoccupations – and perhaps, in so doing, help to minimize the simplifications and superficialities that too often characterize engagements with his work, whether those engagements are dismissive or embracing.[4] My more modest aim in this introduction is to suggest only an *orientation* to the paradox of slavery and freedom I believe is at the center of Patterson's work, and indeed has been in a foundational way. And, in order to do this, what I offer in the next two sections is a provisional map of an itinerary in his work that traces passages from an account of the *existential* birth of freedom from enslavement to the reconstruction of the *historical* birth of freedom from slavery in Western culture. In the last section I seek briefly to situate the text of the interview that follows within the project from which it emerges and the kind of understanding I believe the interview form encourages. I shall suggest that the content and the form of the interview are connected – that it is partly the interview's dialogical reconstruction of the successive *problem-spaces* that mark

4

INTRODUCTION

out Patterson's intellectual formation that enable us to discern the contours of the relationship between the existential and the historical birth of freedom from slavery.[5]

The Existential Birth of Freedom from Slavery

There cannot be many contemporary scholars, of any geopolitical provenance or literary and philosophic sensibility, who have appreciated Albert Camus more thoughtfully or more provocatively than Orlando Patterson. Indeed, the influence runs long and deep. Patterson's 1964 novel, *The Children of Sisyphus*, is a meditation on the absurd and suicide in relation to the abject social-racial conditions of the Black poor in early post-independence Jamaica.[6] Camus' *The Myth of Sisyphus* is clearly one of its influences. Patterson's novel is a reflection on the fundamental moral question that Camus invites us to ponder, namely: How should we judge whether, in the face of its mute exigences and impenetrable opacities, life is worth living?[7] The feeling of absurdity, Camus wrote, a mundane and not a philosophic awareness, arises out of the simple, irreducible fact that our lives and our worlds do not seamlessly correspond. The question is, does the ineradicable fact of the absurd dictate suicide or hope – or, again, *neither*, a way of living, like Sisyphus, with deliberate and stoic resignation? This is the question Patterson explores through his memorable characters Dinah and Brother Solomon and the absurd predicaments they earnestly navigate. Dinah is a prostitute trying desperately to escape the dead ends of her intractable circumstances, and Brother Solomon is a Rastafarian intellectual complicit in forging a false hope of deliverance among his followers. Neither, in the end, can evade the Sisyphean claim on them: Dinah, violently attacked on the very eve of her final, triumphant, escape, returns defeated to the neighborhood of her origins to die; and Solomon, having exhausted the means of sustaining the deception he has perpetuated on his expectant disciples, chooses suicide rather than face up to the implications of his actions.

Arguably, too, *An Absence of Ruins*, Patterson's 1967 metaphysical novel of intellectual despair and postcolonial rootlessness and disorientation, is trying to get to grips with a chronic condition of anomie and alienation of a sort that shapes Camus' *The Stranger*.[8] Camus' 1942 novella, remember, arid and monotone in mood, centers on the character Meursault, the strangely affectless French settler in colonial Algeria who, with seeming indifference, kills an Arab man

5

THE PARADOX OF FREEDOM

and is eventually executed for his crime. He seems a man without the quality of conviction, merely going through the motions of life, a man unable even to deceive himself into conventionally grieving at his own mother's funeral. Meursault, it appears, is a man whose life is a *question* he cannot answer, who intuits the absurd and senses he cannot escape its remorseless claim on him. Notably, in Patterson's novel, similarly restlessly, unsparingly barren in mood, his protagonist, named, suitably, Alexander Blackman, does not commit murder – though, in a cynical critique of cynicism, a self-deceiving attempt to undermine his deceptions and self-deceptions, he does fabricate his own suicide. Blackman, an intellectual recently returned to newly independent Jamaica to teach at the university, feels chronically at odds with the mimicry and bad faith of his fellow intellectuals, radicals no less than conservatives, but also at odds with himself and his own cruel, squalid dishonesty. He refuses the choice imposed on him: either a progressivist believer, on the one hand, or a conformist Afro-Saxon, on the other. What the language of belonging and freedom and purpose should be he does not – *yet* – know, and he lives somewhat adrift, like a castaway, in futile search of an authentic ground that would make the absurdity of his condition habitable, until, acknowledging his failure, he flees, once more, to London, the solicitous city of salvation.

If, in these works of Patterson, it is the dynamics of the absurd in Camus' early work that motivate the fiction, in other work it is Camus' *The Rebel* that is the real generative influence.[9] Readers of *The Rebel* will recall that this sometimes opaque philosophical essay bears a complicated, perhaps even impossibly embattled, relation to the earlier work on suicide and the meaning of life. Published in 1951, almost a decade after *The Myth of Sisyphus* (a work very much of the war years of the Nazi occupation of France), *The Rebel* intervenes in the post-war French debate concerning the legitimacy of violence, and political murder most especially. Patterson, it is true, is not necessarily uninterested in the question of the political justifications for violence – after all, the historiography of slave revolts, to which he has importantly contributed, brings this problem squarely into the historical picture.[10] But what specifically arrests his attention is the way, in *The Rebel*, Camus frames the question of the *moment of refusal* in the interminable cycle of domination. What precipitates the moral crisis in which a subjugated individual no longer "agrees" to be dominated, in which they no longer accept what has for so long been endured? *Here*, at the ontological level of Being, is Patterson's question. Still more crucial is the fact that at the figurative center of

6

INTRODUCTION

The Rebel is the image of the slave. It is through the condition of the enslaved that Camus, albeit in a metaphysical Hegelian idiom, figures the existential birth of freedom. "What is a rebel?" Camus asks, in the memorable opening sentences of his book. "A man who says no: but whose refusal does not imply a renunciation. He is also a man who says yes as soon as he begins to think for himself. A slave who has taken orders all his life, suddenly decides that he cannot obey some new command. What does he mean by saying 'no'?"[11] In the dialectic of *recognition* the book portrays, the emergence of the slave's consciousness of her slave condition is at the same time the emergence of her self-consciousness of the absurdity – and *wrongness* – of that condition. It is the beginning of the experience of *universality*.

In answering the question that he poses (the meaning of the slave's "no"), Camus describes a *borderline* beyond which the slave is not prepared to go, a moral-psychological *limit* beyond which she or he is unwilling to continue enduring the existing wrong. Up until this point, Camus says, the slave has remained "quiet and, in despair, has accepted a condition to which he submits even though he considers it unjust."[12] Then, somehow, the moment arrives when all at once the slave refuses to suffer any longer in abject silence. With newfound voice, she or he says *no* – and, thus, *rebels*. That *no*, however, is not merely a nihilistic act of pure negation. It is also, simultaneously, a vindicating act of *affirmation*, an implicit declaration that there is something worthwhile in her or him that will no longer stand being ignored, violated. In rebellion, the slave also says *yes*. As Camus writes of this moment:

> He rebels because he categorically refuses to submit to conditions that he considers intolerable and also because he is confusedly convinced that his position is justified, or rather, because in his own mind he thinks that he "has the right to ...". Rebellion cannot exist without the feeling that somewhere, in some way, you are justified. It is in this way that the rebel says yes and no at the same time. He affirms that there are limits and also that he suspects – and wishes to preserve – the existence of certain things beyond those limits. He stubbornly insists that there are certain things in him which "are worthwhile ..." and which must be taken into consideration.[13]

The event of rebellion, then, is a profound moment of *self-awareness*, a moment of dramatic self-recognition in which, as Camus puts it, there is, all at once, a perception that there is something in humanity

THE PARADOX OF FREEDOM

with which she or he can identify. In short, the rebel slave abandons the particularity that ties her or him to the imposed – slave – status and identifies with the *universality* of human being as such. For Camus it is the moment when "interest" gives way to "right." This is why, in his view, the act of rebellion has always to be *all or nothing* – because what has been denied by enslavement, namely, *respect*, cannot be repaired piecemeal but only in its immediate *totality*.[14] This feature of universality is also why, in rebellion, what the slave affirms is not a narrow individual self-interest but a value held in *common* with others, even with the perpetrators of the injustice of slavery.[15]

This is the sensibility that shapes Patterson's first monograph, *The Sociology of Slavery*, published in 1967, and also his third novel, *Die the Long Day*, published in 1972, a sort of fictive companion to the work of historical sociology.[16] For Patterson, too, the central animating figure in his moral sociology of the Black Americas is that of the slave, paradigmatically the Jamaican slave. Indeed, more specifically, Patterson, one might almost say, is haunted by the figure of the Jamaican *creole* slave. Born into the abjection of generations of perpetual enslavement (and so without the African slave's first-hand experience of freedom), and governed by the singular institutionalized powers of anomie and systemic violence of the slave plantation (and so without the African slave's prior context of social value), it is with the creole slave that revolt emerges analytically as a distinctive *existential* problem. As Patterson writes in *The Sociology of Slavery*, while most slave revolts in Jamaica through the late eighteenth century were organized by African-born slaves,

> in the last days of slavery even the creole slaves, who had never known what it was to be free, began to organize revolts against their masters, and the last and most damaging of all the rebellions remains a living memory of their struggle for something they had never experienced but for which they felt a need sufficiently strong for which to die.[17]

What accounts for this? How are we to understand the nature of the *decision* the creole slave makes in such circumstances to no longer accept their slave status and to risk life and limb for a value they have never known? The answer to these questions, Patterson suggests, is not to be found in quotidian material determinations or indeed in ideological ones – however important these are as shaping conditions. Something else is required. And here, invoking Camus, Patterson offers the phenomenological picture of the creole slave arriving at an existential crossroads where the burden of injustice

8

INTRODUCTION

has become simply unbearable, not in its brute weight so much as in its moral incongruity, because something has now been traduced, denied, *beyond* what was hitherto endurable. And this violation triggers an event of self-recognition wherein the slave "discovers a universal value" that at once "justifies and stimulates" an act of rebellion, or at least an act of rebellious refusal.[18] What matters to Patterson, therefore, is above all the *moral autonomy of self-determination* that, in the final instance, and born of that moment of simultaneous recognition and affirmation of universality, propels the slave into unprecedented and decisive and irreversible action.[19] It is hard to miss here the strains – however embattled – of a Hegelian phenomenology.

Memorably, it is *this* whole preoccupation that finds a poignant fictive form in Patterson's *Die the Long Day*. Having arrived at the limit of empirical sociological description, Patterson mobilizes the resources of realist literary fiction to explore the interiority of slave ontology, to think about the emergence of an existential threshold beyond which the enslaved will not allow themselves any longer to be shackled to subpersonhood, subhumanity. Notably, Patterson epitomizes this moment in the figure of Quasheba, an enslaved mulatto woman of striking character: strong-willed, defiant, self-possessed, sometimes bad-minded. It is in Quasheba, I would argue, that we see the first adumbrations of Patterson's later idea of "social death," the defining condition of the enslaved that comes to conceptual realization in *Slavery and Social Death*. Quasheba is the embodiment of natal alienation, of the precarity of personal and familial legitimacy and of parental authority, the vivid expression of a condition of impotence and dishonor. Her daughter, Polly, as headstrong as her mother, is the object of the sexual predation of the sickly slave master of a neighboring plantation. Quasheba, who has unsuccessfully pleaded her case to the overseer of her plantation, arrives at length at the drastic point at which she can see no option but to try to kill the offending slave master. She fails, as it happens, and her end is sealed. Now, significantly, Quasheba commits an act of attempted murder, not an act of participation in collective (political) rebellion. Quasheba is not Nanny of the Eastern Maroons. She has arrived, not at a social critique of the *system* of plantation slavery, but at the personal capacity to refuse the degradation, violation, and humiliation to which she has been subjected from the day she was born. Indeed, she has arrived not merely at the rejection of what she has been made into but at the positive *reappraisal* of her selfhood, and with this new perspective she cannot any longer continue as she was.

9

THE PARADOX OF FREEDOM

Quasheba claims for her wounded personhood the priority of an ontological or ethical universality. She is, as Jamaicans say, *smaddy*, somebody. As she admonishes her faithful but apprehensive lover, the ironically named Cicero (ironic because the Roman Stoic was not only a slave-owner but also an avowed humanist), who is urging her to remember her status and beseeching her not to pursue her determined course of action: "True me is a Neager. But me is human too and is only one time they can kill me."[20] This, for Patterson, is a passional moment of freedom's birth: out of the absolute bondage to which Quasheba has been subjected by plantation slavery, she has invented an idea of personal freedom; she has *redescribed* herself as the self-determining agent of her own actions. It is a momentous and revelatory occasion, even if, for Quasheba, a frighteningly fatal one as well. And the cost in her life she pays underlines how, for Patterson, freedom is a fragile and tragic value.

Still, there is another moment in *Die the Long Day* in which the problem of freedom emerges somewhat differently against the background of slavery. I am thinking here of the character Benjamin, the servile quadroon carpenter who, incongruously (or not), in the complex racial genealogies that characterized eighteenth-century Jamaica, is actually Quasheba's cousin.[21] Indeed, the contrast between the actions of these creole slaves couldn't be more different, and yet they are equally relevant for the relationship between slavery and freedom. Benjamin is portrayed as slightly pathetic, cravenly obsequious, endlessly in need of his oppressor's approval, but it is in the quality of his dishonored status and his corollary search for manumission – his legal release from bondage – that the whole predicament of the *hope* for, and *anticipation* of, freedom is vividly explored. (It is often forgotten that, for Patterson, manumission has always been understood as a crucial index of the character of any slave regime, and it plays an important role in the wider story of the birth of freedom.) The episode in *Die the Long Day* that interests me is the one in which Benjamin learns that he is to be allowed at last to purchase his freedom, and he has gone to the capital, Spanish Town, to celebrate the occasion with his friend, the rather philosophical and dissipated near-White free colored Jason, who lives above a tavern of ill repute run by his unnamed mulatto "wife."[22] Benjamin is understandably elated at his coming change of status. After all, freedom is a value he cannot *not* aspire to. But, even as he elaborately prepares to set out on what should be a joyous evening, he has a nagging worry that his happiness may be purely contrived, a cruel deception, and so he has to keep reminding himself, absurdly, of the certainty of

10

INTRODUCTION

his happiness: "He was happy. He had to be happy. How else does a man feel after being a slave all his life and suddenly discovering that he is free? How else but happy? How else ...?"[23] The question lingers. And Benjamin will soon enough find out the unwanted answer. He decides to share his news first with his White Methodist minister, but the visit badly misfires when he falls afoul of the prevailing racial-gendered etiquette, and he begins to find himself roughly "chastised by his new status."[24] But it is only when Benjamin shares the good news with Jason that the full implications of his new freedom are brought home to him.

Jason is not only drunk, he is brilliant and merciless, in a shocking but endearingly empathetic way. He feels for Benjamin's predicament; it is a mirror of his own. Jason tells the soon deflated Benjamin that, in reality, he is about to lose – to *sell* – one of the most "beautiful, simple guiding principles" of his life, namely, "the hope of freedom ... the wish, the dream of freedom."[25] Benjamin, an innocent soul, does not follow. He now *has* freedom, surely, he declares; he no longer has to dream, to hope, to live only the fantasy of freedom. Reluctant to completely shatter his illusions, Jason nevertheless drives home that this is precisely the paradoxical point he is making:

> So now you've got it there's nothing more to hope for. The dream is over. You've gone and sold the goose that laid the golden egg of hope. A slave waiting for freedom is like one of those devout early Christians who lived a little after your Christ died, waiting for his second coming. Now you've lost it. Now you're simply another one of us, lad. And there's the tragedy. That's why I mourn your freedom. Your God has come.[26]

But Jason is not done. Over Benjamin's weak protests, he lectures him on the uselessness of the freedom of the free coloreds, who have made, and can make, little or nothing of their vaunted status. The society has no use for them. In a plantation slave society, only the slaves and the masters have any practical purpose. The society accords free coloreds limited rights and protections and few advantages. Not only in its positive aspect but also in its negative dimension, Benjamin's freedom is virtually worthless. And finally, in a moving concluding gesture, Jason tells him:

> You are like a man buying a primed-up old mule. You are buying all the burdens of freedom and none of its privileges. You say you want to be responsible for yourself. Take my advice, friend, for God's sake.

11

THE PARADOX OF FREEDOM

There's no point being responsible if there is nothing to be responsible for. So you go back home, Ben. Go back to your cozy cabin and your work-shed. Until you are free to be somebody and to be what you know you want to be, it's better to be what you have to be. Go back and try to learn to dream again. Go back home and learn once more to hope for freedom. But this time, promise me, you'll hope for the real thing.[27]

As one might imagine, Benjamin is irretrievably devastated, mortified by Jason's speech. But something hard has registered about the absurdity of his social and moral conundrum, about the inescapable paradox of a free colored's freedom in the viciously binary world of racial slavery. Indeed, Benjamin returns to the plantation and immediately rescinds his request to purchase his freedom, much to his master's bafflement. The whole episode rings eloquently with the reverberating echo of Camus: the birth of the existential desire for, and anticipation of, freedom in a context where the experience of its realization is most poignantly and desperately devoid of actual possibility. To be sure, Benjamin is not the admirably defiant Quasheba whose claim to personhood is her claim to universality. But here too, for Patterson, in the structure of expectancy and longing Benjamin so poignantly embodies in the abject ambivalence of his bi-racial personality, is one of the birthplaces of the value of personal freedom.

The Historical Birth of Freedom from Slavery

While the existential story of freedom's birth from slavery in the specific historical context of Jamaica is told in the monograph *The Sociology of Slavery* and the novel *Die the Long Day*, the general and comparative-historical story of the birth of the value of freedom from slavery is told in *Freedom in the Making of Western Culture*, published in 1991 as volume 1 of a projected two-volume study simply titled *Freedom*. The second volume has not materialized. Almost as soon as *Slavery and Social Death* was published (in 1982), Patterson had begun to plot the ideas that would be central to the later work. *Slavery and Social Death* and *Freedom in the Making of Western Culture* are, in fact, profoundly interconnected books, the one laying out a general account of the nature of slavery and the other laying out a general account of the nature of freedom – the latter depends on the former. Moreover, though it is perhaps not typically read in this way,

12

INTRODUCTION

I believe *Freedom in the Making of Western Culture* is a *key* to understanding Patterson's body of work as a whole, a decisive moment in a single unfolding project driven by the dialectic of slavery and freedom. In a certain sense, this comparative-historical sociology of freedom from slavery closes the hermeneutic circle of Patterson's great exploration of the entangled relationship of these formative institutions that was opened in *The Sociology of Slavery*. Where this early monograph provided the working out of an intuition in the specific historical instance of Jamaica, *Slavery and Social Death* followed, and deepened and widened, the theoretical frame for thinking about the nature of slavery as such, as a system of domination, offering a conceptual idiom for naming and describing what slavery perpetrates on the enslaved. However, in the process of scaffolding this general, comparative work, Patterson discerns that slavery not only deprived and degraded the enslaved, not only produced natal alienation and social death; it also inspired in the enslaved a new, hitherto unheard-of value, namely, freedom. And, thus, the whole project of the social dialectic of slavery and freedom is realized in the last of the trilogy (as one might, in retrospect, call the series), *Freedom in the Making of Western Culture*. Arguably, *everything* about Patterson's consideration of freedom depends on how he *came* to the problem he explores; how it came to *him*. Needless to say, in what follows I am not going to rehearse the argument of this long book in any detail. I intend only to sketch enough to foreground the rationale for the historical dialectic of slavery and freedom it develops.

It is sometimes supposed that *Freedom in the Making of Western Culture* is little more than a Eurocentric paean to the West's achievement.[28] But this is mistaken. Michel Foucault may not be among Patterson's interlocutors, but, properly read, *Freedom in the Making of Western Culture* is a genealogy aimed at displacing the West's most cherished, normative assumptions about the sources and standing of freedom. What Patterson offers is a deeply perturbing redescription of the self-image of Western civilization in which its most vile and despised institution, slavery, is shown to be the fertile source and inspiration of its most honored and celebrated value, freedom. Far from being the pristine and heroic value it appears to be in its own autobiography, a value steadily improved and fine-tuned from the ancient Greeks and Romans to the philosophers of modern liberal democracy, freedom is really a tragic value forever haunted by the dark and violent shadow of its degraded origins. Indeed, the West's history of freedom, Patterson suggests, is a largely self-serving history empowered by *disavowal*. But, taken for granted though it so

13

THE PARADOX OF FREEDOM

smugly and effortlessly is, there is nothing self-evident in freedom's generalized esteem. "For most of human history," Patterson writes, "and for nearly all of the non-Western world prior to Western contact, freedom was, and for many still remains, anything but an obvious or desirable goal."[29] Other values have been venerated more, among them, valor, courage, belonging, piety, glory, honor, justice, and so on. In its "inverted parochialism," Patterson holds, the West has assumed that there was something lacking – wrong, backward, impoverished – in those forms of life that did not – or do not – recognize freedom's virtue. To the contrary, Patterson argues, "it is not the rest of the world that needs explaining for its lack of commitment to freedom ...; rather it is the West that must be scrutinized and explained for its peculiar commitment to this value."[30]

As Patterson makes clear, what he is after in *Freedom in the Making of Western Culture* is not an exercise in the history of ideas or one in moral and political philosophy – though both are certainly involved. The book is meant to be an "historical sociology of our most important cultural value" framed around the following questions: How and why was freedom initially constructed as a social value? And, once invented, how and why did it emerge as the supreme value, as a kind of meta-value? Why did this rise to cultural hegemony take place only in the West? And what forces maintained its status as the core value of Western civilization?[31] Patterson's basic argument, as he says, is that "freedom was generated from the experience of slavery. People came to value freedom, to construct it as a powerful shared vision of life, as a result of their experience of, and response to, slavery or its recombinant form, serfdom, in their roles as masters, slaves, and nonslaves."[32] The insight that slavery and freedom are connected, Patterson allows, is not itself entirely new. For the modern period, the insight is already embodied in the work of David Brion Davis and Edmund Morgan and, for the ancient world, in the work of Moses Finley, Max Pohlenz, and Kurt Raaflaub. What Patterson offers is a sustained argument for recognizing the paradoxical dialectic of slavery and freedom, and one that demonstrates the distinctive role of women in the rise and consolidation of freedom's value.

In characteristic fashion, Patterson starts off by offering a preliminary schema for thinking about the value. Freedom, he holds, is a triadic concept-value comprised of personal, sovereignal, and civic dimensions. Together they form a "chordal triad." In any given context, one or other of the elements or "notes" in the triad may strike more emphatically than the others. The chords developed

14

INTRODUCTION

separately, he maintains, but by the Age of Pericles in the fifth century BC they were identified as dimensions of a single, interconnected idea of freedom. Personal freedom refers to the sense, on the one hand, of not being constrained by another in pursuing one's desires and, on the other, that one can do as one pleases within the limits of another's desire to pursue their own objectives. Sovereignal freedom refers to the power to act as one pleases regardless of the wishes of others. And civic freedom refers to the capacity of adult members of a community to participate in its life and governance.

Part I of *Freedom in the Making of Western Culture* is concerned with the prehistory of freedom, the emergence of the *idea*, prior to the consolidation of the *value*, of freedom in the non-Western world. As Patterson argues, the existence of slaves in "primitive" social formations meant that, almost necessarily, an *idea* about freedom was bound to emerge. But, given the social and economic conditions, what could *not* develop was the *institutionalization* of this idea as a shared social value and common aspiration. "A value emerges, is socially constructed," Patterson writes, "only when a critical mass of persons, or a powerful minority, shares it and, by persistently behaving in accordance with it, makes it normative. Slaves by themselves could never have their aspirations institutionalized, being despised nonmembers of their masters' communities."[33] Freedom as a social value emerged only with the Greek city-states, and the account of this development is offered in Part II of the book. It is, of course, a long and complex story, and it maps a series of fundamental transformations in ancient Athens between the end of the seventh century and the early fourth century BC – transformations that include, *inter alia*, the creation of large-scale agricultural estates dominated by slave and ex-slave labor; the emergence of a large slave population that economically sustained the aristocracy; the invention of the democratic state; the discovery of rationality; and the social construction of freedom as a central value comprised of the chordal triad personal, sovereignal, and civic freedom. Of these transformations, Patterson argues, the development of large-scale slavery was the ground of all the others. He traces the distinctive role of women in securing the ideal of personal freedom and maps the emergence of freedom as an "outer" material value as well as an "inner" or intellectual and spiritual value. Part III focuses on the Roman Empire and what Patterson calls the universalization of the value of freedom. With Rome's "triumph over the Mediterranean and northern Europe," he writes, "the idea of freedom completed its conquest of the Western mind in both its secular and its spiritual aspects."[34] Part IV offers an account of the

15

THE PARADOX OF FREEDOM

place of Christianity as it emerged on the margins of the Roman Empire. What makes Christianity unique, Patterson argues, is that, of all the religions of salvation, the teachings of Jesus made spiritual liberation the foundational plank of its doctrine of deliverance from the forces of darkness. Central here, of course, is the story of Paul the Apostle, whose letters index a theology of redemption focusing on the process by which a suffering soul is released from spiritual slavery into the light of freedom. And, finally, Part V tells the story of freedom in the Middle Ages. Here, Patterson disputes the view that freedom was a negligible value during this period. To the contrary, he argues, "in the serf's yearning and frequent struggle for free status, and the lord's identification of his free status with honor and virtue," one can recognize the "valorization and idealization of freedom in medieval society."[35]

In the Coda that closes the book, Patterson stands back from the details of the historical sociology of the value of freedom from the degradation of slavery just concluded and offers something of a meta-reflection on the paradoxical moral implications of the story as a whole. Significantly (but perhaps not surprisingly, given the discussions of Aeschylus, Sophocles, and Euripides in Part II), it is an explicit idea of the *tragic* that shapes Patterson's picture of the paradox of freedom's emergence from slavery. He writes:

> The history of freedom and its handmaiden, slavery, has bruited in the open what we cannot stand to hear, that inhering in the good which we defend with our lives is often the very evil we most abhor. In becoming the central value of its secular and religious life, freedom constituted the tragic, generative core of Western culture, the germ of its genius and all its grandeur, and the source of much of its perfidy and its crimes against humanity.[36]

All three strands in the chordal triad of freedom – personal, sovereignal, and civic – are marked by an internal and, in fact, ineradicable tension between its vile and degraded sources and its radiant aspirations. Patterson, notably, is suggestively informed here by Martha Nussbaum's great book on the nature of the tragic in Athenian philosophy and literature, *The Fragility of Goodness*.[37] Readers of this book will recall Nussbaum's central argument that the excellence of the good person is always vulnerable to the vagaries of chance and fortune, like a fragile vine (in Pindar's well-known metaphor) always exposed to the contingencies of the elements. For Nussbaum, memorably, if also controversially, it is precisely this vulnerability

16

INTRODUCTION

that helps to constitute and nourish the excellence of the good itself.[38] Now, Patterson's intervention is less to disagree in any fundamental way with this view of the tragic than to subtly shift the emphasis in such a way as to offer a different picture of the intractable relation between good and evil. For him, it is not so much that goodness is fragile, which it clearly is, not so much that the good is always vulnerable to evil – for these formulations suggest too much that good and evil are *external* to each other, that evil comes from an outside to corrupt and subvert the unadulterated good. Patterson offers what strikes me as a more radical view, namely, that what we have learned to appreciate from the story just told is something more paradoxical – the "tragic interdependence of good and evil."[39] The evil of slavery and the good of freedom stand to each other not in a contingent relationship but in a *constitutive* one.

Here, then, is the *historical* arc of Patterson's book mapping the historical emergence of the value of freedom from slavery in Western civilization. It is a remarkable reconstruction any way you look at it, representing the digestion and organization (and indeed *reorganization*) of a vast archive of canonical literature over which a phalanx of professional experts seeks to exert interpretive control. The historical facts matter, of course, not least to an historical sociologist such as Patterson for whom the relevant data are bread and butter to his enterprise. And, as one would expect, there are those who remain unpersuaded by the book precisely as a work of historical reconstruction.[40] But, to my mind, this direction of criticism misses something vital in Patterson's undertaking. In my view, the framing genealogical doubt is as central as the historical reconstruction itself – if not *more* so. Whether or not, in the end, you agree with the complex details of the history Patterson recounts from the materials he assembles (of ancient Greece and Rome, of Christianity and the Middle Ages), it is the provocative critical force of his argument that is to me most important – the intuition that animates and motivates the critical revisionary ambition the work embodies. And, arguably, this ambition is to lift slavery, that degraded but pervasive social form, from its *conceptual* obscurity and to place it (with all the discomfort this entails) at the historiographical *center* of the making of the central value of Western culture – note, not simply at the historiographical center of the making of a Jamaican world, or even of a *modern* world, but at the center of the making of that vaster world of Western civilization itself. To think of freedom, as we are endlessly obliged to do, given its exemplary place in contemporary

17

THE PARADOX OF FREEDOM

life – personal, sovereignal, and civic freedom – is to at least tacitly acknowledge, implicitly invoke, the world-historical place of slavery as an institution, and of the enslaved (foundationally, the women among them) whose struggles against their natal alienation and social death made that value possible – indeed, gave that value its moral life. Those Jamaican slaves with whom Patterson began his intellectual journey – not least his vivid fictional characters Quasheba and Benjamin – are not merely exotic actors within a merely local drama in some peripheral and now irrelevant part of the former British Empire, but universal actors in a world-historical story that birthed the value of freedom in Western culture. *This* is Orlando Patterson's point.

Dialogical Generations, Intellectual Traditions, and Problem-Spaces

Thinking about Patterson's work in this way is, to me, inseparable from the arc of the interview that is the subject matter of the body of this book. It is therefore important to say something about this, something less about its content than its form, or, rather, the content *of* its form. The original interview with Patterson was conducted in his office at Harvard University, in Cambridge, Massachusetts, over a number of sittings between June 2010 and December 2011. It was then published in the journal of Caribbean studies I founded and edit, *Small Axe*, in March 2013.[41] The interview forms part of a larger project of interviews with Caribbean intellectuals aimed at mapping dimensions of what I call an anglophone Caribbean intellectual tradition. I have written about this work in some detail elsewhere and therefore will not rehearse here the entire scope of my concerns or argument.[42] Nevertheless, a number of features of the *process* and *point* are of some significance and bear repeating here, however briefly, in order to properly situate the interview that follows.

To begin with, all the major interviews I have conducted for this project have an expressly *biographical* form. They are, so to speak, intellectual biographies, albeit on a relatively small scale. What is the relationship, they ask, between the circumstances of a *life* and the itinerary of its *work*? This is the question that interests me – or, anyway, came to interest me as I gradually found my feet within this form of inquiry over the decade or so I labored at it. Specifically, the interviews aim both to follow the chronological arc of an individual life (as it is shaped by its familial, educational, social, cultural,

18

INTRODUCTION

economic, and political conditions) and to connect the course of that life with the emergence of a distinctive path of moral, intellectual, and political concerns. The effort, therefore, is clearly one of a certain kind of *contextualization*. But the contextualization offered here takes on a particular *form* and *orientation*, what I have previously referred to as the reconstruction of *problem-spaces*. In a shorthand, by a problem-space I mean the discursive conjuncture in which questions appear as questions demanding answers. Arguably, then, in a conventional way, I am aiming to simply build up a picture of, as I say, the relationship between the distinctive circumstances in which a life is formed and socialized and the intellectual paths it takes. However, the specific aim of the contextualization I have in mind is less to observe the *realized* directions of an intellectual itinerary than to explore the milieu of questions, conundrums, and predicaments to which this itinerary appeared as the best mode of response. What really interests me is how my interlocutors formulated the questions that came to preoccupy them, what the discursive and non-discursive sources were of the hermeneutic paths they pursued. And this interests me partly because the interviews are less contributions to an intellectual history (though there is that too) than an attempt to map the internal contours of an intellectual *tradition* – one to which, admittedly, I also belong. Indeed, the project of the interviews is to link a number of dimensions of temporal experience, including generations, memory, traditions, and criticism, in a conceptual whole. I think of each of my interlocutors as being situated within the temporal frame of a generation, connected in an overlapping way to earlier and later generations, whose experiences of presents, memories of pasts, and expectations of futures are in a constant dynamic tension with one another. The relationship among these generations is one of inheritance – an inheritance less of specific ideas and perspectives than of *complexes* of rival arguments over what is shared from a broadly common past.

Methodologically, the interviews obviously have a *dialogical* character. They naturally unfold in the back and forth of question and answer linked together in a steady and recursive hermeneutic rhythm. Obviously, too, the exchange with my interlocutors is not, properly speaking, a conversation. The attitude and tone of the exchange is more formal, more deliberate, more directed, than a casual conversation. And, as an interview, the *vector* of inquiry is rather more *one* way than the other. My interlocutors and I are not *reciprocally* probing the formations of each other's intellectual paths. And rightly so. There is something *I* want to know about the way

19

an earlier generation formulated their questions and pursued their concerns, because this will help me not only to understand how they came to do what they have done, and are doing, but also how I, in turn, have come to inherit the pasts I have inherited, and in the way that I have inherited them. Here again we are in the embrace of the idea of an intellectual tradition and the agonism of inheritance. Nevertheless, the dialogue allows for an engagement that is at once exploratory, provisional, and participatory. My interlocutor and I are not establishing propositional truths, making final statements; we are engaged in an exercise of question and answer that, while more or less staged and directed by me, is nevertheless relatively open-ended and therefore unpredictable and primed for novelty and surprise. And, even though the dialogue is not symmetrical, it is participatory and cooperative inasmuch as the questions and answers are codependent, feeding off each other in an ongoing process.

Finally, it should be clear that the exercise involved in the interviews is not one of *critique*. Indeed, the interviews I've conducted are precisely one way of *evading* critique – that is, at least of side-stepping an attitude that critique often cannot help but embody, namely, an attitude of *hubris*, of assuming a superior and omniscient reason, of knowing more and knowing better than one's interlocutor. On the one hand, as I have said, my concern in the exchange is not the attempt to discover a real truth below or behind my interlocutor's supposed self-serving discourse. I am not exercising an interrogative hermeneutic of suspicion. Certainly, I am not interested in finding fault with my interlocutor's claims or accounts or propositions. Nor, on the other hand, do I take everything I am told at face value. The interviews do not aim at agreement or consensus. I am not seeking to validate or celebrate or confirm or endorse the direction of intellectual life my interlocutor embodies. My objective, rather, is to challenge myself to listen and learn – and not in a passive but in an active way, in a probing, searching, but nevertheless *receptive* way. The interviews aim to practice a mode of *attunement* and critical awareness. My attitude, one might say, is shaped by a desire for an informed inheritance. And, therefore, my objective is, above all, clarification and elaboration, what I think of as the ongoing attempt to widen and deepen and complicate the contexts of intelligibility by which the pasts in their plenitude are made available to the interpretive present.[43]

It is primarily in relation to this conceptual orientation toward life and work that I have sought to think about the intellectual trajectory

INTRODUCTION

of Orlando Patterson. I would say that the exploratory biographical and dialogical character of the interview form I have described here enabled me to plot the outline of a kind of genealogy of the overlapping and successive problem-spaces in which, on the one hand, Patterson's life shaped his intellectual formation and, on the other, his intellectual formation refracted his life. I do not, needless to say, presume this to be a reductive or transparent relationship in either direction, that one can simply read off the meaning of his life in terms of his work, or his work in terms of his life. Still, a tangled, mutually interpenetrating connection is certainly involved, and one moreover situated in the broader context of an equally complexly tangled intellectual tradition (or several traditions together). So that, across the biographical arc of Patterson's productive life, one can discern the intermeshed network of factors animating the Caribbean – and, specifically, the Jamaican – intellectual tradition. Patterson belongs to a generation of Jamaican intellectuals (writers, artists, scholars, political actors), born between the late 1930s and early 1940s, whose lives are ineradicably shaped (differently, of course, depending on their social location) by the watershed unfolding of decolonization in the wake of the labor upheaval of 1938. The events of this iconic and emblematic year, the centenary of slave emancipation, made it almost unavoidable that, for this generation especially, the immovable center of the quest for a self-determining future of political and economic freedom would have to be framed by reckoning with, a critical working through of, the palpable and inescapable legacy of the slave past. Not surprisingly, then – from one thematic and interpretive direction or another, in one genre or another – the presence of the past of slavery has been the fundamental conundrum to wrestle with. The problem of the moral and material trace of slavery is an intractable inheritance and, in consequence, also an unending – and unendingly rich and unresolvable – debate within the Jamaican (and Caribbean) intellectual tradition.

How and when Orlando Patterson entered this contentious debate, the archives he mined and the materials he mobilized, the perspectives he adopted and those he rejected, the arguments he pursued and those he critiqued, and the itinerary he followed as one thing led to another over the course of his life, is a story I have wished to grasp and document as part of a story of intellectual traditions. As we will see, as is the case with a number of his generational predecessors and contemporaries, Patterson's intellectual life has been an exploratory one, always looking for the register in which to best capture the historical and moral reality he seeks to articulate: the essay, the

21

THE PARADOX OF FREEDOM

novel, the monograph, all have functioned as complementary or supplementary ways into the lifeworlds that have commanded his attention. As we will see, also, there are notable continuities as well as discontinuities in what he has pursued and how. But, above all, what I have wanted to track in the interview that follows is the hermeneutic *movement*, as C. L. R. James might have said,[44] of Patterson's journey: how the specific and immediately familiar level of the historical study of slavery in Jamaica (represented by *The Sociology of Slavery*) prompted the demand for a wider, more generalizable conception of slavery (as articulated in *Slavery and Social Death*); how, out of the vantage secured by these pursuits, there grew the recognition and the conviction that what needed to be brought into focus was not in fact slavery but freedom, or, rather, freedom's paradoxical relationship to slavery (as recounted in *Freedom in the Making of Western Culture*); and, finally, how, after a long and complicated detour of life and work, no moment of which could have been known in advance, there is a return to Jamaica (in *The Confounding Island*) to think the contours of its comparative specificity. Here is the arc of Orlando Patterson's as yet unfinished life's work in all its subtle interconnectedness and rooted and *routed* complexity.

THE PARADOX OF FREEDOM

A Mother's Project

David Scott: To begin with, Orlando, where in Jamaica were you born, and when?

Orlando Patterson: I was born in Savanna-la-Mar, Westmoreland, on 5 June 1940. My parents were actually living in a little town outside of Sav-la-Mar called Grange Hill. My father was the detective there, and my mother – eventually she became a seamstress, but I don't think she was working at the time.

DS: So, you were born in Sav and you lived in Grange Hill?

OP: Not for very long; eventually I think we moved into Sav. I was there when I was an infant but I have no recollection of it.

DS: Where did you grow up?

OP: My parents split up when I was about two years old (after a long separation they came back together). So, the dawn of consciousness for me would have been Kingston. My mom and her sister both left the fathers of their children and went to live – all three sisters – in Kingston.

DS: What year would that have been?

OP: That would have been 1942 or so. My earliest memories are of Allman Town, Kingston, in 1942, 1943, when I was about three – in the middle of the war.

DS: Brothers and sisters?

OP: Half-brothers and -sisters. My father was much older than my mother. He was born in 1897. With his first wife he had six children.

THE PARADOX OF FREEDOM

They were almost as old as my mother was. In fact, the eldest one was, I want to say, a year or so younger than she was. Which made for a complicated relationship, as you can imagine.

DS: That's your father's side. What about on your mother's side?
OP: I was my mother's only child, which was very important. I wouldn't be sitting here with you if it weren't for that fact.

DS: Why do you say that?
OP: Because I'm convinced that one of the main factors accounting for success, especially among children from working-class backgrounds, is simply the amount of time they're exposed to adults. It's as simple as that, and it's something I want to explore: the relation between success and how much attention one has received from caregivers. If you're an only child, especially with a very ambitious mother who was very attentive, just think about it, the adult exposure is just enormous, compared to, say, being one of six children whose parents are working.

DS: So, not only were you an only child, but your mother was *devoted* to you.
OP: Yes, I was her *project*.

DS: In a very self-conscious way, it sounds. You say it as though it was something she *deliberately* committed herself to.
OP: Yes, in a very self-conscious way, which I was aware of from early. She more or less invested *all* her ambitions in me. Because I think she felt she hadn't lived up to her expectations of herself, and certainly the expectations her parents had of her.

DS: Is she still alive?
OP: No, she died in 2002, at the age of eighty-four.

DS: And your father?
OP: He died quite a while back, in 1969.

DS: When your parents split up, did you keep in contact with your father?
OP: Not much. He remained in Sav, and as a detective he was sent around. He was all over the place. He remained in Sav for a while, then he was in Falmouth, and then eventually he ended up in Kingston. As one of the few "native" detectives, he was kept very

24

A MOTHER'S PROJECT

busy by the colonial police force and there are numerous references to him in *The Gleaner*, dating back to the late 1920s.[1]

But in fact, between the ages of two and eleven, sort of the classic period of childhood, I was essentially an only child being brought up by a single mom. Then they came back together. For her, I was the main reason for their reconciliation. I had to go to high school, and he was important in that.[2]

DS: What were their names, your mother and father?
OP: My mother was Almena, shortened to Mina; her maiden name was Morris. My father was Charles Patterson. He was one of the first Black persons to make the grade of "detective" in the colonial police force in Jamaica. As I said, he was born in 1897, so he came of age in about 1920, a teenager even earlier, in 1916. He fought in the First World War. And he would have overlapped in the constabulary with Claude McKay.[3] I never asked my father if he knew him. He would have been his contemporary; it would have been about the same time. I would say, in terms of innate intelligence, he was extraordinarily smart to make that grade in the colonial police force.

DS: Did he have to go for special training?
OP: I don't think so. But he had gone through some post-elementary schooling. He had done the training for the constabulary force, and they must have recognized his special talent. He had one especially interesting talent. Remember, this was the age before the tape recorder. And he was phenomenally good at shorthand. He claimed that he had the highest speed of anyone ever tested in Jamaica! He was virtually a walking tape recorder, the closest thing to that. His notes were quite amazing. And, as a result of this skill, when Marcus Garvey was deported back to Jamaica in 1927 the colonial authorities assigned my father as a detective to tail him.[4] They were scared to death of Garvey. The government had him watched. They wanted to get him on sedition from his speeches, and my father was assigned to take charge and note what he said.

DS: Is this something your father told you, or something you learned later?
OP: He never did tell me about that part of it. I learned about it later and have evidence of it because I have all the notes. Meticulous notes. But a fascinating thing happened to him. He was always a thinking man, and a big PNP [People's National Party] supporter from early. And in the course of listening to Garvey and tailing him,

25

he became radicalized by Garvey and thought that he was saying a lot of good things. Which deeply annoyed the authorities, because he wasn't coming up with anything that they could use. And he kept telling them, "Well, he's not saying anything seditious." And I think he got into a little trouble as a result. He came under suspicion. Then he became even more radicalized, as he got involved with the PNP. He was a big PNP man and a union man. He started to unionize the police. He claimed he was one of the main founders of the Jamaica Police Federation.[5] And this was a no-no with the colonial authorities. But he continued with this, and eventually they booted him out of the police force. He sued and eventually won his case. But they never promoted him. In many ways he was a policeman with the attitude toward law and order that policemen have. It was very unfair not to have promoted him, because he was a very good detective. He was on several major crime cases in Jamaica; he solved several well-known cases and was well known in the police force. I remember as a young person going around Jamaica saying to people in the police force, "I am Charles Patterson's son," and they would know him because he was the person who started the police federation.

But the Garvey thing is fascinating. He never told me about the work he had done; I only discovered this later. But what I do recall, after my mother and father came back together, is that in his little library there was a first edition of *The Philosophy and Opinions of Marcus Garvey*. And I remember reading that book; in fact, it was one of the earliest political books I read. There were two books he had in his library that must have been strong influences on him: one was *The Philosophy and Opinions of Marcus Garvey* and the other was *Black Metropolis* by St Clair Drake.[6] How he got *Black Metropolis* I don't know, but those two books were in his library along with all his lodge books. He was a very big lodge man. The Garvey book and *Black Metropolis* I used to read as a young teenager.

DS: You speak of your father with warmth and even admiration. So, you had a good relationship with him?
OP: No, that's incorrect. This is just me speaking retrospectively. We *didn't* get along, because he had the authoritarian manner of a policeman. And I grew up during the classic period of childhood with my mother, who was pretty strict, but we worked on our relationship. As a single woman with a son whom she was very determined to see succeed, she not only gave me a lot of adult attention, but she treated me almost like an adult companion. We would talk about things. I

A MOTHER'S PROJECT

knew all about our finances; I'd help with them. And she never hid anything from me. Difficult times, I'd know about them. She would read a lot to me, and then, from about age seven or so (by which time I could read very well), one of my tasks was to get *The Gleaner* and read to her while she was sewing.

DS: You had a very intimate relationship with your mother.
OP: Yes, it was *too* close almost, because she was a very strong personality.

DS: This would have been interrupted in some respect by your parents' reconciliation.
OP: I couldn't abide his authoritarian manner. And, of course, I had had eight years in which my mother didn't have very nice things to say about him anyway. And so, by the time he came back I had a thoroughly negative view of him. It was kind of hard, their coming back together. And, what's more, I knew she was doing this mainly for me. Because I'd gotten into Kingston College [KC], and even though I got what they called a scholarship (because we had to do an exam to get in), you still had to pay fees. I remember the surprise my parents had at this, because the amount of money involved wasn't enough to cover the total cost of going to KC. Each parent had also to contribute – they called it "fees," which was still significant for a single person. It was like twelve pounds per quarter.

DS: And in those days your mother worked as a seamstress.
OP: Yes, she supported herself like that. She was a very, very strong-willed person, sometimes to the point of recklessness. Like she would move from one town to another. When I was five, she was living with her sisters, Mavis Hibbert and Myra Morris, and she decided to move. All three of them were good dressmakers, trained, and so on, but there were too many in one location. One of them had to go, and she decided *she* was going to go. So, she packed up and went to Lionel Town, where she had a friend. But to do something like that was a little extraordinary, to just move everything and start from scratch. And that's when I started infant school. I went to Alley Infant School. This was in a place called Alley, which was about 3 or 4 miles outside of Lionel Town, in the cane fields almost, where Monymusk is.[7] It's a little place down there, right by the Rio Minho river, with a church, and it's called Alley. A little village. There was a very good school there. I've been lucky. It was time to go to school. I was four or five. And my mother had tried several infant school arrangements.

27

THE PARADOX OF FREEDOM

There was the private one, which I went to, and after a few days I left. I just literally left and came home.

DS: You mean, on your own, at four or five years old?
OP: Yes. And this is an interesting reflection of the kind of relationship I had with my mother. She could be very strict, and she spanked, and so on. But when to her amazement I came home, and she asked, "What are you doing here?" and I said, "This teacher is no teacher at all because instead of teaching us she is washing her clothes," my mother just laughed. What could she do? At first, she was outraged because this was not a school – the woman was washing her clothes. Her reaction was interesting: "Yes, you're right, that's not what I'm paying for." Then I got placed in the public school. I would have been about five then. They were taking people in but not until they were six or so, but my mother was able to persuade them that I was ready to go. By then I could read. But I hated that school. And I felt that the teachers were hopeless and the place was too crowded. I refused to go to that school, too. So then she said, "Okay, I've heard about a great little infant school in Alley." I think she knew the teacher there; she must have pulled some strings and got me into that infant school, which I loved. It was remarkably progressive. They had clay work. And I loved the teachers, who were very kind – no straps. In the other two schools, the teachers went around with straps hitting the little kids. At Alley the teachers were very caring, and I loved them. I don't know how it happened, but I remember the clay work; I remember the slates; I remember all the things we played with; I remember the fact that all the teachers were very caring; and all the books – like *Percy the Chick*, which was a famous reader from Britain. So, finally, this was the school I liked. But then, the problem was first to get me down there because I lived 4 miles away.

DS: Four Jamaican miles. And your mother worked from home.
OP: Yes. She had set up her business, put up her dressmaking sign. Each day I had to go back and forth, and she arranged with a teacher for me to ride on the back of her bicycle. But the teacher after a while complained that it was too difficult. Then she arranged for me to board with some people: the Marsdens. I lived with them. That was a very happy time. Because this was a family that had about four kids and they were all a little older than I was, and I just loved it. We had a wonderful time. We lived on the Monymusk sugar estate. The father was a foreman there, and he had this nice little bungalow with a screen around it, and all these huge bags of grapefruit from the estate.

28

A MOTHER'S PROJECT

And you could eat all the cane you wanted, because, literally, the cane fields came right up to the backyard. You could just walk in and cut the cane. It had a very, very strong impact on me because of the family. So, while I missed my mom, I had a good relationship with this family. And down the path, going straight into the cane fields, it opened into an Indian village. Indian immigration did not work very well in Jamaica; about 6 percent of the Jamaican population was Indian at that time; and this was one of the places in the district of Vere where there was an Indian settlement. The entire village was Indian. I remember walking down there occasionally to buy things from the Indian shop and seeing people making roti and things like that. It was an incredible experience. And then, walking down for a mile or so, you'd get to Rocky Point, which was a great little beach. I really loved it; for me it was idyllic. And it was a good start, educationally. I learned to read and write properly; before that my mother taught me. I was already able to read basic things, but then I learned to write. It was a wonderful start. I came to love school.

DS: And you stayed at Alley school until when?
OP: For about two years until I was seven. And then my mother decided that Lionel Town was just not the right place to bring up a kid, or for her business. And we packed up again and moved to May Pen. It was nothing like it is now; it was just a little town. My mother set up and established quite a good practice. May Pen was the town where I basically grew up. I went to May Pen Elementary School, when teacher Edgar Whiteman was the headmaster (his son, Burchell, a former politician, is two years older than me, though I do not recall him being at the school). I went right through elementary school there, from age seven through eleven.

DS: What is most memorable to you about the May Pen of that period?
OP: I have mixed feelings about it, because I remained very close to my mother's sisters, who were in Kingston – and my mother of course remained very close to them. May Pen is not the prettiest part of Jamaica. If you had to find one *un*pretty part of Jamaica, you'd go to May Pen. It was in the middle of Clarendon, and it was hot and dusty. There wasn't much going on there. There was the clock tower; there was Clarendon Theatre, and another little cinema called Little Magnet that looked like a shed. There wasn't much else. The thing about that town is that it was a market town. It came alive on Thursday nights and Fridays, with country people (we call them

THE PARADOX OF FREEDOM

"peasants" now) coming in. And May Pen market was the place for the entire area, one of the biggest in the country. They'd come from as far as Manchester. The town simply doubled in size as people came in. I loved it *then*. But my mother was a funny woman. She was not someone who had a lot of friends herself, and I was on my own a lot. That's what I remember, often being *not* with her. I had some friends, and I'd meet them and then come back home and read. Either read for her or read for my own pleasure. But I was on my own a lot. I tell my kids I made my own toys; I spent a lot of time making them. I knew all the cabinet shops around, and I'd collect scraps of ply board and pick up the nails and make toys, kites, gigs [spinning tops], toy trucks, knitted balls for cricket, bats from dry coconut boughs, that kind of thing. And if I wasn't doing that, I was in the woods shooting with my slingshot. So I spent hours and hours and hours alone. She let me go off; she didn't know where I was. I had a fair degree of independence. She'd just tell me when to come back home.

One interesting thing about my years at May Pen Elementary School that I came to realize only recently was that my favorite reggae singer, the great Toots Hibbert of Toots and the Maytals, went to the school at the same time that I did. He was only about a year younger than I am and grew up in the Treadlight district of May Pen, which is less than a mile from Bryants Crescent where I lived. Our paths must have crossed many times in the schoolyard. I may even have played marbles or cricket with him, since, once a game started, anyone could join.

DS: You said earlier, Orlando, that growing up you had a distinct impression that you were your mother's *project*. How did that sense of your mother's commitment get communicated to you?

OP: Well, she made it clear. She was quite explicit about the fact that she was investing a lot in me. I had to be grateful. And one way of being grateful was to do well at school. She wasn't wasting her time or her money. I was aware from very early that she had to *find* money for me.

DS: It was an *effort*.

OP: It was an effort to find money to buy books and so on. But she always went out of her way to make sure that I had my school uniform, my books, and my shoes, and that I was always cared for. Even at the expense of herself. But she made it clear that this was something *reciprocal*. She was doing her part, which was to sacrifice (she was a very devout Christian and dealt with it in terms

30

A MOTHER'S PROJECT

of "sacrifice"), and my end of the bargain was to do well. And I knew from very early also that, in a country without any insurance or anything like that, I'd have to look after her when she got old. She wasn't a perfect person, because she was almost too explicit about this and sometimes would become quite threatening. "If you don't do well, look, I might have to take you out of school and send you to trade school." That was the ultimate threat! "You're going to go to *trade* school." Because, from very early, she had plans for me to go to a *grammar* school, which was quite extraordinary, given that even middle-class people had a low percentage of their children going to grammar school – 1 or 2 percent. The middle-class kids would go to Clarendon College; but Clarendon College wasn't part of her plan. And she told me once that she got into a lot of trouble with people who thought that she was just too uppity: "Who does she think she is?" I remember every morning, early, I'd see the kids going off to catch the "Kalamazoo." Do you know what that is?

DS: A bus, I presume.

OP: It was a single-car train. ... Do you know where Clarendon College is? It's up in the woods, near Chapelton. I don't know why they had it so deep in the woods and not somewhere closer to May Pen. But there was a single coach that was like a school bus, and kids from May Pen would get it in the morning and it would take them there. They called it the "Kalamazoo," for what reason I don't think I ever asked. But I thought, *Wow, this is very exciting!* These were all middle-class kids who had to pay – very well-dressed kids. And my mother decided, *No*, that I was going to go to KC. And she even said to me that several people stopped talking to her because they thought she was just excessive in her ambitions. But, anyway, she had in mind that I would go to a prestigious high school and eventually look after her. As I said, she wasn't subtle about that. That was quite clear. And therefore, if I didn't do well, she would get quite mad with me.

DS: Why did she select Kingston College?

OP: Partly because she thought it was the best in the country, but also because she was an Anglican. She was a devout Anglican, and KC was *the* Anglican school. Bishop Percival Gibson, my headmaster, also moonlighted as the suffragan bishop of Kingston (or the other way around) through most of my school years.[8] He was the first Black person to make bishop in Jamaica – the first *really* Black person. So, ordinary Jamaicans were inordinately proud of him. And, you see, I was lucky in that regard, because my father was more typical

31

THE PARADOX OF FREEDOM

in his authoritarian petit bourgeois policeman attitude. He felt that the thing to do was not to get your kids too uppity. The thing to do was to get all of them to gain a skill. His other children all did practical things, *all* six of them. Obviously, there were good genes on his side, because they were all quite bright. It's significant that every one of them ended up with professions, but they started out going to Kingston Technical High School. You know about Kingston Tech?

DS: Yes, of course.
OP: It was hard to get in, very hard to get in. But you know what the trajectory was?

DS: It's a vocational school. But your mother wanted you to go to a grammar school. That's the distinction.
OP: How she knew that distinction, *that's* the interesting mystery. Because you had to have a certain level of sophistication to know that – to think in those terms rather than the obvious ones. Kingston Technical was a greatly respected school. When she threatened "trade school," she was thinking about Alpha or someplace like that.[9] Given the fact that she was someone with only a primary school education, where she got these ideas from, I really don't know. It could have been through the church, it could have been from reading the newspaper, but, whatever, she was aiming for the very top.

DS: What was the scholarship that you won to Kingston College? And where were you at that point?
OP: At the time, hardly anyone went to high school. Like I said, a few kids went to Clarendon College. And the thing that ambitious working-class kids did at the time was to participate in a system called "first year," "second year," and "third year" exams. We're going way back in Jamaican educational history now. It was a fascinating system that the British set up, a version of "each one, teach one" that involved taking these exams. The "first year" was in fifth class [form], and, when you passed that, you then stayed on and became a monitor. Straight out of grade school, you were a teacher's aide! And while you were a teacher's aide, you'd take your "second year" and finally your "third year" exams. Actually, it was a very efficient system because, essentially, what you're doing is taking the brightest kids who are graduating from grade school and giving them the equivalent of three years of high school. And you got weeded out. If you failed the first year, that was it. You went and cut cane! And if you passed the third year you then went to Mico or one of the

32

A MOTHER'S PROJECT

other teacher training colleges.[10] But, of course, my mom was totally snobbish about that route and would say, "There's no way mi pickney goin' turn pupil teacher." She wouldn't even allow me to entertain the idea. I was all ready to do that. Instead she had me doing after-school classes. I would go home, get a snack, and then head to Miss Palmer's house. Now who was Miss Palmer? Miss Palmer was a teacher, a very good teacher. And my mother basically did a barter arrangement with her. She would sew for her, and in exchange Miss Palmer would have me in her little extra lessons class. She'd have about five kids, and I had an extra two hours with her. Then I'd come home, have my dinner, and do my homework. That's what my mother did instead of having me prepare for these teacher's exams.

DS: And then there was a scholarship that you applied for?
OP: Then, we had to do the exam to get into KC. I prepared for that. You went up to Kingston and I remember staying with my father's family. It was the first time I met them, and I didn't care much for them. We did this exam. And later we got a letter. How well you did would determine how much of a scholarship they were going to give you. I got a letter saying, "Congratulations, you did very well, and all you're being asked to pay is just fees" – they weren't *school* fees, but they called them *fees*.

DS: But not room and board.
OP: Room and board you had to find, but that was okay. I would stay with my aunt. Essentially, the most important thing, which really got my mother, was that they started this ruthless training from the very beginning. They informed her that I did very well, and they were putting me in the very highest class. There were 2A1 and 2A2, which were the top groups, and then there were the B stream and the C stream. They informed my mother that I was in 2A1 and that I was getting the very best deal they could offer. The way they explained it later on was that the government paid most of the fees and the church paid another part of it. And we supplemented it with fees. So, anyway, I went to do the exam and got in. I don't think there's anything quite like this anymore, but May Pen Elementary School was basically just one huge shed covered with zinc (actually corrugated iron sheets), and the classes were divided by the blackboard in the corridor. Now, you know how noisy kids are. Right up to fifth class this was the arrangement in this huge, hot shed. And then in the fifth and sixth class there was a space between them, a wall. But that was it. But, give credit where

THE PARADOX OF FREEDOM

credit is due, there were some good, dedicated teachers in May Pen Elementary. Miss Palmer was one of them. She would encourage my mother to have me take these lessons and told her where I might have problems. But as you went through the school, something interesting happened. First of all, on Fridays the class size always went down because the kids on the farms stayed home. By the time you reached age nine or so, the class size went down because they'd just take them out of school entirely. By the time you got to the fifth class it was down to the reasonable size of about thirty or so. And by the time you got to sixth class, the size would have been about twenty-five to thirty, which was small compared to what you had started with. The average size of the classes for the entire school was about eighty.

DS: Good God! In those terms, then, Kingston College was a radically different experience.
OP: Totally – absolutely, completely different. It was just like night and day.

DS: What year did you start Kingston College?
OP: I went there from 1952 until 1958. Did my Junior Cambridge (the equivalent of O-levels) in 1956 and my Senior Cambridge (A-levels) in 1958. Because the results of the Senior Cambridge exams took so long to be returned – they were all marked in England – it was too late to go to college the same year as when the exams were taken, so I went to UC [University College of the West Indies] the following year.

DS: Were there teachers at KC, besides Bishop Gibson, who made a particular impression on you?
OP: Oh yes. But I should point out that Gibson had an amazing impact on everybody. Because he *did* teach; he taught me Latin. But I'd like to point out the impact of this man. We called him Priest, all of us. He dressed in his robe, his bishop's purple robe. It was very dramatic. He was a little guy, very compact. I have to say that this was when I discovered the nature of *authority*. Like all tropical schools, it was noisy. And KC at that time was just one two-story building. Just *one*. It's bigger now. Bishop Gibson had his office at one corner. There was a lot of noise. And if you stood outside, from time to time, you would suddenly hear a quiet mumbling. Then complete quiet. And what essentially was happening was that Bishop Gibson would get out of his office and stroll down the hallway. Then

34

you'd have total silence. The silence would trail him as he walked down the upper corridor, then the lower one and back up to his corner office. And as he walked away the noise would build back up again. We really were in *awe* of him. Here was a Black Jamaican *in charge*. He was also the bishop of Kingston. But Kingston College was different in the classroom – there were only twenty to twenty-five students. And it was based on real British school lines. You went to chapel every morning. So, it was a *transformation*.

But to return to my childhood in May Pen, there was one very important event that took place there when I was about eight or nine. There was a place called Muir Park, which was where they played cricket, soccer, and so on – the local town park. It had a pavilion. And under the pavilion they decided to build a little library. The library service arrived one day, and I remember a few years ago telling Joyce Robinson, a former director of the Jamaica Library Service, what a strong impression that day had on me.

DS: This would have been promoted by Jamaica Welfare, which was started by Norman Manley.[11]

OP: Yes. So, one day the builders came and built this little one-room library underneath the rafters. And I remember the first day we were told about this whole new concept of "the library." They said you could go there and borrow books. *Borrow* books? You mean you can go into a place and they'll allow you to take books out? And we said, but won't people *steal* all the books? And I remember the first day, the whole school lined up to go to the library, because the concept was such a novel one. Then the lines got shorter and shorter. By about a couple of months on, there was no line. And so, I found myself going to this place with the smell of brand-new books, and I could take any book I wanted. It was amazing! I used to go there and read and read and read. The librarians used to joke about it. *Borrow* books! That was a *transformative* experience. I just read. Instead of shooting birds or swimming in the Rio Minho River, I'd go to the library. I loved the place. It was such a nice, quiet space.

Years of Decolonization

DS: With the emergence of the idea of the public library, and the distinctiveness of Bishop Percival Gibson in the background, it's clear you grew up in an especially momentous period in Jamaica's political development – these are the years of formal decolonization. How did

THE PARADOX OF FREEDOM

this history enter your awareness as a young adolescent at Kingston College?

OP: Well, before I was an adolescent it had entered my awareness in quite a direct way, because my mother was quite a radical. She was also a staunch PNP person. She and my father shared that (and they may well have come back together on that basis). She was politically active. She did canvassing, and I'd go with her. She'd get up early in the morning, before I went to school, to get the people before they went to work. She'd go with her little party leaflets. And, of course, I did everything with her; I went around hearing her encouraging people to vote. I'd take a bag with pamphlets. This would have been 1949, the island's second parliamentary elections. The PNP lost, even though they'd won the plurality of votes. My poor mother was devastated.

DS: In your memory, how did she talk about what was valuable about the People's National Party as opposed to the Jamaica Labour Party [JLP]?

OP: They were just the pits, Busta's party; that was (she had her prejudices) the old-*nayga* party. It was backward. Alexander Bustamante, she said, is only talking about food and old clothes.[1] My mother sang as she worked, and she taught me all the PNP songs, and obviously this had an indelible impact on my political consciousness. Her basic dialogue was that these people were just interested in Black people remaining workers and having handouts. And one of the PNP slogans was that the JLP was simply getting old, secondhand clothes from people and handing them out. And one of the PNP songs, which I used to sing as a nine-year-old (and all the grownups would laugh) went, "Old clothes government / Old clothes government / Ah wha me do you?" I remember those lines. The argument was that they were fooling up the people, giving them handouts, whereas the PNP was the party of progress and education. That was what impressed her: this was the party of education and progress. That was also my father's view; but it was *strongly* her view.

DS: Would you say that *that* context shaped a new kind of horizon for you?

OP: Absolutely. And not long after I was very tied up with the thought of going to high school, and Bishop Gibson, and the Anglican Church. She painted the Anglican Church as very much a progressive one. In her mind these were the heroes: Norman Manley and Bishop Gibson.

DS: It was the beginning of the *new* Jamaica.

OP: Exactly. Education was the central thing, and better jobs – but better middle-class jobs. *Not* trade jobs. Bustamante's party was for people in the cane fields; because the BITU [Bustamante Industrial Trade Union] started in the cane fields. So, she associated the JLP with manual laborers, whereas the PNP stood for education, better housing, urban life, and the new Jamaica where the people would be taking over.

DS: The election years 1944 (the first under adult suffrage) and 1949 would have been seriously disappointing election years for her, then.

OP: When they lost, oh God, yes! Absolutely!

DS: Did she think there was something misguided about the PNP's approach, or did she think that it was a result of the hocus-pocus of the JLP?

OP: Yes, she thought they bamboozled the people and all these old *naygas* voted for Busta, who just tricked them with free food and old clothes and stuff like that. It's the mass of illiterate people who voted for the "laborites"; they were being tricked by the commercial interests. From very early she saw the [Jamaica] Labour Party as the commercial interests supporting Busta, buying off the illiterates and the semi-literates. They won because they had the mass of illiterate people on their side.

DS: Obviously that was a tremendous insight into the character of the early JLP, and obviously one that the PNP would have liked larger numbers of people to share.

OP: She was a *diehard* to her dying day. She *loved* Manley. Manley to her was the ideal of who she wanted her son to be. He had gone to Oxford; he became a lawyer, a King's Council; he won these famous cases that everybody spoke about. And so he became the national role model of what was possible. And there were the local people, too, within the PNP, who ran for parliament, who were of this temper and orientation. Very much more educated, ambitious people than in the JLP. From very early it was clearly the party of the ambitious lower middle class and middle class, not the party of the commercial interests in an unholy alliance with the illiterate cane-cutters.

DS: I want to talk a little bit about your memory of the 1950s and, to begin with, your memory of its *political* character and your memory of your sympathies. One story that has been told of the

THE PARADOX OF FREEDOM

1950s is that there was something of a convergence between the PNP and the JLP: on the one side, there was the expulsion of the left from the PNP in 1952 and N. W. Manley's attempt during the Cold War to distance himself from the early radicalism; and, on the other side, there was the entry into the JLP of more educated middle-class elements – Robert Lightbourne, for example, or Edward Seaga. There's a sense that the radical distinction between the JLP and the PNP of the 1940s gradually disappears and this leads up to the PNP's victory in 1955.[2] That doesn't sound like it's *your* memory of what happened.

OP: *No.* The radicalism I don't think resonated so much at the bottom level. I don't recall my mom seeing that as an issue of much concern to her. She saw 1952 more as a leadership struggle. She never lost faith at all in Manley. That perception of the PNP was probably more an *elite* thing among the educated classes. She still maintained her strong faith that Manley was aiming toward nationhood and a new Jamaica with educational opportunities and housing opportunities: "The man with the plan," later the PNP slogan for the 1962 election.

DS: Interesting, "The man with the plan." And as you become an adolescent in the 1950s these were *your* thoughts, too? For you, too, 1952 wasn't a significant break?

OP: *No.* That was something I read about and felt it to be a leadership struggle, and that maybe that's the best thing that could happen if the left were preventing victory. As a pre-teenager, the 1952 expulsion of the left was not something I saw as a defeat or any such thing. And my mom certainly didn't. My father certainly didn't. He was a trade union man, too. But it's interesting that you ask that, because one has always to be careful not to read history the way the elites and the intellectuals are reading it. From the point of view of someone like my mother or my father it wasn't significant. My father was back on the scene then but having his own struggles because he was expelled from the police force without a pension. They tried to deny him his pension. This would have been just before I was starting high school – 1952. He was fighting his legal battles. He was kicked out of the force for insubordination and for starting a trade union. He was at court with them, and eventually won. Although by the time he won he was burned out and he had become an alcoholic. Those were the struggles he had when he came back to us. As I think about it, I do recall that my father, a covert Garveyite, was bothered by the fact that the more radical and darker elements of the party had been

38

kicked out. But he was a strong PNP man, and he felt that that 1952 struggle was something you read about in the newspaper in which the big boys were having arguments that did not really percolate down as something that indicated a major change in the party, because Manley was still very much the hero.

DS: It sounds as though, in the 1950s, there was still a fairly clear distinction for your parents, as well as yourself, between the JLP and the PNP.
OP: Oh, absolutely. And they'd make fun of the idea that the JLP was a party dominated by these merchants and White people, on the one hand, and that they had an alliance with the not very progressive, not very educated elements, on the other. Whereas there was a strong belief that Manley held the loyalty of people, certainly at my mother and father's levels, throughout Jamaica.

DS: I gather, then, that the names Frank Hill, Ken Hill, Richard Hart, and Arthur Henry weren't names that resonated for you in the early 1950s.
OP: You know, I read about them and I knew that something had happened *up* there, and they were kind of – how should I put it? – maybe bad boys in the party, people who were up to a different course. I had a secret admiration for them, but not anything to make me think it was a disastrous move for the party to get rid of them. Later on, of course, when I went to university and read back, it might have been different. But at the time it happened, they were more or less seen as people who were up to some interesting ideas, but we didn't know quite what they were up to and [the expulsion] was best for the party.[3]

DS: Did you have a sense as you're starting KC in the early 1950s that independence was on the horizon? I'm trying to get a sense of what the idiom of the nationalist movement was for young people like you at the time. Were *you* heading toward independence?
OP: Oh yes, definitely. For the PNP, that was part of their platform. And this was one of the things that people like my mother never forgave Busta for – his *anti*-independence. Apart from the famous slogan that "federation was slavery," independence was being projected by the JLP as a disaster. We saw independence as one of the great *forward* movements. That movement toward nationhood percolated down. It was a period of tremendous *expectancy* and *optimism*, and every time the JLP won we saw it as a tremendous setback. The man with

THE PARADOX OF FREEDOM

the plan was going to transform education and housing, higher standards of living, better middle-class life – but also independence. That was part of the dream we had. "Independence is slavery" was the message that Busta was projecting. So yes, absolutely, I grew up with that vision in mind, against a background where the empire and Empire Day were important during my grade school years. We had Mrs Queen in charge, and on Empire Day we sang "Rule Britannia." You want to talk about the *hubris* and *arrogance* of the rulers! *We* celebrated Empire Day, which I think was 24th May, with ice cream and waving our flags and singing the British anthem. And all that was going to *go* with independence.

But there were other things happening at the same time that reinforced the sense of transition. One of the big events was when the West Indies cricket team beat England at Lords in 1950. And you had Lord Kitchener's calypso "Cricket, Lovely Cricket."[4] So, you see, it was a *cultural* thing also. This was before reggae. And before reggae, too, you had a fascinating renewal of the mento tradition and the calypsos. And the PNP made use of them. Using music did not begin with Michael Manley and reggae, as people sometimes tell the story. You had a lot of songs drawing on the mento tradition during elections. And the mentos became much naughtier. And, at the same time, you had this cricket victory. That victory was very important, and it was also part of a cultural mélange that included sports and politics and the beginnings of educational change.

There was a little movement with the JLP, give them their due, toward the idea of independence. Because by the mid-1950s Busta had come around to the fact that there was no turning back, especially since the British were beginning to push it. And importantly, then, Sir Hugh Foot came to Jamaica as governor. Foot's brother, Michael Foot, was quite a radical. Hugh Foot was a good man.[5] All of these things were coming together, and the British were clearly giving signals that a transition was imminent. They had their push from the Americans, who from after the war were saying the empire is over. (I remember Churchill saying that he didn't win the war to give up the empire.) But you had adult suffrage and I would say by about 1953 Busta saw the writing on the wall. Whether he had got the signal or whatever, the point is that he had come on board. And that just validated Manley's and the PNP's stance. We were moving forward and the plan included not just progressive, domestic politics but also independence. That was the atmosphere. But by then in our minds the JLP was completely identified with backwardness.

40

DS: If in the 1950s there was the emergence, or the expansion, of a sense of national identity, there were also other significant changes taking place in the Kingston of your teenage years, Kingston after the Second World War. The city was undergoing significant demographic changes as people were converging from the countryside. And this was a period also (you talked a moment ago about what was happening with mento) of the emergence of the immediate precursor to ska and the emergence of the sound systems. And you had also the emergence of a new generation of Rastafarians and especially of those who wore dreadlocks. There is a sense in which this was the Kingston not only of, say, John Hearne's *Voices under the Window* but also Roger Mais's *Brother Man*. What was your experience of *this* dimension of Kingston?

OP: Well, I was living through all the shifts, because remember I moved to Kingston from May Pen in 1953 as part of the internal migration. I loved Kingston. The standard of living was significantly better in the city. That would not have been the experience of someone who was moving to the slums – I'll get to that in a minute. But the standard of living was significantly better than what you had in the country. For example, just one purely visual, physical thing – the homes were much nicer. They had electricity (we had electricity too in May Pen); they had internal bathrooms. And one of my distinct memories about going to Kingston was the smell of the porcelain in the bathroom, which was quite vivid! I thought it was a wonderful thing. In the country you had outside latrines, and going to the toilet was an ordeal, especially at night. The place stank. The idea of a place that could be so nice, with white porcelain, and just a purely functional place! The houses had lawns. Wherever we lived my mother shared a house; it was the standard of the lower middle class. My aunt shared a house with a friend, too. So, I had a nice association with Kingston. And I think everybody who moved to the city, at every level, would have felt that. This was true even of the rural poor who migrated to the city. You didn't have to go to the river to get water to wash your clothes. The houses had pipes in them.

Now, Kingston was also much safer than now, and when I was living with my aunts another migration was beginning for us. One of the three sisters *externally* migrated. She migrated to America in 1953, 1954. Of course, there was a big migration to Britain, which started in about 1955. It was *huge*. But even before that people were also moving to America. It wasn't easy to get there then, but Jamaicans were moving and going on tourist visas. They'd work – for

THE PARADOX OF FREEDOM

only about six months – and go back to Jamaica. All three sisters did it. My mom did it twice, working in the US as a practical nurse.

I experienced this also. With internal migration lots of Jamaicans were moving into places like Jones Town and Denham Town. Now, I know those places quite well because my father's family lived in Jones Town. My father's father – I come from a line of long livers – was alive and well. He died at 101 when I was at university. He lived at 55 Myers Street, which was in Jones Pen, as it was called then. Myers Street was just a block away from the border with Denham Town. And Denham Town had this famous cinema, the Ambassador Cinema, and on the other side of Denham Town was Trench Town. The Ambassador Cinema had a huge dusty park around it and all the young men would play football there. Bob Marley and his teen friends would come to play football on Saturdays. And on Friday afternoons at the cinema you'd have a triple bill. You'd start with a horrendous C-class movie, something like *The Three Stooges*, and then you'd have the "Vere Johns Opportunity Hour," and then you'd have another movie. And then you'd have the final feature. It went on for about four hours! And before that there was a whole afternoon of football. From Myers Street, where my grandfather lived, that cinema was in plain sight. So, I used to like to visit him. Now, at that time Jones Town was seen as a respectable lower-middle-class, working-class area. It wasn't a slum. They were these nicely kept units, but closer to each other than middle-class Kingston. They didn't have big yards around them, only a little front one. But these were solid, working-class, churchgoing people in Jones Town and Denham Town. It's not that way now. I used to go there and visit my grandfather, and I actually stayed with them when my aunt decided she was going to New York for visits. I knew that area very, very well. And, of course, you'd walk on a bit and you'd come to Spanish Town Road. And on the other side of Spanish Town Road was where it started getting crowded. The first place you would go in the migration would be places like Trench Town. But those who couldn't afford that spilled over into Back-o-Wall.

DS: You have a *visual* memory of the emergence of Back-o-Wall?
OP: Oh yes, literally – because it was just the poorer people who could not afford Jones Town. Jones Towners held on until the violence that eventually wrecked it, but I was visiting it right through high school, when I would visit my grandfather and stay there. I lived with my aunt in Rollington Town, East Kingston, which was

middle-class Kingston, solid, middle-class Kingston. But you could already see the deterioration, especially in Trench Town, on the west end of the city. You could see from the types of people who were coming in at a certain point that things were getting rough. People were barefoot, for example. They were the first to go, and of course, as more and more people came, they spilled over more and more. Back-o-Wall grew; the Dungle grew; and that escalated really rapidly as the movement from country increased. So, yes, that was very much a 1950s phenomenon. People were just moving. They were moving from country to city and from the city to Britain and the United States.

Now the Rastas you're talking about, there were two phases of that movement. There were *real* dreads before *dread* became a term of admiration. And people were terrified of them; they were seen as the embodiment of craziness. They were seen as strange, especially in a Christian country. And even before that catastrophe of 1959 – the Claudius Henry affair – there was a low point for them.[6]

DS: Are you talking about the raids on Pinnacle?

OP: Pinnacle was one episode, but Whoppy King, that was a major moment in Jamaica's cultural history. Whoppy King became notorious as a serial rapist. Several middle-class women had been raped by a guy with dreadlocks alleged to be Whoppy King. He operated in the Palisadoes area. (There was a time, growing up, when people used to swim in the Kingston Harbor. Hard to believe, because if you tried to do that now, you'd end up dead, poisoned.) But even where we used to live there were several beaches between Bellevue asylum and Kingston Gardens. There were several beaches where you'd pay and they'd have places to change, and they'd enclose a certain section of the beach, like a pool almost. That's where you'd take your girlfriends. Anyway, more adventurous types who had cars would swim either in the ocean, which was rather dangerous, or in the harbor section out there for privacy. Whoppy King eventually raped a woman and I think killed a guy. The whole country reacted. And Whoppy King was known to be a man with dreadlocks. And so the Rastas came in for serious police harassment, and for several years they were really hunted down, and that's when the police started cutting off their hair.[7] It's funny; it's not been memorialized in any writings that I know of. But people were terrified of the Rastas. And then, of course, following that the thing with Reverend Claudius Henry took place. The 1950s was a bad era for the Rastas.

Kingston College

DS: Let's come to 1959 and the explosion into the public domain of Claudius Henry.
OP: But we've left out KC! That's very important.

DS: Yes, of course!
OP: KC is very important. KC was a huge transition. My mother was economically working class but sociologically lower middle class, with a very middle-class set of values. I was never quite clear where she got them. I suspect that, in a way, she was somewhat downwardly mobile. KC, however, meant a complete transition because you suddenly realized that you'd made a major move. I don't know if by the time you went to high school that was any longer the case, because high school was something you took for granted. But back then we are talking about 1 or 2 percent of the population, and going to KC with Priest, Bishop Gibson, and these nice buildings, small classes, learning Latin and French – it was a cultural transition of which you were acutely conscious. You realized that you'd moved into another world culturally. There was that strong feeling on the part of most of us. Of course, not all of us were upwardly mobile. There were middle-class kids there; there were White kids, too, and Chinese kids. These were people who were completely outside of my world. Because the May Pen I grew up in was all Black – except for the banker, and that incomprehensible Scottish Anglican minister whom we made fun of. The banks were still segregated: there were the few light-skinned and White people and occasionally they'd hire a Chinese person – but then *we* never used the bank, so it was only something you saw from afar. But even the local dignitaries were Black people. Teacher Whiteman was the pinnacle of the community. He was a jet-black man. That was my world. The postmaster, the postmistress, the teachers – they were all Black people. Leaving aside this Scottish minister whom you saw on Sundays, I don't think I had contact with any White person growing up. But at KC you suddenly moved into this educationally different world, culturally different and diverse world. You also moved *socially*. It was really a big class and cultural transition.

The teachers were very important. And for me there was one teacher who was very, very, very important. His name was Noel White. We knew him as "Sleptoe." He was a bachelor, and he was

KINGSTON COLLEGE

a very dedicated teacher. He was our master in second form. But we got along so well with him that the headmaster decided that he would move with us. Only this grade did it. It's not quite clear why, whether it was his decision or what. But he moved grades with us. Usually what happens is that each class has its own master, but he moved with us from form to form, right up to sixth form. *Totally* dedicated. White, I think, took a special interest in me, not because he saw that I had special talents in history and literature, but I was always a bit of an outsider; I didn't get totally into the academics of the school as much as I could have. I read voraciously but I didn't pay as much attention to schoolwork. I did enough to move up from one class to the other, always did; out of a class of between twenty-five and thirty I usually ranked about twelfth, or thirteenth, or fourteenth. And I was always aware of the fact that I was doing that.

DS: You weren't making an effort, you mean.

OP: Yes. I could easily have come first in the class or become the head boy for the class. But the kids who were doing that, I always thought they were goody-goody types. I always felt that I was much brighter than they were; I just didn't care to exert myself. My mother didn't like the fact that I was placing twelfth or thirteenth, just enough to stay in the A stream. But I was always comfortable with that. She was always complaining, "Why aren't you doing better?" The school reports were saying: "Could do much better." So, one year I said, "Okay," as if to show her. I remember reading the stuff and, to the shock of everybody, placing second in the class! My mother was ecstatic. Then the next year I went back to placing as before. For the first four years I really was interested in a whole lot of things that I'd read about. I'd go to the library a lot. After Priest left, I did not like the new headmaster, Douglas Forrest, a very light-skinned Jamaican, and he didn't like me either.[1] He thought I was very bratty. He thought I was too independent, that there was something almost insolent about me. He knew I was deliberately underachieving. He knew I was reading a lot, and the reason he knew was because I started writing for *The Gleaner*. I'd started sending short stories to *The Gleaner*. My first short story was published when I was about thirteen or fourteen, on the Sunday literary page. And then what got me in trouble with him (I remember I was about fifteen) was publishing something in *The Star* newspaper. *The Star* was a scandal sheet, and this was the height of the migration to the UK, so people were writing about that. I was very aware of this in high school because there were stories about people going to England and getting

45

THE PARADOX OF FREEDOM

into serious problems. I wrote a story called "A Tragedy of Youth" about a young woman who went up to England, and the people whom she should be staying with, her relatives, were not nice to her and she ended up having to become a prostitute. *The Star* published this in its center spread with a drawing of a prostitute in a brothel (the story, by the way, was illustrated by the renowned artist Albert Huie). And my headmaster hit the roof. "What is a KC boy doing writing about prostitutes in England?" He threatened to kick me out of the place!

This would have been 1955 or 1956. But White came to my defense. So, I was doing this sort of thing. And finally, when it really mattered, I began to take my schoolwork seriously. For my O-levels, there again I did okay. I got a good second-class pass. But the last two years of KC were very interesting, because I quietly settled down and focused. I ended up coming first in the school in my senior year. I just missed winning the Centenary Scholarship. But winning would have been a disaster, since I would have gone for my undergraduate work to England. Instead I went to the University College of the West Indies [UCWI] on an Exhibition Scholarship. I always look back on that as one of the luckiest things that *didn't* happen to me!

DS: You talk about yourself in these years as being unsettled, restless, as doing the bare minimum to keep yourself in the first half of the class. Your head is *elsewhere*. How do you understand this particular unsettledness that you were experiencing in these years? Or let me put it in a slightly different way: What was preoccupying you in these years, do you think?

OP: I enjoyed being at the school. But while I did the work, enough to get through, I always felt there were other things that were far *more* interesting. I thought the teaching was okay, but several of the teachers I didn't like. I'll give you an example. I started doing physics, but I dropped it because I thought the teacher was lousy. But I became very interested in projection and cinema. This is a good example of where my head was. I became really intrigued with movies and the way movies were made. And then I went further. What's the nature of this strange, miraculous thing? So, I studied film and read about how projections are made. I even made my own projector. Then I became the school projectionist. I'd go down to the US embassy and get films and show them. I did a lot of deep research on the nature of light and how a camera works and how a projector works. That's what I did instead of going to my physics class. But after dropping out for most of the semester I decided I'd

KINGSTON COLLEGE

spent so much time reading about light (and they had done some work on that) I decided to do the exam – and I passed it! Up to this day, my physics master, every time he looks at me, he scratches his head, because I hadn't taken a class the whole semester. But I'd read so much around the subject that I could do that. And that was true in a lot of other things. Even in history. You're reading about British imperial history (you had to do that) and European history, but I was interested in West Indian history. And, actually, they had a competition for the sixth form for who could write the best original essay on a local topic. This sounded like something I should do. So I went down to the National Library at the Institute of Jamaica to do research and I wrote an original essay on the Morant Bay Rebellion, which won the first prize. The prize was given by the Jamaica Teachers' Union, and I remember going down to the Teachers' Federation meeting and being given my prize, which was a book. I always felt that the education I was getting, while it was important, was not essentially what I was most interested in, whether it was in science or in history. I was just too independent. The same thing with literature (even though I got a distinction); but you're reading Shakespeare and other set books in English literature when I was interested in reading local novels, Roger Mais and so on. I avidly lapped up all the West Indian novels.

DS: I have, obviously, no first-hand sense of it myself, but this was a fertile period: Vic Reid's *New Day*, for example, was published in 1949; Roger Mais's *Brother Man* in 1953. What was the environment of the literary in which these works came your way?
OP: I got my first exposure to these, believe it or not, at May Pen Elementary, where we read Claude McKay. I used to know some of the poems by heart, especially the constabulary poems. But the one that I remember is "I Shall Return." I loved those poems. Claude McKay, I'd say, was the first local writer I was exposed to. Then of course I'd read the potboilers, like *The White Witch of Rosehall* by H. G. de Lisser. My mother loved that. We read it together. De Lisser's novel opened up a whole new world. You just saw Jamaica in a whole new way. For one thing: the idea that the countryside is beautiful – if you grow up in it you don't see it. You don't think of it as *beautiful*. The picture that was presented of a strange, slightly mysterious countryside, which was evoked in Mais's *The Hills Were Joyful Together*, disturbed me. You saw the country in a different way. Everything you read before had been about England. And then seeing the country through the lens of a local novel sort of *re-creates*

THE PARADOX OF FREEDOM

a vision of the place, as beautiful, as strange, as almost exotic – and as something you want to know more about.

DS: As a provocation as well as an inspiration.
OP: Yes, yes.

DS: Did you also have schoolmates who were involved in this kind of reading, and with whom you would have conversations about the books?
OP: I had a very active teenage life and I went around with a group. We were all bright, we all did well, we all ended up in college. But we were typical: Leroy Walford, Noel and Max Lyon, and my cousin Trevor Hibbert. We went dancing a lot. We were heavily into the music. I grew up with the music, too. As I love to say, I came of age *both* with Jamaican popular music and with the country. I graduated from university the same year that the country graduated into nationhood. But, yes, I grew up with the beginnings of Jamaican popular music. In the late 1950s I used to hear songs when I'd visit my grandfather and stay over the weekend, and I'd go down to Ambassador Cinema and hear "Opportunity Hour" with Vere Johns – this is an important aspect of the country's cultural history.[2]

University College of the West Indies

DS: From KC you win a Jamaica Government Exhibition Scholarship, and you are admitted to UCWI, and this is in 1958.
OP: I entered in 1959.

DS: You won it in 1958, but you entered in 1959. And in that year, 1958 to 1959, you taught at Excelsior. Before we get to UCWI, tell me a little bit about teaching at Excelsior. Was Wesley Powell still the principal?[1]
OP: Wes Powell was still very much in charge. He was a wonderful man, and he was very supportive and put me in charge of teaching history and religious knowledge. One of the classes was made up of girls who had had problems – they'd had babies and come back to school. This was one of the interesting things about Excelsior; it was very progressive for the times, actually. Several of the students I was teaching were older than I was. It was a good transition to university.

48

UNIVERSITY COLLEGE OF THE WEST INDIES

DS: But why did you teach there to begin with, at Excelsior? Why didn't you go straight to university when you got the scholarship? Was there some confusion?

OP: No, it was true of everyone. We all missed a year because it took so damned long for the results of our final exam to come in from England. And by the time the results came, it was too late to get into university that year. Here in America, you do your exams in the spring and you can still get into college that same calendar year if you want to, in the fall. But in Jamaica it took three or four months because, remember, in the old days they sent the exams to England to be graded. It was truly an empire-wide examination.

DS: Did you particularly want to teach at Excelsior, or was that the job that was available?

OP: That was the job that was available. A few people taught at KC, too, but I was not well liked by Forrest so I knew he would not have wanted me to teach there. And I didn't particularly want to go back there because *I* didn't particularly like *him*. People revere Forrest, but I always had problems with him.

DS: And Excelsior, of course, was a distinctive kind of high school experiment in Jamaica.

OP: I liked the atmosphere. It was more working class; it had young women who were trying to get back up on their feet.

DS: Were there principally girls there?

OP: The class I taught was largely girls. It was a coed school, which I liked very much. KC was a boys' school. But the classes I taught were mainly young women. I enjoyed it very much. It was a very good year.

DS: What do you remember about Wesley Powell most particularly?

OP: I remember him as a very disciplined man, very organized – a very proud man, proud of his achievements. But, at the same time, he was very committed to Jamaica and to helping the poor, in a way that added depth and dimension to my education, which I didn't get at KC. KC was very much a Brown people's school, and its role was to educate the next generation of the middle class. Powell had a sense of community and of helping those in the community who were less fortunate.

DS: He was very much a man formed by the 1930s, wasn't he – that whole moment of Jamaican nationalism, the beginning of Jamaica Welfare, and so on?

THE PARADOX OF FREEDOM

OP: Very much so. I got this sense from him, which I didn't get from any of the teachers at KC, who were mainly middle-class people. There was this sense of commitment, of helping build the community, and the school as an important institution in the society, meant to serve the *society* rather than to serve only the individual students. I liked it very much, from that point of view.

DS: Now, you were actually admitted to UCWI to read economics, when in fact you had applied for history. Tell me how that came about.

OP: Well, that was just thoroughly outrageous, authoritarian behavior. Now, as I mentioned, I got distinctions in my final exams at KC. Clearly, I should have qualified to go wherever I wanted with those results. My history teacher, Noel White, had no doubt that I was going to do history because that was my subject.[2] I'd done economics in high school; they'd just started doing it. But what was outrageous was that, even though my grades in history were stellar, and that's what I wanted to do, I got this letter informing me that I was going to be in the first class of economics students. It was the first economics class at UCWI and, basically, they just wanted to make sure they had a good class. And it *was* a very good class. The group included Norman Girvan and some other very good people.[3] So, they simply *told* me I was doing economics.

I was outraged. The first thing I did was to get in touch with Sleptoe White. He was shocked; and we appealed. He contacted the authorities at the university. And we made such a stink that they decided that they would have a hearing at the Senate House of the university. I couldn't imagine it. Here I was, this poor little boy, and Sleptoe White, who was a very humble man; the two of us, we put on our ties and we went up. And I remember sitting outside in the waiting area and they showed me into this formidable room with Hector Wynter (who was then some big-shot assistant principal – what was he, registrar?) chairing the meeting.[4] We're sitting down there, in this big room with these two rows of men with Hector Wynter at the front. And they said, "What's your case?" And I basically told them I wanted to do history, I was not interested in economics; I'd done history all through my school days. White was like my counsel; he sat there and spoke afterward. He said a few words, "You know, this is the best student I ever had, and he just loves history, always did," and so on. And they said, "That's very interesting." They listened, and then they said, "Wait outside." And we waited, and they chatted and they chatted; then they called us back in and said, "We're sorry to tell

50

UNIVERSITY COLLEGE OF THE WEST INDIES

you that we've decided that you will continue with economics." They never gave me a reason. It was just *arbitrary*. Just like that! They said, "We thought you'd do well in economics, and we have enough historians." I was shocked. It was really a letdown. But I got over it.

DS: In retrospect, do you think this was part of a deliberate effort to build up the social sciences as rapidly as possible?
OP: Yes, almost certainly. The fact that I was among the first class of students to do economics at KC also worked against me in that I was among the very small number of applicants who knew anything about the subject. KC was possibly the first high school to teach courses in economics.

DS: I want to understand your sense of the cultural and political moment 1959/1960. I imagine that the collapse of federation must have been a moment of some importance for you and your fellow students. What do you remember most about the atmosphere at UCWI as this was taking place?[5]
OP: Well, I remember that vividly, because my very first political activity was involved with the federation. Because all of a sudden Bustamante started going wild, and he made it quite clear that he wanted Jamaica to withdraw from the federation. The PNP had won the 1959 elections. But they were now on the defensive; they had to find reasons to justify the federation, which Manley had taken the country into in 1958. People were saying, "What is this federation? What does Jamaica gain from it?" Beyond cricket, the only prominent institution that people could point to as regional was the university. And during the referendum campaign of 1961 the PNP thought it would be a good thing to get university students – Jamaican students – to go out with politicians and meet with people as a vivid, living illustration of what the federation could do. There weren't many other institutions at the time, but people had already come to respect the university greatly. UC was the preeminent hospital in the region. Early ska singers were singing about UC, University College Hospital, where you went for treatment. People were very proud of it. And they asked a few of us to go around with the PNP politicians. I was one of the people assigned to go out with Allan Isaacs.[6] I went all around the country campaigning with him. It was a wonderful experience, in my second academic year. I remember Isaacs saying, "Yes, there are lots of important things in the federation, but the most important thing is the university. This is progress." He would say, "And we have proof of it right here. Here is a young man from

51

THE PARADOX OF FREEDOM

the university, a young Jamaican, working-class fellow, coming up. Now he's training, studying to be whatever he wants." Then I'd get up and say a few words. And we did this all over the island. It was a great introduction to politics. But, of course, we lost.

DS: But were you yourself fired up by the prospect of a West Indian Federation?

OP: Oh yes! The University College of the West Indies was a genuinely federal institution. One of the first things that happened when you went there was that you were resocialized out of your parochial nationalism into this *federal* concept. And there were arguments, some of them joking, some of them not so joking, about who were better – nationalistic sorts of contests – at various activities. We would go on about cricket, and the Barbadians would say, "We have the best cricketers," and we would say, "What about George Headley?" – that kind of thing. But, more important, these were friendly contests – you were being socialized into being *West Indian*. For the first time you were living among people from the other islands. You're meeting people from Trinidad and St Vincent in the halls of residence. That was a very powerful experience. By the middle of the first semester you had really gotten the sense of a *West Indian* identity.

DS: But it sounds as though the PNP's mobilization of students to go around with the politicians was itself an index that they were losing the momentum on federation.

OP: Oh yeah, absolutely. I don't know if they were doing polls, but the signs were quite clear. Bustamante was drawing big crowds, and he had a very simple, crude, outrageous sort of argument: "Federation is slavery." They had this crazy thing of ships coming in with chains, which spread like wildfire. But the most effective piece of propaganda was that Jamaica was the most advanced of all the countries. This is all so ironic looking back from this moment, where Barbados has a per capita income more than three times that of Jamaica – but Jamaica was the first one to get the push toward modernization with the discovery in the late 1940s of huge bauxite reserves, which were literally given away, and also the tourist industry. Jamaicans felt like big shots. Bustamante scared the devil out of everybody by claiming that federation would mean that all those poor people from Barbados and elsewhere were going to flood the Jamaican labor market. Between claiming that federation was going back to slavery and that Eastern Caribbean people would flood the labor market, he

52

was way ahead in popularity. You don't win points in politics for presenting ideals that you're striving toward – because you can't yet point to anything tangible. While Bustamante could say something quite tangible: "We have a problem with jobs. And they're going to come and *take* your jobs." It was really awful. The PNP could see the writing on the wall. I don't think *The Gleaner* favored federation either. I can't be sure. But the JLP always had *The Gleaner* on its side because the commercial interests own it.

The Repairer of the Breach

DS: We're going to come back to the university, but adding to the PNP's problems at this point were the events surrounding Claudius Henry, the "Repairer of the Breach," as he styled himself. What do you remember about those events and what, as you remember it, was their significance – the larger social significance, but also their significance for the PNP?

OP: Well, the PNP was the urban party. Bustamante had the sugar belt pretty well sewn up. The PNP had the middle classes and the urban working classes, who were just emerging. Looking back now, those were innocent days as far as violence goes, even though there were troubling cases of political violence even then. And also, on the other side of Spanish Town Road, the Dungle was emerging, and Back-o-Wall (what became Tivoli Gardens). Those were emerging as *badlands*.

DS: The Claudius Henry events take place in this larger context of *fear* of Rastafarians.

OP: People were getting nervous. It wasn't my impression that the PNP suffered from this, but I certainly think that the JLP played up the problems of violence – ironic, since they mainly started it. There were the beginnings of this fear and the attempt by the JLP to blame the PNP for being the party of urban thugs. I don't know how much that played, because it didn't scare off the middle class, which remained solidly with the PNP. What it *did* do was scare the commercial classes and rally them to the JLP.

DS: But do you think that this propaganda around violence encouraged the PNP regime in power to take a hard line against the elements that were associated with Claudius Henry and his son?

OP: Well, yes, something like that may have happened, although, remember, there was a lot of political violence at the time, and the

THE PARADOX OF FREEDOM

PNP was forced to defend itself. And I think the Claudius Henry affair (I don't remember the details) was being seen as an instance of the sort of lawlessness that comes with the urban support of the PNP. That's what they were making it out to be. And there was a big scare when some people had come over from America with threats of taking over the government.

DS: Yes. Henry's son was involved in that.
OP: The JLP tried to cast the PNP as the party that encouraged these elements. I don't know whether the JLP really succeeded in getting people to think that the PNP was behind this, but certainly the crime, the violence, *that* was really becoming a feature of the political rhetoric. The JLP was perhaps more effective in using it against the PNP, though they were the ones most involved in it. The Claudius Henry affair came at a time when there were the beginnings of the first big shift away from a society where people generally never thought much about crime and violence. And remember, too, there was another uncertainty among the elites and, if you like, the more conservative rural groups – we were pushing toward independence. Remember, federation was the way that we would all become independent together. Yet there was still skepticism and fear about independence on the part of these elites. And Manley was seen as a socialist, even though they had kicked out the few so-called socialists. In a way, attacking the federation was attacking the whole notion of independence. But by then it was too late to back away. Bustamante finally decided that the best strategy would be to join the movement and take it over. And I think that his backers felt that that was the way to go. It was too late to take an anti-independence stance.

DS: In the wake of the Claudius Henry events, famously there was a report authored by M. G. Smith [MG], Roy Augier, and Rex Nettleford.[1]
OP: Oh yes. I was at university then.

DS: Exactly. These were all university lecturers you would have known. What is your memory of the publication of the report?
OP: I was a little disappointed not to have been asked to participate in that exercise because I knew more about it than any of them. I was down there [in the areas studied] before that report.

DS: By 1960, then, you had already generated a distinct interest in Rastafari.

54

THE REPAIRER OF THE BREACH

OP: Oh yes. I had gone down at the height of all the newspaper reports. And when I heard that there was going to be this report, I remember writing to MG (who was the anthropologist who taught me sociology) and I told him I was familiar with the area, and if I could be of help in any way I'd love to help. They did it over the course of the summer, and I never heard back from them. And the report was very much a quickie report. But I was a little cheesed off that they had the historian Roy Augier. I don't know what *he* knew about the subject. But I was just a humble undergraduate.

DS: But what was your impression of the selection of the folk who were to conduct the research? I gather that Rastafarians had approached Arthur Lewis, insisting that something be done because they were getting a bad name in connection with violence – and the university responded. Presumably MG, as the senior anthropologist, was tasked by Lewis to lead the research and select his co-researchers?
OP: I don't know *who* selected them. I think it may have been done at the university level, because MG would not necessarily have selected Augier and Nettleford.

DS: Why not?
OP: Because MG was a serious anthropologist who was very skeptical about political types. MG would have seen this as a scholarly activity, and he would have wanted some other social scientists to be involved. The composition was very carefully done to include Rex, who was already "Mr Black Identity" – certainly he was emerging as such. He was also trained in political science and was very keen on promoting the African base of Jamaican culture.

DS: Your sense was that it was politically directed from above because, had MG been able to shape it himself, it wouldn't have taken the form it did?
OP: I think it was certainly done with the advice of the university authorities; and it was seen as a document that could be very important. It took more the form of what the British would call a royal commission. We have that tradition of royal commissions. So, while you may say they were all academics, Rex would represent the politically and culturally important person. And, who knows? Maybe they felt that they would get more of a response from that group.

DS: My impression from my interview with Rex about the report was that, whatever his actual field participation might have been, he

THE PARADOX OF FREEDOM

was seen as an authentic Black person that gave the team legitimacy among Rastafarians, whom he knew.[2] MG basically controlled the process at the level of the research design and writing of the report.
OP: Oh yes. That was always the case. Definitely. MG was used to this. Remember, he had done a lot of work in Nigeria, partly of this nature. Anthropology in the old days was very much tied up with the Colonial Office. All his work in Zaria was partially sponsored by the British colonial government. He was very skilled at that.

DS: When did *you* begin your systematic work on Rastafari and the culture of the urban poor? When you arrived at the university, did you already have a sense that Rastafari was something that you wanted to grapple with?
OP: I was certainly already intrigued by them, but I would say I was more concerned with the working class *generally*. I remember I started writing the first and only play I ever did during that year when I was teaching at Excelsior.

DS: *The Do-Good Woman.*
OP: Yes. By the way, I just recovered the script for that play, which had been lost for over fifty years. I discovered it among the papers of Miss Lou, Louise Bennett, at the Jamaica National Archives. And it came with the pleasant surprise that it was Miss Lou who had starred in the lead role of the play, not Leone Forbes, as I had remembered. I'd also started playing around with an earlier novel that I'd written, and then began to think about the beginnings of what became *The Children of Sisyphus* – this was *before* getting to university. The characters were just beginning to take shape, and I knew that I wanted to include the Rastas. And then of course the Claudius Henry affair became pivotal in all of this. That was one of the reasons why I went all around western Kingston. I was doing that *before* I went to university. It was easy for me to do because my grandfather lived at 55 Myers Street (I don't know why the address sticks in my head). Maybe I should check it out on Google maps; I wonder if Google would dare to go around there now! Myers Street was a long street, and number 55 was near the border of Denham Town, as I think I've told you before. During my high school years, I sort of moved between my aunt's and my grandfather's homes, because my mother was in America. I'd wander off; Spanish Town Road was only ten minutes' walk from where I was. It was easy to get there. I was interested in the religion of the working classes, both Pocomania and Rastafarianism. It started from during that year. And, who knows,

maybe working in Powell's school, with its strong working-class uplift ideology (which you couldn't help imbibing), gave me an even stronger sense of interest in the poor. And, of course, there were the women I was teaching, so many of whom had their problems – these women may well have suggested this idea of uplift.

DS: It is certainly a distinctive feature of your work, your interest not just in the working poor generally but in the *culture* of the working poor specifically. We're going to come back to that. You were at UCWI beginning in 1959. What was your relation like with M. G. Smith and R. T. Smith, who were teaching at the university? They were both at the Institute for Social and Economic Research [ISER].[3]
OP: They were both at ISER. And Lloyd Braithwaite. And they were all three very distinctive, very eccentric people.

DS: Did all three teach you?
OP: They all taught me, as well as a man called George Roberts, the demographer. It was a very good little team.

DS: This was the heyday of ISER.
OP: Absolutely. Alister McIntyre was director of ISER. I think MG may well have come first as an ISER person and then taught in the faculty. MG was very much involved with upper-class, progressive Jamaicans, like the Manleys. And you know he was in love with Edna. He was a ladies' man too, although that wasn't obvious then. MG was very much into Jamaican upper-class society, and his whole set of attitudes would have been quite different from Lloyd Braithwaite's, who was a Trinidadian, who didn't think much of MG's pluralism work. His model of Trinidad was class based. But, also, they had different *styles*. Braithwaite was also a bit of a rogue, a womanizer, and he had a strange way of talking. He never got much published beyond that one article in *Social and Economic Studies* on social stratification in Trinidad. It was rumored that he had hundreds of papers that were unfinished. Now, Raymond Smith was an Englishman, married to a Guyanese woman. He was also a peculiar kind of guy, he was a Yorkshire man; he had a skeptical air about him, which annoyed people.[4]

DS: He was my colleague at the University of Chicago, so I knew him quite well.
OP: He also didn't think much of MG's pluralism. MG didn't like *his* ideas either. And neither of them thought much of Lloyd. Lloyd

was an intelligent man, but he *really* had problems. So, it was a very complicated group. Then there was George Roberts, the demographer from Grenada, but he was also a pretty quirky guy. I remember he was always more formally dressed than the rest of them, and you never knew what George was talking about. He always had this laugh, and everything you said he'd give this little laugh, so you didn't know what he meant. A very bright group of people, but they didn't get along. But I don't think it affected how they taught us. Certainly, we learned a lot from all of them.

MG and Raymond both taught sociology and anthropology. I learned sociology from these two anthropologists, which was interesting. George was the demographer, and the one who was most into sociology would have been Lloyd, who was very much a Parsonian, actually, whereas Raymond was very anti-Parsonian. I remember, once, Raymond was talking about status; he was badmouthing Parsons, but nonetheless he took a book on the family by Parsons, which had just come out, and he said, "I can show you, he's referring to *The Negro Family in British Guiana*." He was very proud of the fact that Parsons had referred to *The Negro Family*. He showed me the reference; the great man had referred to *him*! But he was still very much opposed to Parsons's ideas. So, I was caught in all kinds of crosscurrents. Then Archie Singham came.[5] Archie never taught me, but he was very active in campus life with the students. He was younger and saner than the others. He was a very pleasant person and liked being with the students in a way the others didn't. I didn't see much at all of MG personally. He never invited us to his home. There is one person I should mention, though – David Edwards, who taught agricultural economics and did a little book on small farming in Jamaica.[6] He taught me in my first year and took a real keen interest in me, and was very, very encouraging. He really thought that I was very smart; he was the first person who put it in my head that I should think about becoming an academic. David was an old-fashioned agricultural economist. They don't do agricultural economics like that anymore. But, man, he was very encouraging! The second year was when you really decided what direction you wanted to go in. And MG, of course, insisted that I should do sociology.

The Rise of the Social Sciences

DS: I want to understand here what was *drawing* you to the social sciences. Because you applied to history but you were sent to study

THE RISE OF THE SOCIAL SCIENCES

economics. And, while you have always been a very historically minded scholar, you've also always been very much a social scientist. Now, the 1950s are years in which the social sciences were coming into a certain prominence in Jamaica, partly through the work of the West Indian Social Survey of 1947–9 and the publication of work such as Madeline Kerr's *Personality and Conflict in Jamaica* and Edith Clarke's *My Mother Who Fathered Me*.[1]

OP: I still have Clarke's book; I marked it up. Braithwaite hated it. I thought it was important, and I remember challenging him – one of the first times I ever challenged him. I really thought it was a good book. And I remember Braithwaite saying this woman didn't know what she was talking about. But I remember marking that book up a lot and thinking Braithwaite was just being chauvinistic in this case.

DS: Did you all have to read the Moyne Report, *The Report of the West India Royal Commission*?

OP: The West India Commission? We all had to read that. Because, remember, in the late 1930s *Warning from the West Indies* was published.[2]

DS: What about T. S. Simey's book on welfare in the 1940s, *Welfare and Planning in the West Indies*?[3]

OP: That's right. That was a required text actually. Those were all documents that we all had to read. They came up in more than one course. And, by the way, the man who wrote that last book you mentioned, Simey, I think he actually visited us. He was an elderly man. There was *Warning from the West Indies* by Macmillan, the Moyne Report, and Simey's *Welfare and Planning*. These were volumes published in the 1930s and the 1940s, so they were classics. But, more important, social science was emerging because of development issues.

DS: Yes, indeed. Social sciences were to *inform* social policy around development.

OP: Yes, and ISER was crucial in that regard. The other person who was around was Douglas Hall, but somehow we never really hit it off completely.[4] I did not especially like Douglas's courses. You had to do them; they were required. Looking back now, I think I was also wary of the fact that he was a White Jamaican. It's a complex sort of thing. I had no problems with the White [foreign] scholars there. Edwards was very nice, very encouraging, and had me over to his home.

59

THE PARADOX OF FREEDOM

DS: But the White *Jamaicans* were another matter – M. G. Smith and Douglas Hall.

OP: MG I came to *respect*; he was very much an important scholar. But I never felt *close* to him.

DS: Perhaps you felt you were on the receiving end of Jamaican racial prejudices?

OP: Not so much racial prejudices, but *class* differences. I felt the class differences quite strongly. Because I grew up in the country, in May Pen, a rural environment, a little town. When I came to KC, I had a strong country accent, which I kept right through. Friends who knew me from then keep telling me that I had a very strong creole accent right up to university, which only went away after living in England. I was strongly rooted in the countryside. May Pen, too, was very much an all-Black town. Douglas Hall reminded me of the bank manager in May Pen, whom I saw once a year if I ever saw him, because my mother never used the bank.

DS: He was a kind of Busha?

OP: Way more than a Busha. Because Bushas were not cultivated people; they wore rubber boots. Douglas Hall was more like the landowner. I always felt a little awkward with Douglas; I never really felt close to him at all. This may have been unfair on my part. Sometimes you have responses that are almost automatic; when, years later, he wrote me and asked me to write a chapter on MG for the book he was doing, I remember I couldn't bring myself to do it. I wasn't enthusiastic about it. I wrote back saying I'd do it, but I never did.[5]

DS: During these years the social sciences were coming into prominence. What's interesting is that you've retained a commitment to the idea that the social sciences are important to the question of social policy. That has always been part of your sense of yourself as a sociologist. ISER was the center of a lot of this activity. Indeed, before you entered the university there was that famous Caribbean studies seminar that ISER hosted, enabled or sponsored by Vera Rubin.

OP: Right. Published as *Caribbean Studies: A Symposium*. We had to read that; it was a basic text. Rubin was a funny one, too. She was almost a sort of grande dame. All these guys spoke respectfully of her; she was greatly liked. And I always wondered: Who is this woman? What's her involvement? She edited this symposium, but she hadn't written much, and I kept asking: Who is she? Why is she so

60

THE RISE OF THE SOCIAL SCIENCES

respected? How did she get into this position? Because the way she entered academia was kind of odd. Her husband had died and left her with a lot of money, and she had this Research Institute for the Study of Man. Maybe she had studied anthropology before.

DS: She had studied anthropology at Columbia University.[6]
OP: She had this interest in the Caribbean. Another one of these White people whose real connection I tried to figure out. But the text itself, *Caribbean Studies: A Symposium*, was formative; it had just come out. Then Rubin had a couple of close colleagues, one of whom I came to know a little better, though I've lost touch with him: David Lowenthal, the geographer. Maybe you know him?

DS: I never met him.
OP: He was very interested in me, and he's one of the people who wanted me to come to America to study. He ended up going to London for quite a while. Then there was Lambros Comitas. He had done a bibliography. Quite frankly, I was a little skeptical of this whole group, although I came to respect Lowenthal's work. But I never quite figured them out.

DS: Your years at UCWI were also the incipient years of the New World intellectual movement. Lloyd Best had in fact gone to Mona in around 1958, I believe.
OP: Right, the year before I got there.

DS: Tell me a little bit about your relationship to this project, and tell me in particular about the group that came to be called, I believe by you and Walter Rodney specifically, the West Indian Society for the Study of Social Issues. How did this come about? On Lloyd's account, that group was crucial to what eventually became the New World movement.[7]
OP: We were very serious undergraduates, and Lloyd was a very impressive guy. I was very active in student life. I was president of the Economics Society but also president of the Literary Society. I was into everything. I did what became a notorious study of hall life. You know about that?

DS: No, I don't know about that.
OP: The "Social Structure of University Halls of Residence," published in *The Pelican*, of which I was the editor. It created pandemonium and then the press took it up. It was all over *The Gleaner*.

61

THE PARADOX OF FREEDOM

And the master of Chancellor Hall was so upset by it that he tried to get me kicked out of the hall. Walter Rodney actually did some of the interviews for this project. People were attracted to it because I had a long discussion on the sex life of the students. Oh my God, it created a sensation!

Lloyd, I found, was a very impressive character, and he was *different*. The color thing must have played a part in all of this, because, when you think about it, there were all these essentially White Jamaicans who were involved with teaching – MG, David Edwards, and even Lloyd Braithwaite, he was a Brown man. He looked more like a Busha Brown man. And then came Lloyd Best, who was really a Black guy. I'd say he was the first Black intellectual at UCWI.

DS: But what about Rex Nettleford, who was also at the university then?
OP: Rex didn't count too much. He was into his artistic thing. I didn't think of him as such. I would see him as an arts man. We didn't see much of him; he didn't teach us and kept his distance from ISER and the social science departments. It was never quite clear what Rex was up to. He was supposed to be in political science, but, as far as I knew, he didn't teach a single course. Anyway, he got involved with the trade unions, so we saw him as more of the liaison with the rest of the society. He seemed to feel comfortable with that role. I respected him as a choreographer and a rootsy folk culture person.

DS: But not as an *intellectual*, in other words.
OP: An intellectual, yes, but I never thought of him as a *scholar*.

DS: But Lloyd Best was different in that respect.
OP: Lloyd was the *quintessential* intellectual and scholar. And jet black!

DS: He was also a man of extreme elegance!
OP: Totally. In fact, one of the characters in my second novel, *An Absence of Ruins*, was modeled on Lloyd – I didn't think people would notice, but they did. I really liked him and felt close to him. And then Archie Singham, too, bless his soul, he also reached out to us. The others didn't really reach out in terms of getting personally involved in our lives (except for David Edwards, as I mentioned). But Lloyd, you couldn't get him to stop talking! Whenever you wanted to have a chat, you could talk to Lloyd. I didn't know Rex very much until after I came back from England; then I got to know him a little bit.

THE RISE OF THE SOCIAL SCIENCES

DS: How did this group get going, the West Indian Society for the Study of Social Issues?

OP: It's funny because I'd almost completely forgotten about that. That was the earliest group – coming out of our political activities in the first semester, coming out of the real profound disappointment over the loss of the federation. Then the disappointment – these were really my very radical days – with the independence constitution. We students were very much involved with that. I was writing letters to the editor of *The Gleaner*. And, in the same issue of *The Pelican* in which I published my report on hall life, I also had a long editorial – I was the editor – blasting the constitution as a sellout to the bourgeoisie. It was in that context that we felt the need to start the society.

DS: This would have been in 1961 or thereabouts?

OP: 1961. I graduated in 1962. The debates would have been around then, 1961.

DS: By this time the PNP had lost the referendum, and the constitution-making had begun in earnest. Were there public discussions about the shape of the constitution?

OP: Right. They finally came up with something that the PNP agreed to, and I was very disappointed with the property clause. I remember that made it almost impossible for any kind of government control of business. That was meant to placate the White elites who were scared to death that they were going to get shafted. There is a very explicit, almost crudely written, clause about property in our constitution, which went much further than anything in the American or British constitutions. I obviously must have been following it very closely. It was in that context that people like Carlyle Dunkley, myself, Norman, and especially Walter Rodney founded the organization.[8] I was much closer to Walter then. He was a year behind us, I think.

DS: Tell me a little bit about your friendship with Walter at the time.

OP: We went through an interesting switch. But, at that time, I got very involved with nationalist politics and with Black identity. Walter had a more socialist position.

DS: Walter understood himself to be a socialist at the time.

OP: That's right. I understood myself to be interested in advancing the Black masses and their culture and was very interested in the whole color complex in Jamaica. Which was one reason why, while

63

THE PARADOX OF FREEDOM

I was very influenced by MG, I never got involved with Douglas Hall. Then, when we went to Britain I became more to the left and Walter became more nationalistic. Well, he blended nationalism with Marxism to a degree. ... We had an interesting moment when I realized how far things had gone between us. We used to see each other in London; he was studying in Portugal, but he would come over and stay with us – Norman and I shared a flat in north London.

DS: I want to come to the London period later. But in Jamaica your friendship was very close.
OP: Very close. We were quite close, same hall, and we were the *intellectuals* in the hall, Walter and I. Norman was in Taylor Hall. Carlyle by that time was clearly on a political trajectory and had more or less backed away from scholarship. He did his work, but it was quite clear that he wasn't going to become an academic. But there was a group of us who, from our second year, were clearly going to go into academia. Walter and Norman Girvan and myself, we were the *core*, and we were recognized as such by the faculty and everybody else. Yes, it was very clear that that was the trajectory. We were basically being trained to become the next generation of scholars. Who was going to take over next was very important to them. That was definitely a role cut out for us.

The London School of Economics

DS: How did you come to choose the London School of Economics [LSE] for your graduate work? Did you go to the LSE specifically to work with David Glass, who had been, of course, part of the West Indian Social Survey project?
OP: No. I was being encouraged by several people to apply for the Rhodes Scholarship but I felt on principle I was not going to do that. So, I didn't. And I remember that I was a little disappointed that Anthony Abrahams got it.[1] It was a scandal, because Norman had also applied and he should have gotten it. I remember saying to Norman, "Why are you applying for this? This guy Rhodes was a fascist! Why would you want to do that?" Norman's parents put pressure on him. But Tony had this as his *objective* from the day he got to university. He was going to get the Rhodes. He was in student politics, starting to get involved with social issues. But then the really cynical part was one day Abrahams came and said, "Orlando, you got to come play some cricket." I used to play cricket a lot; I hadn't

64

THE LONDON SCHOOL OF ECONOMICS

played it in the first two years I was there. Suddenly, Tony is saying, "We need a second eleven team. You're drafted." He was going to be the captain. This was all set up for the Rhodes. So, I was really contemptuous of that scholarship and refused to apply for it. I was told explicitly that I'd stand a good chance, because most of the people who'd won the Rhodes before that were White Jamaicans, Rex being one of the big exceptions.[2] However, the Commonwealth Scholarship struck me as being the right thing for me. For the Commonwealth Scholarship you had to select three universities, only one of which could be Oxford, Cambridge, or London – otherwise everyone would put down Oxford, Cambridge, *and* London. I knew I didn't want to go to Oxford or Cambridge. And those were wise decisions, because the people I knew who went to Oxford and Cambridge, I don't know if it was in their best interest. I was also glad that I went to London. I wasn't thinking about studying with Glass; I was thinking about the great LSE. Harold Laski was the person I was thinking about. This was also the heyday of the anthropologists at the LSE.

DS: That was the department of Bronisław Malinowski. Edith Clarke came out of that program.

OP: We'd had to read her book, but, yes, she came out of that. I was thinking of all the greats they still had there, remember them? There was this waspy woman who wrote on East African politics, Lucy Mair. They also had the great New Zealander Raymond Firth. And there were other persons there – Isaac Schapera was there. He was my wife's [Nerys Patterson's] supervisor when she did anthropology. I was more attracted to them, having been taught anthropology by MG.

DS: Firth and Shapera and Glass supervised the fieldwork involved in the West Indian Social Survey. But you hadn't known that at the time?

OP: No, but I'd read them. Anthropologists were teaching us sociology, so my texts were all by social anthropologists. Radcliffe-Brown, I knew his book on social structure by heart. Raymond Firth, I have all of his texts. I knew the work of all of these guys before I knew the work of any sociologists, except Morris Ginsberg and a few others. Anyway, when I went up to LSE I got a letter saying Glass selected me as his advisee. I was told, "David Glass wants to be your supervisor." I couldn't say no. I don't even know if he would have been my choice, but he was very interested. George Roberts had written before that there was this bright Jamaican coming up. And

THE PARADOX OF FREEDOM

I would have been the first Jamaican there since Edith Clarke, who had been in anthropology.[3] I'd opted for sociology. There's a long story to that, a very sad story. I'll tell you when we discuss London, how we fell out.

DS: Okay, we'll come to that. How do you remember your departure from UCWI and from Jamaica? At that point, your mother must have felt vindicated that her "project" was coming to fruition.
OP: Well, yes, but this was a very stormy period in my relationship with my mother. She had come back from the United States and settled in, and I used to visit her. I had a girlfriend from KC days, Jean Amiel – her brother was Keith Amiel, another one of my schoolmates from second form right through. They were middle class. I always saw myself as more working class. They had cars and stuff like that. Keith's sister became my girlfriend. And we were very close, steady, right through university.

DS: Was she at university, too?
OP: Yes, she came the year after me. We were just an item, as they say, right through. Then in my final year, after I won the scholarship, I was going to go away. And there's always a concern about what happens when you go away. So, we decided we were going to get married before I left. Because I couldn't make any promises about what would happen when I left – if we were married it would be different. She felt the same way. And her parents thought it was a good idea. We got engaged, and we set the date for the marriage, and my mother went very strange about this. She did *not* want me to get married. I asked why, what's going on, what's the objection? It seemed totally irrational. I could never get from her what was going on. We set the date, and she got more and more upset. She got sick with being upset – she didn't want to talk to me; she didn't want to talk to Jean. It wasn't that she didn't like Jean; she loved Jean. Finally, to cut a long story short, she said to me one day that she felt that having spent all her life creating this thing, if I just got married right after college, as soon as I graduated from university, she would lose me. It was as psychologically primitive as that. That's what I'd thought, and she finally said so. At first, she didn't want to say it, it was such a deep primitive feeling. I'm not her creature, but in a sense it's almost as if I was. And she finally said so, and, in the end, she made such a fuss, including almost threatening suicide, that we had to call it off. We had actually set the wedding date and sent out formal invitations.

66

THE LONDON SCHOOL OF ECONOMICS

DS: That must have been very traumatic.

OP: In the end, she was literally having a psychological trauma. I thought she was going to kill herself or die of grief. In the end we had to call it off. That was not good, and, of course, as we all feared, I went away to England to this totally different life, and it didn't work out, and I broke up with Jean. But, as far as university goes, the last year was a great period. I was into everything. I was president of the Economics Society, president of the Literary Society, editor of *The Pelican* – I was into everything. And word got out about us, because actually we were the first class of graduating social scientists. Michael Manley and his father had heard about this group, and he came to meet us.

DS: Meaning Norman Girvan, Walter Rodney, and you?

OP: Carlyle Dunkley, Girvan, Peter Fletcher, and me. Fletcher's father was very close to the elder Manley. I think it was through Fletcher that politicians heard about this group, and they actually came to the university, Manley the elder and his son, to visit us.

DS: The PNP by this time – after it lost the referendum – was in disarray. And this was before the emergence of the "young socialists" inside of the party.

OP: That's right. They were now looking at the next generation. They had heard about us; it gave them hope. After that first meeting Michael came and visited us from time to time when we were in England. But that's when I first met him.

DS: He was then head of the National Workers Union [NWU].

OP: He was sowing his wild oats.

DS: In a certain sense, Carlyle Dunkley followed him into the union, the NWU.

OP: Carlyle followed him. By then Carlyle knew he was not going to be an academic.

DS: Do you think it was difficult for your generation at that point, when, as you say, this was the first generation of locally trained social scientists, to imagine yourselves being academics? There must have been some anxiety about what that exactly meant, so that, even for people with good first-class honors, becoming a diplomat or going into politics would have been real options for them?

OP: No, there were *never* any doubts in our minds. The opportunities were amazing. Ninety percent of the other people were literally being

67

THE PARADOX OF FREEDOM

snapped up. The headhunters were there from Barclays Bank (the big imperial bank); they realized the game was up in terms of having those White and Chinese girls serving as tellers. They needed bank managers, and they didn't have any! They didn't even have any bank tellers who looked remotely like us. They realized, then, that they had to act in a hurry. And that first class was just gobbled up.

DS: And you were self-conscious about that?
OP: Oh yes, we were *contemptuous* of people choosing monetary gains when what the country needed was to understand its social problems. We were in no doubt; we had a strong commitment to intellectual life that had a *policy* orientation.

DS: Again, there was the sense that the social sciences are coming into significance.
OP: Oh, absolutely. And that's what ISER did. Because, remember, ISER was a policy-oriented institution. Even though we were undergraduates we were treated almost like graduate students. When they had meetings in ISER, we the undergraduates would attend. We were almost like graduate students. We were acquiring the ethos and the thinking and the orientation of all these people. Scholarship was the thing.

DS: Did Walter Rodney also win a scholarship?
OP: Yes, I think we all got Commonwealth Scholarships.

DS: You arrived in London in the autumn of 1962; and this was a London that, after the Notting Hill riots of 1958, was very aware of West Indians. How were you moving around in London, and who were you connecting with? Other West Indians?
OP: Yes, remember in London at that time we already had a generation there from the 1940s. And they had formed the West Indian Student Union.[4] Where the hell was it? Earl's Court, I think. It was a well-established institution waiting for us. And my older half-brother Victor had been, I think, president of the West Indian Student Union. He had gone off to the war when I was about four. And I never saw him again until my last year in university, when he came over. He was a big shot in the student union. There was a generation before us. That's the generation that goes back to the Eric Williamses. So, we didn't enter a vacuum. But it still was a very, very big change. To go to the "mother country," with the West Indian migrants who preceded us – and Brixton was rising. It looked as if Britain was

68

THE LONDON SCHOOL OF ECONOMICS

going to go the way of America, in terms of ghettos. Notting Hill got violent. It had quieted down by the time we got there. And one of the first places we went was the West Indian Student Union. I'm trying to remember who we met there; it was still dominated by the legal types. A lot of folks had gone to study law. So, in a way, we were the first group who were really spreading out. That's the big difference between the earlier group and us. The earlier group was mainly professionals – law or, in my brother's case, architecture.

DS: Although, of course, interestingly, Lloyd Best had gone to Cambridge to study economics and hung about in London, and then went back to the Caribbean in 1958.

OP: We really were the first *group* of social scientists. There were historians, like Elsa Goveia. Where did she go? Was she also in London? There were a few people before us, but there weren't that many. There was Douglas Hall – I think he studied in Canada.[5] But we were the first significant group. We got together with students from the rest of the Commonwealth, and in my case – and Norman Girvan's case – the New Left group.

DS: That's what I was going to ask you. Tell me what drew you to the New Left group. Indeed, I didn't know that Norman was also drawn to the *New Left Review*.

OP: Not as much. *I* was the one who got really involved.

DS: How *did* you get involved with *New Left Review*, and when?

OP: I got involved from my first year. In my first semester I met Robin Blackburn. It was a little mysterious. It wasn't clear whether he had been expelled from Oxford. What was the term they use when they suspend you, do you remember? They say you are being "asked to step down": both he and Perry Anderson were "asked to step down." But they had also had a row over the old *New Left Review* that Stuart Hall was involved with.[6] It was a little funny because I was Jamaican and there was this other Jamaican, Stuart Hall, but he was at Oxford doing literature. They came to London with the *New Left Review*. Robin was an undergraduate, actually. I don't think he ever did a PhD. But he behaved like a graduate student, because he was very forward thinking. We became friends rather quickly. I'd just met him for coffee. I was still finding my way. He was doing a first degree, while I was a graduate student. He was very much interested in us. (He was also going around with this beautiful Chinese woman.) Robin was always interested in the Third World. And I remember I

69

was then in my Parsonian phase, under Braithwaite's influence. The New Left crowd thought this was very cute, because they were left-wingers, and here was somebody who really thought he was radical but also thought he was a Parsonian! They would have meetings every other week, mainly at Robin's and Perry's. We had discussions, and I remember one of the first things I was asked to do was to lead a session on Parsons, and I *defended* Parsons.

DS: They were, of course, Marxists, and not just Marxists but Trotskyists.
OP: That's right. They were already hostile. The reaction against Parsons was going to take place in the 1970s, but this was the 1960s. They were way ahead of the curve. They thought, "This is American sociology at its worst." And I'd say, "No! I don't think so. There's nothing in Parsons that's opposed to understanding change." So, I became part of the group; I was soon on the editorial board. Then I started writing for them. And then, of course, my novel came out. But I was publishing almost as soon as I went to London. They were impressed.

DS: Publishing where?
OP: In *New Society* – they started publishing me. It was so sad when it eventually folded. But *New Society* was unusual. It was a magazine devoted to the social sciences, like a *TLS* [*Times Literary Supplement*] of the social sciences. I wrote two or three pieces, starting with the one on the Rastas.[7] I got very active. I was doing reviews for the *New Statesman*, for the *TLS*, regularly.

DS: Did you work with or know Stuart Hall in that period?
OP: No. That's the funny thing. I never really got to know Stuart Hall. I met him once when he was doing a series on the West Indies for the BBC, in which he interviewed me. And I never saw him again. I think he was in Birmingham, wasn't he? He was just coming up then, but our paths barely crossed. Isn't that funny?

DS: Yes, that's really interesting. When did you leave *New Left Review*? When did you part ways?
OP: We didn't really part. I left and went back home [to Jamaica], but I'm still friends with Robin. And from time to time I'd write for them. I went back to Britain in 1978, finishing up *Slavery and Social Death*, and I wrote a long piece for *New Left Review*.[8] I think that was the last piece I wrote for them. But when my novel was published, they

THE LONDON SCHOOL OF ECONOMICS

were very excited about it. And I published a chapter from my second novel in *New Left Review*. So, I was very much involved.[9]

DS: In 1962, 1963, you see yourself as a man of the left?
OP: Well, yes. I didn't have any choice, because that's where C. L. R. James [CLR] scooped us up.

DS: Exactly. That's what I want to come to. What was your relationship to James in these years? Were you part of the circle around him?
OP: Well, he made us. We got this note. Girvan, Rodney, and I were ordered up to his flat and were told that every Friday evening we would turn up and study Marx. It was an indoctrination session, that's what it was! And we were given stuff to read – Marx, Trotsky, and all the rest of it. It was almost a seminar. We were literally sitting at the feet of the great man.[10]

DS: Just the three of you?
OP: Just the three of us.

DS: And he would pronounce.
OP: He gave us the stuff to read, and he pronounced. I was writing *The Children of Sisyphus* then. And during the course of doing that I told him I was writing fiction. He said he would love to see what I wrote. For weeks we would be going up to the great man. But I was already reacting against my earlier Afro-Jamaican nationalist position and becoming more left-international, while Rodney was going in the opposite direction.

DS: You referred to "sitting at the feet of the great man," so there was that sense already that James was the "great man."
OP: Oh my God, yes. Even before we left Jamaica – from university days. The Trinidadians used to boast about C. L. R. James. No, no, no, James was already a *legendary* figure. The Trinidadians never let us [Jamaicans] forget that. We'd have discussions about who the respected intellectuals were. *We* Jamaicans would talk about Vic Reid and the people who wrote fiction. *They*, Trinidadians, would say, "Those are all lightweight." Eric Williams and C. L. R. James were the intellectual heroes – the Trinidadians would always remind us they had a superior culture to Jamaica. "You have anyone anywhere close to the Doctor?" They not only had the Doctor, they had another figure, CLR. Yes, he was legendary *before* we graduated from UCWI.

THE PARADOX OF FREEDOM

DS: But it was James who sought you students out.

OP: Yes, we were quite flattered. Somehow, he always knew everything. CLR was almost a mysterious figure. He was a legend, and he was writing *Beyond a Boundary* at that time. But his version of Marxism was a little too dogmatic for me – I think for all of us, except Walter perhaps. We all three felt that we were being indoctrinated, but we were sufficiently smart to resist that. But we still thought it was wonderful talking to the great man, because we didn't just talk about Marx. We related to the Caribbean.

DS: Right. With which he was once again intensely preoccupied.

OP: Very much so. He suddenly went off; there was a time when we didn't see him.

DS: Yes, he was in Trinidad.

OP: He got locked up by Eric Williams. We read about it. We only saw him for a little while before he went over and got himself into trouble. Then we saw him on and off; he came down to the University of the West Indies when we were down there. But, in London, we also knew his wife, Selma, who was very much involved with the sex workers, organizing them. She was quite a character. Anyway, it was a very active period. I plunged into British intellectual life at all levels pretty early. That would never have happened in Oxford or Cambridge. I was living in the city, and I was all over, and getting involved personally, too. And LSE was just the best place to be. We had a lot of friends, and then you had people from the Commonwealth. And the faculty was receptive. It was very nice that the leading demographer in Britain – David Glass – more or less said, "You're going to be my student."

West Indian Fiction

DS: By the time you went to London in 1962, there was an existing body of West Indian fiction: from Vic Reid, Roger Mais, George Lamming, V. S. Naipaul, John Hearne, Samuel Selvon, Edgar Mittelholzer, Andrew Salkey, Sylvia Wynter. And, of course, there was a growing body of poetry: from Martin Carter, Derek Walcott. Did you have a sense of yourself in 1962, 1963, as wanting to make a distinctive contribution to this body of work?

OP: Well, I was the second generation, so to speak. I saw all of those guys as the older generation. We were already reading Vic Reid in school. When I was in high school I had to read John Hearne. I remember him coming in and lecturing to the sixth form association meeting; they'd invited him in to speak. And there was Roger Mais. These were all people I was already reading in high school; certainly Vic Reid, because he was beloved by the teaching establishment. He was a protégé of Edna Manley. I think he was working for the Ministry of Education. And then of course there's even an older generation, if you want to go back.

DS: You mean H. G. de Lisser and people like that?
OP: And Claude McKay, whom I'd also read in grade school. So, when we went up to London, many of those still alive were there. There's a big overlap. We saw Andrew Salkey as part of our generation almost, just a little older.

DS: You thought of yourself self-consciously in relation to this older generation.
OP: Yes, sure, in relation to West Indian literature.

DS: Were you ever tempted to leave scholarship for a life of fiction?
OP: Well, yes. I started off quite successfully in fiction, published two novels within a couple of years – *Children of Sisyphus* in early 1964 and *Absence of Ruins* in 1967. But, more important, I was in with the literary crowd, so to speak, doing the things they did. I was reviewing for the *TLS*, the *New Statesman*, and things like that. And moving with a left-wing crowd, who were as much literary as anything else. They were into Jean-Paul Sartre – they were very much into continental philosophy and literature. That's how I got into Sartre. I'd read Albert Camus long before.

DS: You'd read Camus in Jamaica?
OP: I started reading Camus the year before I went to university, that year between KC and UCWI when I was working at Excelsior. I was always interested in philosophy, so I went to the library looking around, and I was just pulled by the title. I thought, "This is interesting."

DS: Pulled by which title?
OP: *The Myth of Sisyphus*. It was a very odd sort of book to be at the Cross Roads Library, where I was a member. I don't know if it's still there. It may have been the headquarters. Camus' book could also have been – as I strongly suspect – a gift from the

THE PARADOX OF FREEDOM

French embassy because there were several other French works there. I was, from KC days, from my early writing, very interested in French literature, especially the French *realist* literature – Guy de Maupassant, [Honoré de] Balzac, and [Emile] Zola. Zola in particular; in fact, I'd say I modeled several early essays on Zola, *Germinal*, and so on, the low-life sort of culture. And I liked the fact that Zola was also a public intellectual and critic. I especially loved the short stories of Maupassant. That's so funny, I haven't read them in years and years. The only reason why I went on to do high school French, even though I didn't get along with Forrest, was because I wanted to be able read both Zola and Maupassant in their original.

DS: So, it wasn't, then, as you told Forrest, that you might want to marry a Frenchwoman!

OP: I was just being bratty. I just wanted to irritate him. But Maupassant in particular, I loved his short stories. I loved the atmosphere they created; it was just wonderful. Maupassant has this technique of a story within a story. Two guys come, sit in a café, and start talking, and the story is about the story they're telling. It's a technique that he perfected. Some short-story writers – and I had initially thought of myself as a short-story writer – used that technique, which I was initially very attracted to. Anyway, I would have been drawn to the French section of the library. And that's when I saw Camus, purely by browsing. And I plucked it out and started reading, and I was hooked by it. I liked its style, and so I read it compulsively through college. At first, I didn't really understand it; I related to the themes. I kept reading and rereading it. I was thoroughly immersed in Camus by the time I left Jamaica.

DS: Did reading *The Myth of Sisyphus* then lead you to other works by Camus?

OP: Sure. His novels, which I also liked very much, and the other philosophical works. It was kind of sad, Camus' career. He had this big tension with Sartre, and it became increasingly clear to me that he was ambivalent about Algeria. When I first read him it was because I liked him, but as I got more into the writing, and more into Third World issues, I started thinking: Who is this guy? Where did he grow up? He grew up in Algeria. What was he doing? He was a poor White there. And then there's the big debate with Sartre. In fact, the left was suspicious of Camus, because he was kind of more centrist. And it's quite understandable. He's a bit like White South Africans

74

WEST INDIAN FICTION

now saying, "Look, sure, I agree with the transition, but we had a life here, too. This is where I grew up. And I didn't exploit anyone anyway." That began to turn me off a little bit. And then his own reputation really plunged right after he died.

DS: There's now been something of a revival of interest in Camus. But let me ask you this way, the Caribbean writers you were reading at the time – Reid, Mais, Hearne – were not writing *philosophical* novels. What was capturing your imagination about the possibility of thinking about your Caribbean realities through this kind of philosophical lens?

OP: It's just the coincidence of being very attracted to Camus while I was writing this novel. He was a major philosophical inspiration. I also was attracted to Camus because the whole issue of *meaning* in life became important to me about this time, partly for personal reasons. It was very much late teenage years – I'd had some angst about having gone through this very religious upbringing. My mother was a devout Anglican and I went to KC, and so giving up on religion and on God did create some angst, which was one of the things that led me to philosophy. It's one of the things Camus was exploring – the meaning of life, the fact that life can be meaningless. Life can be worth living even if it's meaningless. *That's* the attraction. I was bothered by that. I was bothered by my personal relationship with the girl I was going around with since I was quite young, and it's one of these things where you're dating and you're going steady, and I knew that I liked her – we'd started going around from when we were about sixteen, seventeen – but that sort of thing doesn't work out. By the time I was at UCWI, I realized that. I don't know how much I was in love with her, but everybody assumed that we were going to get married, and we planned to get married. But part of my ambivalence toward my mother was what got me. Her manner was totally unreasonable, but, in a way, I was also having doubts about the relationship. If anything, I persisted in it precisely because [my mother] was being so difficult. I felt very guilty about that, too. In that sort of state Camus was very good.

DS: Because Camus had a philosophy of *subjectivity* and of personal identity.

OP: Right, in a way none of the others did. And he addressed real existential issues. He himself didn't like the term "existentialism" too much, but, in a sense, he was even more existentialist than Sartre,

75

THE PARADOX OF FREEDOM

who had a very, very abstract kind of philosophy – talking about existentialism, but not really living it the way Camus was.

DS: Could you say more about what you mean by giving up on religion? We will talk more later about your knowledge of Christianity – Paul in particular – but can you walk me through this crisis you went through in your belief in God?

OP: I may not have emphasized it enough, but I had a very religious upbringing. My mother, as I've already mentioned, was a devout Anglican and I had to go to church every Sunday throughout my childhood. Occasionally I rebelled, but my rebellion took the form of attending the Methodist church, and on one occasion even the little Catholic church a few times. That was weird. The only people who attended the Catholic church in May Pen were the Chinese and the small group of light-skin people and Middle Eastern traders. They all stared at me as I walked up the aisle, made the sign of the cross and said my Hail Mary, the only Black kid, the only Black person in the church. I also once explored the fundamentalist Maranatha church, and when Billy Graham came to Jamaica in early 1958 with his American-style religious crusade, not long before I did my higher school exams, I remember being saved and was very righteous and went to Bible study for all of three weeks. But I always came back to the Anglican church. At KC I joined the choir from my first year and had to go to service sometimes twice on Sundays. My voice broke late in adolescence so I sang soprano, was soprano number 2 on the KC boys' choir, and would sing solo at the weddings of the school's old boys: "Oh Perfect Love, All human thought transcending," was my specialty. Christianity was thoroughly ingrained in me up to my late teens and early twenties, and then I began to have my doubts the year before going to university. It was a quiet kind of crisis. I didn't talk about it much or express much external angst. Instead I read Camus and developed a serious duodenal ulcer. I lost weight. I sometimes vomited. I had constant intestinal pain. Actually, there were two internal crises going on, one based on my growing doubts about God, the other based on my doubts about my relationship with the girl I had been dating since I was sixteen. I felt compelled to love both – she and God – and couldn't bring myself to break them off. So, I read Camus and bled inside. Camus was a kind of savior. The ulcer receded the more I came to understand what he was talking about. I broke off with God just before I left for England and the LSE, and I broke off with Jean not long after plunging into the cultural and intellectual whirlwind of London in the sixties.

The Children of Sisyphus

DS: Tell me in detail now about the making of *The Children of Sisyphus*. How did you come by the central idea and the plot of that novel?

OP: The plot came to me early. I was always concerned with women who were struggling. The central idea turns around struggling women.

DS: You had this fascination from Excelsior.

OP: Yes, but it's also a fascination with my mother, who was for many years a single person struggling until she and my father got back together. Some early short stories, including one I mentioned to you, which I published in *The Star* and which I wrote when I was about fifteen, were about women struggling. I'd started playing around with that theme of a woman against the world, which in many ways was suggested by my mother's experience. And then going into the slum areas I saw all of the economic suffering and sexual abuse of women. People didn't really talk about it then; they're starting to talk about it a bit more now. In any case, that began to gel. I was playing around with those themes in a few short stories, especially during that critical period between high school and Excelsior. There was a period just before I started going around with Jean, whom I mentioned earlier, when I used to go around with another girl. She was a bit older than I was and was brought up by a single mother. I remember she didn't do too well at high school. She had gone to Excelsior after dropping out. This was before I worked at Excelsior. I was about sixteen or seventeen years old. It was very interesting. I remember she broke it off right after I passed my senior Cambridge exams and did well. She just said we couldn't get along. She saw herself basically as going along a trajectory different from my own. It was very sad. It took me a long time to figure out what she was talking about. Even after she'd gone to Excelsior, she still messed up. She got her results the same year I got mine. I was on track, doing well. She was doing her exams for the second or third time, and she messed up completely. And I heard some time after that she had started going around with a real rascal of a guy, and I knew she wasn't going to come out well. I think she got pregnant later on. In a way, she almost predicted her future. So, I had those experiences, a lot of them focused on women. And then there was the first play I wrote, *The Do-Good Woman*, about a woman who had been trying desperately to get married and

THE PARADOX OF FREEDOM

was ditched by her fiancé. All of those things were in the background building up to my writing *Sisyphus*. I'd written a previous novel, *Lilith*, which is lost. It was completed when I was a teenager. It is also focused on a woman. So, all of the early characters were of women struggling.

DS: When was *Lilith* written? When you were at KC?
OP: Yes, I finished that in the period after I graduated, when I had that long break. I lived on Windward Road then. I do not recall the exact address, but the house was on Windward Road. My parents later moved to a quieter road off Windward Road, but in the same East Kingston area, basically working and lower-middle class.

DS: What, in brief, was *Lilith* about?
OP: In a way it was expanding on a Dickensian theme. It was about a young woman who got betrayed and ended up in the low life and I think got jilted. I haven't thought about that in so long, but I think it was partly inspired by Dickens's *Little Dorrit*, which I read many times, partly by stories in the Bible. Most of all, I knew all the characters, all these young women. Then of course I had a half-sister I should mention, Ermine. My father had a family before, much older than me, as I said earlier. My mom went to America a couple of times to earn money. The second time she went, I was doing my junior Cambridge exam (the equivalent of what later became O-levels). Those were critical years, sixteen to eighteen. My father was there, at home. And this sister came, and she was basically going to look after the house in my mother's absence. She was my father's youngest child by his first marriage, eight, nine years older than me, in her early twenties. She was known to be very smart. I liked her very, very much. Like all my father's other kids, she'd been sent to a technical high school. She came in to look after the house, and then something funny happened. I was wondering why she wasn't working, why she'd dropped out of school. And then she slowly started getting fatter and fatter, and I realized she was pregnant. I thought this was incredible; I couldn't believe that, because I admired her a lot. Then she had the baby, which was really quite traumatic for her. The father was totally out of the picture. I remember going with her to look for him, as she got more and more pregnant. He didn't want anything to do with her, and that traumatized her because she thought the guy was the love of her life. It was a very bad experience for her. And her way of responding to that was to go and have another baby for somebody

THE CHILDREN OF SISYPHUS

else. My father by then was really angry. Now she was very much a *fallen* woman, a disappointment. A Jamaican Little Dorrit. And, like Dorrit, her salvation was migration. She picked herself up and went to England and got married over there. Migration is good from that point of view. However, she basically abandoned her two Jamaican kids, whom my mother largely brought up. So, I had these experiences, which fed into the writing about the predicament of working women.

DS: Now, *The Children of Sisyphus* is not only crucially about the predicament of working women or poor women, it is *also* centrally a novel about Rastafari. Had you done systematic research on Rastafari when you were at UCWI? I mean formal, systematic work?
OP: Yes. Remember I first became attracted to them with the failure of the millenarian movement of Reverend Claudius Henry, when the ship with Emperor Haile Selassie was supposed to come and take them back to Ethiopia. When Henry got arrested it was all over *The Gleaner*, so I went down to see his people, with their paper bags – it was very sad, they just looked stunned. And I saw the Dungle, and the smell was in your nose even after you went back home. It was a horrible existence. I'd never been over to that side of Spanish Town Road. I used to go to West Kingston a lot, as I told you. And on one of my mother's trips to America I stayed with my father, who decided he wasn't going to keep a house, so we went and stayed with *his* father, who was then in his late eighties or early nineties and lived at Myers Street in Jones Town. From my grandfather's place I would start wandering around. And I was very attracted to religious groups. I loved the music more than anything else. I'd hear the Pocomania music and I'd be drawn to it. I'd go and sit in the back of the little church shacks; I don't know what the worshippers thought, but I'd be there going from church to church watching them laboring and working themselves up to states of spirit possession. The Pocomania scenes in *Sisyphus* were based on these visits. I still love that music, by the way. And the Rastas were all around. So the thing with Claudius Henry got me really interested. It was easy to bring together the Rasta story with what I was already playing around with – the woman who becomes involved with a Rasta but also was involved with a Pocomania preacher.

DS: Your interest in Rastafari was really part of a larger interest in popular religious practices, including Pocomania, and popular Jamaican music as well.

79

THE PARADOX OF FREEDOM

OP: Oh yes, Jamaican working-class people and sufferers. The Dungle horrified me; and I was also fascinated with the Rastas. At that time the Rastas were being seen as *dread*, in the original, literal sense.

DS: The question I want to come to now is the relationship between the frame of *Sisyphus* and the story of Rastafari, on the one hand, and of Dinah, on the other. Why does Rastafari illuminate something of the philosophy of the absurd?

OP: There were these people, what were they doing? They were searching for meaning, when you think about it. And their way of finding meaning was millenarianism – escaping to Africa. As I thought about it, I asked myself: What exactly drove these people? I could understand why they were attracted to Rastafari. But what I saw *especially* was their profound disappointment when the millenarian promise didn't come true. And that paralleled a lot of other things; it was similar to *my* loss of faith in Christianity. Remember the scene with the university student wandering among them? That was me. Their sense of meaning was devastated. You looked into the faces of these Rastafarians; some of them had sold off their land. They were wandering around the Dungle with paper bags, and they just looked stunned. It was a look of utter despair. I don't know how they managed, how they continued, but it was definitely a look of *meaninglessness*. Because they had put everything into this hope; they really believed it. What happens when belief dies? It was the same as my own loss of belief in Christianity, but they faced it in a *traumatic* way. I think Rastafari, at that moment of millenarian disappointment, posed the question of meaninglessness in a very profound and existentially direct way. They weren't philosophers of meaninglessness; they were *living* it.

DS: You think the people who were disappointed because Henry's ships didn't arrive in the harbor suffered a *loss* of faith?

OP: That's a very good question. I *thought* they had, but of course I subsequently came to learn from the work of Leon Festinger and other psychologists that, "when prophecy fails," that doesn't necessarily happen.[1] I think that the movement went through a radical change and became more spiritual. This is like what happened with Christianity when the Messiah didn't return. They sort of reinterpreted it as an *inward* search. And that's how I interpret Rastafarianism. There's a lot of special pleading in most of the academic scholarship on Rastas. A lot of the current scholarship blasts my early popular piece on the Rastas. And for me it's so symptomatic of the patronizing view

80

THE CHILDREN OF SISYPHUS

of bourgeois scholarship. People become extremely sympathetic to the Rastas, are very protective, and project their own interpretation of what happened during different periods in the evolution of the movement. It's also very *presentist*, a failure to see that the creed evolved and is very different now from what is was then. But it was quite clear to me that the failure of millenarianism just posed the problem: What do you do when the thing that you most intensely believe in is shown to be false? Of course, one of the characters in the novel, Brother Solomon, led me to ask whether one can create the environment in which one can force oneself to believe.

DS: Can one *fabricate* the conditions of hope?
OP: That's essentially what Solomon did. That's my thinking.

DS: I want to come back to Brother Solomon and focus on him specifically. But pausing for a moment around the 1964 essay on Rastafari, the one critique of it that readily comes to mind is Rex Nettleford's, in his essay "African Redemption," in *Mirror, Mirror*.[2] In your essay you characterize Rastafari in terms of a psychology of withdrawal, saying roughly that Rastafari represents an aggressive, extroverted type of withdrawal. What's interesting, of course, is that this is one of the first essays that I know of that is trying to use *theoretical* language growing out of that sociological literature on millenarian movements. You write, and I'm quoting here, "The initial outward looking nature of the belief system is really a guise for and a function of the withdrawal which is an index of the total involvement in the society and a passionate need to be accepted by it, expressed in terms of a denial of any wish to be accepted."[3] These are terms that I imagine someone like Nettleford would object to. But what you're trying to capture here is the *paradox* of Rastafari: a desire to be accepted and an aggressive denial of any such desire.
OP: Right. Exactly. From talking to them, that was my sense. I spoke to a lot of them, a few well known – Mortimo Planno, for example – and lots of others, ordinary people.[4] And it was quite clear that these were Jamaicans who were badly dealt with by their society. It's hard to understand it now because Rastas have almost acquired a certain kind of cachet, but then they were seen as the dregs of humanity – and they *knew* that. This was reflected in police behavior toward them; they would just laughingly cut their locks off. There was a profound *rejection* of them. They were held in contempt. I felt nonetheless that I was talking to *real* Jamaicans here, and they wanted to be part of the society. They wanted the things I wanted. One way you

THE PARADOX OF FREEDOM

react to this is to reject the people rejecting you in this aggressive withdrawal; but the aggressive withdrawal was also indicative of a desire to belong to the society, which they later in fact got involved with. They became very involved with reforming the society, at least spiritually and culturally, and they're the most thoroughly *Jamaican* group there is. I saw *both* sides, and I knew in the end that most of them wouldn't be ending up in Africa. A few took up the offer from Selassie, but most didn't.[5] But I could see from talking to them that these were people who were suffering and who just wanted to live a better life in Jamaica.

DS: At the center of the sociopsychological problem that you're trying to describe, both in the essay and in the novel, is *anticipation*. And in the novel, but also in the essay, anticipation is *everything*. Thus, the paradoxical question arises for you: What if the ships, by some miracle, were actually to sail into the harbor? What would Rastafarians do?
OP: Well, I think they'd be overjoyed. The question is whether they'd also *go*.

DS: But your argument seems to be that something would be defeated by that reality.
OP: Yes. You want to live in anticipation. Their anticipation was glorious, a moment of tremendous camaraderie; before the debacle of Henry being arrested and the whole thing falling down, they were very, very happy. Solomon is making that point about *living in anticipation*. Some of this can be gotten in Camus, but also in Immanuel Kant, discussing freedom as paradoxical. Because there is a sense that you accept that, ultimately, we're all determined, but the idea of freedom is profoundly necessary and you have to live *as though* you are free. That is something that attracted me to Kant later on, his theory of freedom. But, for Camus, that was *his* way out, too. It was true of the Pocomania people. Except the interesting thing about *them* was that their anticipation was satisfied every time they had a long meeting, culminating in their transfixed state where they got possessed. It worked because they got immediate gratification. The Rastas were more traditionally Christian, and more *ambitious*.

DS: More eschatological?
OP: Yes. In a funny way, Pocomania was almost the *reverse* of Rastafari because they had given up. This is why I say I think the Rastas were offering up a profound criticism of society: precisely

82

THE CHILDREN OF SISYPHUS

because they were so profoundly *disappointed* with it. How could you do this? It was a demand for Jamaicans to take notice of them. This should *not* happen; this was bad; this is not what Jamaica *should* be like. Criticism explicitly, in the final analysis, indicates that at some level you feel that the society could have done better. The society *betrayed* them and it had the capacity to do otherwise. With the Poco [Pocomania] people, they'd just given up. They'd resigned themselves; they just felt about the society, that that's the way it is. There was no criticism of it. In their meetings they genuinely withdrew without any criticism. In fact, they didn't even want to have a conversation or talk about betrayal. That was the way the world was. They just withdrew into their own spirituality and got their satisfaction every night in this laboring, which is quite an amazing physical experience, as they climaxed in complete possession. They had essentially given up on Jamaica. They didn't expect anything from it.

DS: Whereas Rastafari was making a defiant demand on society.

OP: Yes, exactly. There was a class element to it, too. There is no ideology in Pocomania. There is no politics in Pocomania. It's *pure* spirituality. Rasta ideology was a critique, which in a sense embraces its antithesis. It's thesis and antithesis, which are intimately implicated with each other. The Rastas took the society *seriously* and were betrayed by it. For the Pocomania people, you just give unto Caesar the things that are Caesar's. So, yes, I saw Rastas as wanting desperately to *belong*. In a sense what happened subsequently bore that out. Because the next phase was to move away from millenarianism and to start to internalize the notion of Africa and of Zion as a spiritual state, with all the ritual food and aesthetic life, and the rest of it. But, also, the critique became an *involvement* with Jamaica, and they began to criticize bourgeois society. But, clearly, they had moved from total withdrawal to a critical engagement with society. I find that sociologists are a little bit irresponsible in the way they approach Rastafari. They're too subjective, or in a way it becomes almost a *confessional* kind of analysis. You can be sympathetic to a group, as I was, without having to feel that you have to defend it or endorse it in every way. Even Rex got a little bit like that sometimes, because in purely objective terms this idea of going back to Africa on a ship is absurd. It's absurd in any objective sense. As absurd as the Christian belief that all Christians will rise from the dead on Judgment Day, or that they are literally eating the flesh and drinking the blood of Christ in the Eucharist. Christian belief also rests on everlasting anticipation of the return of Christ. But, as Tertullian

83

THE PARADOX OF FREEDOM

famously said, "I believe because it is absurd." There was a point in my own spiritual development when I was drawn to fideism, the idea that religious belief was its own form of life, quite independent of reason, and even hostile to it. I was also very drawn to the existential theologian Kierkegaard, himself a kind of fideist, in my early years, about the same time that I was under the spell of Camus. You can only begin to understand the Rastas and their millenarianism in terms of what it meant and what drove them.

DS: Anticipation in your view is what sustains Rastafari. And anticipation embodies, in a certain sense, an investment in a *future* that objectively will not come. It is an *irrational* investment, therefore, in the future. For anticipation to *be* anticipation, there has to be, at some level, rational recognition that the future will *not* come. Perhaps this is the place for the role of hope. There is a paradoxical relationship between rational and irrational understanding.

OP: That's right. In a way, that's the Christian state. Because you know that the true Christian is anticipating, being prepared; as Augustine pointed out, this is Jesus' primary teaching – be prepared, anticipate the Second Coming. But, in a way, you *don't* want it to come. You want to live this life, and there'll be a real crisis if it happens. The faith is really about living in anticipation of a state that is forever in the future. That's the great thing about Christianity; it's the only way you can explain why people have been waiting for two thousand years. It can be very powerful and motivating. Just looking at my mother's attitude toward me, it was one of endless anticipation. She had no real reason to think this would ever work. Because, in my village, what she was anticipating was considered almost absurd. *Nobody* went to university except for White folks and a couple of the middle-class estate people, who were quite well off. She was an amazing anticipator, living in constant preparedness and anticipation of this happening. But she was so committed that it becomes self-fulfilling. And that's the good thing about anticipation sometimes.

DS: But one of the troubling things about anticipation, perhaps, at least in *The Children of Sisyphus*, is that anticipation can be *manipulated*. And this is the interesting thing about the character Brother Solomon. I am puzzled by what you meant to do with him as a literary device. Because, as a Rastafarian, Brother Solomon is, in a certain sense, *atypical*. He is abandoned by his mother on the doorstep of the Anglican parson, is brought up by the White parson and his wife, and is given a kind of theological education. Then he

84

THE CHILDREN OF SISYPHUS

has a sexual encounter with the parson's wife, which produces in him an intense and contradictory, almost violent, set of emotions. He has a breakdown; and it is *through* this breakdown that he becomes a Rastafarian – frustration, futility, agony, and so forth. So, what were you *doing* with Solomon in relation to Rastafari?

OP: Well, he was obviously the philosopher. He was, to some extent, the philosophical mouthpiece for my own musings. I saw Solomon as voicing my own philosophical thinking. And certain reviewers were quite intrigued by that. *The Observer* review said that Brother Solomon was the most engaging fraud in modern fiction.[6]

But anyhow, to get back to Solomon, I was probing this question of belief: How do you sustain hope and belief or meaning when the traditional source, religion, goes? And he is making the case that you can live a religious kind of life, and, quite surprisingly, quite a few philosophers have used religion. I was surprised to see this in Kant and his idea of freedom. Kant was also something of a fideist when he argued that we must "deny knowledge so as to make room for faith," which I see as the religious parallel to his idea of the necessity of believing in freedom in the face of the fact that all is ultimately determined, by nature and by God. So, it really was the beginnings of my thinking about freedom and the nature of the meaning of life. Of course, for Brother Solomon it didn't work. When the ship did not come he lacked the power of spiritual reinterpretation and self-redemption – or what the social psychologist Festinger referred to in *When Prophecy Fails* as the capacity to come to terms with cognitive dissonance. Instead, he caved and killed himself, in part because there was no faith behind his anticipation. He was a false fideist. *The Observer* was right in calling him an engaging fraud. However, the great majority of the Rastas gathered in the Dungle waiting for Jah Selassie were genuine in their faith. They did what the majority of the group studied by Festinger, and the vast majority of early Christians and other millenarians after the non-show, have done: they doubled down on their belief. Selassie had not betrayed them. Rather, it was they who had betrayed him in misreading the signs. They were still being tested by Jah in their *downpression.* What followed was a new post-millenarian phase of the movement in which they lived and showed their faith in Jah through *livity,* which is righteous living, expressed in ritual, *iditation* (meditation), *ital* (diet), the spiritual transcendence of *kaya* (ganja), and, famously, *bingis,* the inspiration for reggae.

DS: Exactly. This is the point. For Camus, in *The Myth of Sisyphus,* at least as I understand it, it is important to be able to recognize the

THE PARADOX OF FREEDOM

absurdity of reality, the resounding silence with which reality regards one, and yet *refuse* suicide.

OP: Right. My answer is that it didn't work. *I* was beginning to doubt.

DS: Brother Solomon does not refuse suicide. One question that I come away with, thinking about Brother Solomon, is, What is the nature of the *failure* of Rastafari that you're pointing to with Solomon? The failure is not simply that Solomon is a deceiver, or fraud, but there's something about Rastafari, the nature of its belief or self-understanding, that you are pointing to, it seems to me.

OP: Well, I was moving more toward Marx and certain kinds of political realism, and the view that you've got to take politics seriously and logically. In the final analysis, Rastafari is a religious solution that doesn't work. It was as simple as that. Which is also, in a way, a criticism of Camus. And the fact that I had Solomon dying off in the end, committing suicide, was the beginning of a rejection of Camus. I just felt that, *no*, that's not going to work, there have to be other ways for Camus to turn to the problem of meaning. And maybe one way is to become *politically* engaged.

DS: We will come back to this, because there is the political Camus of *The Rebel*, which is perhaps an auto-critique, and which you were also very interested in. But, before we get there, I want to talk about Dinah. She is manifestly trapped. There is in Dinah no fold of self-consciousness in her striving. There may be a sense of the absurd in Rachel, the toothless old lady who regards Dinah ironically and admonishes her that she will never escape her circumstances. But Dinah in the end *surrenders* to her fate. So, one could ask again, What is it that you want us to understand through her? Dinah can't overcome fate. It's not a matter of committing suicide; her fate *overwhelms* her.

OP: She tries, she moves from one to the other, but eventually she goes back to where she comes from.

DS: What's the connection, or disconnection, between Solomon and Dinah?

OP: Well, Dinah to me is someone who is just blind ambition. She really was determined to get out. And I was making the somewhat pessimistic point about her that is just the Sisyphean argument in its most non-philosophical, starkest way: you're destined by fate.

86

THE CHILDREN OF SISYPHUS

DS: She's *doomed*.

OP: Doomed, no matter what, to keep trying and trying again. She was, in a way, the Sisyphean character at its most direct and least philosophical. She's fated. This, almost literally, is the Greek view. As you can imagine, I went back to the Greek myth, trying to figure out what Camus was up to. Then I got into the Greek idea of fate and the endless repetition of trying to get out from under it. It was metaphor; but it was also literal. (It's funny because, right now, I'm heavily into rereading Saussure and the whole theory of semiotics, because I want to do a critique of the current sociological approach to culture.)[7] Now, Dinah is both signifier and signified, because in one sense she's signifying the Sisyphean condition, if you like – the most philosophical sense of endless strife, meaningless strife, meaningless efforts. But the metaphor is also real; she's also living it. Her life is both a metaphor of this deeper meaning and the real thing. So, it's signifying and it's also what's signified in that she's representing the Sisyphean idea or Greek idea of fate and meaninglessness; she's literally living that experience, too. And, in that sense, she's no longer a signifier. She's the real thing. I wasn't thinking in such elaborate terms then, but I did see her as symbol and as real. Because there's the philosophical idea of the meaning of life but also the fact that, literally, their life was Sisyphean. And that's the direction that I more or less went in as I got more and more into Marx and more into the question of social reality.

DS: Prior to *The Children of Sisyphus*, so far as I know, there is only one profoundly significant Jamaican novel featuring Rastafari, and that's Roger Mais's *Brother Man*, published exactly a decade before, in 1954. Is there a connection or direct relationship for you between *The Children of Sisyphus* and *Brother Man*? Is there something that you felt was unresolved in the Rastafarian character in Mais's novel?

OP: That's a good question, because I'd read it when I was in high school. I remember I was struck very much by the atmosphere of that novel; it's very evocative. But I never really got into the characters at all. I got more into what was evoked about Jamaica. I was drawn – I'm sure by that novel – to learning more about the Rastafarians. I can't even remember the plot now, as I think about it. But I do remember that, in both *Brother Man* and *The Hills Were Joyful Together*, Mais was a powerfully evocative writer. I got some sense of the mournful beauty of Jamaican life. In certain parts of it there's almost a desolate beauty. In the area where I grew up in May Pen it's very dry, very flat, in the cane fields. I don't know if you've ever been,

THE PARADOX OF FREEDOM

but if you go into a cane field you really feel as if you are surrounded by ghosts, because the cane field makes this very eerie sound.

DS: Well, you probably *were* surrounded by ghosts in the cane field. But I'm just wondering whether there is a connection between the crucifixion of Brother Man and the suicide of Brother Solomon.
OP: I think there must have been influence, but it was very subconscious, because I'd read it much earlier. It was one of the earliest novels that I read. I can remember it being very much talked about and Mais being *the* Jamaican novelist. I liked his style of writing much more than John Hearne – I always felt Hearne was very much a *poseur*.

DS: We'll come to you and John Hearne later on. I've read somewhere that C. L. R. James was important to your finding a publisher for the novel. Tell me about that.
OP: This was the period when we were in London and were sitting at his feet. Norman Girvan, Walter Rodney, and myself went up to his apartment every Friday to be indoctrinated in the gospel according to Marx via Trotsky.

DS: And *via* James.
OP: Yes, via James. I went for a couple of months, and after went less and less. But we spent pretty much the better part of a semester doing that. On one occasion I told him that I had just finished the novel – this was 1963. He said he'd like to see it, and I brought the manuscript over. And I didn't hear anything. Three or four weeks later, he said that the publisher Hutchinson was interested. That was his publisher for *Beyond a Boundary*. He didn't even ask me! I was waiting to hear comments. He read it, and without saying anything to me, he sent it to them. And the next thing I knew, he said, "I think they're interested in it. You should go talk to this guy, the editor." Just like that, no agent, nothing. *He* was my agent, I guess. And it is the easiest book I've ever published – simple as that. They *grabbed* it.

DS: And they ran with it. What was your discussion about the novel with James like? Did he say anything to you about the novel?
OP: *No.* His comment was to write an essay on it.

DS: You didn't talk with him about it at all?
OP: *No.* He sent me the essay, which he then sent to *New Left Review*. That was his comment: "This is what I think, and by the way, I'm publishing it."[8]

THE CHILDREN OF SISYPHUS

DS: Your relationship with James was still very close at the time.
OP: It was quite close then. We grew apart, just from distance. I went back to the West Indies. Then he had his troubles with Eric Williams. And then we didn't see each other for a while until he started his lectures here. And we had lunch a couple of times.

DS: These were lectures at Harvard University?
OP: Yes. When I first came here as a visiting lecturer on sabbatical, they'd just started the African American studies program, which didn't have many people. They had several visiting lecturers. James came and gave a regular series of lectures. He would fly up from wherever he was; I'm not quite sure where he was then. We overlapped a little bit. And then he disappeared again. The only other time I saw him after this was once in Canada, when we were on a panel together at York University. That was the last time I saw the old man. He went back to Britain and our paths didn't cross again. We didn't correspond or anything, but we'd had this quite intense interaction in London: with Norman, Walter, and myself.

DS: In 1964, famously, Martin Luther King passed through London on his way to Oslo to receive the Nobel Peace Prize. And Claudia Jones, I think, was one of his hosts. Do you remember hearing him speak in 1964 at Africa Unity House?
OP: No. Malcolm X was the person whom we met with, because he came to the LSE not long before he was assassinated. It was after his famous visit to Mecca. The other person who came through the LSE, whom we also met, was Stokely Carmichael. One person I forgot to tell you about was Michael de Freitas. He had an outfit called RAAS. You know who de Freitas was?

DS: Michael X.
OP: He ended up being executed in Trinidad in 1972. I was asked by Ruth Glass, the wife of my supervisor, to do some research on West Indian organizations in London – which I did. The other research assistant was Robin Blackburn. Ruth hired the two of us – we were the smart ones there. I was hired to the faculty right after my PhD. She was a professor at one of the London colleges. I needed some money between the end of my Commonwealth Scholarship in June and the start of my first teaching position at the end of August 1965. There would have been a gap, and I was getting married. Everyone warned me against working for her. She knew what her reputation was so she got her husband to ask me – and how could you say no

89

THE PARADOX OF FREEDOM

to your supervisor? And, as everyone predicted, it was a disaster. Anyway, I mention this because in the course of doing the research I canvassed all the organizations, and one of them was RAAS. So, I met with de Freitas.

DS: Is it RAS as in R–A–S?
OP: It was a play on the Jamaican *raas*.

DS: The expletive? Not "Ras" the honorific, as in Ras Tafari?
OP: No. It's Racial Adjustment Action Society. I don't know if it got much off the ground. But I went to see de Freitas and interviewed him at length. He was very welcoming. He was a hard man to get hold of; people said he'd never talk, because he had this reputation. But he took a liking to me. Here I was, a young lecturer at LSE. So, he promptly turned around and said he'd like me to be his advisor, the counselor for his organization. I thought this would be a great way of getting into this research. He had me over to the place he lived in, a very luxurious apartment, where these women would come. I remember it was very strange. On a couple of occasions, I would go over there when we were supposed to talk about the organization. He'd say I should wait. And then suddenly this glamorous looking woman, looking like Christine Keeler or someone like that, would turn up, and he'd disappear for a couple of hours. I would be sitting down there wondering what the hell is going on! After this happened a couple of times I kept my distance, but he insisted on our talking. So, I got to know him quite well.

DS: What sort of character was he?
OP: He was a fine-looking fellow, but he used to be the enforcer for London's most notorious slumlord, which means he was the person threatening people with knives and guns to pay their rent. Then he got the revolution bug and decided he was going to become an activist. He took the name "Michael X" because he saw himself as the direct British counterpart of Malcolm X – he was a hustler, he was into drugs, fast women – a pimp, for all I know.

DS: His prominence as a Black Power activist in London was later than 1964, wasn't it?
OP: Much later. Because when I met him he was still working for the slumlord. He was literally enforcing *against* West Indians. And it didn't work out with Ruth.

Figure 1. Oil Painting of Orlando Patterson by Steve Coit, displayed in the Junior Common Room of Leverett House, Harvard University.

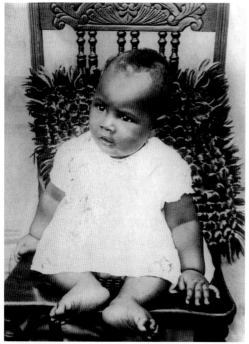

Top Left
Figure 2. A curious Orlando, age under a year, in Savanna-la-Mar, Jamaica.

Top Right
Figure 3. Orlando age ten in a photographer's studio, May Pen, Jamaica.

Bottom Left
Figure 4. Between age six and ten, Orlando and his mother occupied two rooms in this house on Bryants Crescent, May Pen, Jamaica.

Bottom Right
Figure 5. Orlando's elementary school in May Pen. It housed all classes from 1 to 6, which were separated only by an easel and blackboard except for the 6th class, which was separated by a board wall. Each class had about sixty students grouped on either side of an aisle down which the teacher walked brandishing her leather strap.

Above Left
Figure 6. Orlando's paternal great-grandfather, possibly a freeman born during last years of slavery, and the father of William "Captain" Patterson, 1862–1962.

Above Right
Figure 7. Adolphus "Daddy" Morris, c. 1884–1979, Orlando's maternal grandfather, a sugar estate foreman and later barber and small farmer. He was a descendant of slaves of Y-S estate, St Elizabeth parish, owned by heirs of John Morse. The surname Morris may have been a misspelling of "Morse," it being the custom of Jamaican ex-slaves to adopt the name of their former owners as their surnames.

Above
Figure 8. Orlando's father, Charles Altamont Patterson, 1897–1969, a detective in the Jamaican colonial police force and co-founder of the Police Federation, its union. His reports on the Jamaican meetings and speeches of Marcus Garvey are in the Jamaican National Archives.

Left
Figure 9. Orlando at age seventeen with his mother, Almena, known affectionately as "Aunt Mina," 1918–2002.

Opposite page
Top
Figure 10. Graduating class, Chancellor Hall, University College of the West Indies, 1962. Patterson is in glasses, kneeling, second row, 5th from right.

Bottom
Figure 11. Orlando writing *Children of Sisyphus* in his Belsize Park flat, London, 1963. Photo credit Bill Patterson.

Above
Figure 12. Orlando in his Leverett House apartment, Harvard, where he was Allston Burr Senior Tutor, 1971–73.

Left
Figure 13. Orlando (in glasses), with Manley, announcing Orlando's Urban Upgrading Project to constituents of South Central Kingston, 1975. Photo credit *Jamaica Gleaner*.

Middle
Figure 14. At the White House, explaining the white ethnic revival to President Gerald Ford, with Daniel Patrick Moynihan and Nathan Glazer, 1975.

Bottom
Figure 15. With Ralph Ellison, his wife Fanny McConnell Ellison, and Henry Louis Gates, at the 1991 National Book Award ceremony in which Orlando won the non-fiction award for his book *Freedom in the Making of Western Culture*.

Figure 16. Orlando with his wife, Anita Patterson, professor of English at Boston University.

Figure 17. Orlando with his daughters Kaia (mother, Anita), Barbara and Rhiannon (mother, the late Nerys Patterson, novelist).

Figure 18. At the White House with a group of experts called by Obama to advise on police brutality and victimization of black youth, 2015.

Figure 19. Presentation of *The Confounding Island* to Prime Minister Andrew Holness at his residence, with the minister of finance Nigel Clarke, 2019.

The Sociology of Slavery

DS: I want to turn now to the making of *The Sociology of Slavery*, your PhD thesis at the LSE. When and how did you decide that you were going to work on slavery?
OP: Before I went to London I knew that was what I was going to work on. I had always wanted to be an historian. And when I went to London what later became known as historical sociology was what I clearly saw as my aim.

DS: How did you perceive that what Caribbean historiography, or the historiography of Jamaican slavery in particular, needed was an *historical* sociology? What is it about the character of the debate about slavery and history at the time that drives you there?
OP: Very simple – I was interested in the *slaves*. Everything previously had been written about broader social and economic factors – even Eric Williams's book was about "capitalism and slavery." Elsa Goveia's book was about West Indian slave society.[1] I thought what was missing was a central focus on the slaves, on their *lives* – where they came from, what they did, how they survived. They had been treated merely as a *category*, whether in the Marxian or Parsonian traditions. In a way, the closest to what I wanted to do would have been James's *The Black Jacobins* – he looked at the slaves as revolutionaries.[2] But if you look at every other book that had been published before that, they were more involved with the *structural* issues.

DS: Douglas Hall's *Free Jamaica*; Phillip Curtin's *Two Jamaicas* ...
OP: Curtin's *Two Jamaicas* was subtitled *The Role of Ideas in a Tropical Colony*.[3] No one had done that before. But I have an interesting story about another West Indian at the time, Eddie [later Kamau] Brathwaite.

DS: You'd met him in 1964, I believe, in Jamaica.
OP: Yes, after *Sisyphus* was published, in 1964. He was working very much in the old tradition, on missionaries – that's what his thesis started on. He met me in the West Indies working on slavery. We had a long talk, and he went back to England and promptly *changed* his subject to doing what *I* was doing. It seemed obvious to me; I've always known that I wanted to work on the slaves. Even as an undergraduate. I remember, in my final year, there was a very

interesting lecturer, a Trinidadian guy, in political science, and he'd have sessions at his home on Friday evenings with me, Norman, Walter, and some other students. He was the first Black political scientist who taught there – a very dapper fellow. Each of us did a presentation, and I did one on the lives of the slaves. *That* was what was missing. No one had done anything on that – both the social structure and the culture of the slaves. Everybody was concerned with the *system*, and the slaves as a *category*, their exploitation, and so on. Eric Williams was concerned with how slavery influenced British development. He'd done one little thing on race earlier on, but never wrote a treatise on the slaves *themselves*. James came closest to that, and therefore *The Black Jacobins* was an important text for me. So, the penny had dropped, Eddie realized, and I must have teased him about it: "Why are you working on missionaries?" Toward the end of my undergraduate days I was very much in a *nationalist* phase, interested in Black culture and things Black, Black Jamaicans. I took that interest over into my PhD. I was very much into Black culture and the urgent need for scholarship to start writing about the Black *experience*.

DS: Brathwaite would have just come back from Ghana, but then he left in 1965 to go to the University of Sussex (though I think he lived in London).

OP: Exactly. But then he was in the archives working on missionaries, and I was in the archives working on slavery. He did one very terrible thing that I never said much about, because we soon became very active in CAM [Caribbean Artists Movement]. The book from my thesis, *The Sociology of Slavery*, came out very soon after, in 1967, and he was sent a copy of it by the journal *Race*, to do a review. He did the most snide, nitpicking review of a book I've ever read.[4] And he took all the sources and used them in his own book. It was unbelievable. I'll never forget it. I read it and thought, "This guy has a problem," because, clearly, he had gotten from me the idea to write on almost the same thing. And, basically, his agenda was to tear it down as much as he could, because he was going to be coming out with *his* book. I saw another side of him. I remember when it came out I said to him, "Wow, I saw your review. You must have done a lot of work on that. Thanks for doing the review." And he said, "Oh!" – because he's an incredibly sensitive guy – "You don't mind?" I said, "No, you had to write what you had to write," and changed the subject. But then he brought out *The Development of Creole Society*.[5]

92

THE SOCIOLOGY OF SLAVERY

DS: I'll come back to your relationship with Brathwaite in a moment. But I want to stay a bit with the making of *The Sociology of Slavery*. Did the dissertation have the same title?

OP: Yes, same title. But I went there [LSE] knowing that's what I wanted to work on. And, while Glass was a demographer, I made it clear to him that I thought there was this important need to study the slaves. And to understand slavery you've got to understand the *slave's society*.

DS: It's fascinating to me that you say the one text that came closest to the kind of perspective you were looking for was *The Black Jacobins*. I hadn't remembered that *The Sociology of Slavery* is in fact dedicated to James. And, of course, *The Black Jacobins* had just been reissued in 1963, when you were starting at the LSE. Was that the first time you'd had read it? Did James introduce it to you earlier in the study group?

OP: No, I knew about *The Black Jacobins*, and I'm pretty sure I'd read it before meeting James – the first edition. I read everything that was written on the slaves, especially from the perspective of the slaves. I do not recall what edition I read, but certainly in reading secondary sources I read everything that was available.

DS: When you read *The Black Jacobins* while you were doing your research, did it form part of your discussion with James? Did you discuss *his* reading of that slave past while constructing your own?

OP: I can't recall discussing slavery with James. Definitely Marx. But we were talking about *The Black Jacobins* from UCWI. James was already a celebrity. And we were all reading everything he had written. We were all reading *everything* on the Caribbean – *voraciously*. That's when we were meeting with this lecturer Archie Singham. There were lots of seminars very much focused on the Caribbean, and James was featured.[6]

DS: I wonder whether there isn't another dimension of the attraction to James. Because, in *The Black Jacobins*, part of what makes its focus on the slaves a dynamic one is that it has a *political* agenda. And, interestingly, the preface to *The Sociology of Slavery* evokes Frantz Fanon. So, one has a sense of *The Sociology of Slavery* as, if not a directly insurgent text, then a very deliberately *engaged* text.

OP: Absolutely! By then I was very much into Fanon. In fact, George Lamming did the independence issue of *New World Quarterly*, and he asked me to do a review of Fanon because I was so much into

93

THE PARADOX OF FREEDOM

Fanon at that time. And I did it. And the title he gave – I didn't give it, *he* did – was "Frantz Fanon: My Hope and Hero."[7]

DS: But a title with which you had no quarrel, I assume.
OP: I had no quarrel, no. But that would have been about when I was writing the preface to *The Sociology of Slavery*. Because, remember, we are now in 1967. I read *The Black Jacobins* as having a political agenda, but I read it as a serious academic text, too, that focused on the slaves as revolutionaries. I have a long chapter on Jamaican slave revolts in *The Sociology of Slavery*. It was much, much longer in the earlier drafts of the thesis. It was the only part of the thesis that my supervisor, Glass, objected to. It was too long. In fact, it was so long that I cut it out and did a more sociological interpretation that formed the foundation of the long piece on slavery and slave revolts that came out not long after that.[8]

DS: You describe *The Sociology of Slavery* as concerned with the society and culture of the slaves. But, in a certain sense, *The Sociology of Slavery* can also be described (and I think this is language you would also use) as a social psychology of slavery. A social-psychological perspective informs your preoccupations.
OP: Absolutely, yes. I was interested in getting into what the slaves were thinking, what it was like to be a slave, how they survived the system mentally, socially, and culturally. *That* was my main concern.[9] One important book that had come out, and that partly influenced my work (I was partially countering it while absorbing some of the ideas), was Stanley Elkins's book *Slavery*.[10]

DS: I want to talk about Elkins, because your engagement with the "slave personality" thesis is important.
OP: Elkins was *big*. And, of course, he got attacked a lot. I was part of the criticism, but at the same time I thought he was on the right track in terms of trying to figure out the psychology of slavery. Some people just totally dismissed him; I didn't. I was critical, but I thought "Sambo" was *there*, definitely. But on whether it was "real" or not, whether it was "dissembling" or not – that was where we differed.

DS: What would you say to the proposition that Elkins and yourself at that point are writing out of a similar paradigm, informed by the "individual and society" framework? So, there are real intersections at that moment. This would change later.

94

THE SOCIOLOGY OF SLAVERY

OP: The individual and society framework was big at that time. Three works that I read as an undergraduate, mainly at the urging of Lloyd Braithwaite, that strongly influenced me were Abram Kardiner's *The Mark of Oppression* [1951] and two books by Gordon Allport, *The Nature of Prejudice* [1954] and *Becoming* [1960]. Kardiner's book on how racial prejudice and discrimination influenced Black Americans, based on twenty-five psychoanalytic interviews of Black men, led me to consider one aspect of oppression that is out of favor today, namely, the self-inflicted wounds of immiseration, the ways in which the response to oppression traumatizes the oppressed and leads them to turn their anger on themselves and those close to them. Freud was still very much in vogue then, and Kardiner's work encouraged me to read Freud more closely, both to understand my own inner struggles as well as the ways in which racial and colonial oppression internally traumatized the oppressed. Allport's work on prejudice is still, in my view, the best work ever published on the subject, and I have returned to it time and again over the years. His Terry lectures at Yale, published in 1960, was an argument for social psychology to take the study of personality more seriously. It was also an implicit critique of both behavioralist – which was big at Harvard at the time under Skinner's influence – as well as Freudian determinism. Above all was the idea that, while we are strongly influenced by our environment, we also have the capacity to influence, and to change, our circumstances and social environment. I've remained strongly influenced by social psychology and by the interplay of culture and psychology in human life.

DS: *The Sociology of Slavery* initiates a perspective that I think you have come to be associated with – the view that New World slavery was a fundamentally *destructive* experience. And, for you, Jamaica is a paradigm instance of this destructive experience. In fact, slave Jamaica constitutes a formation that you cannot call a *society*. That's emphatic in *The Sociology of Slavery*, and it doesn't just set your agenda. One has the sense that there is an unstated view you are arguing *against*. What is the view of society, of the social, or of Jamaican society, that you're challenging?

OP: I don't know if *I* was challenging. As it turned out, *others* were challenging *that* view [that slavery was primarily destructive]. Eddie Brathwaite sets up a challenge with his creolization argument. There was nothing *there* to challenge before. To the degree I was challenging anything, it was more the American study of slavery, which saw slavery as *stable*. U. B. Phillips's racist book was still the classic text at that time, *American Negro Slavery*; and Kenneth Stampp's book *The Peculiar Institution* came out as the counter to Phillips.[11] So, Phillips reigned from 1918 until Stampp's volume first came out in 1956. I'm actually doing a paper on all of this now because John Hope Franklin died recently, and I've been asked to give several commemorative lectures on him and his work.[12] It's been a little awkward because when people die you can make exaggerated claims about them. And while people have been saying he [Franklin] changed the whole course of the debate on slavery, this isn't true. *From Slavery to Freedom* is of course a great textbook that educated generations of people about slavery. But, in terms of changing the debate, that honor goes to Stampp. He was the person who finally toppled Phillips.

DS: Did U. B. Phillips's work shape the discussion of slavery in the Caribbean?
OP: Yes, to the degree that you're talking about slavery in the Americas. But the interesting thing is that Phillips was one of the historians who actually looked, in part, at slave *life*. He was doing it from a conservative, racist perspective, but the point is that this was the only major book that looked at slave life. He also wrote a paper on Jamaican slavery.[13] In a way, *The Sociology of Slavery* was relevant even to the United States, which was why it was widely reviewed here. There had been few modern books that looked at slave life in the US and the Caribbean. There was one other person who influenced me – the cultural anthropologist Melville Herskovits. He was very important in my undergraduate education. Remember, I was taught sociology by two warring anthropologists.

DS: Yes! The two Smiths: M. G. Smith and R. T. Smith.
OP: So, the people I would have been dialoging with were Herskovits, who was emphasizing the continuities with Africa, and U. B. Phillips, who was emphasizing the civilizing influence of slavery on Blacks. And a few others, mainly on America: Carter Woodson, Herbert Aptheker, John Hope Franklin, and W. E. B. Du Bois.

DS: In some sense, though, you emphasize the *discontinuities*. And, more than discontinuities, you are emphasizing the *destructive* character of a form of systemic violence.
OP: Absolutely. Which was the worst of any kind. I think Jamaica may have had the harshest slavery in world history.[14] However, I also examined how, in spite of the catastrophic impact of slavery, Blacks

THE SOCIOLOGY OF SLAVERY

were able to eke out creolized syncretisms between the surviving remnants of the African cultures from which they were torn and elements of the British cultures to which they were forced to adjust: Jamaican creole, Kumina, Pocomania, and the other Afro-Christian religions, the reinterpreted Anancy folk tales, the agricultural slash-and-burn techniques of farming, and, of course, the music are all examples of these syncretisms forged on the anvil of slavery. And Herskovits's work *The Myth of the Negro Past* was very important in my study of these patterns of cultural adjustment, although I did not go as far as he did in his claims of the survival of the African past. So, my account, while it emphasized the destructiveness of slavery, was not solely about destruction but also about survival, social survival and resistance, expressed in the large number of revolts, psychological resistance expressed in the Quashee personality complex, cultural survival expressed in the creole language and other syncretic patterns. It's interesting that Brathwaite's book has come to be identified with the tradition of creolization in Jamaica, but that is only due to the title of his book. In fact, *The Development of Creole Society in Jamaica* devoted less than a quarter of the work to the lives of the slaves, and Brathwaite did not invent the idea of creoliz-ation during slavery. Elsa Goveia's work, which he drew on heavily without sufficient acknowledgment, was the first to use the concept of creolization extensively in the study of Caribbean slavery. And *The Sociology of Slavery* was the second major study of Caribbean slavery to explore the processes of creolization. Indeed, the book was the first to be wholly devoted to the process of cultural survival and trans-formation, to a far greater degree than Brathwaite's. Nonetheless, because it has the word "Creole" in the title, people simply assume that it was the work's major concern and that he pioneered the study of creolization, both of which are completely false.

DS: Exactly. This is what's interesting to me, that, for you, Jamaica is the paradigm instance of slavery. This is my speculation, that you see a Jamaica in independence that understands itself through a nation-alist idiom, "Out of Many, One," and therefore the supposition is that it constitutes, however diverse, a social *order*, a society. And I read *The Sociology of Slavery* as a critique of that assumption – that it does not in fact constitute a "society."

OP: Yes. And I was giving my own view of Black culture and a critique of the racism in Jamaican society. Remember, I used to write a lot of articles for *The Gleaner* on Jamaican race and color problems. I was criticized for seeing the culture of Blacks as the product of the struggle against, and survival from, slavery and colonial denigration, but also for seeing the potential for violence in the society. I was taking what I later came to call a "catastrophic" view, namely, that the history was very *destructive*, and the behavior of people, both of the elites and of the masses, had to be seen in that context. So, it was not an "Out of Many, One" society. I was very critical of that ideology, of that love-fest of the "Out of Many, One People" idea.

DS: Memorably, in the concluding chapter of *The Sociology of Slavery* you connect this catastrophic view of the slave experience to the evolution of a fragmented social order, the emergence of social groups that do not share common social values. Two interconnected things are fascinating to me. One, you're involved in a whole critique of the Durkhemian–Weberian–Parsonian thesis that presupposes that social formations have to rest on commonly shared values; and, second, one hears an echo there of M. G. Smith, also a critic of the dominant sociological thesis.

OP: It's *more* than an echo. I shared MG's view *very* strongly that there were two different societies and there was very little holding them together besides the imperial system. My only difference from MG is that I saw a more *dualistic* system, whereas he saw a tripartite one.

DS: You mean Black/Brown/White?

OP: Yes. I saw Brown and White as very much *one*, what I called Anglo-Jamaica. I included that dualism theory in the thesis of an essay that I wrote in the early 1970s, "Context and Choice in Ethnic Allegiance,"[15] but it was buried away and has not received much attention. The essay was primarily a critique of the ethnic revival movement of the 1970s which challenged the view that there was something primordial about culture and ethnicity. In regard to Jamaica, the essay was a point of departure from MG, in which I gave a more dualistic analysis of the system in contrast with Smith's tripartite view. I also argued, contra Smith, that there was a kind of agonistic interaction between the two cultural systems in Jamaica, in the way, for example, that Black Jamaicans would go to their Pocomania and Kumina religious gatherings during the week, then dress up in their best clothes and attend the Anglican service on Sundays.

DS: Well, at the point of your writing, the colonial period is over, and, if you like, the Brown sector has inherited power from the White.

THE SOCIOLOGY OF SLAVERY

OP: They were the main purveyors of European civilization. They were, in many ways, *more* European than the Whites, many of whom didn't even go to college. The lawyers and doctors and the people who were going to Oxford were the Brown-skinned people.

DS: But, of course, MG initiates that debate in the *colonial* period, in the early 1950s.
OP: He was my *main* teacher, actually, more than anyone else. That was the background. So, I saw that final chapter as in fact saying that there were *two* societies.

DS: Let's return to the "slave personality" debate that *The Sociology of Slavery* engages in. The question of the slaves' adaptation or not to domination has always seemed to me one of the most interesting issues that *The Sociology of Slavery* engages. One of the things about Stanley Elkins is that he is turning his lens on the formation of New World slavery while listening in the background to the debates about the Holocaust and to the stories about survival in the camps. He is reading some of the autobiographical literature on the transformation of personality during that period. But Elkins's social psychology of the personality of subordination is also emerging at a period when there is a good deal of work on culture and personality – Abram Kardiner's famous work, for example.
OP: Which, as I said, I read and liked. *The Mark of Oppression* – I liked that.[16]

DS: There is, in *The Sociology of Slavery*, then, an interest in this question: What is the mark of oppression on the Jamaican slaves?
OP: There also is another book by a social psychologist who came to Jamaica.

DS: Yes, Madeline Kerr's *Personality and Conflict in Jamaica*, of course.
OP: Fanon also – he was a psychologist. That perspective was very important to me. I was reading everything that could inform that. I was thinking: What was it like to be a slave, to mentally survive that holocaust? I liked the use of the concentration camp, because the plantation was just one extended concentration camp that went on for hundreds of years.

DS: But does Erving Goffman influence you?
OP: Not much, at that time.

99

THE PARADOX OF FREEDOM

DS: What was your essential critique of Stanley Elkins?

OP: The main critique I have of Elkins is that I thought that the behavior of the slaves was one of *dissembling*. Yes, there was Sambo. The initial crude criticism by the chauvinists, by the nationalists, was that there was *no* such thing – Sambo was only in the heads of White people. I was critical of Elkins, but my criticism was *not* that. My own data showed that Quashee and Quasheba were real. And, very importantly, Elkins did suggest that this personality emerged contextually; but you can see how this would have irritated Blacks in the middle of the civil rights movement! This was bad timing. He was clearly indicating that Blacks *became* Sambos. Now, I was saying that Sambo was real enough, but it was a form of dissembling, part of that chaotic system in which slaves used this behavior as part of their psychological warfare. Blacks were "playing fool to catch wise"; that's my favorite Jamaican proverb. But I also suggested that, if you played fool to catch wise *too much*, you could get trapped in that game. So, my critique of Elkins was a more sympathetic one in the sense that I was saying, you can't say that this is all some White man's fantasy. It *wasn't* a fantasy. And it was part, too, of the saturnalia that you had, and the pictures are there, by Isaac Mendes Belisario. His figures are a really great resource. There's nothing like that in the annals of US slavery. Those prints are amazing, and they had a strong influence on me.[17] They were mocking the Whites right in front of their faces, as several astute analysts clearly saw. *Lady Nugent's Journal* made it quite clear that she saw what was going on – a very interesting woman.[18] Jamaican proverbs and Jamaican Anancy folk tales are examples of the oppressed getting back at their oppressors by mocking and outwitting them; they are examples of what James Scott calls the "weapons of the weak" – and Scott, by the way, uses my discussion of the Quashee play-acting personality as one example in his famous discussion of the weapons of the weak.[19]

DS: *The Sociology of Slavery* is importantly, to my mind, not only an exercise in the virtues of a certain kind of sociological analysis. It is also an exercise in demonstrating the *limits* of sociological analysis. By that, I mean to point to the moment in *The Sociology of Slavery* where you are interested in the possibility of revolt. In the structure of *The Sociology of Slavery* you have produced a complex historical and sociological apparatus, and then there comes a moment when you mobilize Albert Camus' *The Rebel* and Gabriel Marcel, the Catholic existentialist, to make the point that, as you put it, there is

100

THE SOCIOLOGY OF SLAVERY

a "line" beyond which the dominated will not go. What triggers the particular moment of revolt may be contingent and have a lot to do with various psychological factors (we'll come back to this when we talk about *Die the Long Day*). But are you suggesting that there is a limit to specifically *sociological* analysis when, say, an *existentialist* reading has to inform our understanding?

OP: Well, I've always felt that, in the final analysis, you have to almost do a thought experiment and place yourself in the position of the slave to understand what was really going on, which goes beyond what data make possible. At this point, the chapter of the thesis got so out of hand that my advisor, David Glass, said, "You have to cut that back." He actually said, "This is no longer sociological." So, I cut back a huge chunk of that. You're right, that was clearly important. And, even then, I didn't withdraw from the complexities of the situation because in that revolt situation you see Sambo, and you see the playing and the complexities of the reaction. Now, I got into a little bit of trouble with the nationalists, and even the White supporters of the nationalists, in the essay I did that is published in *Social and Economic Studies* and reproduced in the book on Maroons.[20]

Eugene Genovese expressed horror and shock at that essay because I noted that Cudjoe did this weird thing. Because after forty years of struggle, he signs [a treaty], and he was playing this Sambo game with the British; and then he signed away the rights of future generations of rebels. I couldn't just render that as *heroic*; that was something I had to comment on. What I wrote on it upset Genovese like crazy. In his own essay, which he did later on, he had some really snide remark about me.[21] But the evidence was right there. I wasn't playing games at all with that. When it came to understanding what was going on, I read it as I saw it in all the complexities of that response. How could a slave rebel have made that decision? What was going on? Slavery did lead to a tortuous way of adapting psychologically. And these are problems that are still Jamaica's. (In the introduction to the new, 2022, edition of *The Sociology of Slavery*, I include a print of Cudjoe signing the treaty with the Jamaican Whites that gave the Maroons autonomy within their own communities, but also agreed to return all future runaways and assist the Whites in putting down all future revolts. I entitled the print, "Snatching Treachery from the Jaws of Heroism." Jamaicans are still having a hard time coming to terms with the Maroons. Were they traitors or heroes? The truth is, they were both. But Jamaicans, like most people, find it hard to live with, or come to terms with, contradiction.)

THE PARADOX OF FREEDOM

DS: Well, that is, to my mind, a characteristically Orlando Patterson perspective. Another aspect of this question of revolt that you set out here – and *all* of your books wrestle with this thesis – is that, for you, the dialectic of slavery and freedom turns principally on the *creole* slave; it's less about Tacky, who came directly off the slave ship. The 1760 revolt is less perplexing to you than the 1831–2 revolt, because Sam Sharpe was born and brought up within the very engine of slavery. Sharpe is interesting, in part, because, in order to become a deacon in the Native Baptist Church, he obviously had to *play* some game. But that didn't make him less critical; in fact, it shapes his whole ideological approach.[22]

OP: Absolutely. He used Christianity and Christian organization to rationalize revolt. This, by the way, is the origin of the *Freedom* book, which spent a lot of time on Christianity and the ancient revolt against slavery. *That* was the basic thesis of *Freedom*. In fact, the book I'm working on right now is a short history of freedom for Princeton University Press. I did a public lecture series at Princeton University in which I see Christianity as essential for the survival of freedom from the ancient world. Anyway, it comes back here to the fact that Sam Sharpe interpreted Christianity in a radical way, when in fact the missionaries (who were being criticized by the planters) were saying, "No, no, we're going to teach the Blacks how to be obedient, we're not teaching rebellion." But it didn't prevent the rebels, the slaves, from reading it *their* way. That becomes a very important thesis later on when I'm looking at the Middle Ages and at serfs who were all very much like Daddy Sharpe in being able to read the *radical* version of Christianity, even though the elites were projecting a version of Christianity and Christian freedom that involved obedience and submission.

DS: When I was a student at the University of the West Indies (in the late 1970s) the historiography marked the distinction between the revolts of the eighteenth century and the revolts of the early nineteenth century – the distinction between the African slave and the creole slave. But you were writing this in the early 1960s. I want a sense of how that problem emerged for you.

OP: Between the creole and the African? That became clear to me from the data. Again, if you're trying to figure out the psychology of the slaves, knowing Jamaicans, growing up in rural Jamaica, they were going on about "saltwater Negroes" and "guinea birds," and it was quite clear that there was deep contempt and resentment between the two, and you wonder, What the hell is going on in the mind of

THE SOCIOLOGY OF SLAVERY

these creole slaves? Almost all the early revolts were led by the Akan slaves. So, reading the literature on the historical development of slavery, it comes as quite a shock when the creoles start rebelling. The question to me becomes Why? What's going on here? Why now? Why then? How did they get the fever, the bug? And why was there this transition? It was perplexing. One answer, of course, is that they were getting it from the missionaries and from Christianity, and from what they'd learned from the talk about liberty and freedom from the Whites – but primarily it was from Christianity and from the missionaries. That, for me, sufficiently explained it. But it was a very important transition, because it was so startling. If you read the estate accounts (and the Whites themselves constantly referred to this), they saw it as one of the sources of their insecurity. Later on, people were making a big deal about it. But it was always clear to me.

DS: Let's turn to the relationship between *The Sociology of Slavery* and *The Development of Creole Society in Jamaica*. You have given me a really interesting glimpse into the origins of Brathwaite's research into that book. You say that he got the idea from you to shift his focus from missionaries to slave society. But, in some sense, he takes the *opposite* view from you about the *nature* of slave society.
OP: Well, yes, he *had* to take the opposite view. In a way, he just basically transferred the perspective he had on the missionaries. He was working on missionaries, looking at the way they fashioned these communities, like Jericho in St Catherine – except he suddenly realized that what he was doing was working on what *White* people were forming. *He* became increasingly radicalized, too. Eddie didn't *start* off as being all that radical, though much of the Black nationalist thing was developing with him too. He had gone to Africa and come back. But when *I* met him, he wasn't all that into Black nationalism. I'd say he definitely became *more* radicalized in the years after.

DS: Brathwaite's view is that what we have here is a *society*, however debased, and it has a logic that derives from the Afro-slave community. Do you think that Brathwaite's thesis is simply mistaken? Do you think it's a thesis that contradicts yours?
OP: It really doesn't. I think it was premature to make the claim he made about what was happening then.

DS: Ah! It was a *premature* claim.
OP: Originally, he was working on the nineteenth century; then he shifted. After we spent the summer talking and he saw what I

THE PARADOX OF FREEDOM

was working on, he suddenly realized, "Wait a minute. Why am I writing another book on missionaries?" I think slavery *remained* very chaotic, very destructive, and indeed the missionaries were very important in building some order in the system; there was a lot of creative work being done after slavery. The nineteenth century was the critical period.

DS: I see what you mean.

OP: He was originally on the right track, except he was dealing with the wrong group. Not the wrong group, there is no way that one could argue that the missionaries were not important in institution-building. They were important even for the Africans themselves. Because Daddy Sharpe used the missionary organization, he used Christianity. And similarly, as Curtin and others have pointed out, the roots of Black Jamaican culture go back to the way the Black Jamaican preachers used the organization and the fervor of the missionary activities – they virtually appropriated it in creating the base of Afro-Jamaican culture. So, they were drawing not only on African culture but also on the organization and other aspects of missionary Christian culture to create the foundations of Afro-Jamaican culture, which has a strong Christian element. No matter how African you go, it *still* has a strong Christian element. For me, Pocomania constitutes, if you like, the purest form of what the African Jamaican created. And there's no denying the Christian element there in the music (although it's also profoundly African). That's why I call it a sort of *syncretic* creolization, which is the term I think I use in that chapter I mentioned earlier. But a lot of that cultural work was in the nineteenth century. And claiming that it went back to the eighteenth century was, I think, misreading what was going on, because, for one thing, there weren't many missionaries around. There weren't many models, because White society was totally chaotic. Now, people like Barry Higman have been working hard to show that the system was much more robust. But I don't believe it.

I think the best model comes out of the diaries of that planter Thomas Thistlewood.[23] *That* was Jamaica. They're screwing themselves stupid, right, left, and center; they're smoking too much, they're drinking too much. The preachers were all debauched; it was a *chaotic* society. Whites provided no models; and there was this tension – more than a tension – between the Africans and the creoles. Obviously, it wasn't *totally* chaotic; people had to have some stability in their lives. But it was very much a continuous process

104

THE SOCIOLOGY OF SLAVERY

of transition in which there was such a high mortality rate – unlike the United States. The creole population never reproduced itself in Jamaica. There's no *demographic* continuity. It was protracted genocide.

DS: You would want to argue that that itself is an indication of the absence of a *societal* base.

OP: Yes. As I pointed out in the introduction [to *The Sociology of Slavery*], it was the closest people came to a society that lacked basic social order. It was Hobbesian. It came as close to a Hobbesian society as one could imagine. *That's* how I thought when I was twenty-three, starting the thesis, and that's what I think now. And the most recent work on Jamaican slavery, drawing on the amazing diary of Thomas Thistlewood, completely supports my position against the revisionists such as Barry Higman, who, in spite of the very valuable work he has produced, has tended to normalize Jamaican slavery and to underplay its uniquely catastrophic and near genocidal cruelty.[24]

DS: I know that's what you think! Let me ask you the question more polemically, to provoke you a little bit. Suppose one were to say that the only difference between Kamau [Edward Brathwaite] and yourself is that you see the glass as half *empty*, whereas he sees it as half *full*; you see the conflict and disorder and a hopelessly debased formation, whereas he wants to look for the moments that are integrative. Would you agree with that?

OP: Sure. That's right. I pointed out clearly that a creole social order did emerge. In fact, I theorized it as a syncretic Afro-Jamaican social order. So, I wasn't denying that; I didn't say that chaos existed throughout. We differ in terms of the *timing*, and he perhaps emphasized more, if you like, the *stability* in the system during the last decades. But, in the end, there were important continuities. I see slavery as the primary source for continuities later on, whereas he goes back so much more. Again, I was the first person to write about continuities from Africa in some of the customs. Anancy, for example. But even then Anancy had changed from being a messenger of the gods, a moral figure, to the *ginal* that he became. So, even when I talk about the African continuities I saw *changes*. The real source of that society is, on the one hand, the chaotic situation and, on the other, the adaptations and adjustments made to that problem. It's still the source of major dysfunction in the society. But in the nineteenth century there was a really strong effort to overcome some

105

THE PARADOX OF FREEDOM

of these. And, in some cases, there was success. Here, an important person was Edith Clarke. I saw her work as very important. And so did MG, by the way.[25] In a way, we, Clarke and I, share the same view as far as the peasantry goes, except for the timing. I see the peasant as making a really incredible effort to overcome the problems of slavery. The dynamic for me was how you overcome the slave past, and which groups did. Because I didn't see all groups succeed in doing that. Edith Clarke emphasized that there was a peasantry and there was a stable pattern there, different from Europe, and different from Anglo-Jamaicans. And this is where I talk about a syncretic creole; I talk about African syncretizing with the European culture in response to the challenges of slavery and the economic hardship to produce the Afro-Jamaican creole. But then, there was still chaos reigning on the plantation.

People keep talking about the shift from slavery to peasantry without realizing that the plantation continued right through. There was chaos *there*, and, if anything, it expanded again in the nineteenth century, as Clarke clearly showed. If you went to the plantation belt, it was a zone of total instability, very different from the orderly peasantry. By the time you get to the late nineteenth and early twentieth centuries you did have some stability among the peasantry, and people often see that period as a golden age of peasant stability. They had largely withdrawn and were living their own lives. They had their farms. I think of figures in my own family past – my grandfather, my great-grandfather. These farms were very stable; there was family life. R. T. Smith got it right. It wasn't European, but it was a stable developmental cycle. They all got married in the end, but they all got married at the average age of forty-seven. So, I just found Brathwaite got the timing wrong. He also neglected the persisting problems of those groups who really didn't make it as the peasants did. And then, of course, there's a persistence of the instability in the urban areas. Because one of the criticisms people have made of me here, in the United States, and there, in Jamaica, is that I say there is this peasant movement and this period of stability, so how can I also claim that slavery was still having a negative influence? This criticism only sticks if you take the view that there's a monolithic Black community and fail to note that there's a clear pattern of continuity between the instability of slavery and the plantation belt that, as I think Edith Clarke quite rightly said, sometimes permeated the peasant area, and then fed right into the urban slums. I just had a more complex view of the society than Brathwaite did. The fact that he was a Barbadian may have partly influenced it, too. Don't forget

106

THE SOCIOLOGY OF SLAVERY

that Barbados was a much more disciplined society, more *disciplined* in the Foucauldian sense.

DS: Meaning that they had been disciplined *by* slavery?

OP: And colonialism. Because, in Barbados, ex-slaves didn't have a chance to withdraw from the plantation. There's no land! So, there wasn't much of a peasantry in Barbados, and what you had then was that, when the Whites got their act together, they created a *society* in Barbados that definitely had a disciplining effect. The Blacks then had a model of a disciplined society in the Whites. Jamaica *never* had that. But in Barbados they were tightly packed together; the modern plantation became a much more powerful influence there. And there's another factor, too, which I'm working on right now with one of my students. I'm trying to explain violence comparatively, and a case that I'm using is comparing Jamaica and Barbados.[26] I have several explanations for why Barbados has such a low rate of violence. It's a good comparison, because in many ways they have the same history, the same trajectory, the same colonial past. But then Barbados has been very successful economically and has a low rate of violence. And this has to do with the higher proportion of Whites who are there, the fact that this is a much more coherent White society, and they succeeded more in establishing hegemonic control over the Black Barbadians. One reason for this was that the British went around their empire recognizing certain groups as being good at certain things and creating in effect a kind of self-fulfilling prophecy in which, by following up on their own prejudices and myths, they created what they claimed to have found. A classic example is the Gurkhas, who they claimed were noble savages. The Gurkhas were no better fighters than anybody else in that part of their world, but the British decided that they were noble savages, put them in uniforms, trained them, and then turned around and said, "You see what I mean? They're good fighters." I think they did something like that with the Barbadians. They thought Barbadians were the smart Blacks. They made that decision from quite early. And [on the same principle as with the Gurkhas] if you think they're smart, then you educate them. And of course, *because* you educate them, they ended up being smart. Barbadians from very early were being used as missionaries all over Africa. I'm not so sure that Brathwaite didn't end up in Africa as part of that tradition. A lot of Barbadians were educators there. Anyway, the important thing is that his creole thesis applies perfectly to Barbados. And whether he knew it or not he was imposing a Barbadian model on Jamaica.

THE PARADOX OF FREEDOM

The Caribbean Artists Movement

DS: Very interesting, Orlando! Now, talking about Brathwaite allows me to turn to CAM (the Caribbean Artists Movement), specifically. Tell me when and how you came to be connected to CAM.[1]
OP: I was at their first, founding meeting.

DS: I know that you were part of that founding meeting, and I want to come to the details of the internal debates within those first meetings. But, late 1966, what was going on that you were being drawn to, what kinds of discussions?
OP: Well, there were several meetings in which we were getting together, talking. Several of us would meet. We had a nice big apartment.

DS: "We" meaning Nerys and yourself? Or was this before you got married?
OP: This was before, just a little before. But prior to the first meeting, we had preliminary meetings and get-togethers. And one was where we were living, Norman [Girvan] and I, in Tufnell Park, London. But then we were also getting together at various events. One of them had to do with several prominent artists.

DS: Like Aubrey Williams?
OP: Aubrey Williams was very important. He was a very warm person, a very nice man. He'd invite us to his home, and we'd have meetings. He was an *intellectual*, too.

DS: And what about Ronald Moody?
OP: More Aubrey than Moody. Aubrey had all kinds of explanations of his paintings to do with Guyanese culture, and so on. Then also there was Wilson Harris, who would come and talk to the West Indian Student Union then. Brathwaite, I guess he was the moving force. There was also the poet Anthony La Rose.[2]

DS: John La Rose, as he called himself later. And Andrew Salkey? Had you known John and Andrew prior to CAM?
OP: John and I were just meeting. But I knew Andrew because he interviewed me after *Sisyphus* came out.

DS: For the BBC?
OP: Yes. So, we had connections; we were meeting. Andrew would

108

THE CARIBBEAN ARTISTS MOVEMENT

invite us over to his home. He lived very well then. He had a very nice apartment. I remember meeting John Hearne there. In my first year at UCWI, Andrew's *A Quality of Violence* had come out.[3]

DS: That's right, 1959.
OP: I remember discussing it with the poet Dennis Scott, in Chancellor Hall. I remember Dennis coming to me with this book, asking me what I thought about it.

DS: How interesting! Dennis was a teacher of mine at Jamaica College.
OP: Dennis was not only on the same block at Chancellor Hall but the same floor, just three doors down from me. I remember reading his poetry. He was a member of the Literary Society when I was president.[4] So, to return to Salkey, he lived well. He was always formally dressed because of the BBC connection. We would be meeting at each other's places. And then Brathwaite decided to formalize it with this organization.[5] Many things were happening. Aubrey was very productive – he was doing quite well. And Andrew brought out another novel.

DS: Yes, *Escape to an Autumn Pavement*.
OP: And he was busily doing the anthologies. He did two anthologies, which had short stories by me.[6] I was in fact reviewing Harris for the *TLS* [*Times Literary Supplement*].

DS: You reviewed Wilson Harris's *Palace of the Peacock*?
OP: Yes. And there's the Negritude thing, too, which was the model for Brathwaite.

DS: Oh, of course – *Présence Africaine*! I can see the connection.
OP: And then the *Times Literary Supplement* had a special Commonwealth issue in which the centerpiece article was an essay I wrote on Negritude, "Twilight of a Dark Myth."[7] They were all anonymous then, but they've attached names now. I was very much at a crossroads at the time, uncertain whether I would lead a literary life or not. I was reviewing for the *TLS*; I was reviewing for the *Guardian*. I was doing pretty well. I had two novels out. But then Andrew was also publishing, Wilson Harris was publishing, John Hearne was publishing. So, West Indian fiction was out there, and the BBC was very interested. So, we were meeting, and Eddie decided to do a *Présence Africaine*, if you like, because that project was very

THE PARADOX OF FREEDOM

much on our minds. I was reading a lot of Negritude literature, and I was writing about it. I'm pretty sure that was the model, whether he admits it or not.

DS: So, you were there at the inaugural meeting at Eddie Brathwaite's flat on 19 December 1966, when the project was, I think, launched. Do you remember who was there?
OP: Aubrey Williams would have been there – though I can't be sure. I know it was myself, Brathwaite. La Rose, definitely; I'm pretty sure he was there. Was Norman there? No. Oh, you know who was there, believe it or not? Or did he come later? Oliver Clarke, who later became editor of *The Gleaner*.[8]

DS: I think his involvement was later? I didn't realize that he was directly related to Edith Clarke, his great-aunt, I believe. He was at LSE, wasn't he? Doing economics. What was the discussion at that first meeting about?
OP: The first meeting was that we want to establish an organization, and we should have a journal. CAM, the Caribbean Artists Movement, was the name decided. The name came from Nerys, my then wife, who was at the first meeting. We had just gotten married. She was Welsh and a student of Irish history and culture, and she pointed out that the word CAM, in pronunciation, means "step" in Irish [*céim*]. So, this was the step toward a new movement in Caribbean culture. You know who may have been there? I'm not sure. He attended a lot of meetings. An English guy.

DS: Louis James. *The Islands in Between*. Yes, he was there.[9]
OP: There was also another guy who later came in and out. He was very interested in what was going on, and we went to his place a couple of times – a very successful White Jamaican. Jones.

DS: Evan Jones! The poet.
OP: He wrote several successful screenplays. *Funeral in Berlin*, for example.

DS: Yes. But, you remember, "Song of the Banana Man" was also by Evan Jones. We had to learn that in school.
OP: That's right. We had these Whites who were digging into their roots. Who else? I can't recall who else was there. Of course, Eddie's wife, Doris, a warm, lovely person, was there. There must have been six or seven of us. I'm sure there was somebody else. Gordon Rohlehr?

110

THE CARIBBEAN ARTISTS MOVEMENT

DS: No, I don't think so.
OP: From time to time, he would come down from Birmingham.

DS: The second informal meeting took place at your and Nerys's flat on 19 January 1967. Where in London were you living?
OP: 83 Anson Road, in north London.

DS: And this was a larger gathering. In fact, Gordon Rohlehr was at *that* meeting, I believe.[10] And my understanding from Anne Walmsley's book about CAM is that you proposed to lead a discussion on the West Indian aesthetic. Why did that question seem to you to be a pressing one – the question of formulating an idea of a West Indian aesthetic?
OP: Well, that for me would have been partly a reaction to the Negritude work I'd read most thoroughly for my article in the *TLS*. I was well versed in Negritude literature, more than everyone else at the meeting, because I'd devoted a lot of time to it. That movement was certainly a model, to my mind, of what we were doing.

DS: As I understand it, part of your presentation of a West Indian aesthetic turned on what we were talking about earlier, the traditionlessness of Caribbean society and the implications of this for the Caribbean writer. The Caribbean writer is *not* like the writer in Asia or Africa, who is anchored in a solid, continuous history.
OP: That was when I was finishing up *An Absence of Ruins*. Eddie was there, so we had a good discussion.

DS: One of the interesting things about what I gather your presentation turned on was the importance of a *sociological* perspective. Given the fact that the writer is not embedded in a culturally continuous past, the artist has to have an eye on the social formation.
OP: Right. Was John Hearne there?

DS: Not yet, not at that meeting. Hearne was at the 5 May 1967 public meeting that I will come back to in a minute.
OP: Because that was what drove John Hearne crazy. And I was definitely putting forward a view of the novel, too, which was very social realist. This was very consistent with my reading of literature at that time. Because, as I said, the people who most influenced me in writing were the French realists. Zola is the novelist I read self-consciously and whose craft I studied. The review of *Sisyphus* that most pleased me was the one in the *Daily Telegraph* that featured it in

111

THE PARADOX OF FREEDOM

its very prestigious literary page. And in the headline I was described as a "Caribbean Zola." I was very happy with that. I thought, My goodness! They saw through me. And, of course, this was very different from the kind of precious individualistic, personality-oriented, character-based novel that John Hearne was involved in.[11] So, I was bringing together my sociology and my literature at that time. It was the time in my life when the two were most in alignment. They later came *out* of alignment, and I had to *choose*. And I saw this as very critical – that the artist could no longer live or die in London outside of his society, that you had to be immersed, you had to be committed, you had to be involved. This was consistent with existentialist writing.

DS: Of course, that is pure Jean-Paul Sartre.
OP: That was the basis of my argument.

DS: Presumably Brathwaite disagreed. Rohlehr perhaps also disagreed. Do you remember?
OP: Well, yes. Rohlehr was doing his dissertation on Joseph Conrad, the quintessential character-based novelist. They all gave me that look, as if to say this is nothing they'd read. Rohlehr changed later on. It's really very sad that he never published that dissertation on Conrad. He was a strange fellow. I read that dissertation; it was very good. In fact, it led me to respect Conrad in a way that I hadn't before. But he just dropped it. But what he wrote on Mighty Sparrow later was very much consistent with social realism. In fact, we became friends later on. There was a little period when we were very close.[12]

DS: Really? How interesting!
OP: Because when Rohlehr came back to Jamaica he stayed with me for a while. I'd gone back, and he came back not long after – he'd gotten his PhD and he was looking for a place.

DS: He taught in Jamaica first before he went to Trinidad? I didn't know that.
OP: Oh yes! We overlapped. When I was in the University of the West Indies, he was there, too. And we were pretty close then. I remember it was an interesting dynamic because he was a very dark-skinned guy, and he went to Britain, worked on Conrad, and came back. He was getting back into his West Indian roots. He was never into the Black identity thing in an overt way, but it was interesting. He and my wife got along very well, even though she was Welsh. He felt

THE CARIBBEAN ARTISTS MOVEMENT

very comfortable with us; he stayed with us for a while as he looked for a place. I liked him very much. And then he went to Trinidad and I came here to Cambridge, and we lost touch. We actually did reestablish contact and became good friends again in the year he spent here in Cambridge. I always thought he was a little awkward with White people, but he was always comfortable for some reason with Nerys.

DS: Interesting. The third informal meeting of CAM was again held at your flat, on 3 February 1967, and this one centered on a presentation by Brathwaite. It was bits of what would be published as "Jazz and the West Indian Novel."[13] My question is whether you heard Brathwaite's presentation as a critique of your view.

OP: It could have been. I didn't interpret it that way. I just thought it was far-fetched. I remember taking it very seriously and us having a long conversation. I thought it was too literal.

DS: But do you read Brathwaite's argument as saying, contrary to your view that these societies are traditionless, that there are musical and oral traditions of the folk that shape cultural forms such as the novel. His big example, in that respect, has always been Roger Mais's *Brother Man*, as a novel with a kind of syncopation and style that he thinks of as connected to the jazz tradition.

OP: That was definitely his thinking, which was quite clearly a different view from my own.

DS: But why couldn't he see that there's a certain sense in which in *The Children of Sisyphus* one can hear – maybe I'm of a younger generation, the reggae generation – a reggae soundscape?

OP: Absolutely. And several people noticed that. As a matter of fact, the review in *Newsweek* (by Art Mifflin) referred to the musical quality and the poetic quality. We were clearly emphasizing our *differences*, but obviously we had a lot in common, too, which I think we recognized. We were West Indians trying to make sense of West Indian society. And his poetry, which I liked very much, became very important for the group, too. But, then again, I remember when we went back to Jamaica I offered an interpretation of *Rights of Passage*, which I saw in terms of the way I saw the society.

DS: *Rights of Passage* is what he was writing at the time. But you're saying that, while there were differences, what was shared was at least as important as what was not shared.

113

THE PARADOX OF FREEDOM

OP: Absolutely. And I think we both recognized that: this is how we could always meet. It was always a friendly debate. Which was why, when he did that pretty nasty thing with the review of *The Sociology of Slavery*, I just thought it was out of character. Because we saw ourselves as being very much focused on understanding our society and going back home and changing things. Let a thousand flowers bloom – that's how I saw it. But we had a common agenda. We were all in Britain, and we were all focused on going back home, even though I'd taken a job at LSE. But I then broke contract. The overwhelming focus on home was such that it would bring us together; it was a powerful common thread in our discussions. The odd person out in that respect would have been Andrew Salkey, who really was not going back.

DS: Perhaps also John La Rose?
OP: John La Rose kept on with it for quite a while, and even had a little publishing house, New Beacon Books. But, as far as Eddie and I were concerned, we were heading back: we were very West Indian in that sense. Andrew spoke with a British accent. In a way, there were two groups of us then. It was a very interesting meeting point. People like Andrew, even Stuart Hall, Wilson Harris, George Lamming – that whole generation was going to stay in Britain. They were involved, but they weren't going back. Lamming would, later on, half go back, and in the end he retired there. But Lamming was settled in a bedsitter in north London – and I may have mentioned it to you, I told myself, I'm not going to write novels if that's what I'm going to end up doing at the age of forty-five. That's what I told *myself*. I didn't tell *him*. We'd meet occasionally. He had me up to his home to tea. And I went – it was way out in north London. You had to change trains three times. He didn't have a car or anything. This man was by then a very established person: *In the Castle of My Skin* was out; he had won prizes and all the rest of it.

DS: Not only *Castle* but also *The Emigrants*, *Of Age and Innocence*, *Season of Adventure* – they were all out.
OP: Oh yes! And he was lecturing all over. So, I went up, and got off the train – finally. I don't know if you know the wilds of north London, it goes on endlessly! I got off and there were these neat English cottages. I went to this place and I thought this was the man's house. I said, "Hmm, a pleasant house." Turns out the man lived in a studio bedsitter, upstairs in this place. I remember that experience very well, because I thought when I left, "Well, this is not the life for

114

AN ABSENCE OF RUINS

me." I thought it was a little pathetic, quite frankly. I had responsibilities, my parents to look after. I knew then that the writing life was not one I was going to do full time. And I certainly wasn't going to stay in Britain – which, in a way, I was on the verge of doing. I could easily have gone the Stuart Hall route; in fact, I was being pulled in that direction.

An Absence of Ruins

DS: Let's talk about your second novel, *An Absence of Ruins*. This is a short, intense novel, one that has in a sense a literary-philosophic preoccupation. It is preoccupied with the question of the very possibility of an authentic Caribbean intellectual-artistic life. And what's interesting, as a matter of form, is that the social-realist frame of *Sisyphus*, or much of it, is gone. It is a meditative, very internally driven novel; what you have is the internal moral-psychological landscape of Alexander Blackman. Also interesting is that gone, too, is the reading through Albert Camus, *The Myth of Sisyphus*, and so on. And much more present is Jean-Paul Sartre's *Nausea*. So, the first question about *Absence* is, what prompted you in that direction?

OP: Well, remember, most of *Sisyphus*, more than half of it, was written while I was still in the Caribbean, and the final half was written in my first year in Britain. By the time *An Absence of Ruins* came along, I was in Britain, and I really was in the midst of contemplating my situation. It was this transition I mentioned, whether basically I was going to live in Britain and abandon the whole Caribbean thing.

DS: Is there a connection, though, between the form and content of *An Absence of Ruins* and your thinking specifically about the question of a West Indian aesthetic?

OP: Yes, if you like. It was the most negative period of that process of thinking through the destructivist view of the past, and one in which you could interpret what came out of that chaos in more positive terms. But it was the climax of the most negative, destructive period, and written at a time when I was seriously thinking of not going back. It was right at that point. The novel was more or less like writing it out, and then I moved back to a more positive stance.

DS: How would you now, stepping back, articulate the sense in which Alexander Blackman embodies the predicament, as you see it, of the Caribbean intellectual artist?

115

THE PARADOX OF FREEDOM

OP: You know, I used Walcott's poem about "an absence of ruins" that was trying to come to terms with the chaotic past, devoid of things that one could anchor on.[1] It's a problem to live that way.

DS: I want to draw a connection between Alexander Blackman and Brother Solomon from *The Children of Sisyphus*. They are, of course, as characters, resolutely *cynical* characters. They both are tempted by suicide – one carries it out. Interestingly, Blackman dissembles *his* suicide, and it might be important to think about the difference between the kind of cynicism that causes one to go through with it and the other to *play* at going through it. You say of Alexander Blackman at the very end of the novel that he was "a being deprived of essence, a willing slave of every chance event."[2] Brother Solomon is not exactly "a willing slave of every chance event"; he is not a being "deprived of essence." What is interesting about Solomon is that he understood himself to have a cause that was *betrayed*, in a certain sense. Not so Alexander Blackman; *he* is deprived of essence. Not only that, but there is, even in that description, a *bitterness* attached to that cynical self-appreciation.

OP: I guess I was at a point where I hadn't yet seen how it might be possible to construct or draw out a positive interpretation of Caribbean, certainly Jamaican, life. It didn't seem possible at the time. Or I was pessimistic about it.

DS: You mean your view has changed?
OP: Sure – from the "Blackman" thing, definitely. I moved quite significantly away from that, in a way, even interpreting slavery differently.

DS: So, *Die the Long Day* might be read as a critique of *An Absence of Ruins*.
OP: Yes. *Die the Long Day* goes back to slavery and begins to see how there might be something reconstructive. How to create order from chaos. How to construct meaning from meaninglessness. In *Die the Long Day* I went back to a single day, the most hopeless possible, a mother's despair and resistance over the impending rape of her only daughter by the syphilitic overseer. My description of the novel on the cover jacket was that it was an exploration of survival during slavery, "morally, spiritually and physically." I added that it was not only about Black survival but "a prototype of the potentially debasing aspect inherent in all human relationships. Every form of interaction – between lover and loved, husband and wife, father and son, boss and employee, God and worshipper – runs the risk of

116

AN ABSENCE OF RUINS

debasement. But whenever this takes place the human spirit rebels. There are limits, limits beyond which one refuses to be dehumanized or debased." Here I quoted Camus' *The Rebel*: The slave "affirms that there are limits and also that he suspects – and wishes to preserve – the existence of certain things beyond those limits. He stubbornly insists that there are things in him which 'are worthwhile ...' and which must be taken into consideration." Whatever the forces stacked against it, man's humanity will survive, and this novel is an unpretentious celebration of the survival of the human spirit.

DS: How interesting! But I don't want to let you off the hook so easily with that, because I remember reading *An Absence of Ruins* as a student at university in the late 1970s and feeling that I could identify with Alexander Blackman – with the sense that, even as he is playing himself (as the Trinidadians might say), he is watching cynically a society play at being a "society." And that perception, I think, is incredibly acute, and as relevant today as it was in 1967.
OP: It was partly that, but I think Alexander Blackman was an archetype not just of Caribbean Blacks but also of Blacks generally. I was thinking of the Black experience; I was thinking of Blacks within the context of Western civilization. How is it possible to survive, to build a meaningful tradition, within the context of a very dominant Western culture? I was thinking of the whole question of what had been achieved, and whether it was possible or not to accept the nationalist answer, "Back to Africa"; I began to see the dilemma of where you go from this very catastrophic past – especially if you're not into Negritude, or Eddie Brathwaite's interpretation. So, *Absence* was more of a novel about the broader Black condition – broader than just the West Indian condition.

DS: It's interesting that you put it that way, because in that very brief passage that I just read – "A being deprived of essence, a willing slave of every chance event" – one notices its deliberately paradoxical character. The passage notes the power structure, that he's not merely devoid of essence but *deprived* of essence. He's both a willing being and an enslaved being. He's caught in a web of paradoxes.
OP: And that, of course, is a very powerful philosophical trope, which is behind that Sartrean dictum that "existence precedes essence." You may be deprived of essence but you still have an existence. It's like a pure existential state, which I was trying to argue and which may well be the basis of a viable way of survival. I have an essay, which I wrote not long after I came here, "Toward a Future That Has No Past,"

117

published, oddly, in the journal *The Public Interest*, in 1972. It was the most radical thing that *The Public Interest* ever published.[3] The argument there was precisely that not having a past may be a liberating condition. We're the people of the future. That was the theme. I linked up the West Indian experience with the Black experience all over the Americas. I was thinking in broader terms, even though I was using Jamaica, obviously, as the site for the novel. "Blackman," as the name indicates, is about Black people and the Black condition. I found working through existentialism very valuable then, in that you didn't need an essence, you didn't need a tradition, you didn't need the bourgeois sort of anchorage – that, indeed, in the world in which we live, it may well be that you have the possibility of starting from scratch and creating a world for yourself.

DS: Alexander Blackman is an attempt, then, to create that kind of figure.
OP: Yes. And, by the way, I saw jazz as very much a part of that, as the most successful model. I seem to recall having an argument with Brathwaite about that. Because, where he was seeing it in terms of continuities, I was seeing that the *spontaneity* of jazz was only made possible because you weren't trapped in tradition.

DS: But it's interesting because the challenge, I suppose, is to create a fictional figure that is simultaneously essenceless *and* creative. And Alexander Blackman turns out himself not to be a creative character. He wanders around London lost and adrift at the end.
OP: Right, that is the end, but it's also the *beginning*. And it is sort of simply saying, let's forget about the past; forget about any essence; just start in this moment to create. And there may be advantages to that. That last paragraph of the novel was deliberately written in a more poetic way to almost suggest a sort of spontaneous kind of John Coltrane expression. So, it was not creating something out of nothing but creating something out of *chaos*.

DS: It's not as if there was no past. All of your work is preoccupied with slave past. There is a past, but there is no *continuity*.
OP: Right, but there's the knowledge and weight of the past. There is, in fact, a *kind* of continuity, the continuity of problems and chaos – a continuity of *discontinuity*.

DS: Indeed. This is one of the novels that was part of the discussion at that famous third CAM public session of 10 May 1967 – the colloquy, as it was called – on *Sisyphus* and *Ruins*. And there are three discussants: Gerald Moore, Kenneth Ramchand, and John Hearne. And the gist of your presentation, I gather, was this question of the artist and sociologist. Do you remember what your argument was?

OP: I don't remember at all what the argument was, and I hope *somebody* took notes.[4]

DS: There are, apparently, bits and pieces preserved.

OP: Was this at the West Indian Student Union? Or was it at somebody's home?

DS: It was a public session, so I think it was at the West Indian Student Centre.[5]

OP: I don't remember, except that I was deliberately being *provocative* then. Because I knew John Hearne's work and I did not like his style of writing. I thought it was precious. So, I was *deliberately* provoking him. But, no, I don't remember the details, except it just would have been an extension of what the earlier argument was, just the public version, maybe more formal.

DS: And, as you suspected it would, it *did* provoke Hearne, apparently to apoplexy.

OP: Absolutely. By the way, when we went back to the West Indies, because that talk became well known, Lucille Mathurin, who was a really very vibrant, beautiful woman, had this idea to have a debate, a conversation, between myself and John Hearne, which she taped. This would have been the year after I came back, in 1968. She came over to my place; she got a tape recorder and a bottle of rum, and she had John and myself, and we talked for almost two hours. Everything recorded: our views on literature, and so on. This was a very good discussion. And she made the very big mistake of giving John the tape. John was then heading the Creative Arts Centre, so he had the facilities for transcribing it. He said, "Okay, I'll take the tape and have my secretary transcribe it." The conversation took both sides of a tape. He took the tape and then we waited and waited, and finally I said, "Lucille, what happened to the tape?" And Lucille said, "Yes, I'm waiting to hear from John." Finally, John said the tape was spoiled. But I think it was a lie. He may have listened to it and felt he didn't have the best of the conversation and just threw it away.[6]

DS: How unfortunate.

OP: That discussion was interesting, but I was just presenting my

THE PARADOX OF FREEDOM

own view of the novel, the social realist view, against his. He was going on in the most extreme way about the novel of character.

DS: What were the responses from the other people in the CAM audience?
OP: The audience? We had a lively debate and I think a lot of people were sympathetic to my view, but the literary types were obviously more inclined to his view. We had a good debate. Did you ever meet Hearne?

DS: No. But in my time he was a familiar figure because he was also writing a column in *The Gleaner*. The columns were superb as a kind of informed and literate journalism. But the turn *against* Michael Manley was sharp and abusive, and to some extent slightly vulgar. But that was John Hearne. It was a moment, too, at the University of the West Indies, when there weren't many people who were sympathetic to him. He was still the director of the Creative Arts Centre, but it wasn't uncommon for him to be booed. He used to wear his Busha hat; he would be deliberately provocative in some ways.
OP: I know. I'll never forget, a little after I came back from Britain, he asked me this stupid question: "What was the hunt like this year?" What a stupid question! I never went hunting.

DS: The hunt? Like hunting wild pigs or something like that? Really?
OP: The upper-class thing. I don't know. Or hunting as in chasing foxes, or whatever. He knew I never did that. I thought he was a pathetic figure, myself. And he had this not very healthy relationship with Morris Cargill. He was just an ass licker. Cargill just used him right down to having him co-write novels, which they thought were going to make money for them.[7]

DS: Were there women in CAM discussions, beyond the wives of its principals, or was CAM largely a male affair?
OP: Good question. I'm trying to think now, who would have been the women. You're right, there isn't a single woman that I can think of. There weren't many West Indian women writers at the time, certainly not among the poets that I knew. And there's not a single female novelist, was there, at that period?

DS: Sylvia Wynter had already returned to the Caribbean by the time of CAM.

120

AN ABSENCE OF RUINS

OP: She returned to the Caribbean, and then she went off to California.

DS: She was in Guyana, then Jamaica. She would have overlapped with you in Jamaica, I think.
OP: Yes, a little bit. We never hit it off. We never had any conflict, but we never spoke very much. Jan Carew was wandering around up there, in his strange kind of way. You never knew what he was doing, where he got his money. He always lived well. He had gone to Russia, he was writing some book.

DS: *Moscow Is Not My Mecca.*[8]
OP: But I never figured out where he got his funds. He kept referring to the plantation in Guyana. He was a mysterious fellow. Is he still alive? The last time I saw him he was very ill.

DS: I think so. I haven't heard anything to the contrary. Upon reflection, how significant was CAM for you at that moment of your literary intellectual formation?
OP: It was a lot more significant to Brathwaite and other people. I felt it was a good way of keeping in touch, coming out of that moment of existential despair. It was good to be with West Indians, and I think it was very important in my decision to go back home. I really felt strongly about that, and I would say that it was important in keeping me from making that fateful decision – to *stay*. One of the factors, anyway. Because, also, I'd gotten married to a Welsh woman.

DS: When and how did you meet Nerys?
OP: We met at LSE. She was in the Anthropology Department. Anthropology and sociology were very close; we used to have a Thursday morning seminar in which the anthropologists and the sociologists met. I wish we would do that here, but that would never happen. It was a great period for anthropology: Lucy Mair, Raymond Firth, Isaac Schapera (who was Nerys's supervisor). And so, we would meet in the seminar. She was an undergraduate and I was a graduate student. And just one thing led to another. She was a very beautiful woman. She would have been attending all those meetings. The high point of my engagement with the Thursday seminar at LSE was when Lucy Mair discovered that I had written the essay on Negritude in the special edition of the *Times Literary Supplement*. She was very impressed with it and was chairing the seminar that year (1965–6). She decided to make it the focal reading for a special

THE PARADOX OF FREEDOM

session on Negritude. I think it was the first year of my lectureship at the LSE and a special privilege to have all those great men and women from anthropology and the other social sciences focused on my work. I remember Nerys was very proud of me – we had just gotten married, and her supervisor, Isaac Schapera, one of anthropology's big shots at the time, was in attendance.

Returning Home

DS: What was it that finally decided it for you, to return to Jamaica, and at that point?

OP: I think it was primarily a desire to help in the development process and to teach at the university. Several of my friends were planning to go back, Norman Girvan in particular. We were very close. We were at university, came up together, and shared an apartment. He was going back. It was just the possibility of helping in the nation-building process. Also, Michael Manley had visited us. He was passing through and made a special point of meeting with Norman and myself. We had met him before, when we were undergraduates and student leaders. He and the old man, Norman Manley, came up to meet us at UCWI during our final year. Michael would remind me on his visits to England that Jamaica needed us.

DS: That's right, you told me this.

OP: He was very impressed with us. Michael was in transition then, and he was beginning to think about politics. He came up to London on some trade union thing, I'm not quite sure, but he was wandering around. I'm sure some woman was involved. But he had time on his hands. He sought us out. So, I thought, "Well, things are really happening." Of course, the JLP government was still in power, but I really felt the need to return, to help in the nation-building, to help at the University of the West Indies, which at that time was going through a period of expansion. It was less that I felt homesick – that never occurred; it was more that I felt a strong *commitment*, partly political but partly also academic. I was going back to the University of the West Indies having left the University College of the West Indies.[1] It was more or less a public intellectual kind of role that I saw for myself, and I felt that was very attractive. I'd felt that I'd come to the end of my phase in Britain. I was very involved with *New Left Review* in the early days, as I mentioned. And then something interesting happened in the late 1960s, following the failures of

122

RETURNING HOME

communism and the rising tide of student protests that culminated in the Paris protests of 1968. There was a kind of introspection on the left, and the New Left group took a very European turn. That's when Perry Anderson got into writing his books on Europe.[2] I just lost interest basically.

DS: So, prior to this point, *New Left Review* had a much more capacious, global, international, Third World kind of outlook.

OP: More so, yes. Robin Blackburn had gone to Cuba. They were into Latin America very much; Cuba and the broader Caribbean was on their minds a lot. Then there was a shift. It was after the failure of Labour and Harold Wilson, who was a huge disappointment. Anyway, I just felt a parting of the ways. And, having written *The Sociology of Slavery*, too, I felt I wanted to go back and work more on the Caribbean. And Nerys, she was very keen on going, too. That had to do with her Welsh background. She was something of a Welsh nationalist, *culturally*. In her later life, after we parted, she became very involved with Welsh national politics. So, she was keen on leaving London and looking forward to going to the Caribbean. I also felt that it would be a better life. I was getting fed up with just living in a bedsitter. Because even after you became an assistant lecturer, which was the equivalent of an assistant professor (except you could stay for life), my salary was the grand sum of twelve hundred pounds a year, plus fifty pounds London allowance. Of course, this was the 1960s. But then, you're hearing about people going back to America and getting ten, twelve thousand dollars a year. In the case of the University of the West Indies, their salary scheme was still geared to Europe, but you could live a much better life, much more comfortably, instead of being crammed in one room. You couldn't think about children, living in a bedsitter. Academics were paid quite modestly in Britain. By contrast, I saw how at home people lived quite well. So, from abroad the atmosphere at UWI looked very attractive. You lived on university commons; the houses were not architectural gems but comfortable. Basically, all these things came together: wanting to start a family and not being able to imagine it in London, the attractions of going back to the university and to Jamaica, and then Manley's visits.

DS: Yes, so tell me, what do you remember about that meeting with Manley? What did you understand his purpose to be in coming to seek you out?

OP: I think he was thinking about taking on the leadership of the PNP. Manley was an intellectual. And, in many ways, that would

123

THE PARADOX OF FREEDOM

have been his alternate life course if he hadn't also been a very charismatic man of action. He wanted to meet with the up-and-coming young Turks up at LSE.

DS: But was it a discussion urging you to return?
OP: Yes, and to work with him in the PNP. When did his father, Norman, die?

DS: N. W. Manley died in September 1969. He'd retired in July that year, after which Michael became president of the PNP.
OP: Right. I think maybe Norman was thinking about retiring. Michael was still in the trade union, but he may have been beginning to think about electoral politics.

DS: Because, remember, in the elections of 1967, Michael, who had been an appointed senator since 1962, becomes an elected member of the House of Representatives, he becomes an MP. So, there's a sense then that he was beginning to think about a more active political life.
OP: As I said, he had earlier come up to the university [UCWI] to meet with us, me and the gang. We had made quite an impression because we were the first generation of social scientists, and we were quite active.

DS: Still, politically, Jamaica in 1967 could *not* have been a very attractive prospect. The JLP regime had won a second term and Donald Sangster was prime minister, until he suddenly died and was replaced by Hugh Shearer. Politically, my sense of the period is of a fairly *repressive* regime.[3]
OP: *No*, that is exaggerating. This was why everybody was shocked when they sent the troops to the university during the Walter Rodney affair. It *wasn't* repressive, no. Shearer was going on about violence (I remember he had a funny way of pronouncing it). But it would be very unfair to say that people had that sense. Certainly, as a student I didn't feel that way. And I think history has been a bit rewritten on this through the 1960s. Shearer himself, he was not a repressive person – he was a "face man," as we called him, a lady's man; in a sense, he was just a darker version of Michael. And they were friends. He was a very pleasant guy; he was not a repressive person. As a person it would have been hard *not* to like him. But then he got onto this thing about the violence, but this was domestic violence. Jamaica started having problems even before then, although nothing compared to what later happened. So, when they sent the troops up

124

to the university during the Rodney affair, this just came out of the blue, because nobody was being harassed before.

DS: But books were being banned, weren't they?
OP: Well, you know, this was the beginning. Yes, they had banned books; but the PNP later on had censorship, too. It was slowly building up, maybe. But if you are asking me if there was a general atmosphere of repression in Kingston – *no*. You had a womanizer as leader; it was politics as usual, and the JLP, they were for business. But that *tone*, and this goes back to Bustamante, you felt the same way. He's a character, he's a loveable rogue – we saw Shearer in that tradition. As a matter of fact, Shearer was his protégé. I didn't particularly like Sangster; *he* looked like a repressive sort of Brown man, but he didn't last very long. He died of a heart attack a year right after.

DS: Yes, within a couple of months of coming to power; although of course he had in effect run the country from about 1965, when Bustamante became debilitated.
OP: Exactly. I didn't feel that way; *nobody* felt that way. This was why we were all so absolutely shocked when they had a thing about censorship. We thought it was heavy-handed. The one person we thought of as a little sinister would have been Edward Seaga.[4]

DS: Already in the mid-1960s, among you intellectuals Seaga was seen as a sinister character.
OP: I thought he was a sinister character from the first time I heard him give a speech. Let me see. I heard him speaking in West Kingston – I would have been eighteen, nineteen years old. He had just come back. It was the period between high school and going to university. I remember hearing about this guy and went and heard him speak in West Kingston, and I thought there was something sinister about him even then. We always had our suspicions about him. Although he himself was at the university for a little while and was into culture. But no, until the day that they stopped me from leaving the university, the soldier with the gun, I never felt intimidated.

During the Rodney affair the soldiers came up and closed the gates. I lived on University Close. I was through with my lectures and was going home. I drove down to the main gate and was stopped. The soldier had a gun. And my reaction was *outrage*. I felt this was absurd; like something out of Naipaul, was my reaction. I got out and argued with him. I said to this soldier, "You are violating my

THE PARADOX OF FREEDOM

constitutional rights, and I want to speak to your supervisor!" And he was intimidated. He went for his supervisor, and I said to him, "I want to go to my home! You're violating my rights and I want to get your number." They backed off, and I drove away. I didn't feel terrified; I just felt this was a joke and an outrage. And I don't think that anyone really felt that the system was becoming repressive. I just think it was a heavy-handed reaction. Who was behind it? It could have been Shearer, it could have been Seaga – it could have just been the White elites who backed the party who panicked. Or it could have been the CIA. Because I didn't even know that they had enough competence to find out all these things that they claimed Rodney was doing. It clearly was a surprise to me, by the way, because *I* didn't even know that Rodney was involved with the Rastas. The reason why it came as a surprise was that *I* was involved with the Rastas. In preparing for *Sisyphus*, I used to wander around West Kingston; I knew Mortimo Planno, I knew Ras Daniel Heartman, from my undergraduate days. I would go and visit them from time to time. So far as I knew, Rodney had had no interest in the Rastas when he was a student. I would have known about it. I was the person who was working with MG; the only reason why I did not work on that famous project was that I was in America on my first undergraduate visit out of Jamaica.

DS: You mean the *Rastafari Report*?
OP: Yes. I talked to MG about it, but I wanted to visit America. I would certainly have done work for them. Because I talked to MG about the people I knew down there, especially Mortimo Planno, whom I kept in touch with even after I came to America. So, I was outraged by the reaction to Rodney and, of course, demonstrated, but I was surprised, quite frankly.

DS: Surprised by the reaction of the state?
OP: I was *outraged* at the reaction of the state.

DS: Or surprised by what they were saying Rodney was involved in.
OP: Yes. That took me *totally* by surprise. Rodney never said a word to me. Maybe it was because I was married to a White woman or something like that. I guess we had drifted apart. I think Walter disapproved of my marriage to a Welsh woman. I remember that we arranged a lecture series at UWI for the public on Africa and its relation to the Caribbean, and when we discussed possible lecturers on Africa I suggested Nerys, who had done her master's thesis on

126

RETURNING HOME

African kinship with Isaac Schapera, and Walter flatly rejected the idea. When I asked him why, he said that he was not going to preside over a White woman lecturing on any aspect of Africa. I remember being jolted by his attitude and at that moment realized how intensely committed he had become to Black nationalism during the course of his graduate studies. Ironically, during our undergraduate days it was I who was more into Black consciousness and the racial and color iniquities of Jamaica, as well as the Rastafarians, and Rodney much more a Marxist. And here's something interesting. When *Sisyphus* was published, Walter, who was working in the archives in Portugal, wrote me a long and very appreciative letter saying how much he loved the novel and what it meant to him. I suspect that it was one of his earliest exposures to the realities of Rasta life. I can't be sure. What I do know is that he had little or no interest in the Rastas when we were students in the early sixties. He obviously became deeply transformed by the research and writing of his thesis, "A History of the Upper Guinea Coast," and the work that later became *How Europe Underdeveloped Africa*. I was shocked by the naked racial chauvinism of his attitude toward Nerys, and we basically parted company after that. It later came out, of course, that by that time he was already deeply involved with the Rastas of Kingston, which he told me nothing about. As I mentioned earlier, I was utterly surprised to hear that he had been politically engaged with them, or, as the government claimed, plotting rebellion with them, which I simply do not believe.

DS: What do you make, though, of Philip Sherlock's response? He was vice-chancellor, wasn't he, of the university? It was Sherlock who locked down the university.[5]
OP: Yes, I'm really not in on all the details. I just assumed he was ordered to lock it down. What could he do? It was a crisis, and everybody saw it as a crisis.

DS: What was your view generally of Philip Sherlock in that period?
OP: I thought he was a man of the past by then.

DS: Anyway, you returned to Jamaica in late 1967, and there was a job waiting for you. How did you negotiate the position at the University of the West Indies?
OP: They were eager for me to come back, and they knew I was interested in coming back. I'd written to them.

DS: And you went back to the Department of Sociology, not to ISER.
OP: No, my wife went to ISER. But they wanted me back. We kept in touch all the years I was in London. I had gone back a couple of summers to do research in Worthy Park. And I lived in university housing when I went back. And people would come up to London. I remember Gladstone Mills. He was already a lecturer or professor when I was a student. He came to London on sabbatical when I was a student at LSE.[6] So, I was always in touch.

DS: October 1968 happens, and Rodney is expelled from the country. Is that the last time you saw Walter Rodney?
OP: No. I saw Rodney again on two occasions. One was in Waterloo, at a conference arranged by Michael Craton, in which he deliberately set the two of us up against each other. "Roots and Branches" was the theme. He asked Rodney to respond to a paper I'd written, which was an early comparative piece. The whole thrust of my scholarship was different from Rodney's. By then, Rodney was into Caribbean "groundings," and so on, so he knew that Rodney would not like a comparative perspective. It was an early version of the thesis of *Slavery and Social Death*.[7] And Rodney was snide about comparative work, because he took a historical particularist position. We were at our conference for several days, but we never talked much to each other at all, except in that exchange. He avoided me and I avoided him. That was one occasion. Then we met again at, I think, Trinity College, in Connecticut. They brought us up for a Caribbean conference. I don't remember the details, but I spoke and he spoke. That's the last time I saw him. He was assassinated not long after.[8]

Not Much of a Joiner

DS: In the wake of 1968, famously, there was a transformation, or the beginnings of a transformation, of cultural-political consciousness in Jamaica. There was the emergence, first of all, of *Abeng*, the newspaper, and various activities around *Abeng*. What was your relationship to *Abeng*?
OP: I'm not much of a joiner, but I got pulled in. I was in *New World*, among the early *New World* people. But then, again, the New World group was such that I attended a few meetings but not on a regular basis. I was the sociology voice in that and was involved in some of the earlier issues. Then *New World* shifted its focus to Trinidad

NOT MUCH OF A JOINER

and Guyana. *Abeng*, I was partly involved with that, but, again, not centrally. George Beckford was the main person behind that.[1] I liked G-Beck and I attended a couple of the meetings, but I was more on the sidelines.

DS: So, *Abeng* didn't attract you as a forum for criticism of the status quo.

OP: As I said, I participated in several of the meetings, but I was not a central member of the group. I did *not* see it as a political process or something to try to change the system. I was still very committed to the PNP. I was a lifelong PNP person. It was one of those things where you grew up in it. My father was almost a fanatical sort of PNP man. And my mother was also a fervent supporter. As I mentioned, she took me as a young child with her during her canvassing for the PNP early in the mornings before school. So, I could never bring myself really to take that kind of critical stance toward the PNP.

DS: You mean the stance that *Abeng* adopted, much to N. W. Manley's dismay, I think.

OP: I never could. I later became more involved with the party, but I never departed from the idea that we have to win the next election. There was another group, the Young Socialists.

DS: That's what I'm coming to. Before you returned, the Young Socialist League emerged and was initially, I gather, encouraged by Norman Manley as an attempt to generate new voices within the PNP in the wake of the referendum defeat in 1961 and election defeat in 1962. But later he began to disapprove of them very strongly, and Hugh Small was even expelled from the party. What was your sense of the Young Socialist League?[2]

OP: Well, I was very good friends with a person who was centrally involved with it – Leroy Taylor, the economist. He was very much a founding member and a leading advocate. I knew everything that was going on, but, again, I was not a joiner. This goes way back now. I didn't take it very seriously. Leroy and myself, we'd have lots of arguments. We were very close. He came to LSE for a little while; we overlapped for a year when he finished his thesis. I got to know him and I liked him – but he was a strange character. And he got stranger and stranger. And funnily enough, when I used to work for Manley, he was working in the planning office, but we never saw much of each other at that time, during the seventies.

129

THE PARADOX OF FREEDOM

DS: By the time you came back in 1967, the Young Socialist League was basically over. One of the things that troubled you about *Abeng* was the critical stance that it took toward the PNP. Now, this was a PNP that was itself in transition because of Michael's role. Did you have a sense then, in 1968, 1969, when *Abeng* emerged, that there was some interesting, progressive future in the PNP?

OP: Oh, absolutely. In fact, I met up with Manley again, and we saw each other quite a lot. I used to help him with his speeches. We'd talk; he'd discuss them with me. We were closer then than when I formally became his advisor. I've talked to Rachel Manley about this – I wrote the foreword to *Slipstream* – and we both agreed that it was the best period of his life.[3] It was one of the great ironies and tragedies of his life that the one woman whom he really loved, and to whom he would have perhaps remained faithful, Barbara Lewars, died young. She was a stunner. But the nicest time I had with him was when the four of us, just me and Nerys and him and Barbara, spent a whole evening together. So, I was much too involved with the PNP and Michael to really be taking any critical stance.

DS: In these discussions, did you have a sense at that time that Michael would become president of the PNP – because it wasn't at all self-evident, I don't think, in 1967, 1968 – it wasn't self-evident that his father would back him for president over Vivian Blake.

OP: Yes, but you know my position was that I was still working within the system. I saw Manley as the progressive part of the system, and that's where my political energies were focused. Manley was just interested in what was going on, and, in a way, he saw me as one of the progressive young Jamaicans who was as much connected to *Abeng* and the other groups through friendships. I was very much advising him on what was going on. Because he wanted to tap into that, too, the same way he wanted to tap into the reggae thing. He was wide open, and I was very optimistic, though I became quite pessimistic after the Rodney affair.

DS: Pessimistic about what?

OP: Working within the system in Jamaica. Because I didn't think he was going to win. It didn't look like it. 1969 was a really bad period, because it looked as if the JLP already had everything going in its favor. And whatever polls there were weren't good. But I didn't see the alternative as going through *Abeng* or a revolutionary route.

130

NOT MUCH OF A JOINER

DS: In 1967, 1968, 1969, was Marxism back on the table in those discussions as a serious theoretical question?
OP: There was the New World group.

DS: But by this time who would you have identified as New World?
OP: The core was still there, whether they were meeting and calling themselves New World or not, they were still talking about the same ideas – still the plantation, still the socialist kind of thing. And it didn't make any difference to me, because I was never a group person. I met with them, all of them; we were having lunch every day, but I tended to avoid formal meetings. We had one famous one that may have startled the White elite there. That was when I had the article on sugar, the plantation. We met publicly then, and we had Sir Robert Kirkwood, who was the very embodiment of sugar in Jamaica. I'd done a searing critique of the sugar plantation and why we should get out of it. And Kirkwood was very upset. He was more upset by my criticism than he was of the socialist talk. And he wrote a long piece in *The Gleaner* attacking me.[4] I'd come, with my background, studying the sugar industry and slavery and did my usual thing talking about continuities and disruption in social life. G-Beck offered the economic critique and I offered the sociological critique. But, for some reason, Kirkwood got more upset with the sociological critique. I think he felt he could handle the economic critique. I was drawing on my own work and I was drawing on Edith Clarke's work. Anyway, that was the closest I came to a real political involvement with New World.

DS: The moment of 1968 is often narrated as an *explosion*, when ideas that had been percolating – ideas about the critique of the plantation and the status quo, the critique of racial structures in Jamaica – were now beginning to gel as the ideas around which different kinds of political organization develop. Is that your sense of that period?
OP: Yes, there was definitely that. I remember giving several talks around, and there was a sense of the need for more serious change. Now, as I said, I remained close to Manley right up to when I left. I was still committed to doing something within the PNP. But I too began to feel really disillusioned after 1968, in the sense that the JLP seemed to have things really sewn up and was perhaps moving in a more authoritarian direction – meaning military direction. And, certainly, my decision to leave – or rather to stay here in Cambridge – was made much easier.

131

THE PARADOX OF FREEDOM

DS: Before we get there, you mentioned a moment ago that platform you shared with George Beckford in the critique of the sugar industry. Tell me a little bit about your relationship with George Beckford.

OP: George was an economist who was very interested in sociological issues. He was more of a political economist. He liked the work I had done on slavery. He used to cite *The Sociology of Slavery* a lot. We always had a good, cordial relationship. We would drink, and so on, but never close in the sense of visits. George kept his private life to himself. I don't think many of us ever went to his home. We hardly ever saw his wife. And there was a kind of Jamaican element. It's funny, but he remained a *raw chaw* [roots, natural] Jamaican, and he kept his private life that way. And my sense was that it was almost as if he lived in two worlds. There was his Jamaican world and the way he treated his women – he wanted to keep that separate. We spent a lot of time in the senior common room. But I was much closer to Leroy [Taylor]. Norman [Girvan] and I basically just grew apart and remained apart right through the Manley regime; even though he was working for the government, he disapproved of my role in the Manley regime. They were very critical, a grumpy group of lefties. And they were very much thinking that they could work with the big communist in the party who was scaring everybody – D. K. Duncan.[5]

DS: D. K. Duncan and Hugh Small were the principal members of the PNP left. Let's stay a bit longer in the late 1960s. The CAM people were returning, you among them. Brathwaite, Ramchand, Rohlehr, were all returning. Give me a sense of your literary, cultural engagements around this period.

OP: I was still writing fiction then. When Brathwaite came back he did try to bring CAM back, and we had several meetings. I remember one meeting in the common room of Chancellor Hall. And I distinctly remember discussing *Rights of Passage*. I was then writing *Die the Long Day*. That's incorrect. I wrote another novel that I did not publish, called *Jane and Louisa*.

DS: What's happened to that manuscript?

OP: It's somewhere around. It was in my mother's place for a long time. I think I have a part of it, but most of it has been lost. I did publish one chapter from it in *Jamaica Journal*.[6] I was writing that novel then; so, yes, I was still thinking in literary terms. And when Brathwaite came back, we met; we actually used to meet quite a bit. Eddie, come to think of it, would be another person in terms of social life I was involved with. We would have dinner with each other

132

DIE THE LONG DAY

beyond the faculty club scene; I liked his wife, Doris. And she got along very well with Nerys. So, we used to meet quite a bit.

DS: Was there a discussion then to begin what eventually becomes *Savacou*, the journal?
OP: Yes, we had begun the journal then, definitely. And I remember Brathwaite pressed me frequently to publish. I think he actually published something of mine without even telling me.

DS: What made you abandon *Jane and Louisa*?
OP: I read it, and in fact I remember asking Brathwaite to read it. And he didn't sound too enthusiastic about it. But, then, I don't know if Brathwaite ever sounds enthusiastic about anyone else's work. He said, "Well, this is the urban experience," or something like that. But I very much had a strong urge to write this historical novel anyway, which was pressing on me.

Die the Long Day

DS: When did you begin working on *Die the Long Day*?
OP: Almost as soon as I gave up on *Jane and Louisa*. I went straight into this because I'd wanted to write an historical novel. And I'd spent years immersed in the materials on slavery, so I wanted to work on it before it got stale.

DS: You were propelled in the direction of *historical* fiction.
OP: I'd always been interested in historical fiction. I thought it was a natural place for me. I started on that almost in a hurry. I was writing it during my last year in Jamaica and my first year in the United States and submitted it then.

DS: And published in 1972. Now, *Die the Long Day* is in many ways shaped or framed by the question of Quasheba's *humanity*, and it's of course significant that you so name her, given the whole debate about the slave personality (Quashee and Quasheba). The narrative is framed by the idea of a *limit* beyond which she refuses to submit to the humiliating power of the slave master. But what is interesting about the novel form in which you work out this idea (which has been part of your work from so early) is what *triggers* Quasheba's act of refusal. Because there may *abstractly* be a limit beyond which one's humanity will not accept domination, but then there is the *contingent*

133

THE PARADOX OF FREEDOM

situation that triggers the active refusal. And you stage that refusal around a mother's relationship to her daughter. Why is that? Why does that appear to you to be the most poignant, the most arresting situation to employ?

OP: For some of the same reasons it appealed to Toni Morrison, I guess. By the way, I met Toni Morrison and spent an afternoon with her, just before *Die the Long Day*. And we talked about it. It came out in 1972, so this would have been 1971. I met her through Jan Carew. He was in Princeton, doing one of his many visitorships. He was like a spirit that sort of appeared. So, there he was in Princeton. Toni was a friend of Jan Carew's. I don't know what their relationship was, but she came up to Princeton. She had just gotten divorced [from the Jamaican architect Harold "Moxie" Morrison]. She came up with a couple of little boys. We spent the afternoon together. I'd gotten to know Jan fairly well in England. We'd last seen each other in 1967 or so, when I left. *Die the Long Day* was already either in press or just about to come out, and I remember talking to Toni Morrison about it. I was always intrigued, because in a way *Beloved* is focused on that relationship between mother and daughter. For me the most powerful, the deepest, the most lasting set of ties among Blacks was between mother and daughter – in slavery, and afterward, too. I think it's still the case. When I did my studies in West Kingston and up in Standpipe, what came out clearly was the relationship between women and their daughters. Women were clear that they preferred daughters to their sons. And I always thought that was the most powerful relationship. The relationships with men were all fragile – there was a mother–son relationship, but even that was not as strong as the mother–daughter relationship. Historically, mothers and daughters tended to remain on the plantations (if slaveowners were selling anyone, it would be the sons). I always saw that as the strongest bond there is in traditional Jamaican society.

DS: But at the same time that it is the strongest bond, as you suggest, or *because* it is the strongest bond, it is also the bond that pivots on an axis of sheer *vulnerability*. The loss of the daughter – and the loss of the daughter to the sexual predation of the White planter – appears in some way to be a most acute violation. What I'm trying to get at here is that it is that potential loss that Quasheba fears that *propels* her into her act of rebellion.

OP: Yes. No other relationship would have generated such a reaction. Certainly not a male–female relationship. Absolutely none. It was the closest thing to a precious, inviolable kind of relationship, one that

DIE THE LONG DAY

would last for a lifetime. One couldn't expect lifelong relationships in slavery in any other circumstances. Men were beaten, brutalized, died young, or they had other relationships and other attachments. And even one's son would start straying with other women. Daughters remained forever.

DS: At the start of the novel, when Quasheba's disappearance is being talked about, and we meet her circle of relations on the plantation, we meet her lover, Cicero. Cicero is a *very* different kind of spirit than Quasheba. Indeed, *he* is a kind of Quashee character: stable, but willing, a little submissive, or playing fool to catch wise, in some respect. What a contrast! Why did you make Cicero Quasheba's partner, do you think?
OP: Because that's what I saw from experience in Jamaica. It's one kind of relationship I observed. He's that kind of man who would most likely have a lasting relationship with another woman. And that strong woman–weaker man is something I've noticed.

DS: At least fictionally it helps to draw the contrast-effect one recognizes in the two characters. When Cicero says to Quasheba that she's a "Neager" (or Naygah as one might spell it today) and she must know her place, you have Quasheba respond, "True, me is a Neager. But me is human too and is only one time they can kill me."[1] What's fascinating about this is the way in which you have her assert a claim to *universality*. So, I want to ask, to begin with, where would she have found that kind of language? Where would a slave on a plantation at the end of the eighteenth, beginning of the nineteenth century find the language of universality to assert their claim to humanity?
OP: That, in a sense, harks back to Camus again. At a certain point, the slave discovers his or her humanity in saying *no*. You reach a limit. When you reach that limit, it's a *human* limit, and it generates the questions: What is this? Why protest? Why not just give in? And, to justify that, you have to think of yourself in more universal, *human* terms. As long as you're thinking in particularistic terms, you're being a Naygah. But what I was saying, and what Camus was saying, is that the act of defiance is what brings you closest to the recognition of your humanity. Because that's the only reason why you'd protest. Why not just be a Naygah?

DS: In other words, why not simply accept one's particular condition.
OP: Right. The act of protest forces you to recognize that there is something in you that demands dignity, and that *couldn't* be your

135

THE PARADOX OF FREEDOM

particular life situation. It has to be something *more* than that. Because your life situation is telling you to survive by doing all the things you've done before. Something *extraordinary* happens in the act of defiance in which you go against *everything* you've been taught. You wonder what that could be. That could only be your *humanity*. In a sense, your act of resistance, that very extraordinary act, lifts you out of the normal, the everyday circumstances of your oppression. So, you cannot explain what you are doing in terms of anything that is common to your existence. It has to be something very special. And, invariably, that's where you discover your human dignity. And I think that's the point Camus was making, too, about slaves. It's interesting that he used slaves as the archetypal rebel who discovers his humanity in rebellion.[2] That's essentially what I was getting at.

DS: And you choose to figure the rebel in the novel as a woman rather than as a man. The male characters – Cicero, but also Africanus, a man of deep knowledge – are nevertheless unwilling to risk what Quasheba is willing to risk.
OP: Africanus never gets to that point. He's very deep, very African, very wise. But he's in the system, so he never shakes himself out of it. He'll accommodate it as best he can, in the most humane, dignified way, but he never discovers that profound existential dignity that comes in the act of rebellion and which requires you to transcend yourself, to transcend the ordinary ways you've fashioned over a lifetime to survive with some dignity.

DS: When you were writing *Die the Long Day*, there weren't many historical novels that turn on slavery, as there are now.
OP: Not really. They almost all come after.

DS: What models *did* you have?
OP: There were no models, to tell you the truth. And I think that novel doesn't get the credit it deserves, because there were not many others like it. Later, there was an outpouring, but I had no models, only my own imagination. Toni Morrison's *Beloved* was much later.

DS: But when you wrote *The Sociology of Slavery* you already had a sense that this might be the making of a fictional project as well.
OP: Yes, because I had done that before. In a way, *Sisyphus* was from sociological research that I decided would work better as a novel.

136

DS: It is interesting that you figure the Maroons as the folk who kill Quasheba.

OP: That's also related to my own historical research. I was writing "Slavery and Slave Revolts" while I was writing the novel.

DS: Because what's interesting about the Maroons, of course, is that, having crossed that line of revolt and claimed *their* humanity, they had in some sense then been reconstituted by the 1739 treaty with the British as another part of the system.

OP: Yes, but those acts of defiance and discovery of one's humanity tend to be heroic *moments* in one's life.

DS: And *fleeting*, therefore.

OP: Many people go back to accommodating, one way or the other. Africanus, for all we know, may well have had such a moment of rebellion, but then he had to go back to *living*. The Maroons had their moment, but then they had their own accommodation to the system. They became slave catchers, which their historians prefer not to dwell on. It's just amazing how people just neglect historical facts. People talk about these heroes, yes, but there are also the sad facts.

DS: For you, then, that moment of revolt is not interesting *because* it is the guarantee of a permanent state of defiance. What you're interested in is the *moment* in which there's an *absolute* claim against one's domination, and in which one's humanity is asserted.

OP: Right. And, in a way, Quasheba's is unusual in that it's a *sustained* moment for her. She knew it was not one she could live with but one she had to die for. Not many people make that choice. The only way you can sustain that is if life, as you know it, is going to be terminated. It's almost like a suicide – a long-drawn-out suicide.

DS: Thus the title, *Die the Long Day*. The novel, though framed by Quasheba's long act of revolt, is largely concerned with giving us a picture of the *life* of a plantation, the various kinds of negotiations, accommodations, and so on, through which plantation life was lived: in some sense, the everyday character of a plantation.

OP: Oh yes. I wanted to do that. It was my tribute to them, reliving the memory of the life they lived. I wanted people to know what it was like. The novel definitely was meant to do that. In many ways, also, I felt the novel would be more popular than *Sisyphus* was, in terms of being adapted in classrooms.

137

THE PARADOX OF FREEDOM

DS: But it wasn't?
OP: It had certain scenes that made it difficult.

DS: You think so? It seemed to me that, relatively speaking, the story of slavery was a kind of academic abstraction and that the story of revolt and accommodation (the big questions) were drafted very quickly into various kinds of political debates – nationalist ones, by and large. Thus, for me, anyway, when I first read *Die the Long Day* many years ago, one of the interesting things about its reconstruction of the modus vivendi of everyday slave life (the ordinariness of slave life in extraordinary circumstances) was that it made the picture of enslavement that much more complex, less flat.
OP: That was exactly what I wanted to do, and I think I achieved it. By the way, one of the persons who really liked that novel (I think he liked it more than any of my other works) was Sidney Mintz.

DS: How interesting! What was Mintz's response?
OP: He wrote me once and told me how very important it was. He felt the same way you do: that it brought slavery *alive* more than any other work he knew of. By the way, talking about models, there was one sort of romantic, or more Gothic, novel, which was H. G. de Lisser's *The White Witch of Rosehall*. But that wasn't really about slavery, but about a slave mistress.[3]

Arrival at Harvard

DS: How did you come to leave the University of the West Indies for Harvard?
OP: Well, I didn't have any great urge to come to Harvard the way the typical American does – because I didn't grow up in the system. Where I grew up, it was Oxford, Cambridge, and LSE that mattered. And I had already done that. Two things happened. One, I'd become a little disillusioned with what had happened after the Rodney affair; not that I was a great fan of Rodney, but I was horrified by the soldiers up on the campus. That really dampened the enthusiasm with which I'd gone back home. I'd gone back home to settle down. I'd immediately built a house on Coopers Hill; my dream was to have a house in the hills, drive down to campus, and so on. I'd settled in. And one of the things that stood out, symbolically, was that I had had a dining table made from the blue mahoe at a workshop that built blue mahoe furnishings near Port Antonio – a dining table built

138

ARRIVAL AT HARVARD

to seat ten. I was figuring I was going to have six kids in Jamaica! My brother Victor was the architect, and we sat down and designed this house together on the hillside. So, I'd dug in. And, as I said, we were having this good relationship with Manley, whom I was seeing quite a bit. But then the soldiers came up. I was disappointed, too, with the intellectual life, to some extent. I felt that if I stayed I'd move more and more into public life. Manley was already hinting that I should think about going with him into public life. He had already made up his mind he was going to make the move. He wanted very much to be very closely aligned to the intellectual life of the younger generation, and we hit it off very well. But then, as I said, after the Rodney affair, it seemed from a couple of polls that the JLP had things wrapped up. They gave the PNP little chance. So, I became a little restless intellectually because it was clear to me that, if I stayed, *that* would be the way I'd be going. Because I felt the campus didn't provide me the academic resources I'd need for the kind of scholarship I wanted to do. And I really had to decide whether I wanted to go the academic route rather than a more public intellectual-cum-politician route, which is what Carlyle Dunkley did. He always had that in mind. He never had any ambition to be an academic intellectual.

Anyway, I had a sabbatical coming up; it was just half a year, from January 1970. I applied to several places asking them if they had the space for me. I was really looking for a place to hang my hat, but I said, if you want me to teach a course I would. I was interested in coming to America because I had never had any academic experience there. There's one more thing I should mention. In the summer of 1969 the famous Black sociologist St Clair Drake invited me to come to Chicago. He was at a place called Roosevelt University. He was a funny guy; we got along very well in Jamaica. And then he invited me to Roosevelt. He eventually went to Stanford, but for a long time he was faithful to Roosevelt University, which was the only place that would give him a job up north. When he graduated, he had to go down south, even though he had written this great book, *Black Metropolis*. Roosevelt seemed an interesting place, the way St Clair Drake described it to me. By the time I got there, it had already begun to decline; if it was ever *up* there, I don't know. Anyway, I spent a summer teaching in their summer program, teaching on West Indian literature and society. I was there the whole summer by myself and I was very fascinated. That was the summer of the Black arts movement, which was focused on Chicago. There were people there like Nikki Giovanni. Every street corner had a poet spouting. It was amazing! A bit like the Harlem Renaissance, except it was less elite

139

oriented. So, I figured I'd like to come to the States, and I wrote to several places saying I'd love to come and spend a semester.

About the same time that St Clair Drake invited me, I had written to just the usual suspects – Harvard, Yale: they had African American studies programs just starting that I was very interested in. I think I may well have written to Columbia, too. Anyway, when I was at Roosevelt, out of the blue I got a call from Talcott Parsons. I was really shocked! He asked me if I was interested in coming over, so I said yes! They actually flew me over while I was there in Chicago. And right there on the spot he said, "You can come, and do sociology and African American studies as a visitor." I said, "That sounds great!" I didn't expect Parsons to call me!

DS: The great man himself!
OP: They had Ewart Guinier heading up the Afro-American studies program, but he was really a disaster.[1] He and I did not get along. He was not a scholar, was completely out of his depth, and rather authoritarian. We argued, and when things got so bad that he locked me out of the faculty bathroom I went to the dean and said, "I'm going home. This is ridiculous. This is not what I came to Harvard to get, and I don't need this. I'm sorry, I'm going to quit my course and go home." He realized that Guinier had acted like a moron. But he said, "Okay, please, can you stay and finish your course at least? And we'll ask the Sociology Department if they will provide you with an office space." So, the Sociology Department provided me with an office space. And that was the only reason why I didn't get on the first plane out of here. My life would have been very different.

DS: Who was the chair of the Sociology Department then?
OP: At that time, the chair would have been George Homans, with whom I became very good friends. He was an old "Brahmin"; he liked the fact that I'd written novels, because he was a very literary man. And then David Riesman and I got along very well, too, and he rapidly became my mentor, as did Marty Lipset. David and Marty basically adopted me. Then people at Princeton heard about my problems here, and I got this note from the Sociology Department (there was no Afro-American studies department at the time, just a committee) asking if they could come and talk to me. And I said, "I don't know, but I'll come and give a talk." So, I went and gave a talk to Sociology. Next thing I know, I get a letter from the chair of Sociology, asking if I'd be interested in joining them. And I said, "We'll have to talk, because I really was seriously thinking of going

ARRIVAL AT HARVARD

back home." And the chair flew to Cambridge to talk me into coming to Princeton. I said, "No, I've really got to go back home. I don't want another visiting position; I am on sabbatical." George Beckford was also writing me at that time saying that there was a professorship at UWI coming up and I should apply for it.

At the same time Sociology here [at Harvard] asked me if I would be interested in staying for another year – because they'd now gotten wind of the fact that Princeton was interested. So, there was a kind of little competition going on. I decided to stay here an extra year. I'd never had a leave before – it was only one semester – but it had been a pretty unpleasant semester. I didn't get much done. So I said, "Okay, I'll stay for the following year." I told the people at the University of the West Indies; they were not entirely happy with it, but they said, "That's okay." And then, early in the fall, Princeton offered me a position in the Sociology Department as a tenured associate professor. David and Marty heard about this and immediately went to the dean and said there's no way that they can have Princeton grab me from under their noses. And they then said to me they were going to try to get a tenured position through. But at Harvard there's no such thing as an associate with tenure; you go straight into a full professorship. I told them to go ahead. Princeton then started putting pressure on me. It was a little tense at one point because they knew that there was a counteroffer coming from Harvard, so at one point I had to literally decide whether I was going to take the chance of going through the ad hoc committee here and saying no to Princeton, which was a tenured position. But Marty and David and George Homans said it's worth taking a chance. So, I went along with it, turned down Princeton, and took this one. That's how I ended up here. I pretty easily could have gone to Princeton or gone back home. For me, I saw little difference between the three. The one thing I knew I wasn't going to do was to have anything to do with the Afro-American Studies Department under Ewart Guinier.

DS: And your wife, Nerys, was willing to stay?
OP: She was willing to stay and she did a joint degree in Celtic studies and sociology under George Homans's supervision. So, I came January 1970 and I got tenure on 1 July 1971.

DS: When in 1972, shortly after you come here, the PNP under Michael Manley won the general elections in Jamaica on the "Better Must Come" platform, were you tempted to return?
OP: Well, almost immediately, Michael got in touch with me and urged me to come home. After I got tenure, it was announced in *The*

141

THE PARADOX OF FREEDOM

Gleaner. Michael read it and sent his congratulations, but then said, "We must talk." He formed something called the Technical Advisory Council, which was chaired by none other than M. G. Smith, who was on a very long leave from University College London. MG and I worked together down there. He was full time. He left his London position for a couple of years. The idea was to have a group of social scientists to think broadly about where we were going.

I would go there four or five times a year. Manley gave me an office in the prime minister's office; I had a secretary there. So, basically, I had two jobs starting almost immediately. I would spend all my summers and all my Christmas vacations there. I was spending the better part of five months each year in Jamaica. I usually left the day after my last lecture. That went on for most of the 1970s. But I was never tempted – and Manley, in fairness to him, never pushed me – to return permanently. Because he knew that I was at heart an academic. But I did a lot. He had me working in his constituency; he trusted me. I set up this urban upgrading project.

DS: Did UWI encourage you to come back at that point?
OP: No. The university has maintained its distance ever since. Through all the years I would go down there working for Manley I didn't have much to do with the university. Once, Rex Nettleford asked me to speak to his trade union group, but that was it. They kept their distance.

DS: Was Norman Girvan on the Technical Advisory Committee?
OP: Norman was on one of those committees in the planning office, but we didn't see much of each other. Norman was on the left wing of the party, fraternizing with D. K. Duncan. And I was advising Manley to be wary. One of the things that Manley liked was that, because I wasn't in the hurly-burly of daily politicking, I'd see the situation and I'd tell him what I thought. I made it quite clear: "What we have here with the left is an 'empty barrels make the most noise' situation." They really didn't have all that much power. But they were given the information ministry, which is in many ways the one with the least power, but it was also the one through which they could make the most noise.

DS: I didn't know that D. K. Duncan was *that* prominent in the early part of the 1970s. I thought that he became prominent from around 1974 onward.
OP: Well, even before he won a seat he was seen as the ...

142

ARRIVAL AT HARVARD

DS: The *firebrand*?

OP: Not only the "firebrand." Even before he ran, he was seen as the person pulling the strings behind the scenes, the real power, plotting revolt, and was going to kick out Manley. There was a real terror of this guy. I would go to cocktail parties, and people would talk about D. K. Duncan like he was some kind of ogre. And I kept saying, "Guys, I think you are just wrong." But Manley gave them a voice, and they used it. For me, quite frankly, it wouldn't have been a great loss if tenure at Harvard hadn't worked out and I'd had to go back to Jamaica or go to Princeton. It was a very good opportunity, I thought, and I felt I wanted to stay in America. I was interested in what was developing from an intellectual point of view in terms of studies of Black life. *That* was what the challenge was for me, much more than being at Harvard. There were two big events in my youth: one was Jamaican independence; the other one was the Black movement, which from LSE we were all following very closely. We saw this as the great revolution of our times, the civil rights movement. That's the main reason I wanted to be in America, the main reason why I was so fascinated with African American studies departments here.

DS: Those were, of course, the early 1970s, the immediate post-King years, wrenching years for the civil rights movement, and a transforming moment for the Black Power movement; and it is also a significant moment – 1969, 1970, 1971 – for the making of Black studies, the making of these African American studies programs.[2]

OP: You must remember something else about this, intellectually. I was used to *African American studies* even before the term was used here. Because, when I did my undergraduate studies, we read Melville Herskovits. I mentioned that Lloyd Braithwaite may have been critical of him, but we *did* read Herskovits thoroughly. I liked Herskovits a lot, as I told you. Herskovits was the first person to use the term *Afro-American studies*.[3] Herskovits actually has a chapter called "African American Studies," laying out the basis for it. And that's what we were doing in Caribbean studies, which we saw as part of African American studies in the Herskovitsean sense: both were part of New World Black studies. I thought this was the intellectual background I was going to bring to African American studies, except I was more in the metropole here, as opposed to being in one of the peripheral areas. And the Black revolution had shifted toward a more *cultural* orientation by the early 1970s.

THE PARADOX OF FREEDOM

DS: Do you think that the rise of Black studies provides one of the contexts in which Harvard and Princeton were interested in you?

OP: Oh, absolutely. They were desperate for people who were not just in it rhetorically and politically. And I was a serious scholar involved in doing just that. Writing in that vein, studying slavery. I'd had a major book on slavery out. I had a major paper on slave revolts out. These were subjects that everybody was very interested in here. There were two major essays I wrote not long after I started here. One was published in *The Public Interest*. The other one was called "Rethinking Black History," which I published in the *Harvard Educational Review*.[4] So I was all set intellectually to move in this direction and take the leadership in this area. It didn't work out that way, because of what happened in terms of the *identity* movement, which, as it turned out, was not all that interested at that time in scholarship of the kind I was involved with.

DS: Before we turn to those essays, I wonder whether there wasn't a question of adjustment, also, to US sociology. Of course, you were steeped in Talcott Parsons from earlier on, but did you find that the cultural tradition in the United States was significantly different from the British sociological tradition?

OP: I saw what I wanted to see and left what I didn't want to get involved with. I saw myself as an historical and cultural sociologist coming out of the British tradition with a somewhat Marxist background. Not long after I came, sociology went through this big shift, as it desperately tried to redefine itself in quantitative measures. I saw that, and, in a way, I could be seen as the last of the appointments in the Harvard tradition of Homans, Riesman, Marty Lipset, and Daniel Bell. They were all very much for me because they saw me in their own tradition. And I also was bringing a European kind of perspective, too, which they liked a lot. And my own left-wing connections, *New Left Review* connections, they thought that was cute, but they didn't see it as a big problem. They liked my LSE background. So, I fitted in very much with that group who were still in control. If I had come here ten years later they would not have been as interested. But I was very much in the mold – the Third World was very much in vogue. Marty wanted to teach a course with me, and we ended up teaching a course together. I was interested in ethnicity, race, and slavery.

DS: *Big* issues.

OP: Big issues. David loved it, so did Marty. It's hardly surprising that they liked what I was doing. And I taught a graduate course

ARRIVAL AT HARVARD

on development, which I had done with one of my mentors at LSE, Ernest Gellner.

DS: Oh? I didn't know that!

OP: Yes. I met Gellner in 1962, during my first year of graduate studies at LSE, where he had been a professor of sociology since 1949. Gellner and Ron Dore ran a popular "Sociology of Development" seminar which I naturally attended (and continued to do as a faculty member after my appointment in 1965). However, I was even more excited by the celebrated Thursday morning interdisciplinary seminars of the Sociology and Anthropology departments. Ernest, as you know, did his graduate studies and later empirical works in anthropology, and several of the major stars in anthropology at the time often attended the seminar. As I mentioned earlier, I was both pleased and flattered when, during my first year of teaching at LSE, Lucy Mair, who was then chairing the seminar with Ernest, asked me to present a paper of mine on Negritude, "Twilight of a Dark Myth," that had appeared in a special issue of the *Times Literary Supplement*.[5] In 1965 I was appointed as an assistant lecturer in sociology at LSE, and I'm sure that Ernest strongly supported my candidacy. At that time, assistant lecturers, in addition to teaching their own courses, had to assist the senior professors in their courses in the one-on-one tutorial system for students taking their course; there were no graduate teaching assistants in Britain at the time. As soon as I was appointed, Ernest got in touch with me and asked me to be his teaching assistant in his social philosophy course. This meant not only attending all his lectures but closely reading the texts he taught, which was a great education for me. The work on which he based his lectures was the now classic *Thought and Change*, which appeared (to mixed reviews) that same year I first taught with him.[6] It was a wonderful learning experience discussing Gellner's ideas with him as I prepared for my tutorials at that crucial stage of my development (I had just turned twenty-five). Gellner was a warm and humorous person who, without any trace of condescension, patiently responded to my questions, including issues I had reservations about, especially his functionalism, which bothered me, as it did my New Left colleagues at the time, one of whom, Perry Anderson, was later to write critically on this.[7] In addition to his ideas, I was strongly influenced by Gellner's methodology and style of thinking. His interdisciplinarity – he was social philosopher, sociologist, anthropologist, and social and cultural historian – and his mode of doing historical sociology, especially his emphasis on the role of ideas and culture in

THE PARADOX OF FREEDOM

their historical interactions with structural forces, what he described in *Thought and Change* as the "genuine time- and context-bound roots" of social processes and major developments in the emergence of modernity. Traces of his influence are already there in my work on Negritude and the early Rastafarian movement; they're more marked in *Ethnic Chauvinism: The Reactionary Impulse*, even where I departed sharply from his modernist theory of nationalism (for me there are clear traces of nationalism in the Davidic kingdom three millennia ago), more subtly at play in *Slavery and Social Death*, and clearly evident in *Freedom in the Making of Western Culture*. It would be fair to call my method of historical sociology *Gellnerian*.

DS: At the time, were there other Black faculty members in the Sociology Department?
OP: No, there were no others. I was the second Black faculty appointment in the entire faculty of arts and sciences at Harvard. Martin Kilson was the first; I was the second. Then there was Peter Gomes. But intellectually I felt very close to Marty Lipset, Dan Bell, and especially David Riesman. I dedicated *Ethnic Chauvinism* to David and Evey Riesman. David had read it very carefully and loved every page of it, because it was very much in his spirit. So that was a natural appointment in terms of where the department was at that time. But then, the department was headed for a big crisis after that. We were the leading department in the country then, with Parsons, Homans, Marty, and David. Parsons dominated sociology at the time. I came at a critical moment in Sociology when it broke away from Social Relations. The year before I came was the end of Social Relations.

DS: Is it Parsons who engineers the transformation?
OP: No, Parsons didn't want it. Parsons *created* Social Relations! The whole point of Social Relations was the Parsonian model of integrating psychology, anthropology, sociology – that was Parsons's baby, created in the 1930s and 1940s. He was working with Robert F. Bales upstairs, and this was one big happy family. He was working with anthropology people, Clyde Kluckhohn downstairs. Parsons hated the change. This was the beginning of the end for Parsons.

DS: Right. In fact, he died shortly thereafter.
OP: In 1978. I overlapped with him for almost a decade. I liked him a lot. He liked me. We had very happy moments, dinner over at his house; but Alex Inkeles was the person who broke it up and then left. In fact, I moved into the office that Inkeles left and have been in it to

146

this day. We became a department the very same year that I joined it. I was the first person appointed to Sociology when it became a separate department. Because, before that, we were part of Social Relations and we had different wings – the Anthropology wing, the Sociology wing, and the Psychology wing.

Engaging Black America

DS: In the early 1970s you published a number of essays on Black America. Two of these essays, "Toward a Future That Has No Past" and "The Moral Crisis of the Black American," were published in *The Public Interest* – indeed, in both cases they were published alongside essays by Daniel Patrick Moynihan.[1]
OP: I got to know him quite well.

DS: Tell me more about Moynihan and your relationship with him. In some respects, for many African Americans, he is the very embodiment of the "damage" theory of the Black family.
OP: Moynihan was, and remains, one of the most unjustly maligned figures in American intellectual history. I came to know him fairly well when he was at Harvard. He was a good friend of my colleague Nathan Glazer, with whom he had co-authored *Beyond the Melting Pot*. While at Harvard they edited a volume, *Ethnicity: Theory and Experience*, and asked me to contribute a chapter, which I did.[2] Moynihan edited my chapter, and I came to know him more closely as a result. He was not a racist; just the opposite. He was a deeply progressive guy whose views were strongly fashioned by his working-class Irish-American background, growing up in Manhattan's Hell's Kitchen, where his mother ran a saloon. He was also arguably one of the most pro-Black and left-of-center persons to advise an American president, one of the architects of Lyndon Johnson's "Great Society" program. The policy brief for which he has gained notoriety was nothing more than a summary of standard sociological and social-psychological views of the time – the Black Columbia social psychologist Kenneth Clark, the sociologist E. Franklin Frazier, the psychologist Abram Kardiner, and, yes, W. E. B. Du Bois's *Philadelphia Negro* and his edited volume *The Negro American Family* – which held that slavery had devastated Black family life and that its consequences lingered up to the present in the high rate of female-headed households and its problems among lower-class inner-city Blacks. The problem was partly that it was stated perhaps too starkly,

147

THE PARADOX OF FREEDOM

without the standard academic qualifications, but, more importantly, it came at a time when there was a shift toward the assertion of Black pride, accompanied by a parallel shift in sociology and public policy away from cultural-historical explanations toward more structuralist ones. However, Moynihan himself never said that socio-economic factors were not important. He held that they reinforced the pre-existing problems inherited from past oppression – the same "marks of oppression" that Kardiner had written about. Furthermore, he was one of the authors and strong advocates of the Family Assistance Plan, which sought to replace welfare with a guaranteed income, the very first legislation in American policy history that guaranteed, as a right, an income floor for families with children. The fact that Moynihan was White and sometimes talked too much made him the perfect foil for the new Black identity movement, which wanted to hear nothing about Black internal problems. Moynihan was lumped with another social scientist whose work had suddenly become out of favor – Oscar Lewis – of "culture of poverty" infamy. Ironically, like Moynihan, Lewis was left of center in his politics and social thought. Both became targets for the Black identity movement as well as the movement toward anti-historical structuralist thinking in sociology. The phrase that summed up the hostility toward them was one coined by William Ryan in the title of his 1971 book, *Blaming the Victim*.[3] It was all this posturing and intellectual dishonesty that led me to write *Ethnic Chauvinism: The Reactionary Impulse*.

DS: Now, on any view, *The Public Interest* was not an *uncontroversial* magazine, even then, and, certainly, its editor, Irving Krystol (I think Krystol and Daniel Bell were the co-editors at the time), was not an uncontroversial figure. What drew you to publish in *The Public Interest*?
OP: I don't really think about the politics of journals I'm publishing in. That calculation is not one I make. The point is, I was more interested in the editors. I'd met Krystol; I saw him once or twice. But Bell was the person whom I was interested in.

DS: But Bell was not at Harvard then?
OP: Oh yes, Bell was here. He came *before* me, and he would have voted on my appointment.

DS: I see. You were more interested in the fact that *The Public Interest* was a much more of a *public* intellectual platform than a straight academic type of journal.

148

ENGAGING BLACK AMERICA

OP: Yes, absolutely. And I'd admired Bell greatly from even before I came here. In Europe with the New Left we argued about and condemned *The End of Ideology*. I loved Bell and we got along very well, and he loved the fact that I wrote fiction. In fact, his wife reviewed *Die the Long Day* for a major journal – *Commentary*, I think. We got along great; they were all my people.[4]

DS: That's very interesting!

OP: So, when Dan told me he was editing this journal and asked me if I would be interested in writing for it, I said, sure. The whole question about Jews and Palestine was out of my orbit. We weren't obsessed with that in Britain. At that time the question for me was "anti-ethnicity."

DS: Right. But it seems to me *more* than that. The question of Black America, race in particular, was one thing. But one of the registers through which both of these essays in *The Public Interest* are written is a critique of a certain kind of US *liberalism*. And Bell, Moynihan, and Krystol, in different ways (some of which eventually come to be called "neoconservative"), were all critics of a certain *liberal* strand in American political discourse. Bell, it is true, breaks with Krystol shortly after this, partly on the grounds that he is taking *The Public Interest* in too conservative a direction.

OP: Right. And I was very much in tune with that criticism of liberalism, too. It came partly from my lingering left orientation. I saw a wishy-washy kind of liberal guilt thing that I felt was not good for Blacks. And I saw the Black identity movement, especially the middle class, playing into that. And I didn't like it. I was for a tough-minded facing of the role of class in Black life, the way Martin Luther King Jr was going toward the end of his life. I brought that over from Britain with me. And I saw a dangerous identity movement emerging that I felt Blacks were getting into. I also saw the dangers of the *White* ethnic movement, which I saw as a clear backlash against this. Black identity was legitimizing a kind of [White] neofascist development in America, which I thought was dangerous for Blacks. I went to Princeton [to the Institute for Advanced Study] to write an earlier version of *Slavery and Social Death*, but I was so disturbed by what was happening with the "ethnic revival" that I decided to put aside the slavery book and write *Ethnic Chauvinism* instead.[5] I did a good part of the research for *Slavery and Social Death* in the Princeton library. But *Ethnic Chauvinism* was my blend of an academic and public intellectual style, really in the Riesman tradition. I felt it was

149

THE PARADOX OF FREEDOM

more urgently needed at that time, so I was very critical and wrote op-eds, because I saw dangers for Blacks, I saw dangers for America. I thought this thing was *neofascist*. This view was partly prompted by my neo-Marxian position. But it was prompted, too, by what I saw in the whole identity movement as a clear, anti-intellectual, wishy-washy, and unproductive or counterproductive symbiosis between liberal guilt and Black identity.

DS: Yes, that's clear in both essays, which I want to talk about.
OP: There's another essay that I wrote at that time published in *American Scholar* on Black–White relations.[6] Those were all my ways of dealing with that whole phase.

DS: But this was also your coming to terms with America. This is your thinking *through* America.
OP: Right, absolutely – coming to terms with it, thinking through it. And also rethinking Black history. That whole bunch of essays were definitely about coming to terms with America and positioning myself intellectually. But, of course, by the time I finished that, people were pissed with the position I was taking.

DS: I can imagine. In the 1972 essay "Toward a Future That Has No Past," you draw a picture on a very large canvas of slavery and post-slavery societies in the New World – the United States, the Caribbean, Latin America – to intervene in a debate about the supposed essential *unity* of Black experience. This is where the argument got traction and got going.
OP: That's the origin of the "Black Atlantic" idea, and several others made use of it. Others got credit for it.

DS: Yes, and I'm going to draw that connection in a moment. But what is the context of this intervention? Was it specifically Black American, or were you hearing at the time resonances from the kinds of discussions you had had in Britain and the Caribbean?
OP: It was very much a *hemispheric* perspective, even bringing in the European one, and positioning myself and seeing and encouraging Black Americans to get out of what I saw as a terrible *parochialism*.

DS: Exactly. Your perspective is hemispheric, but your *address* is to African America specifically.
OP: Absolutely. And I keep telling them they're too parochial. They ought to see the linkages. It's very important that they do so.

150

DS: Now, in this essay you argue that there is more diversity in the hemispheric Black experience than Black American leaders might typically admit, and there is also a fundamental similarity, namely, the historic erasure of the past. This notion of the historic erasure of the past in the present of the Black experience is a familiar "Orlando Patterson theme." But here you maintain that the *sense* of pastlessness lays upon the Black intellectual a challenge to imagine a future *unburdened by tradition*.

OP: Right. It's a complex argument in that I was saying it's more a *sense* of the past rather than the past itself. Because I was also pointing out that there are continuities in the cultural experience coming from slavery, many of them negative, but also continuities in terms of survivals from Africa, in music, and so on. But the sense of the past and of continuity that was so badly disrupted offered the opportunity to be unburdened by tradition and to be a people of the *future*. This future could be defined as America in many important ways. I love to use jazz as my model of perfect Americanism. It's music very much of *now*, in its nature, and in the sense that it's not burdened or bound by scripts. But there is still *influence*; there's a *consciousness* of being unburdened by the past. It recognizes the influence of the past but doesn't romanticize it; it doesn't allow itself to be bound by the past.

DS: One of the things that you emphasize in this essay is a distinction between the Black American intellectual's preoccupation with history and the larger sense of carrying an embodied sense of the past in one's present. You say the obsession with Black history on the part of Black intellectuals does not and cannot substitute for the *absence* of that lived sense of a tradition.

OP: That's right. And this may have advantages, especially in America.

DS: Exactly! It has advantages, but, even more than that, part of what you're arguing here is that there is a real challenge, and perhaps a *responsibility*, for Black American leadership to give up *Blackness* as a ground of political solidarity. "Beyond Blackness" is what you term it.

OP: Right, exactly. And, in a way, the thing I like about Tommie Shelby's book (which I reviewed for the *New York Times Book Review*) is that I saw in his writing a fruition of this issue.[7] He distinguishes between *thin* and *thick* identity. And he rejects *thick* identity and promotes the idea of *thin* identity, which is exactly how

151

(if those terms [had been] around at that time) I would have used them. He's simply saying that there's no basis anymore for this sort of *deep* identity, navel gazing, but only for an identity based on the experience of discrimination and lingering racism and inequality, which we still continue to share, and which we have to mobilize on the basis of having to eradicate it. But, in doing that, of course, you are also radicalizing America in a way that I saw at that time as one important implication of Black relief of the burden of the past and promoting a kind of egalitarian vision of America (which had implications for women and for other groups, as it turns out now). I still think that's the right position, and I think Tommie gives a beautiful philosophical treatment of what I was trying to get at, which is *not* to abandon concern for Black people but to see a thick identity as counterproductive. He arrives at thin identity, which recognized the need for struggle.

DS: There's a kinship, of course, with Tommie Shelby. But there's also, perhaps, a kinship between what you're saying and Paul Gilroy's argument against Black particularism and *for* a Black cosmopolitanism and planetary universalism.[8]

OP: Well, that's the argument of *Ethnic Chauvinism*, published in 1977.

DS: I want to talk about two more aspects of this essay, "Toward a Future that has no Past," that are very striking. One is the redescription of the passage from Aimé Césaire's *Notebook of a Return to My Native Land*, in which you suggest that Césaire should *not* be read as an essentialist (as he often is) but instead should be read as saying that those who have invented nothing have an opportunity in the future to invent something unburdened by the past.

OP: That's how I read Aimé Césaire. It was ironical that all around me he was taught in African American courses as the embodiment of Black ethnicity. And I just felt, "Did they read the same poem that I read? Maybe the translations they read were all bad!" I was able to read it in the original, because I told you my French was pretty good at that time. That's how I interpreted Césaire. He was an old Marxist, so it's very likely that that was the correct interpretation.

DS: But when you were writing "Toward a Future That Has No Past," were you conscious that these were themes from the 1960s, from *Sisyphus*, from *An Absence of Ruins*, the critique of a certain conception of the past, the present of the Black experience, that were being rearticulated as you try to think about Black America?

ENGAGING BLACK AMERICA

OP: I don't know about being self-conscious. I knew about the continuities. That was clearly how I'd been thinking. That essay and *Ethnic Chauvinism* were the culmination of that thinking.

DS: Yes. But before we get to the book itself, to my mind the sense of your responding to America, of explaining Black America to yourself, is heightened in the second essay published in *The Public Interest*, "The Moral Crisis of the Black American." Here it seems to me that you are building on your doubts about Black solidarity. Black Americans inhabit a paradoxical situation here (the idea of paradox is *methodological* for you). And that paradox turns on the horns of the dilemma of two incommensurable moral systems – a moral system that embodies individual responsibility, moral autonomy, which you identify as the American creed, and a rival morality that embodies a conception of determinism. And, for you, Black Americans aspire to that creed of individual autonomy; their politics is articulated in terms of the horizon of being included in that moral system. At the same time, rubbing against that, so to speak, is the familiar need of disadvantaged groups to articulate their morality in terms of *determinism*. And that dilemma is where African American politics is; it sits on the horns of that dilemma. Before we tackle the direction of your resolution, which again carries us back to the Orlando of the 1960s, how would you trace the intellectual genealogy of your recognition of this dilemma? You had literally just arrived and were settling in America. But somehow this distinction was eminently clear to you, even as it was invisible, by and large, to the African American leadership?

OP: Well, as an outsider coming here, it was much easier to see than insiders could. And the contradiction just struck me everywhere I turned, in the sense that people were screaming for self-determination and insisting that what they wanted, in extreme cases, was to withdraw into a separatist heartland or go back to Africa. I was convinced that, deep down, there's a strong commitment to this basically American ideal of self-ownership and self-determination, which goes all the way back to slavery. It's the only position an ex-slave could take, when you think about it. Because the thing that's most precious to them is being able to determine their own lives. This is an insight Camus saw *philosophically*; but it's an insight that comes out of many slave studies. If you know the literature on African American and Caribbean ex-slaves, you know that there's almost an *anarchic* sort of desire to be independent. After emancipation, the slaves just wanted to experience the joy of being on their

153

THE PARADOX OF FREEDOM

own. It explains some other things, too, some of which, if you follow through, can get you into trouble. And one is the attitude toward authority, and toward work. It's not that people don't want to work; it's that people have this almost visceral disdain and revulsion toward working for others. And you get that in Jamaica. Nobody works harder than the Jamaican countryman on his little plot of land. Some of these people put in seventeen, eighteen hours a day, getting blood out of stone on these little lots, hardly the size of this office. But they have a hard time working for others. And you get the same thing here among African Americans. This is an insight that had emerged out of my slave studies. It's the hustling tradition. Hustling is hard work.

DS: In the essay, you quite tellingly describe a number of positions that, while self-consciously seeking to underline a quest for individual autonomy, end up in the clutches of determinism. The way *out* of this dilemma for you is interesting. Because, for you, as you put it, what is needed is an act of sheer *will* – in particular, the will to *rebel*. In the essay you call for an existential rebellion following Camus. The will to declare "the limit," as you put it, the will "to say no, that simultaneously affirms humanity." The aim of this is to renovate a Black American sense of moral and political responsibility – a responsibility not so much for the past, which cannot be changed, but for the present that will become the future.

OP: Right, and that I still hold to be the case. And I think it's the position that former President Barack Obama holds. But it's been a hard lesson to learn. I just felt I was ahead of the times then. There's been a reaction to this identity movement in academia now. Again, they don't cite *Ethnic Chauvinism* much. But there's certainly a sense that we have to go beyond this. Obama's dilemma is that he sees that instinctively, and that is his agenda, too.

DS: I wonder whether you think Obama sees it instinctively because, like you, he's a *kind* of outsider to the African American experience.

OP: Oh yes, definitely, having spent part of his life in Indonesia, as the Tea Party people never fail to mention.

DS: But also, I think, more than Indonesia, is that he did not grow up inside of an *African American* socialization.

OP: Absolutely. And it's no accident, you know, that the other African American who came closest to the presidency, Colin Powell, is also a kind of outsider, his parents being Jamaican. Yes, he's second generation, and he talked in a way that was very self-determining;

154

and at the same time he doesn't see America as the enemy but as a place that allowed him to achieve his own goals. He's very much a Black American. And he has been a very interesting model, puzzling at first for many of the arch-identity types. Jesse Jackson had the same problem with him that he has with Obama. Different, in that Powell didn't go around making speeches about Black fathers having to take responsibility. One of the essays that Skip Gates has in *Thirteen Ways of Looking at a Black Man* is on Powell. He interviewed Jesse Jackson, who expressed total puzzlement about Powell; he said, "Who's this guy? Where'd he come from? What's this all about?" What he in fact was saying was, "He's not one of us. He didn't go through what we went through. He didn't talk the talk the way we talk it; he's not into the identity movement. How is that possible?" It was just not possible to Jesse; he couldn't see how America made someone like Powell possible, a Black man who could talk like a chief of staff and *claim* America.[9] I think what pissed them off was when he did this Jamaican thing about how he had some Scottish blood. Jamaicans unselfconsciously talk that way. Less so now than they used to when I was growing up – my jet-black grandfather would talk about his Scottish nose. When I read Powell's autobiography, with him going on about his Irish traits, I was thinking about my grandfather.[10] But I also thought Jesse Jackson, reading this, would say, "What the shit is this?" But that is a view that Black Americans have got to come around to sooner or later but are resisting mightily.

In my work *The Ordeal of Integration*, I stuck my neck out again on the whole business of segregation, which is still a big puzzle right now – why the Black middle class is so segregated. We've still got a long way to go on this debate. They're messing themselves up really badly, and for a reason that they will not admit. Because the fundamental assumption of Black identity politics is that all cultures are equal and you can achieve anything from any cultural standpoint in a society such as America. It refuses to recognize what in a sense Pierre Bourdieu has almost legitimized – because the whole notion of "cultural capital" is very antithetical to cultural identity. Because the fundamental assumption of any identity movement is that any culture can do anything; it's all just different ways of skinning the same cat. The notion of cultural capital is that, no, there are certain kinds of cultural resources that are essential to skinning one kind of cat, such as being successful in a competitive, capitalist society. Bourdieu comes at it from a very Marxist perspective. He's saying, "It is horrible that it is so." But he's still saying that this is so. And the concept of cultural capital does admit that there are certain ways of doing things, just that, for example, the bourgeoisie monopolizes them. And the bourgeoisie monopolize it even before they go to school, and the school legitimizes and reinforces their control of this. But the point is, according to the idea of cultural capital, "If you got it, you're going to succeed. If you don't have it, you won't succeed." The critique of that, in a way, is the standard cliché response: "That's a cultural deficit argument." That's the implicit critique. Because you're saying that we *lack* something.[11]

DS: Absolutely. But, in emphasizing *will*, the way you do here, it's clear that you haven't left the moral world of existential philosophy; that is still the implicit space in which you are operating. Now, for you, this notion of moral responsibility for oneself, as I read the essay, is not necessarily a purely private or individualistic one. It does not necessarily preclude acts of collective rebellion. How would you elaborate the conception of solidarity and responsibility that this kind of *collective* will entails?

OP: Well, for me at that time (again coming out of LSE), there was an idea of solidarity that characterized what was called "coalition politics" in the early phases of the civil rights movement. While Black Power was a turning point, in a way, Charles Hamilton (with whom Stokely Carmichael wrote the book *Black Power*) went on to articulate a kind of coalition-building solidarity, and that struck me as essential.[12] *That* was the great tragedy of racism: the whole point of Jim Crow was to prevent that kind of solidarity. I saw this kind of coalition as essential and that "Black identity" was in fact just doing for Jim Crow what Jim Crow had always done. You're segregating yourself, you're saying you can do it on your own; you're advocating policies that lead to the racialization of poverty, when in fact poverty should be seen as a *national* problem. You have to find ways of establishing some type of solidarity with other groups, whether it's Latinos or the White working class. But, of course, we went the opposite way. And, exactly as I predicted, Richard Nixon saw clearly the opportunity there. His wedge politics was precisely to play on that. Nixon was the most Machiavellian person. One of my very best students, John Skrentny, pointed out in *The Ironies of Affirmative Action* that one of the greatest promoters of affirmative action and of Black identity was Nixon.[13]

DS: This brings me to the themes and positions that come together with such force in *Ethnic Chauvinism*, which was published in 1977 – because these several earlier essays converge on the argument in that

ENGAGING BLACK AMERICA

book. Before we get to the substantive issues in *Ethnic Chauvinism*, though, there are a number of features of the book that strike me as interesting. I didn't know, for instance, that the book was written at the Institute for Advanced Study, and that you were, as it were, overwhelmed by what was going on around and put aside the slavery work to focus on that.

OP: When I was at the institute something interesting happened. I was invited to the White House to advise President Gerald Ford on ethnicity and the whole ethnic revival movement, which was in its heyday at that time. I was already taking a stand. Ford was an intelligent man. It was very unfair what Lyndon B. Johnson did, saying Ford couldn't chew gum and walk at the same time. But Ford was very *parochial*. He came out of Grand Rapids, which is like the heartland of the White middle class. He wrote an op-ed (which I was pleased to see appeared on the same page where I had an op-ed once) pointing out that when he was at Michigan he played with a lot of Blacks – he was a football star and became close to many of them. But anyway, that was his *only* experience with Blacks. And he knew nothing about ethnicity. He was appointed, you remember, in the throes of the ethnic revival. But he was plucked right out of the Congress, a man whose focus was entirely on upper-middle-class, suburban Grand Rapids. He really didn't know very much about what was going on in the rest of the country. So, they decided to have a crash course to educate him on basic civic issues in American culture and the economy. Essentially, they'd put on little mini seminars for him in which he'd sit and listen. We'd debate the issues. And they did this in different fields. They did this in economics, because there was the whole question of stagflation. And then they did it with ethnicity, because at that time we were in the heart of the White ethnic revival and the *backlash* against Blacks by Whites. Michael Novak was running around writing books about his Czech identity and all the rest of it.[14] Ford actually asked, "What's this ethnicity thing?" The very word he didn't even know. *Ethnicity* was a new word; according to the *Oxford English Dictionary*, David Riesman was the first person to use it.[15]

DS: Really! I never knew that. How do you come to be involved in the group?

OP: In fact, this is the biggest irony. Because here we have what was supposed to be a right-wing or fairly conservative president – he had this famous headline telling New York to drop dead, remember? I was in my office, in the prime minister's office, in Jamaica, in the

157

THE PARADOX OF FREEDOM

thick of left-wing politics (this is 1975) when I got a message saying the White House is desperately trying to get a hold of me. It actually got me into trouble with the Jamaican leftists, because the word soon got out that the White House had summoned me. And the group invited was me, Moynihan, Nathan Glazer (who had written one of the first books to have "ethnicity" in the title, and it was still the hot seller on ethnicity then), Michael Novak (who had an extreme position celebrating the ethnic revival), and John Higham, an historian of immigration from Johns Hopkins. Glazer and Moynihan, the moderates, were the intellectuals who were going to promote ethnicity's good side. But they needed one person who was critical of ethnicity. They couldn't find anyone except me. And we spent nearly the whole day in the White House. But I lost that debate because, two weeks after, I heard that Ford announced that he was supporting the ethnic movements and giving funds to people – Poles in Pittsburgh and others – and I thought, "What the hell is that?" The issue came up in the presidential election when Jimmy Carter made the famous *faux pas*. That was when the ethnic revival, I'd say, peaked. Jimmy Carter went to Pennsylvania and made a speech in which he said, "I believe in the purity of ethnic neighborhoods." Now this is supposed to be the liberal champion! He was trying to *outdo* Ford in ethnic support, because there was the suggestion that he wasn't supportive enough, and he had Black support. Carter was innocently, though naively, repeating what he thought was the correct position, namely, the celebration of ethnic identity. But the way he phrased it suddenly led people to gasp in disbelief. He accidentally pulled the curtain to reveal the dark side of ethnicity, the idea of the purity of one's neighborhood and traditions. That, no one wanted to hear. People suddenly thought, "How can we be headed in this direction?" But that's exactly my argument in *Ethnic Chauvinism*. There is little or no difference between celebrating one's identity and thinking in terms of the purity of one's neighborhood and culture.

DS: There are two features of the book's form that I want to just note and hear how you respond. The first is the book's obvious relationship to David Riesman and his work. Indeed, the book is dedicated to David and Evey Riesman. It owes a great deal to the form of Riesman's *thinking*. Perhaps not only in its sociological *style*, in the way in which it takes up large normative issues and takes positions on them, but also in the book's *temperament*, in the *nerve* of the book (to use one of the terms that you take from Riesman)

158

ENGAGING BLACK AMERICA

– and, more substantively, too, in the sense that *Ethnic Chauvinism*, like *The Lonely Crowd*, is a critique of *conformity*.

OP: Absolutely. David was a very influential person. I'd read David when I was an undergraduate. *Individualism Reconsidered* and *The Lonely Crowd* were in the university [UCWI] library.[16] David was big in the 1950s. *The Lonely Crowd* was a best-seller; it was the last sociology book to be a best-seller. I remember borrowing that book at the UCWI library (I was the only person to read it; it had never been taken out!) and reading all of those essays, and liking his style. For someone like myself coming out of literature, his was the perfect sociological style to emulate. We were kind of kindred spirits. Right to the end of his life we remained very good friends. I taught a course with him, too. That's how I came to know much about America. Now, David did something interesting. He didn't have graduate students teaching in his course as assistants. He had various people who were at the faculty level. I was already a tenured professor, but I enjoyed the experience. The way David taught the course was that, from months before, the summer before, we met at his place and we went through all the texts. It was like a salon. The excuse was to review these books. But we'd talk about America. We used the books as a point of departure for long discussions, which started with cocktails at about five o'clock – Evey was a wonderful hostess – and went on until about ten. We met every week right through the summer. By the time we got to the course, we all knew everything. He lectured in the course. And we all took sections. It didn't bother me. People raised eyebrows: "You're taking a section? You're a tenured professor?" I said, "What's wrong with that? I'm teaching a course with David. He's the lecturer, but I want to meet students talking about America." And that was a great learning experience for me. I just plunged in at the deep end, into America, working with someone who knew America better than anyone else.

DS: That's my sense too, of what you were doing. The second thing that's notable about *Ethnic Chauvinism* is the *methodological* stance that you adopt in this work (and in work after), in which you imagine your work as a kind of *pursuit*, an intellectual *quest*, in which, *paradoxically*, the thing that you understand yourself to be in search of is not the thing that you eventually find. You are in search of windmills, you say here, but what you find is the discarded skin of a serpent.[17] Whence this methodological self-understanding?

OP: I'm not quite sure, because it's the same thing with *Slavery and Social Death*.

159

THE PARADOX OF FREEDOM

DS: Exactly; and also with *Freedom in the Making of Western Culture*.

OP: Right. You go looking for one thing and then you find what I call a "shadow" concept. It's like a ghost that you discover. But it's a mode of intellectualizing in which you are open to surprises and always willing to see the unexpected in what you're doing. It's the total opposite of your normal science type who has a hypothesis, who goes out to get data that almost always *confirm* the hypothesis. I used to teach a qualitative methodology course for the graduate program here in which it was quite explicit that you do *not* begin with a hypothesis. I do usually have some ideas I may begin with, but am *open* to finding not only something else but often something which may be totally the opposite of what I'm looking for. It's a *dialectical* style, in a way. And it's the Jamaican thing, too, to believe in a shadow concept. You don't know what's lurking behind the bushes in your exploration.

DS: But that's the key word, though – *exploration* – because the work is exploratory, open-ended.

OP: Yes, it's a mode of analysis, which as you say is genuinely exploratory and open to surprises. And it makes for an interesting life, because things get really boring to me if you begin knowing what you're going to find in the end, and find it.

DS: To now turn to the substance of the argument in *Ethnic Chauvinism*, it's striking, of course, to see the figure of the "sorcerer" standing in for the earlier figure of the existentialist rebel. The sorcerer is the embodiment of the existentialist. And as I was reading *Ethnic Chauvinism* and thinking about that, it struck me how interesting the convergence with, and divergence from, Camus. Oddly, one can hardly imagine Camus using the figure of the sorcerer.

OP: But it's Camus, in the sense of using this archetypal figure as a way of exploring an idea, the way Camus does with the slave, as he does in his novels. The style is similar. It's not a style that sociologists are accustomed to using.

DS: Absolutely not. Nor might the sociologist recognize James Joyce as the kind of literary sorcerer you do.[18]

OP: I remember reading Joyce thoroughly. And there's a great passage of Joyce's that I discovered, buried in the heart of a very obscure journal, in which he talked about Irish nationalism being a sow eating its litter.[19]

160

ENGAGING BLACK AMERICA

DS: In fact, you use that image when you talk about the relationship between nation-state nationalism and ethnic chauvinism. But speaking of Joyce and that image of the sow eating her litter as a way of thinking about the way nationalism devours its children, it is a striking feature of *Ethnic Chauvinism* that part of the critique is a critique of nationalism and of nation-state nationalism. For you, nationalism is one of the modern embodiments of *ethnic* allegiance. As I read that (it hadn't struck me when I first read it), I suddenly remembered the arc of Anthony Smith's work on nationalism. It is in one of the later books that he turns to thinking about what he calls the "ethnic origins of nations," which is already there in your argument.[20]

OP: I had a correspondence with him once. That was interesting.

DS: For you, the problem is that, while ethnic allegiance speaks in the name of freedom *from* constraint, or freedom *for* the recognition of destiny, it can, and very often can *only*, realize itself by *denying* freedom to others. So, this is the conundrum of ethnic allegiance that is at the center of your critique.

OP: Right. And a lot of people have come to recognize that problem as central to ethnicity. Ethnic cleansing is the ultimate manifestation.

DS: For you, then, and here is partly where I want to press you a little, the problem of ethnicity as a *moral* mode of politics is that it is internally flawed – it is flawed from *within*. Is there no ethnic politics that has virtues? I ask the question because there are moments in your earlier essays when you say that the moment of Black ethnicity has passed, partly because of the backlash (Novak and company). The suggestion is that it had *once* had a positive moment.

OP: Right. What I eventually try to point out is that it's a necessary evil at *certain* points, as a form of mobilizing. If you're being attacked on ethnic terms, you have to respond and mobilize on that basis.[21] And if you've been demonized for being Black, as being unattractive, ugly, and all the rest of it, or the way Black culture was denigrated in Jamaica and other parts of the Caribbean, it becomes necessary to counter that and assert your own beauty, and so on. Even though it has its dangers, there are moments when uprooting the psychological "marks of oppression," the self-hate, the denigration, is important. So, I felt there are dangers, but there *are* times when it's certainly *strategically* important and necessary; but it's a two-edged sword, and it can start eating itself in Joyce's famous image. Joyce obviously must have felt exactly the same way, in terms of the necessity for the

161

THE PARADOX OF FREEDOM

Irish to kick the English out; he supported the movement for nation-building and independence but felt that it had started eating itself. And that's essentially what's happened with Black Americans.

DS: *Ethnic Chauvinism* is partly a rereading of the story of Western civilization, and a rereading of the story of the making of the modern West in particular, and of the role and place of the French Revolution in our understanding of the making of the modern world. And you take a nice dig at the idea that the important legacy of the French Revolution is the idea of liberty, whereas for you the lasting legacy of the revolution is the *illusion* of the nation-state. You point to the way in the unfolding of anticolonialism, the decolonizing movement, the political leaders were hoodwinked into believing that nationalism was the *only* resource through which to prepare and create the possibility of the new nation-state. But you also say that these were not political leaders who could have been entirely naive to the dangers of nationalism. And so, you ask the question rhetorically: Why, then, did they adopt this form? And you answer the question: For the same reason that it was adopted in France, namely, this was a bourgeois project. Again, your neo-Marxist background is there. That is to say that, for these political leaders, the objective was to replace one elite with another. Nationalism for you is an essentially *cynical* ideology.
OP: Yes, one mobilized and used by elites. You see the tragedy all over Africa – look at the disaster in Zimbabwe. We saw it with Kenyatta; I hope it doesn't happen in South Africa. In every one of these states the leadership used nationalism in this way, rather than the alternative, the sociojuridical idea of the *state* in which it's the laws and policies that enable sharing in a democratic polity in which everyone participates.

DS: But isn't that the model of the US state?
OP: That is the model of the US state, the American model, which is what I like about it as opposed to the German. The French model is kind of in between. But it's the Anglo-American concept of the state that I admire. The great thing about it is that it rests on the constitution and on fundamental legal principles. You can become an American, as I did, by *juridical* means, within a certain period of time. Which is not to say that there's no American *culture*, but it's not allied to the state. And that's not to say that these African states shouldn't have their own culture or the Jamaican state Jamaican culture – it's the *conflation* of statehood with nation that is a great danger. That's bad news for minorities, *always*. And I think that's

162

one of the good things about America – there were conservatives who tried to develop some notion of the American state as
resting on its culture, but it's insignificant. It's like the English-only
movement.

DS: But someone may say that it's hard to imagine the kind of
mobilization that was required to overthrow colonialism without the
attempt to create a sense of *national* identity and national investment
in a particular future, without the creation of the symbolic modes of
solidarity and allegiance.

OP: You can have civic pride in a state and recognition of the
purely *political* processes without necessarily specifying a particular
cultural experience as being the embodiment of that state. And this
is especially important where you have multiethnic countries. When
Kenyatta tried to make the Kikuyus the foundation of the state, there
are so many different cultures in Kenya that they were laying the
foundation for disaster. The same goes for Nigeria, and, as you know,
with Biafra there was an attempt at a breakaway on the basis of a
nation-state. It's not to say that culture isn't important, it's not to say
that you don't have traditions developing in a culture – it's to deny
the claim that the *legitimacy* of the state should rest on a particular
cultural experience.

DS: Ethnicity may be seen, as you articulate it in *Ethnic Chauvinism*,
as an extreme form of *ideology*. But is yours an anti-ideology
argument?

OP: No, I think ideology is important. You're always going to need
ideologies; it depends on what the *content* of the ideology is. Ideology
is important and ideology matters, because people need to believe
in things. And the content of ideology is important, too, which is
why I don't agree with the culture-as-toolkit argument – what I call
"toolkittery," that you can use it in any way. Now, it's true that
people have varying interpretations, wildly different. Just take the
Bible; you can interpret it in many different ways. But there's also the
fact that certain ideas can be dangerous, and you don't have much of
a choice if you commit yourself to them. Fascism or Nazism is one.
There's no toolkittery there; you couldn't say, "I'm a good liberal, but
let's adopt this racist ideology." It has certain consequences, though
you may fool yourself into thinking that it doesn't. I think there are
limits to which you can take this, what amounts to almost a ration-
alistic point of view. Ideologies are important. Racist ideology does
have implications – and liberal ideology does have implications.

163

THE PARADOX OF FREEDOM

DS: What was the response to *Ethnic Chauvinism*?
OP: People were very curious. Most of my colleagues were, but obviously Black Americans didn't like it very much.

DS: Do you remember any *particular* African American response?
OP: It got a good review in the *American Sociological Review*, in fact, quite to my surprise, because it was not written necessarily as a very academic text. But *Contemporary Sociology*, which is the journal of the American Sociological Association, gave it a special kind of [treatment], I forget the term they used, but they had three people review it, one of whom was Andrew Greeley.[22] And it was respectfully reviewed in *The Times* and a few other places. But comments from Black Americans suggest they thought it clearly was not in tune with where things were going at that time. Remember, it came out in 1977. There was, by the way, a long review in the *Daily Gleaner*, by the guy who is a very distinguished journalist now, the sort of a Tom Brokaw of Jamaica: Ian Boyne. He did a long piece on *Ethnic Chauvinism*, drawing the conclusion that it's antinationalistic and may even be critical of the way things were going in Jamaica at the time, which got a lot of raised eyebrows. In fact, I had to write Michael Manley a note, because Boyne was suggesting that it was hostile to the whole way the PNP was going. I thought that was overdoing it.

DS: Just one final question on *Ethnic Chauvinism* that occurred to me afterward: you don't use the word *race* in any prominent way in the book; you talk about *Black ethnicity*. Is there a particular reason why you avoid using the term *race*?
OP: Yes, and I explain that at some length in *The Ordeal of Integration*.[23] The term *race* is problematic for me, in the sense that race is supposed to be a largely constructed category; there's no biological foundation for it. But the thing that bothers me is that sociologists and others use the term *race* in a manner that almost essentializes it. That's true also even for people in the identity movement. "My race this and my race that, and you're a member of this race and I'm proud of this race," and all the rest of it. Now, bracketed in every one of those statements is, "As you know, race is a social construct, but it's one that's so meaningful that I can use it in this way." But if you keep doing that, you end up in fact essentializing it. And sociologists do that, too – it's almost one of our standard master categories. And the question is, do you end up using the concept so much that it ends up as an essential fact, a fact that has almost as much weight as a biological fact? It's this looseness

164

and this fluidity by which the thing is being essentialized by constant repetition that I object to.

DS: And you were self-conscious and concerned about this in the 1970s, as you wrote *Ethnic Chauvinism*.
OP: Absolutely. Actually, I had an op-ed on this in which I criticized the census for validating the category *race* and *ethnicity*. In what sense are they a race? Except that the basis of ethnic identification is color – it's somatic. So, I use the term *ethno-somatic*, and I've introduced it to sociologists, and I've suggested that this is the proper term, or *ethno-race*; when you must use the word "race" I put it in inverted commas. But *ethno-somatic* is my favorite term. In other words, it's one kind of ethnicity.

DS: But that's a term you introduce much *later*, isn't it?
OP: Yes. I use it in the paper "Four Modes of Ethno-Somatic Stratification."[24] And some people have picked up on it. But I hate using the term "race" by itself because I think it leads to this essentializing. But when I wrote *Ethnic Chauvinism* I was very much aware of that, so I just avoided the term then, because I saw Blacks as an *ethnic* group, one that has suffered greatly, much more than other groups. But, in terms of identification, I didn't see any difference between what they were doing and what Michael Novak was up to, or Irish ethnicity advocates like Andrew Greeley were up to.

DS: So, White and Black are ethnicities, and within that you have subethnicities. Afro-Jamaicans and Indo-Jamaicans are distinct *ethnic* categories. Or, again, Irish are a particular ethnicity of White.
OP: Oh yes. And the term *White* itself as a category – it's doubtful whether it properly marks an ethnic group. To the degree that you have Barthian-type boundary making, White does become an ethnic group vis-à-vis Blacks, but it's a very weak one in many ways because people do not, in most cases, identify as a White ethnic group *except* in the context of distinction from Blacks.[25] They define Whiteness as very much a negation of Blackness, rather than anything like Jewish ethnicity, which is positively defined as constituting some kind of ethno-religious "essence." And most White people do not define themselves as a group in this way. So, as I love to point out, Whiteness has no meaning in Sweden. Or even in Ireland. Everybody's White. In the same way, Blackness has no meaning in the Congo. So, Whiteness is really not an ethnic term except in the special circumstances where it's being defined contradistinctively against Blacks. And, even then,

165

THE PARADOX OF FREEDOM

it's a weak category. That's why I'd rather use "Black Americans," with subcategories within it. In fact, one of the things that's happening right now is that Black Americans are being befuddled by the fact that there are subethnic groups within Black ethnicity. But I think it's dangerous hearing kids talk about their "Blackness" – it's gone full circle. It's just as if it's something essential. And that's dangerous, even though it may be done sometimes in a favorable way. But whether it's done favorably or not, it's still essentialist and still has implications. That's why I avoid the term. If you take seriously the view that there is no biological entity that is Blackness, then I don't see any other logical position for you to take. Because not everybody's as sophisticated about race as a sociologist. You can't assume that the ordinary person has a social constructivist view of race.

DS: But you don't think that "ethnicity" potentially suffers the same dangers, that it may not be biology that is essentialized but tradition or culture?

OP: That's what *Ethnic Chauvinism* was about, because I'm critical of that, too. I think, from a sociological point of view, you can justifiably use it to refer in a Barthian sense to groups that make boundaries and define themselves in this way. So, you go back to the question of whether you're talking sociologically or normatively, and *Ethnic Chauvinism* shifts between the two. Especially the chapter on the Chinese in the Caribbean, I was making the point that there's nothing inherent in ethnicity or in race that would lead people to identify on that basis. I was being sociological there, even though I was still very critical of the primordial view. But I was also taking the view that *questioned* people who normatively celebrate this ethnicity. The book was making a sociological argument about the non-primordial nature of ethnicity, insofar as it is an objective social phenomenon, which it is: people do indeed get defined externally by other groups who differentiate themselves from them, and people do internally and subjectively define themselves as belonging to groups. That's just a sociological fact. Whether you should *promote* it is another matter. And so, I was arguing on both fronts in *Ethnic Chauvinism*.

Making Public Policy in Socialist Jamaica

DS: I want to turn now to a somewhat longer discussion of your relationship to the Jamaican state in the 1970s, which we have already touched upon. In 1972, Michael Manley came to power, and

166

MAKING PUBLIC POLICY IN SOCIALIST JAMAICA

you and others were appointed to a Technical Advisory Committee to provide an intellectual context in which Manley could make decisions in the course of governing. What exactly was your formal title when this happened?

OP: My title, which was given in a formal letter from the Civil Service Commission, was special advisor to the prime minister for social policy and development. That was also, I think, the title that M. G. Smith had.

DS: Oh, it was the same title. But you were nevertheless responsible for somewhat different aspects of development.

OP: Yes, MG was full time. MG had his fingers in everything. He was really a full-time advisor paid by the government.

DS: But did the government also pay you?

OP: I was also paid, but he was paid much *more*. He had resigned or had taken leave from University College London, and so that was a full-time job. I was part time. I don't know how much he was paid, but obviously he must have been paid a living wage. And he saw Manley every day. I would only see Manley occasionally *when* I was there. We'd have a meeting whenever I would come down, within a couple of days of my arrival, and he'd tell me what he wanted me to do in that particular period. He often had some specific things he wanted me to do. I wrote quite a few reports on these specific projects. For example, there was a bagasse factory, and the people had decided to give up on it for various reasons. And we didn't want it to go under. So, I was asked by Manley to join with another guy, Barclay Ewart, a businessman whose ex-wife, Glynne, Manley eventually married. I did a study with Ewart on the bagasse industry, and we eventually advised that the state help to preserve it. And then Ewart eventually bought it out from the state and made a go of the factory. That was one thing. He also asked me to help set up community councils, which still exist. It's one of my main achievements working with him. They had me go all over the island to create community councils; this came out of the Technical Advisory Committee, actually. I worked with a man from what was then the Ministry of Youth and Community Development, and we went all over the island. From way back there were little community councils, going back to the West Indian Commission.

DS: Going back to Jamaica Welfare, perhaps.

OP: Right. They'd become moribund, or non-existent, or barely

THE PARADOX OF FREEDOM

existing. We met with community leaders; I was all over the country, and established, reinvigorated, and, in some cases, created from scratch these community councils all over the island. Then I wrote a long report on it, "Community Councils in Jamaica."

DS: So, you acted by and large on assignment? You didn't bring ideas of what *should* be done?

OP: No, I brought ideas, too. It was both general and specific. Manley was especially interested in how I thought things were going as an outsider coming in. So, we had long discussions on policy in a *broad* sense. But he would then suggest *specific* things to do. But the biggest project was the urban upgrading project, which is what I spent most of my time doing, which I was also interested in doing. It was in South-Central Kingston, Manley's constituency. I introduced the idea that we should get away from housing schemes. Because I saw, even then (they didn't call them "garrisons" yet), that this was a major source of violence and problems. I advised him strongly that we should get away from building housing schemes. They were *iniquitous*. The model was Tivoli Gardens. You clear out ten thousand people, you spend millions of dollars of taxpayers' money for three or four hundred people – it wasn't many – whom you selected, and who would fight to the death to keep their units. That was the model: it was as simple as that.

So, I worked with many ministries, depending on what the project was. But then I fell out with Anthony Spaulding, because Spaulding wanted housing schemes. I wrote a long government report called "The Condition of the Low-Income Population in the Kingston Metropolitan Area," which set out a model of urban upgrading, in which, if you have x amount of money, instead of spending it on a housing scheme and throwing people out of their homes, you should try to *upgrade* it. It would still look like a slum, but it's a much more *livable* slum.[1] In other words, you bring in services. The aim would be to bring a standpipe to every yard. You still wouldn't have running water in every home but, if every yard has a standpipe, people wouldn't have to walk half a mile to get water, as they did in Waltham Park. You bring in health services by having a clinic in the area. I had a fairly radical plan, in fact, of building communal units in which each modern site would be assigned a unit for the adults and a section where the children would sleep. I also had a plan to train mothers to set up daycare programs, women with whom those without work could leave their children. And the clinic would link up with the daycare program to provide healthy nutrition

168

MAKING PUBLIC POLICY IN SOCIALIST JAMAICA

for the kids. It was a well-worked-out program. And I went and persuaded the American government, USAID [United States Agency for International Development] to invest 15 million dollars in it – a lot of money in the 1970s. I led the team that negotiated the grant. I had the clinic built in South-Central Kingston. That was the political *payoff*. Manley went along with the concept, much to Spaulding's disgust. Spaulding went around talking about "Patterson's African backyard concept." He wanted to give people housing schemes. It was cynical, and I confronted him once. I said, "Okay, show me the money, and let's look at the figures. How many units can you build? You've got five thousand people in your constituency. Even if we spend the entire government budget we'll not be able to provide housing for everyone. So, what's the fairest way of building with the amount of money you have?" I remember him saying to me, "I cannot, as a leader, say to people [that] I'm just going to give them an improvement to the slum they're living in. I've got to let them hope and give them the goal of having a two-bedroom unit." I said, "That's just being cynical. You'll never be able to do that, except for a select few. What about the 90 percent you kick out?" And he refused to answer that; so we fell out. Because we were quite close in the beginning; we used to *lime* [hang out] together.

DS: Really! You and Anthony Spaulding?
OP: Yes. We used to go around. He was a hard drinker; we would drink, we would go to all his little hangouts and hideouts. He had a woman in every housing site. He was a slightly manic personality. Some people thought he was drunk; I think he may have been manic-depressive, what we now call bipolar. That wasn't diagnosed in Jamaica then. But he drank a lot, so people thought he was drunk. But very often, quite frankly, I'd be with him and he just had a manic way of dealing with people. He could be quite charming, too.

But then we fell out big time over this, because I told Manley we should move away from housing schemes. But, as minister of housing, Spaulding wanted to build houses. My office was originally in housing. So, I went to Manley and said, "This is not working." And that's when Manley said, "Okay, we'll move your office to the prime minister's office." He went along with the concept, but I must tell you the end of this story. The thing was working, and we hired (this was my big mistake) an architect who would be a director of the project, and it was coming along nicely. We had a clinic; we integrated the Ministry of Health in there, and we had women coming in with their babies. We started training women in

169

THE PARADOX OF FREEDOM

daycare. They were paid initially by us but, ultimately, we hoped, by the women who were hiring them. This happens naturally; when a woman gets a job as a domestic, she leaves her kids with a woman in the yard who is unemployed. But it's done on an ad hoc basis. We were going to systematize that. Pay them but also bring in the services from the clinic. But, to end the story, I had an architect whose job was to survey the state of the existing buildings, estimate what it was going to cost to fix them up and how much each landlord or owner would need. And we had an arrangement with the bank, which at a very low rate would provide the funds, partly supplemented by us. We would guarantee the loan for fixing up these places. This was the whole point of upgrading – no housing scheme. This architect (there were lots of unemployed architects at that time, because there was a slump), as soon as I went back to Harvard, as soon as I turned my back, he went into alliance with the local leaders who would benefit from a housing scheme. And they were able to persuade Michael that, for the sake of his political interest, he should have a housing scheme. So, I came back to Jamaica once and found it was a fait accompli. Michael gave in because people said it was a political necessity; and in the end Michael was a very political animal.

DS: Two questions here, Orlando. First, do you in retrospect, or did you at the time, think of that as a very familiar kind of Manley move, thinking creatively about new forms of practice and then at the last minute pulling back and giving in to short-term political interests?
OP: That was very much Manley, yes, because he was a *political* animal. It was very amazing seeing him; it was like a transformation in the field, on the ground politically. He was hero-worshipped, and, of course, he loved it. And when all the members of his local office, who then had a vested interest in this, came and said, "We have to have a housing scheme," he gave in to it. It's a payoff. And that's how "garrisons" got developed. They started as payoffs so that the people who were very active in the constituency would get a first shot at the new units.

DS: The second question is whether being an advisor was a mode of thinking, of acting, that appealed to you. You said earlier that, when you first went back to Jamaica from the LSE, you had to decide about whether you were going to have an academic life or yield to the pull toward policy.
OP: Well, it was being a public intellectual. But I was doing more academic work at the same time.

170

DS: But operating in the community, moving around the country, *applying* ideas – did this appeal?

OP: Sure! Part time. I don't know if I could have done it full time, even if I'd wanted to, but I essentially divided my time between doing this in the summer and my academic life at Harvard.

DS: Is it your sense that Manley (and maybe the story you've just told is answer enough) took his advisors seriously?

OP: He was very interested in what we had to say. But it could have been that he operated at different levels. He was very much an intellectual, Manley. And he would have been quite happy as an intellectual. After he retired he wrote his *History of West Indies Cricket* (although Rex did a lot of the writing and research for him).[2] He loved intellectual discussions. He was quite serious. But then he'd put on his bush jacket and go out into the field, and maybe he just thought in a different way and acted a different way then. I think there was an element of that. It's like his relationship with women. In many ways he was a very upright person, strong moral views; politically he was totally uncorrupted. As Rachel pointed out, they didn't have any money when he left office, which is the best sign of a complete lack of corruption. This is a trait of all the Manleys. This is why he had to start the lecturing series; he needed money to support his kids. So, he was not corrupt in that sense at all. But once he got out there in the constituency and in the public, he just got into another mode. And, as I said, the same would have been true of his relationship with women. He was an upright man but he was totally ruthless with women. Look at the preface I did for Rachel Manley's *Slipstream*.[3] I spent a lot of time on this; it's the area where I reflected most on Manley and the kind of person he was. He had a bit of a dual personality that way: Manley the politician as opposed to Manley the intellectual. And that division can be found in many other areas. He was a man of the people and he was greatly beloved, but, in his private life, he still remained an upper-class Jamaican. And his closest friends were these types whom I didn't especially like. These light-skinned Jamaicans, commercial types. I always thought it very odd, and I felt uncomfortable with them.

And in fact, as I told you, before he became prime minister, we'd have these lovely dinners together. And after he became prime minister we did occasionally go around for more personal kinds of activities. Manley was very close to Russell Graham, who owned Palace Amusement Company, and I remember we'd go to private showings. He was just married to Beverly at the time.[4] I'd known her

THE PARADOX OF FREEDOM

from high school days. And we'd go over to his place and you'd see some of these types. One of his closest advisors was O. K. Melhado. It's with that group of Jamaicans (if you can picture them) that he seemed most comfortable. MG himself was a near-White Jamaican – I called him a White Jamaican once and he got mad with me; he wrote back and was very upset, and said he always thought of himself as a Brown man. But, anyway, *that* was Michael's group. Rachel herself mentioned one interesting little detail, which I think is very significant. He didn't like Jamaican food. He liked British-type, bland food, which was his mother's cooking. Nor was he into reggae music; he liked classical music. His tastes were very Anglo-Jamaican, from the strong influence of his mother. And eventually our social relationships became less and less personal. It happened slowly, in the second year or so. This went on for eight years. We just did not socialize.

DS: Reflecting on the aspect of his personality that you've just sketched, do you think of him in contrast to his father, N. W. Manley?
OP: I only met his father once, but, in many ways, yes. His father was a genuinely upright man who was consistent throughout. What you saw is what you would get with NW, and he paid a price for this, because, though he was charismatic for middle-class Jamaicans, he didn't have the same popular touch. He actually lost his seat once. But he was not, in public office, any different from what you saw as a barrister or as a leader or in private.

DS: I remember once in a discussion, I think with Rupert Lewis, and I was speaking as though, color/class-wise, N. W. Manley and Michael Manley were similar figures. And Rupert stopped me and said that NW was a Brown Jamaican man from the country, whereas Michael was a middle-class, near-White man, whose social setting would have been very different from his father's. Do you see a similar contrast?
OP: Yes, there's a difference. Michael was close to being White, whereas Norman was a Brown man.

DS: A classic Brown man.
OP: A classic Brown man – "good hair," as Jamaicans say, but you wouldn't call him near White. And growing up in the country, too, would have meant associating with other Brown people, *and* with Black people. But you shouldn't underplay Norman's middle-class background. Norman was totally middle class, close to *upper* middle. But Lewis is right about the rural thing, as opposed to Michael's

172

MAKING PUBLIC POLICY IN SOCIALIST JAMAICA

upbringing. It's the *parenting* that was different. Edna was a strong British woman – but I'm ambivalent about her myself. I remember once being at a small dinner party thrown by the Grahams for her. My wife and I turned up and we spent a good part of the evening together. Of course, Edna was a formidable woman, and of course she did a lot to develop the arts, but she was essentially a British woman. I could never take to her art. Those horses! Michael loved her, and he had this big horse sculpture in his office.

DS: Perhaps her *Horse of the Morning*.
OP: The horse is not part of our tradition. However you want to put it, it is not part of the African tradition. The British didn't bring them over with them. Horses are very much part of the English countryside. And then she had those figures like *Negro Aroused*. I never took to it.[5] There's a whole room devoted to her at the National Gallery. I've never been totally inspired by her. And I didn't take to her that evening at all. "Imagine," I just kept thinking, "this woman has been here for decades and decades, and she still had the manner and bearing of an Englishwoman in the tropics." She was very White. There's no getting around it. N. W. Manley wasn't brought up like that; he was brought up by *Brown* people. There's that difference. But the old man Manley, of course, was also the embodiment of Anglo-Jamaican culture – *all* the virtues of the British – even *more* so than the son. Michael would have had more of a direct British influence from his mother, whereas Norman was rooted in that thing that goes all the way back to the free coloreds of the late eighteenth and nineteenth centuries. His ancestry was more George William Gordon. *That's* Norman. Whereas Michael was more influenced by the mother and European culture. In a way, Norman was influenced by English culture but in a *creolized* aspect of it.

DS: That's a very interesting way of putting it, yes.
OP: Michael would have had a more direct influence from his mother. There's a real split, because *he* – unlike his father – was a man of the people. And it's reflected in his tastes in women. His first wife was British, and his last wife was also a Welsh woman. His marriage to Beverly was – I wouldn't say it was cynical, I'm sure they liked each other – but it was certainly politically *expedient*.

DS: From the vantage that you had, living outside of Jamaica but at the same time formally close to the political leadership in Jamaica, how did you see the radicalization of the PNP and the government

173

THE PARADOX OF FREEDOM

on both domestic and international issues in this period, the early 1970s?

OP: I had an interesting experience with this, because I'd read about the radicalization of the party and of Jamaica, and the middle classes were just scared to death for the reasons I mentioned – that there was a lot of loudmouth proclamation of socialism by people like Arnold Bertram, D. K. Duncan, and the rest of them. But working closely with Michael, the thing that was clear to me was that the people who were running the country were basically very middle and upper-middle class, somewhat middle-of-the-road Jamaicans. It was never the case that the radicals had any critical ministry in Manley's government. The party was never any more radical than what you'd find in the platform of the British Labour Party, which was the model, in fact, for Michael.

DS: For Michael himself, it was never more radical. He never flirted really with a more radical socialism?

OP: No, but what he did flirt with was Fidel Castro. One of his biggest disasters was the trip to Cuba in 1973.

DS: When you say his visit to Cuba was a mistake, you mean it was a PR [public relations] mistake?

OP: It was a PR mistake. And I kept telling him so. The left wing of the party really had no real power, but they had a *voice*. And they made the most of it. And they scared everybody to death. And then he went to Cuba. And then, of course, in the rhetorical heat of the moment, Manley would give speeches in which he would sound a lot more radical than he was. Like when he came back from Cuba and he made that speech at the airport that there are five flights daily to Miami – he was all revved up with the Cuban visit and visiting Fidel. But he was never a communist and he never wanted Jamaica to go in that direction. But they – Michael and Fidel – were two charismatic figures who identified with each other. Michael *loved* Fidel. And in a way they were similar personalities, because Fidel was also a man whose private life was very different from his public life, and who was a bit of a womanizer, too. So, they hit it off very well. Fidel was a world figure; and Michael always yearned for the global limelight. And he got some of it from the fact that he was seen as this radical leader of the Third World, the champion of the concept of a New World Order. So, in a way, he almost promoted that rhetoric, even though in fact he was never any more than a social democrat, a *left-leaning* social democrat. And all his friends knew that, which is why

174

MAKING PUBLIC POLICY IN SOCIALIST JAMAICA

they all remained close to him and saw the public Manley as the rhetorical charismatic figure.

DS: And were those *your* political sympathies as well? Would you define your political sympathies at the time as that of a left-leaning social democrat?
OP: That is exactly where I was, and I thought that what the loudmouth left was doing was dangerous. And I frequently said that to Manley. And it may have gotten back to them, because I never made any secret of my own views. I thought D. K. Duncan was just a bad idea.

DS: In 1976, shortly before the publication of *Ethnic Chauvinism*, Manley won a second term by an historic vote. And that election was won on a socialist platform. By then, socialism had become the rhetorical stand of the PNP. Were you sympathetic to that platform? You sound *not* to have been.
OP: No. And I began to be less and less involved with them. Michael and I began to pull away from each other then. I'd even contemplated just breaking off, because I thought that was foolish what they did. But Manley would always insist on my coming over. In 1977 I was in the thick of writing *Slavery and Social Death* anyway, and I decided that maybe it was time I backed away. But he got in touch with me, rang me and told me that he very much needed me there, so I had to come over. So, I went back. The same thing happened in 1978. I was kind of backing away because I didn't have much respect for the left. I really was openly hostile to D. K. Duncan, and I told Michael that several times. I thought this guy lacked any substance or subtlety and he was doing far more harm than good. I saw one of my roles as being someone who could openly tell Manley what was what, which other people might not want to do, because I wasn't dependent on the job. I spoke my mind. And I think he appreciated it, too.

DS: Of course, in the immediate aftermath of 1976, there was the massive crisis, when the question of whether or not to go to the IMF was on the table. And in this period Norman Girvan was very important as an advisor in the National Planning Agency, and in the attempt to create a People's Plan as an alternative to the IMF. The WLL [Worker's Liberation League] left was also writing an alternative and seeking to influence the process.
OP: Well, I was definitely not with that group. I thought they were in cloud cuckoo land. And it was obvious that the People's Plan was

175

THE PARADOX OF FREEDOM

just not viable. We were in deep trouble financially. The situation had evolved, the left voiced this radical position, and by then I was completely fed up with what they were up to. I wasn't on speaking terms with any of these people. I didn't see Norman for years, even though we were in the same party. We were in different worlds. I would do my thing down in West Kingston, trying to carry on, but it was getting violent – we got shot at several times. The violence began to escalate in 1976; the woman who worked for me as the assistant to the director who was my main contact, she almost got killed once – they just shot up the place that was my little headquarters there.

DS: When the left emerges in the WLL/WPJ (1974 is when the WLL is formed, and it gets transformed into a formal party structure in 1978) around academics at the University of the West Indies – Derek Gordon, Don Robotham, Trevor Munroe are principals – I assume these are academics with whom, politically, you are *not* sympathetic. You had nothing to do with them?[6]
OP: No. I never saw them. I'd come down, I'd go to my office in Jamaica House, I'd talk to Michael, and I'd leave.

DS: Did you have a connection to Carl Stone at all, outside of the cooperative work?
OP: Not much. We knew each other. We were at KC together, in the same form. Carl was a funny guy; I don't think he had any involvement with anyone, right or left. I don't know.

DS: He was very independent.
OP: He came to the university late. He came in my last year to UCWI. Then he went to the University of Michigan, mainly through Archie Singham's influence. Then he came back as a lecturer at the university, and he largely kept to himself.

DS: Of course, he taught in the Department of Government. He taught me.
OP: But Carl, even at KC, he was like that. He was in the same form, but he was a mystery man. We knew he smoked his ganja, and he smoked cigarettes, too. You could smell the cigarettes on him. At lunchtime he'd come back stinking of cigarettes. But he had this funny style about him; there was something almost *stiff* about Carl. And he had this way of laughing, this almost false laugh, which he gave to everything, a grim laugh. You never knew what he was thinking. And he remained like that all the time. His personal life was

just totally a mystery to everybody. And, of course, he died of AIDS. He was one of the early victims of AIDS in Jamaica.

DS: Rosie Stone, his wife, wrote a very moving autobiography dealing with both his infidelity and his death. She became subsequently very involved in agitation around HIV in Jamaica.[7]
OP: He did his writing for *The Gleaner*. I didn't see much of him.

DS: Were you sympathetic to the work he did, though, when he came back from Michigan? He developed a "behavioral" approach learned in American political science.
OP: Yes, I thought *Democracy and Clientelism in Jamaica* was pretty sound.[8] I thought he did good solid work, and also his political survey work. He introduced professional polling to Jamaica, and I thought it was very good, very sound.

DS: I always think of Carl and you in similar terms in the sense of Jamaican scholars who meld disciplinary kinds of approaches. Carl always thought of himself as a political *sociologist* – that is, the methodologies of his research were deeply sociological, although the direction of the work was an attempt to understand *political* behavior. And, in your case, there's a deeply *historical* way of rethinking what the sociologist does.
OP: Exactly. That's true. And, in many ways, I'm sure we would have come from similar backgrounds in terms of the Jamaican class system. In KC we used to talk. In fact, I was one of the few people who would actually speak to him. Because he joined us only in sixth form. I don't know where he came from. There were several people who came into KC's sixth form, because we had very good teaching resources for the A-levels. Peter Fletcher, in fact, also joined our sixth form from whatever school he was going to. But unlike Peter Fletcher (who was Richard's older brother and became a distinguished surgeon later on), who integrated immediately and whom we all liked a lot, Carl kept his distance. And he was seen as a somewhat older person. He was, in fact, almost nineteen, twenty, when he graduated. And he always had the manner of a serious older man, involved with serious business. Some Jamaicans are like that, they're involved with the business of life, and you felt he didn't have time to mess around with teenage things. I don't know how much he was into music. I had a full, rich teenage life. I was thoroughly immersed in the musical culture that was emerging, the parties. Carl was always a very quiet fellow. We'd have exchanges. But we never became friends.

THE PARADOX OF FREEDOM

DS: That was also my impression, of someone independent-minded. It wasn't simply that he wasn't drawn to either side of the political conflict in the mid- to late 1970s, but you always had the impression from him that he knew *better*. That distance was not simply naive, but he knew better and was more mature and was above it. But, interestingly, the story that Rosie tells in her autobiography is partly one of Carl's humanity and his particular loves, his children, and Jamaican music. You get a different take on Carl, and his death, I think, is an enormous loss. Anyway, the whole Manley experiment came tumbling down at the very end of the 1970s, 1980. And there was the emergence of a kind of violence that Jamaica had not quite seen before.
OP: By then, I had more or less withdrawn from my role as advisor.

DS: Yes, I think your association ended by 1979, so you were no longer an advisor. But did you see the fragmentation coming? By this time, Jamaica was an incredibly *polarized* society.
OP: Yes, and even here in Cambridge, Massachusetts, the *Boston Globe* had front-page stories on Jamaica, on the violence. And I remember vividly we were seen as a real problem. In 1978–9 I was a visiting fellow at Wolfson College, Cambridge, at the invitation of someone I admired greatly, and I was heavily into writing *Slavery and Social Death*.

DS: Moses Finley?
OP: And Jack Plumb: they were the people who had invited me. I was definitely not going back to Jamaica after 1977–8. I definitely did not go back. By then Manley was heavily into his political mode anyway; politics dominated everything. I stayed away then in the sense that I gave up my advisory job.

DS: By then MG also had serious conflicts with the left, and he had broken with Manley.
OP: Oh yes. He had gone to Yale University by then. He, too, saw the writing on the wall.

DS: Upon reflection, do you think that Vivian Blake would have made a better leader of the People's National Party than Michael?
OP: That's an interesting question. Might have. He would have been a less *political* figure.

DS: Less *ideological*, perhaps.
OP: Certainly *less* ideological. And less enamored with being in the

178

SLAVERY AND SOCIAL DEATH

world spotlight – in which Manley was. Clearly, that was part of his problem, best seen in the Cuban escapade. It was a bit reckless, embracing Fidel so openly at the height of the Cold War, knowing how the Americans would react to it. But he just couldn't *resist* it. He was overcome with all the attention. And then giving that speech, which was a very reckless speech, which he himself later on regretted doing. So, he got caught up in a way that was almost irresponsible. I think Vivian Blake would not have been like that. Blake, I think, would have stood up more to the left-wing loudmouths, as I call them, and would have told them to tone it down – whereas Manley got caught up in it. Even though he was solidly a social democrat and in no sense a communist, the left-wing thing he did get into, and wrote a couple of books, as you know. His intellectualism in a sense *ensnared* him into this involvement with the rhetorical left. I call them the "rhetorical left" because they never really were serious analysts of the situation.[9]

DS: In your view, can one read *Ethnic Chauvinism* as in part a critique of the Jamaican 1970s?
OP: Well, yes, I was certainly thinking of the loudmouths in Jamaica as I was of people here. You have to live through it; there's a certain kind of mean-spirited solidarity that you get on the part of the left, a sort of self-righteousness. It was very similar, whether it was the identity movement or the socialist solidarity movement. And I saw similarities in both.

Slavery and Social Death

DS: I want to turn now, Orlando, to the making of *Slavery and Social Death*. During the 1970s, which was obviously an amazingly fertile period for you (working along a variety of different lines, so to speak), you were also continuing, and indeed in some respects perhaps also altering, the character of your work on slavery – expanding and deepening the canvas on which the question of slavery is to be understood and moving in a comparative direction. Could you already see the outline of this direction as you completed *The Sociology of Slavery*?
OP: It was a gradual evolution. What I saw at the end of *Sociology of Slavery* was my interest in slavery in the New World. My interest was very much in American slavery and in Latin American slavery. And that came partly out of my reading of Stanley Elkins.

179

DS: And Frank Tannenbaum, perhaps – had you already read Tannenbaum?[1]

OP: I read Tannenbaum as an undergraduate; it was one of the required texts. But Elkins's book was important, and remember there's that chapter on him in *The Sociology of Slavery*, discussing slave personality. I became very intrigued with American slavery and the similarities between American Black life and Caribbean Black life. The essay "Toward a Future That Has No Past" was really, as I said, bringing all that together. That was a comparative essay; it was the first development toward a comparative approach to Black life in the Americas. Then I wrote an academic piece on slave revolts, which was published in *Social and Economic Studies*. And that work marked the first time I became very interested in the ancient world, interested in ancient slave revolts. And I remember discussing it with classicists. I was still in Jamaica then, when I was writing that piece. I was already thinking about how slavery, initially slave revolts, operated *comparatively* in the ancient world. But my first comparative interest, if you like, was in the Americas. And then I signed a contract with Harvard Press from very early for *Slavery and Social Death*. I signed in 1973 or so.

DS: Really? Which means that you already had an outline of the project in your head.

OP: Right, from very early. Obviously, I'd made up my mind I was going to do that. It was very long in the making; I was working on it whenever I wasn't in Jamaica.

DS: What I want to understand is whether, as you finished *The Sociology of Slavery*, the need you felt for a *comparative* direction was in order to distill an idea of the *general* question of slavery – that is, to answer the question: What essentially characterizes slavery?

OP: Yes. And to really understand Jamaica you have to understand what slavery was like. What was *distinctive* about Jamaica? How does slavery influence other societies where it was important? My plan was eventually to come back to Jamaica. But I got more and more involved with the comparative work. Clearly the agenda was there from the early 1970s. In a way, the reason why it took so long was that it became secondary during the couple of years I wrote *Ethnic Chauvinism* – although *Ethnic Chauvinism* was drawing on lots of the material I was collecting for the comparative slave study. And then, of course, I got back to it in a pretty serious way in 1978–9, when I went to England.

SLAVERY AND SOCIAL DEATH

DS: Now tell me how and when you meet Moses Finley. That seems to me an extraordinary connection.

OP: When did I get connected with Moses now? I think Finley had read *Sociology of Slavery*, must have. Oh! I think I remember now. There were two things that I'd done. The sociologist Neil Smelser asked me to do a piece on slavery for the *Annual Review of Sociology*.[2] That would have been 1975, 1976. So, I was already deeply immersed in this. Finley read it and liked it a lot; I think that was when he first came across my work. Then he must have gone and read *The Sociology of Slavery*. And also, the essay on slave revolts referred to ancient slave revolts. And Jack Plumb had read *Sociology of Slavery* and liked it. *Sociology of Slavery* did quite well in Britain; Eric Hobsbawm reviewed it for *The Guardian*. Again, like several of the things I did, it was really one of the first of its kind. I think I may have mentioned that there was no book that was completely devoted to the social life of the slave before *The Sociology of Slavery*. People were quite intrigued with the book. And Plumb invited me up. And I had a good year, because I saw a lot of Moses, who, of course, did something very important for me in the sense that he was the preeminent classicist on slavery. He was an enormous authority, and the fact that he liked my work more or less gave me a lot of credibility with the classicists – because I am not a classical scholar. And *Slavery and Social Death* later became accepted among classicists as one of their important works.[3]

DS: How would you describe the nature of Finley's intellectual influence on your thinking about slavery?

OP: Oh, very important. Even though he was a classicist, Finley read sociology and he was very interested in the sociological approach. In a sense, what he wrote was sociological history. Take *The World of Odysseus*. I read his work thoroughly and was guided by it. His seminal essay "Was Greek Civilization Based on Slave Labor?" was very important in my thinking, and I'd read that from my LSE days.[4]

DS: Oh, right, in which he describes ancient Greece as a "genuine slave society." Then he also wrote that book *Ancient Slavery and Modern Ideology*?

OP: That came later.

DS: After you met him, certainly.

OP: It was not very well reviewed. It was very unfairly reviewed in the *New York Times*. I remember writing a note and complaining

181

THE PARADOX OF FREEDOM

about the review. But I liked him; he was a greatly revered person. He was an interesting guy, an American who was hounded out of America by Joseph McCarthy.

DS: I gather it was Karl Wittfogel who gave evidence against him.[5]
OP: Now Wittfogel, that was interesting. I'd always had a comparative interest because I'd read Wittfogel as an undergraduate. M. G. Smith was a big fan of Wittfogel. I think he put me on to him. So, I had a strong comparative interest from even then. It was very sad to hear about Wittfogel giving evidence against Finley. But then, you know, Finley went to Britain and found his feet. He writes in this wonderful essayistic way – I like that, too. And he had very powerful ideas, which he expressed in a very succinct manner but with a wealth of scholarship behind them.

DS: He was also very close to a certain kind of critical Marxism, influenced by the Frankfurt School, wasn't he?
OP: Very much. Interesting guy – chain-smoked. And was very close to his wife. There are some differences between Finley and myself in that he felt Greek civilization was based on slavery in the sense that the elite depended on the slave system. It was more like it was what supported their leisure and hence their ability to conceive of freedom. He didn't take the antithetical, somewhat Hegelian position that I took that slavery and freedom were intimately linked. We differed on that. On the slavery book, I remember sending him the early draft, and there was one thing he didn't like. He was funny; he didn't like any differences, any hint of criticism. And I remember writing some section in which I said I wasn't completely in agreement with him. And then he fired off a very caustic piece, which, upon reading, I thought, "Boy, it really isn't worth having a disagreement with him." He also hated all the tables in the first draft and asked me to clear them out. He thought they were pretentious. When I finished I sent the final draft to him, and I remember he wrote me this very sweet note. And he's not given to writing notes like that, saying how very proud he was of me. It was very nice; I should have kept that piece. It's somewhere in my files; God knows where it is. So, he was just very interested in the sociological approach I brought to it; he felt that it was very valuable, and just encouraged me and offered me protection, so to speak. Because classicists are, or were, a pretty parochial group – if you're not out of the classical tradition and you start messing around with their literature, they can be unkind. I never had that experience, partly

182

SLAVERY AND SOCIAL DEATH

because everybody knew Moses was on my side. I was very lucky from that point of view.[6]

DS: What about the influence of David Brion Davis's books, *The Problem of Slavery in Western Culture* and *The Problem of Slavery in the Age of Revolution*?[7]
OP: More the *first* one. The first one I read and was very inspired by, definitely. And then we got to know each other quite well.

DS: Yes, and he in turn is inspired by your *Slavery and Social Death*.[8]
OP: He did a great review of it for the *New York Review of Books*. But, yes, *The Problem of Slavery in Western Culture*, that book was *very* important as a model.

DS: A model of a *comparative* approach?
OP: Yes. In a way my approach was somewhat different in that his was more of historical narrative, whereas mine was more of a comparative work based on cross-cultural anthropological and historical data. I was dipping into two other academic areas. One was the ancient world and the other was comparative anthropology. I used the Murdoch sample. Although Cliff Geertz was unsympathetic to this kind of anthropology, he nonetheless invited me to spend a year at his institute.

DS: The Institute for Advanced Studies. Were you in historical studies or social sciences there?
OP: Social sciences. Geertz was surprisingly sympathetic. He obviously did not like this whole mode of analysis, but we got along well. The year I was there was very important for me. The theme they focused on that year was symbolic anthropology. That's how I got into symbolic anthropology – because I became very good friends with Victor Turner.

DS: Oh yes, of course! You met Victor Turner at the institute?
OP: We spent the year together, and we had wonderful parties. To see Victor try to do his Central African dances when he got a little tipsy was the funniest thing. He threw lots of parties. And we had a ball.

DS: Was he also close to Clifford Geertz then?
OP: No. I remember one of the last conversations I had with Victor Turner. And he said to me, "Orlando, why does he hate me? Why does he hate me?" I was so much younger than them, and they saw

183

me as an outsider trying to master what they were doing. So, Geertz could tolerate me. But he was vicious with Turner. I don't even know why he bothered inviting him. I guess because he *was* Victor Turner, after all, and he had to. Anyway, we limed a lot. I introduced him to Jamaican rum and he introduced me to good scotch. In the end I was very much on Turner's side, which was comparative in a way that I found very valuable in *Slavery and Social Death*.

DS: You use the concept of "liminality."
OP: That came straight out of Turner.[9]

DS: But to return just for a moment to the contrast between your orientation and that of David Brion Davis, *The Problem of Slavery in Western Culture* is in a sense a kind of history of ideas, whereas you have always differentiated the kind of project that you're involved in from that.
OP: There was one chapter, chapter 6, "The Legitimacy of Enslavement and the Ideal of the Christian Servant: Moral Doubts and Rationalizations," in *The Problem of Slavery*, that got away from the history of ideas and was more what I did. And that chapter in my copy you'll find very marked up; it was *very* influential. David could write that way, but still what I did differed very much because I was focused on the *substantive mechanics* of slavery and the *process* of enslavement.

DS: The idea that slavery should be defined as a structure of "natal alienation" producing a condition of "social death" has become, in some ways, relatively common now. How would you sketch the genealogy of that idea?
OP: Partly from Moses Finley. Actually, it goes back in a way to Henri Lévy-Bruhl, who was a late nineteenth-, early twentieth-century French scholar who influenced Moses, and who was the first person who broached the idea of the slave as being quintessentially an *outsider*.[10] Then Moses picked up on that – the slave as an outsider. And then French anthropologist Claude Meillassoux developed it. He had a whole team working on the Sahel. I read them very carefully, and the whole idea gelled with reading what they wrote on the Touareg, who actually had a term they used to define the slave as dead. The term literally came from a Touareg expression. And I remember one that I quoted, which I thought was almost blasphemous in Islamic terms, which went something like: "Everyone is subject to Allah. The slave is subject to his master." Making the

184

master out to be a god. And one of these phrases describes the slave as one who is dead. This evolved in a grounded way, too, because it's not only the Touareg who speak of the slave as symbolically and socially dead. There are also accounts of tribal slavery, in which the idea is that, ultimately, the slave was a *kinless* person. And kinlessness is social death in kin-based societies. All of them had this idea of being an outsider and then associated that with the idea of being socially dead. And then, finally, there are two other sources from which the idea came. One was Roman. The Romans had this idea of the slave being *legally* dead. But, funnily enough, coming back to the Caribbean, the indigenous Caribbean, the Caribs, our notorious, funky Caribs, the ethnography on whom is really wild. They had all these strange customs. They had a ritual that you cut your hair a certain way when you're in mourning. Slaves had to cut their hair like that too. They're *always* mourning their *own* death. The idea is pretty universal; and it was just a matter of bringing it together. It emerged in a grounded way, because it was not a concept or hypothesis I went and imposed upon the data. It emerged, starting just as I described it.[11]

DS: One of the things that *Slavery and Social Death* aims at is the very prominent notion that the institution of slavery was a *peculiarity*, was an anomaly. And *Slavery and Social Death* aims to undermine that pervasive assumption, embodied in Kenneth Stampp's famous book *The Peculiar Institution*.[12] Tell me how you conceive of that intervention.

OP: There was an ideological component, if you like. It was partly motivated by my earlier view on ethnicity and on Black life and culture, but here one of the universal views, in American studies primarily, was to think of the quintessential slave as a *Black* person. In a way, I was very interested in *undoing* this idea, both to be clear to Black Americans that their condition was not so peculiar, but also to make it clear to Whites that most of them had ancestors who were slaves. It was part of my general comparative move, to expand the experience of slavery. That partly motivated it. It raised the whole question of the origins of racism. And it also harks back to the Sambo thesis in Elkins that I still had in the back of my mind. There is a long section on Roman slavery in my book. The Romans' attitude toward the Greek slave was very similar to the Sambo image. Graeculus was the Latin version of Sambo. To the Roman slaveholders the slaves were stereotyped with all the same characteristics. So, yes, there was a bit of that agenda in writing the book.

THE PARADOX OF FREEDOM

Also, I was very concerned about the parochialism of American studies. I wanted to point out the fact that, not only was slavery *not* a peculiarly American institution but, seen within the context of broader slave studies, there were indeed *oddities* in American slavery that people had come to see as the norm, because American slavery had been so much more thoroughly studied than other areas of slave life in other countries. It wasn't that slavery was peculiar, but US slavery was very distinctive and had come to be seen as the norm when, in fact, it was the odd man out. And one of the best examples of this, which *Slavery and Social Death* worked hard at demonstrating, is that the United States had one of the lowest manumission rates of all large-scale slave societies. The way Tannenbaum had framed it was, "Wow, isn't Latin America peculiar in having such a high rate of manumission?" But that turns out to be a very parochial view of it, because it treats the United States as the norm. And then we have to *explain* why Latin America was an exception. The truth is, *most* large-scale slave societies had a high rate of manumission. What's more, one of the more original sociological points of *Slavery and Social Death* is that manumission was an *integral* part of any thriving large-scale slave system, because it's the way you *motivate* the slaves. When you make someone socially dead, dishonored, totally without any sort of stake in your society, no past, no future, you're demotivating them, in a way, so that it's hard to imagine why they would want to work for you, or serve you. And the way to solve the problem, the best incentive, was manumission. Nearly all large-scale slave systems found eventually that this was the best way of motivating the slave. Of course, that was the root of what later became the *freedom* idea. So, the point I was making was that the United States, not slavery, is very peculiar in being so hostile to manumission.

DS: I wonder whether there is a way your global conception of slavery is being read through your intimate sense of New World slavery, and slavery in Jamaica in particular? One might say that it is in Jamaican society especially that you see (and identify in *The Sociology of Slavery* specifically) the absence of that social fabric, that familial fabric, through which the slave might potentially become a new social person, to acquire a new social life. What would you say to that proposition? Indeed, in *The Sociology of Slavery* in your description of the Jamaican social order, you describe the set of circumstances in which the slave *cannot* be anything other than socially dead.

186

SLAVERY AND SOCIAL DEATH

OP: It gets complicated because "social death" doesn't necessarily mean a *lack* of community or community life. Remember, this was 1982, and you had developing, then, the "slave community" argument. And you'd had, in 1974, *Time on the Cross*. And that whole historiography was undoing what I called the "catastrophic theory" of slavery. They were saying there was *continuity* – there was *family*. And I just thought they were *wrong*. John Blassingame took this argument to its ultimate conclusion; his book *The Slave Community* did very well. As I said, in this work the slave family looked like a suburban, two-parent family.[13]

DS: This would be the direction that Kamau Brathwaite also took with the idea of the "folk culture" of the slave.
OP: Yes. I just thought it was wrong. But that argument became very big, very important for the new identity movement that wanted to see *Black community*. In a way it's a departure from Malcolm X. Malcolm X gave a series of lectures on Black history here at Harvard, which Archie Epps edited and which contains my favorite reference to the catastrophic theory. He said, "We didn't land on Plymouth Rock; Plymouth Rock landed on us."[14] That's the best summary of the catastrophic theory. But Black identity politics was moving in a totally different direction. You had strange bedfellowships, in a way: cliometricians joining with the identity historians, culminating in the slave community theory, which was overturning a whole tradition of scholarship about the Black family that goes back to W. E. B. Du Bois and E. Franklin Frazier, who, by the way, had a big debate with Herskovits about this. Now, Herskovits, of course, did have a view of the continuities of Black life, but he recognized slavery as being destructive, in the sense of the removal of the father. His theory was more like a residue theory. He wasn't holding that there was a two-parent family; he had done his fieldwork, so he didn't see that.

Now, as you know, my own position is borne out, because there's a huge reaction against the revisionist theory now. And the important point is that I wasn't saying people didn't have relationships. People will always try to have relationships and build community. What they lacked, what they did not have, was *legitimacy*. They lacked any recognized rights in their children, and in their spouses, and in their ancestors. In *Slavery and Social Death*, I used the term *genealogical isolates* for this – because you can't separate legitimacy from kinship. The whole *point* about kinship is *rules of legitimation*. That's what happened on a massive scale in the United States. The way that America solved the problem of not having an external slave trade

187

THE PARADOX OF FREEDOM

was the massive internal slave trade, in which children were sold off from their parents. What a catastrophe that must have been! Can you imagine it, the tremendous demand after the 1830s when the system started to boom with the perfection of the cotton gin? And as the slave system moved south and west, the entire supply was coming from the north. These guys were just selling off younger slaves. And the basis of that was that families had no custodial claims on their children. Women were losing their husbands, but, more important, all the male kids were being sold off. There was a massive, catastrophic, forced movement and trafficking of younger slaves, in which families were torn apart. And, even if you weren't torn apart, imagine living in that nightmare scenario in which you were never sure whose kid would be next. So, I was trying to tell these people, you're just looking at the figures without trying to *imagine* what this community life was like for a slave. Imagine living in a society in which suddenly a cousin or a dear one disappears. That's how it was. People just disappeared, but on a massive scale. Women they tended to keep, to breed, partly, and also because of the closer ties. And that's when I think a lot of the real problems between Black men and Black women began. Because the women and their daughters formed a much stronger bond that was much more respected, if that's the word, than fathers and sons, or even mothers and sons. I just never believed this revisionist story, and, though I remained good friends with Bob Fogel and Stanley Engerman, both knew that I felt they were wrong, wrong, wrong. Then, in Jamaica, Barry Higman, of course, took up the cliometric revisionist position. And it was perfectly clear to me that he was wrong, concentrating as he did on a small period of Jamaican slavery and being terribly misled by the quantitative data he drew on. But, also, there was a lack of imagination about what it was like living in a system like that. I think Higman is a fine scholar whose works, on the whole, have made major contributions to the study of Jamaican slavery, but we differ greatly in our understanding of the destructive impact of the institution. My advice to those who lack the imagination and simple human empathy to recognize in Jamaican slavery a genocidal reign of terror, a holocaust, when it is staring them in the face, is to read the 1400-page and thirty-year diary of Thomas Thistlewood, which leaves nothing to the imagination. Revisionist works on Jamaican slavery that fail to see its genocidal nature are akin to the denial of the Jewish Holocaust.[15] But, anyway, things have changed again. There's been a reaction *against* that revisionist literature. I was in the thick of those intellectual battles. *Slavery and Social Death* was written within that context, though in a way also

THE PARADOX OF FREEDOM

getting out of it, because I didn't want to get into the nitty-gritty of
the debate by writing about American slavery. So, I took this side
step, pulled away, became interested in civilizations of slavery in the
broader aspects of the evolution of Western culture that *Slavery and
Social Death* plunged me into.

It's a natural development from that to work on *Freedom*. But
the work on *Freedom* originated in the idea that manumission was
an integral part of what slavery required, with the United States
being one of the exceptional cases – made exceptional by the very
unusual fact that it was the only large-scale slave society where the
system started to expand massively precisely when external supplies
were being cut off. That's the significance of 1807. The slave trade
ended, and 1832, 1833, cotton soared. It's one of the tragedies of
Black American history because, if the cotton revolution had come
just a little later, the whole system might just have ended, gone the
way of the North. The South came very close; the Virginia Assembly
actually debated whether they should abolish slavery; that's how
close it came. But then cotton came. And that was the end of that.
The economic incentive then just turned it around.

The Paradox of Freedom

DS: In 1991, Orlando, almost ten years after *Slavery and Social
Death*, you published volume 1 of the freedom series, *Freedom in
the Making of Western Culture*, with its argument that freedom as
an idea and value was generated out of the experience of slavery.
Again, one of the things that intrigues me is the preface, intrigues me
for the *methodological* predicament that you outline – the way you
stage a methodological paradox that you seek to work out. You say
in that preface that you began in search of a "man-killing wolf called
slavery," but you kept stumbling upon the tracks of a lamb called
freedom. A lamb, you say, that stared back at you with "strange,
uninnocent eyes." And this propels you to shift gears. It turns out
now that it is not slavery that is the real target of your preoccupations but *freedom*. I find that very fascinating, and I have a number of
questions around this. The first one goes something like this. You ask
yourself in the preface if you were supposed to believe that slavery
was a "lamb in wolf's clothing." And you answer, no, not with your
past. What do you mean by that?
OP: Well, it was just Jamaica. If you grew up in Jamaica it was quite
clear that you could not view slavery as anything other than horrible.

189

THE PARADOX OF FREEDOM

But Jamaica, too, is a source of this paradox, because Jamaicans are a very freedom-loving people, *chaotically* freedom-loving, in fact. And there were several experiences in Jamaica that planted the seeds of this view. One of them I've already mentioned to you – growing up in elementary school, going to high school, during the colonial period; *you*, David, came of age *after* the colonial period. But *we* celebrated Empire Day seriously; people look back at this now and almost smile, but they don't realize how serious it was. It was the biggest holiday of the elementary school year. On Empire Day we literally waved the flag, and we literally sang "Rule Britannia." We were forced to sing that anthem that ends "Britons never, never shall be slaves." And it struck me, even as a kid, that this was strange.[1]

DS: You mean the relation between the assumption of innate, uncompromisable British liberty and the practice of overseas slavery?
OP: Right. You know the song. The question is: Why would they say that? *We* were the enslaved people. But no one threatened the British. The British were the ones going around enslaving *other* people. Why were they singing about Britons not being slaves? It's bizarre. It struck me even as a kid as strange, that they would express their glory in that negative way. Saying "Rule, Britannia, Britannia rule the waves," yes. "We've conquered India, we've conquered Africa, we've conquered America" – that's what you'd expect the following lines to be. But it struck me as unbelievably or strangely anticlimactic, to say the least, to say, "Britons never, never shall be slaves." Why would an imperial group want to celebrate the fact that they would never be slaves? As a kid, you didn't think much more about it. But it did strike me, as someone who was sensitive to words and lyrics and poetry, as odd.

But then there's also the fact that I grew up in the sugar belt. May Pen was a little town when I was there. Now it's a ghastly city. But it was just a little one-donkey town when I was there, a market town for the villages and the estates. All the big estates, Vere, Sevens, Parnassus, were around there. *That's slavery breathing on you.* There is something about Vere (I don't know if you know Vere) that I find *oppressive*. And I lived there as a little kid, when I was about five or six, in Lionel Town. Now, Vere is one of the few flat parts of Jamaica. If you go from Lionel Town down to a place called Alley (the name itself is significant), you go through the estates there, and you're just walking through cane. It's like walking through history, walking through a strange time zone to the past. The atmosphere is still very strongly reminiscent of something oppressive, as if some

190

tragedy had happened there. Partly it's reflected in the fact that there are lots of Indians there, and they give a certain post-emancipation quality living exactly the same way. So, I had a strong sense that slavery was *there*, and we knew about it and were taught about it even at elementary school.

Those were the beginnings of my interest. But I started off, remember, trying to understand freedom in Jamaica, studying the effects of slavery on the slave. Because, don't forget, in all history Jamaica has probably the highest instance and record of rebellion of any slave society anywhere. Much more than Haiti, which had the *big* one, but not many before that. We had many major slave revolts. So, that was always in the back of my mind.

DS: But let me hold you to that image, Orlando. It turns out that, in search of this wolf called slavery, you stumble upon the lamb of freedom. But when the lamb looks back at you, what is shocking is that the lamb doesn't look back at you with clear, innocent eyes. The lamb looks back at you with *un*innocent, strange eyes.

OP: Right. Freedom itself carries a good part of its origins. It's a very complex, almost *contradictory* value. Freedom for me is about power. The social scientists argue a lot about freedom. Essentially, where I'm at now (and what I was getting at in the coda of *Freedom*) is these three ideas in a chordal tension with each other – freedom *from*, freedom *to*, and freedom *with* is the way I express it. The three require each other: freedom from power, freedom to exercise power, and freedom with others in sharing power. I've received some interesting criticisms – one from a neighbor of mine, Amartya Sen – but I've been able to quite satisfactorily get at them in the new book. Amartya is very much a cosmopolitan, but he doesn't really like the claim that a value might be "Western" – especially one he thinks of as a universal value. He's not happy with my claim that freedom is *socially constructed*. His view is that it's universal, and that in any event the Indians had it, too, from way back. My way of dealing with it sociologically is by saying it's a *cultural* construct. It's *not* just a set of ideas. It's an *institution*. And one has to explain how it came about. If you see it just as an idea, then of course there are any number of sages in China, India, or wherever who can come up with the idea of being free. But celebrating freedom as an *ultimate* value is quite unique. Anyway, the complexity of what I was getting at there can be seen in the fact that, in ancient Greece, one of the three components of freedom was "freedom to," which involved freedom *to enslave*. Now the idea that you can exercise your freedom

THE PARADOX OF FREEDOM

by enslaving someone else is totally incomprehensible to a modern view of freedom, which is the negative view of freedom celebrated in liberalism. And so, you have someone like Isaiah Berlin (whose essay I thought was totally overrated) celebrating negative freedom and simply claiming, *prescriptively*, that positive freedom is invalid.[2] He's trying to write it out of the semantic field of freedom. But you can't do that. You're just writing out two thousand years of history. I argue that, if you read my view of history, you can begin to understand the American South in a way you couldn't before. Southern slaveholders were totally obsessed with liberty – they led the revolution. But part of their liberty was the liberty to *enslave* others. You can only make sense of that if you know the history. It's a very good example of how you can only understand a concept *historically*. If you try to understand it in a purely prescriptive way, then of course you'd think these people in the South are totally crazy. Anyway, the lamb of innocence is the fact that freedom involves the freedom to empower yourself and to overpower others. There is, however, a good and an evil dimension to this idea of freedom as power. The good meaning of the positive view of freedom is empowerment, to have control over one's self and one's destiny, the power to define one's goals and to achieve them. This is what, in effect, Amartya Sen was saying when he defined freedom as capability. It's an ancient idea, going back to Plato. The evil side of freedom as power is the idea of being free to hold power over others. The Greeks accepted this without any sense of contradiction; the idea persisted right down to the slaveholders of the US South, who also saw no contradiction, who held that their freedom to have power over their Black slaves was actually a virtue and a good thing for the slaves in that it was a way of civilizing them. And this was justified by racism, the view that Blacks were inherently inferior and keeping them under control was in their best interest. The ancient version of this idea was Aristotle's view that some people were inherent slaves, born to be slaves.

DS: You're running ahead of me. But now you've also answered one of the questions that I was going to ask you, which is why you thought freedom required a *sociological* history. You've answered it in saying that, for you, the philosophers erred inasmuch as they wrote a purely abstract, prescriptive theory of freedom. But I want to hold you a little bit longer around the paragraph about the wolf and the lamb, and what you say about Jamaica is in fact provoking me further. The paragraph is enigmatic. But what strikes me, as in *Slavery and Social Death*, is the *consistency* of the problem that bedevils you, namely,

192

THE PARADOX OF FREEDOM

the *internal* relation between slavery and freedom. One could say that the problem is already at the center of *The Sociology of Slavery*, and it is what you try to illuminate through Camus' work *The Rebel*. It is slavery as an extremity of the human condition that *internally* generates its limit and the urge and the demand to go beyond that limit. Is that a fair assessment?

OP: Camus was quite clear on that in *The Rebel*.

DS: Right. But, for you, it is in the creole slave that the problem of freedom emerges. And one of the questions that I want to ask is whether, in a sense, you haven't been always rewriting the story of Jamaican slavery.

OP: Yes, that's where things started. In a way you can see *all* of what I've been doing ever since [*Sociology of Slavery*] as a way to try to understand Jamaica – but then I went wider and wider afield in trying to understand the people who were enslaving Jamaica, and how they themselves were so obsessed with freedom. I may have mentioned this earlier, but the very first historical essay I wrote, which was based on actual research, was done in high school. There was an all-island prize that was given (I don't know if it was still being given when you were in high school) by history teachers; I think it was called the George William Gordon Prize. It was given by the History Teachers' Association for the best student essay based on some research. And I won that prize. I almost forgot about that. This would have been 1959. The essay was based on the 1865 Morant Bay Rebellion. Now, for me, what was really intriguing was that you had this really extraordinarily brutal repression, but at the same time you had this complete outrage in Britain led by John Stuart Mill and these liberal types. Later Bernard Semmel wrote about it in *Jamaican Blood and Victorian Conscience: The Governor Eyre Controversy*.[3] But I thought this was strange even as an eighteen-year-old high school kid. Because this was a serious thing; he was impeached. He was hauled back to Britain and impeached. And you wonder, "Wow. Why would they want to do that?" So clearly there was this real paradox; these people were brutal, and no one was complaining about the brutalities of the Jamaican system of slavery, but they were very upset by the fact that this guy had gone against constitutional principles. That was the issue in my very first academic or semi-academic research (this was before I went to university). I was thinking from very early about these constant paradoxes. Plus, the fact that the biggest paradox of all was that, in Jamaica itself, the Whites were more freedom loving – as they were here in the American South – than any other group of people

193

THE PARADOX OF FREEDOM

and, in fact, almost led the way in their rebellion against Britain. If you read the records of the Jamaica House of Assembly, they were a cantankerous group, always going on about their freedom. And one of the interesting things, of course, is that they established institutions that we inherited. That partly explains our own commitment to democracy. In a way, it was partly the inheritance of an institutional framework that they themselves had established but that excluded Blacks. And the idea of freedom is also part of the religion, too. So, in *The Sociology of Slavery* I discuss the Daddy [Sam] Sharpe rebellion, which I spent a lot of time working on. Daddy Sharpe, of course, was inspired by Christianity. It was called the Baptist War. And what we saw here was Sharpe reading or being read to and interpreting the scriptures. And, as you know, Christianity became an important part of explaining the institutionalization of freedom in Western civilization afterward. Well, all that is there in Jamaica. As someone brought up as an Anglican very strong in that faith, I could see the very strong commitment of Christianity to freedom. But it was also paradoxical because the Jamaican ministers were among the most oppressive of the lot.

DS: Indeed, and the Anglicans in particular.
OP: A bunch of drunkards and tyrants. They were the rationalizers of the system. You don't have to leave Jamaica to see the paradoxes of freedom; you just have to think about it.

DS: Interesting. In some sense you are, I think, rewriting in later work that dialectic of slavery and freedom that first gets sketched or worked out in *The Sociology of Slavery*. But, clearly, writing *The Sociology of Slavery* and thinking about the predicament of that creole slave, you don't yet have a sense that her or his resistance to slavery, desire for freedom, will become a frame in which you recognize that the source of the value of freedom in Western culture writ large lay in the social death of human slavery. That relationship seems to me to be a very important one for the way your work has unfolded.
OP: You see the idea of freedom as power among the British in Jamaica. You see the idea of freedom as negation in the behavior of Jamaican Black people, who are among the most freedom loving in the world. If you reflect on your own society in Jamaica in this way, it's hard to resist that. Though, I must say, not many people have come to this conclusion. I remember Hilary Beckles was not in agreement. I gave one of the Elsa Goveia lectures on freedom. But

194

THE PARADOX OF FREEDOM

when Beckles published the lectures he left it out.[4] He just couldn't see what the *connection* was. I gather he is now a knight.

DS: Yes, it's "Sir Hilary"! When you published *Slavery and Social Death*, which was 1982, did you have a sense then that your work was *headed* for freedom?
OP: The last chapter clearly hinted strongly at that. And several reviewers actually picked up on that because, in the last chapter of *Slavery and Social Death*, I did mention freedom.

DS: Because I'm struck by the fact that the first lecture that you give that begins to sketch out the freedom book was given in 1983.
OP: Yes, in fact I did a piece for *Slavery and Abolition*, which outlined it, just a little after they started publication. The antislavery society in Hull brought me over because they were celebrating, I think, the two hundredth anniversary of the birth of Wilberforce. And they brought me up to lecture. And that's when I did the first sketch, which was then published in *Slavery and Abolition*.[5]

DS: Although you express some hesitation about doing so, you do venture in the early part of *Freedom in the Making of Western Culture* a definition of freedom that then, if you like, drives the project of the book. And you say that freedom can be defined in terms of this chordal triad of "personal freedom" (which is the freedom as non-constraint), "sovereignal freedom" (the freedom to act regardless of the wishes of others), and "civic freedom" (which is the capacity of adults to participate in the life and governance of their community). Is this an *arbitrary* definition? You do say that it *doesn't* stack the cards of your historical account, but one might argue that *it can't but do so*, inasmuch as these are already the virtues of freedom that are valorized in Western culture.
OP: As an historical sociologist you try not to be anachronistic but, rather, to put yourself back in the earliest possible period – in this case, it would have been early seventh century BC – and try to see how the institution evolved. And, no, it's not arbitrary; in a way I did depart from the current position, because many people still find it very difficult to comprehend or to accept the idea of freedom *as power*. Now we're living under the hegemony of the liberal conception of *negative* freedom. I thought *that* was one of the first things I had to come to terms with. For the Greeks, there was no problem whatever in talking about freedom as power, or *areté*. It was a term the aristocrats loved; it gave the impression of the aristocratic dignity and

195

THE PARADOX OF FREEDOM

ability to *best* others, either in the Olympics or, as Pindar expressed it, in terms of the conquest of others. It was also a natural concept among the Romans. So, it took me some time to formulate this idea. Using current lenses, it's a very hard idea to come to terms with, and some people just completely refuse to accept that this was ever the case and just go into prescriptive mode. But I don't say "They were wrong." Because you can't say history is wrong.

There were two important ways in which I had to completely overcome present prejudices and present conceptions. One way is what I just mentioned, namely, the idea that power has historically been a central component of freedom. But there's also another thing that has to do with being a Jamaican, which is that my whole upbringing intellectually was one of hostility – like Amartya Sen's – to any view that great things originated in the West. My natural tendency as a young intellectual was to say, "There they go again, claiming every-thing originated there." If anything, I was more inclined to take a *universalist* view that *all* people want to be free. It took a real effort to come around to what I think, as an undergraduate, I would have seen as almost a repulsive idea: that this thing really originated with the Greeks. And, in a way, I can say that many conservatives love this idea. But what saved me was *how* it originated. What I gave with one hand, I took back with the other. "You can have it, you originated it, but you want to hear the rest of the story?" It's very interesting how conservatives view that book *Freedom*. Because many of them like it very much, they find it intriguing, but they still balk at my expla-nation. It's widely cited and used in all kinds of strange circles. But I could take some comfort from the fact that I wasn't just saying that this is something that Plato and Aristotle cooked up in their heads, and this came out of the great wisdom of the West. It came out of the oppressed and the oppressors of people. What I'm saying is that Jamaicans' love of freedom comes out of oppression. Those were two things I had to overcome: repulsion at the idea that the West indeed invented freedom and my attraction to the idea that the oppressed discovered freedom in resisting their oppression.

In fact, Martin Bernal, the Cornell historian and philosopher who wrote *Black Athena*, reviewed *Freedom in the Making of Western Culture* in the *American Journal of Sociology*. He was slightly patronizing. He said it was interesting but I'd been misled by Western historiography. Remember, *Freedom* came not long after *Black Athena*. It was quite predictable what his position was. Any argument that makes any claim that anything originated in Greece he would oppose – the Egyptians had it first, and so on. That's not

196

THE PARADOX OF FREEDOM

true. I had to overcome that, but that's a position to which I would have been very sympathetic as an undergraduate, even as a graduate student at LSE. At LSE I was very sympathetic to Karl Popper's book *The Open Society and its Enemies: The Spell of Plato*, in which he attributed every sin, including that of the Nazis, to Plato.[6] This was one of my favorite books; I read that book, both volumes, from page to page, beginning to end, a couple of times, and thought it a great book. And it was with that background that I approached this material. But then the data *transformed* my view on it. And then of course the third thing was Christianity itself. Because I had grown up as an Anglican but had completely discarded the idea that Christianity had a lot to do with freedom by the time I was a graduate student, even by the end of my undergraduate days. Again, my position was the standard one that Christianity had sanctioned slavery because its history included slavery. So, all of these things involve, if anything, *abandoning* the current, the present views, everything I had stood for in my view of the past, of history and slavery, about how freedom came about.

DS: You know, I can imagine people reading that volume on freedom as in some way a celebration of the West – as I did too on my first reading. But, thinking about it again, there are very crucial ways in which, as you're suggesting, it is a *critique* of the West. The critique partly hangs on a distinction that is made very early in the book, the distinction between the *idea* and the *value* of freedom. The story that unfolds in *Freedom* is, crucially, I think, not merely the story of the emergence of the idea of freedom but the story of its predominance as a personal and social *value*. Its institutionalization as a value is the principal point of distinction between non-Western people, such as the famed Tupinamba of French ethnology, and Greek and Roman traditions. The crucial thing is not simply the emergence of freedom as an idea; the crucial thing is the *institutionalization* of freedom as a value, which is the story of the making of Western culture.

OP: Right. And that's where I differ from intellectual historians like Quentin Skinner. He claims to be writing a *new* intellectual history that is supposed to be context-sensitive, but it's not. It's just totally *disembodied*. I don't know if you've read his work *Liberty before Liberalism*.[7] It's intellectual history. Totally disembodied. By context he simply means taking account of other people. He wouldn't know how to think about how these things were institutionalized. Now I'm fairly influenced by "symbolic interactionism." Because essentially what I showed is that the whole thing began with a struggle

197

THE PARADOX OF FREEDOM

with the semi-slaves, the serfs, and then went right through the sixth century – it's a class struggle. And out of this emerged the value of freedom. It was as if they were making sense of this, as the symbolic interactionists would say, *in the course of* interaction, in the course of people making meaning, making sense of what's going on. I have a section in the preface in which I pointed out that there are two parallel histories, because one meaning was made out of the struggle, and basically consolidated by the end of the fifth century BC. The meaning then becomes part of the process. It informs *both* action *and* other thinking. Intellectual historians are looking *only* at meanings – it's like a disembodied thing – without considering that it is both influenced by, and influences in turn, what is going on in the struggle by real people to be free.

And that's where the Middle Ages are important. The new book spends a lot of time on the Middle Ages. Contrary to the prominent idea in Western historiography that the Middle Ages were the dark ages of freedom, I argue that this wasn't true. The symbolic meanings were *there*, embodied in Christianity, which took over, lock, stock, and barrel, the whole tripartite notion of freedom: freedom as redemption (which means to buy somebody out of slavery), freedom as power (which became the dominant notion), and freedom as sharing the body of Christ. Paul was clearly very knowledgeable about these ideas. The problem is that the Church knew the radical implications of freedom and tried to keep it away from the masses, which is one reason why they never made the common language the idiom of Christianity. They kept it in Latin. But people did find out the Christian doctrine of freedom, just like Daddy Sharpe did. Right through medieval history you have a lot of Daddy Sharpes, often religious types, renegade priests (like Sharpe), translating the doctrine back into the secular meaning. A large number of peasant revolts were inspired by Christianity, in exactly the same way that Daddy Sharpe's revolt was. I'd already written about that in the essay for the book in honor of David Brion Davis, *The Problem of Evil*, and which I'm just going to incorporate into the new volume.[8]

DS: One of the ways the argument in *Freedom* is critical of the West also turns on your view that the West has, in fact, *misunderstood* itself and its difference from other cultures. Because, for the West, its own institution and valorization of the value of freedom is taken to be the universal norm in relation to which other, non-Western, societies are judged, and, it is urged, *ought* to be judged – whereas you say it is not the *lack* in non-Western culture that requires

198

THE PARADOX OF FREEDOM

explanation but the *peculiar* history of the West's valorization that requires an accounting.

OP: And the fact that they've been the slave-mongers poses other problems in the history of the West. But forgetting all that [the relation between slave-mongering and their idea of freedom], they turn it around and then universalize the value. It's paradox within paradox. In celebrating the value, they universalize it, and then find it very strange that other cultures don't have it – and further claim superiority in having had the genius to discover this universal thing and celebrate it.

DS: I wonder whether, as an extension of your argument, one could say that one way of reading that distinction you're making between the *idea* and the *value* of freedom is that, in those societies and cultures in which freedom is not institutionalized as a value but exists as an idea, freedom is not reified and its sources in slavery are not obscured; but where freedom is institutionalized as a value, it becomes reified, universalized, taken as a norm, and its relationship to its origins in slavery are obscured, and perhaps indeed distorted.

OP: And *denied*. In cases where you have slavery in non-Western societies, the idea of freedom was obviously clearer. People say, going back to Homer, that that was the first time you see the word *freedom*; that was essentially the first time you had a freed slave. But this book, *Freedom*, simply pointed out that, *no*, there wasn't any *institutionalization* of freedom. There's a simple explanation for why that doesn't happen, and that is that you don't want to celebrate a value that is important to the lowliest of the low in the society, who are the slaves. The fact that you go around celebrating freedom meant that you were once a slave. And, in fact, most slaves in that kind of situation would want to shut up about it. And wouldn't want to identify themselves by saying, "We're free." So, it presents an even greater paradox, a greater challenge, as to why it is there was this perverse thing happening (perverse in the eyes of most other slaveholding societies), that a value invented in the catastrophic condition of the slave, and in the slave's desire to be free, could become such an important value.

There are so many other things you can celebrate as your primary value. Why would you want to pick up on something that had, as I said in the book, such a lowly pedigree? That's one of the biggest questions about the West. In all its major periods you find a large-scale growth of slavery. You start with the Greeks, where you had for the first time a large slaveholding society. In all of the other slave-holding societies, slaves are never more than a small portion. They didn't need them. But then people are saying, by the time you get to

199

THE PARADOX OF FREEDOM

the fifth century AD, slavery was slowly being replaced by something called "serfdom," where you're a slave to the land but *not* to somebody else. That is hogwash. Slavery existed alongside serfdom, and in the ninth century there was a huge expansion in Carolingian France. And then you realize slavery was booming in Renaissance Italy, and *they* were the first people to establish sugar plantations run by slaves in the Mediterranean islands – Cyprus, Crete. In fact, these were models for the New World sugar plantations. The first modern slave plantations were in the Mediterranean. The Venetians ran them, too. And then you had the British. And, with the rise of capitalism, what do we find? Large-scale slavery again. It's a very extraordinary situation, and in no other civilization do you find this. It's very interesting; it's fascinating. It's not a flattering history of the West, by any means. And if people read the work carefully they will recognize that, in many ways, this is a severely critical interpretation of the West.

DS: But the thing, though, it seems to me, is not just that it offers an unflattering picture of the West's self-understanding. What's *more* interesting to me is that, for you, the picture of freedom is in fact a *tragic* one. And on rereading the book it struck me that tragedy has a crucial place in your understanding of the rise of freedom. Obviously, tragedy is connected to the idea of paradox: if you like, freedom forms a part of a tragic pair, the other member of which is slavery. Freedom and slavery form a tragic pair. There is a tension between them that is inescapable and untranscendable. What the institutionalization of the value of freedom inscribes is not just a seamless transparent freedom but also a *tension* and a tragic paradox.

OP: Absolutely. And the history I'm writing now deals with that tragedy. Among the more controversial chapters is the one [that shows] that Nazi Germany was in a sense a horrendous distortion of the culture of freedom. One of the things I try to show is that freedom only works when the triad is in equilibrium, so to speak: each element in tense equilibrium with the others so that each note balances the others in the chord. But once it's fragmented you have trouble. You get in parts of Europe, but especially in Germany, a continuation of the medieval idea of freedom as power and freedom as surrender – which Christianity validated, by the way. That's Paul's letter to the Romans. And then Augustine picked it up. It ran right through elite medieval thought – the idea that you can be free by surrendering to the absolute freedom of God, of the King, and of the Church. It never left. The Germans picked it up – Hegel – and it culminated in the Nazi notion that you're ultimately free if you're

THE ORDEAL OF INTEGRATION

all-powerful. And you can only be all-powerful if you're one with the state. And, I tell you, surveys of Germans all indicate that they felt they were very free. This was seen as an abomination, but you have to think of it in sociohistorical terms to understand it now. We see Nazism as the antithesis of everything we value. It's a very familiar liberal view. But Nazi Germany had a perverse form of freedom.

DS: Liberals see freedom as the antithesis of domination.
OP: Right. But that's not what the history of freedom tells us. And even liberal freedom in its heyday, before it was reintegrated and tempered by the welfare state, was a pretty brutal system. It's the dark, satanic mills. And it's the South.

The Ordeal of Integration

DS: Let's turn to *The Ordeal of Integration.* In 1991 the first volume of what was to be a two-volume work on freedom was published. And then, instead of publishing the second volume, you opened a new multivolume project. So, first of all, why is it that the second volume of freedom isn't published?
OP: Because it was just so *vast* a subject. I spent about six years or so collecting notes, writing chapters, a lot of which are still there, and indeed my plan is to do a collection of essays on modern freedom. But to write a coherent, fully detailed second volume of modern freedom was a very daunting task and was just taking up too much of my time. And I usually like to do at least three things at a time. And the other problem I had was that, once I've worked out an argument, if I don't write it out very quickly, I get bored with it and move on. I think I worked out pretty well what it is that happened with the modern world. Which is why I'm just going to get it over with in the new book. And there are lots of chapters, very detailed chapters – about the Renaissance and the Reformation – and I think I'm going to bring them all together as a collection of papers.

DS: *The Ordeal of Integration* was published in 1997 and *Rituals of Blood* in 1998. They are part of a trilogy dealing with race – or "interethnic" relationships, as you prefer – in America. The final installment of the trilogy is to be called *Ecumenical America.* Will that be published?
OP: That is going to be a collection of essays, nearly all of which have been written and published in other places, like "Black Americans"

THE PARADOX OF FREEDOM

in Peter Schuck's volume *Understanding America.*[1] There's a long, long piece that is used a lot by students, on ethno-somatic stratification in the Americas and Europe, which was published in the book by Glenn Loury.[2] And there's the "Ecumenical America" essay and several other essays I've done.[3] I think I'm just going to bring these together, including my Caribbean pieces. It's going to be on race in the Americas and in Europe – a volume of essays like the other two.

DS: *The Ordeal of Integration* and *Rituals of Blood* have about them the quality of *interventions.* Much more so than with *Slavery and Social Death* or *Freedom in the Making of Western Culture,* one has a sense of you wading, knee-deep, waist-deep, into the middle of contentious debates and staking out your positions, your sociohistorically backed-up positions.
OP: Right. That was definitely the case with *The Ordeal of Integration,* which I've kind of gotten away from somewhat. At the time I thought things had gone too far – at least in sociology, in which there was this totally negative view of whatever progress had been made. As an outsider, it seemed to me that they were missing a great deal. There's definitely a political point being made there, which is that, seen comparatively, while America has got its problems (and this is before Obama, by the way), in the political realm the society had gone way beyond any other majority White society in the world. Where I've shifted, though – and that's going to be one of the big essays for the new volume (this is already indicated in the Peter Schuck volume) – is that, while the society has become almost completely integrated – not almost, it's *fully* integrated politically (and in terms of its public culture it's disproportionately influenced by Blacks) – I've become much more critical of the level of *social* integration. I saw the trends in somewhat too optimistic terms in *The Ordeal of Integration.*

DS: Interesting! Even though you add a caution in *Rituals of Blood.*
OP: But I have been disappointed with the way things have been going, where you have a society that is publicly integrated much more than any other majority White society but in which the trends, if anything, have reversed (I'm drawing on the materials from the 1990s). What really disappointed me, and caused me to step back, is what's happened with middle-class integration. It's *not* happening. There's been tremendous growth in the middle class, but they're just as segregated. They are as segregated almost as the Black working class and poor. And this is happening at a time when there's been a genuine revolution among young White Americans. It's not academic;

202

THE ORDEAL OF INTEGRATION

it's not periodic; there's been a *real* change. It's not just a life-cycle change the young ones have overcome. I think all the evidence points to the fact that, outside of the South, we are genuinely going through a sea change among young Whites' attitudes on race.

DS: Meaning that young White Americans are more non-racial?
OP: Meaning that they're non-*racist*. I think so. The educational system did have a powerful effect, and the media, and hip-hop, and all the rest. They're all living with each other, Whites and Blacks, but they're not marrying each other. There's still this social distancing, in spite of the change in attitudes and this cultural acceptance. In fact, this is one of the many paradoxes that I see in life: How can you have the assumption and celebration of Black culture, Black athletes, Black music, and yet this complete social separation? It's one of the bizarre aspects of American life. And who is staying away from whom? The liberal sociology language, which I'm never willing to go along with, is that it's all racism – it's subtle racism, *subtler* forms of racism. Larry Bobo would say, "laissez-faire racism."[4] You can also explain it in terms of class, with respect to the Black poor.

DS: In your view, then, it's the Black middle class that is staying away from the White middle class, not the White middle class that is shunning the Black middle class?
OP: I'm not going to say that Blacks don't want to live with Whites. When I was doing the book tour for *Ordeal*, I had one of my most depressing moments when I went to Atlanta, Georgia, which has maybe the largest group of Black millionaires anywhere in the country. A woman who was assigned to me from the bookstore took me around, and she said, "Do you want to see where the rich Blacks live? I'll take you to where the rich Whites live first." She took me up to the northeastern part of the town. Then she said, "I'm going to take you now to where the rich Blacks live. Really rich." This is in the southwest end of town. Totally, absolutely, completely segregated. *Voluntarily*. I was, shall we say, a little disappointed with that development. My own view – and interpretation – right now is that of a paradox of full public integration with persisting private segregation. That's how I see it: the public sphere of America is fully integrated, more so than any other majority White society; the private sphere is as segregated as ever.

DS: In your introduction to *The Ordeal of Integration*, you seem to feel compelled to say something about your intellectual orientation and its sources. Is this prompted by specific misunderstandings of your work? There's a certain tone of exasperation there.

OP: Oh yes. In America, because of the position I take, and my interests, writing about ancient civilizations, and so on, and there's some suspicion on the part of Black intellectuals – in fact, some people call me a Black conservative. So, I just had to make it clear to them that, *no*, on the contrary, where I come from, people would consider me just the opposite. And also, I have an LSE background, and my own interpretation of the situation in class terms didn't sit well with a lot of people who still see Black America in *race* terms.

DS: But what stands out in your remarks in that section of those introductory pages is your refusal to be pigeonholed, your assertion of a sense of intellectual *independence*, and your very interesting remark that we – intellectuals, academics – tend to read mainly for cues about *identity* rather than reading for the *argument* itself and its implications, which seems to me to be a very pointed critique of the academy.

OP: Absolutely. But isn't that the way it is? People just want to know, "Where's so and so? How do I categorize this person? What box do I put them in?" It's a very crude set of boxes. I think the situation is getting a little better; hence my very favorable review of Touré's book *Who's Afraid of Post-Blackness?* I don't know if you saw that. It was a front-page review in the *New York Times Book Review*. The reason that I like it, and presumably the reason why the editors asked me to do the review, is that this is what post-Blackness is all about – you really can't box or pigeonhole us. There are many ways of Blackness. It's an interesting book.[5]

DS: I wonder, though, whether "post-Black" may itself become another box.

OP: He made it quite clear that *post-Black* doesn't mean post-racial.

DS: Now, interestingly enough, in this, as one might say, most American of your books to date, you frame these remarks about intellectual orientation by pointing to the distinctly West Indian or, indeed, Jamaican formation that you have, that in some sense shapes, you suggest, your academic irreverence and your public intellectual commitment. Do you think of *The Ordeal of Integration* as a book looking at America *through* Jamaican eyes? Or, even, a book about America by a Jamaican *becoming* an American?

OP: It's a book looking at America through the eyes of a West Indian *cosmopolitan* – an idea that seems to be declining quite rapidly *in*

THE ORDEAL OF INTEGRATION

the West Indies now. My generation was very much a cosmopolitan one – you talk about the University of the West Indies, it began there with a large number of nations coming together. And then we all went to Britain, and everybody became much more involved with British culture and ideas. The writers, most of them were in exile, as they used to say. That was the tradition, C. L. R. James being the leading figure in it. And, in a way, you can see *The Ordeal of Integration* as very much in the tradition of James writing about American civilization.[6]

DS: You don't think of *Ordeal* as in some sense a manifestation of your own changing relationship to America?

OP: Oh, absolutely! I saw myself as becoming very much an American, and one who is part of the growing diversity of Black American culture. Which has become increasingly a factor, by the way, in second-generation studies – people have been talking about the heterogeneity of Black American culture. One of the criticisms – very, very mild, it's just one sentence – of Touré's book was that he completely neglected that; the fact that this is another basis of tremendous heterogeneity in the Black population. I saw myself as very much a Black American in this mold. I was coming of age in America and recognizing myself as a *transnational* Black person.

DS: Central to the thesis of *Ordeal* is the philosophic argument that threads all the way through your work, namely, the importance of the moral autonomy of the individual – the idea of our ineradicable powers of self-determination. We are the products of our past but we are *not* determined by our past. For you, even the slave can, and does, make choices. This is the great point, of course, of Quasheba in *Die the Long Day*. So that, in *Ordeal*, one sees again the influence of Sartre, your criticism of identity politics and the politics of victimhood, in particular. One has a sense, in your staging this argument – one can feel it here, as one feels it in much of your work – an irritation both with White American liberalism and with what you sometimes call Black racial advocacy, the sense of there being a collusion between Black racial advocates and White liberals who seem unable to get beyond the politics of victimhood.

OP: Right. But here's the interesting thing that came out clearly in the volume on the cultural dimension of Black American youth. A graduate student and I wrote a third of the book, in addition to editing it, and looked at the attitudes of disadvantaged Black youth. There's a lot of survey data on attitudes, and one of the remarkable

THE PARADOX OF FREEDOM

things is that Black people themselves, and Black youth in particular, take exactly the position that I take. In every survey that's ever been done, you ask them, "Try to tell me why you're in the situation you're in," and they say, "Well, I just fucked up. Bad decisions." They'll mention race if you ask them, but they always say, "Yeah, race is a problem. I've got racist cops to deal with," and so on, but in survey after survey they say race is not their biggest problem.

DS: This is in fact the crux of *The Ordeal of Integration*. What you are concerned with problematizing is the contrast between discourse about race among ordinary people and discourse about race among intellectuals. One can see, you're arguing, a considerable transformation in the way young Blacks think about their life chances in America.

OP: Young Blacks are taking absolutely the opposite position to Black intellectuals. They're saying, "Yeah, the system has been pretty bad, but we don't think that, in my case, while I've experienced racism every time I deal with the policemen, I don't think that's the primary factor." It comes out, amazingly, in every survey. And sometimes it presents real problems for my colleagues, who are approaching it from a systemic point of view (which I think is important but, in a way, can be patronizing) but who don't know what to make of this popular view when they come across it. Are they going to say that these people are cultural dopes who don't understand their position; they don't know that they're really being screwed by the system? In fact, people say they *do* understand their condition, they do know that there's racism. And they give you instances of racism. But they say, "No, I don't think that's the main reason why things are so screwed up with me." Then they list all the *decisions* they've made. "I dropped out of school. I didn't have to. Nobody put a gun to my head and said, 'Drop out of school.' I knew when I dropped out of school that I was screwing myself. Because you can't lift yourself out of poverty in this society without a high school diploma." You get that over and over, both in open-ended interviews as well as in surveys. And so, my fellow sociologists are in this weird position where they're simply saying – they *have* to say, although they don't want to say it, because it sounds so horribly patronizing – that these people don't know what they're talking about when they're talking about themselves.

DS: Is this sense of Black youth what drove not only the favorable reception of Touré's book but also the collaborative work embodied in *The Cultural Matrix*?

OP: Yes. Certainly.

206

THE ORDEAL OF INTEGRATION

DS: The historical sociological problem for you about systemic analysis, however, is not its focus on systems per se, which you share, but that systemic analysis can be systemically *reductionist*; and that systemic reductionism leads to the assumption that the people that you're speaking to, the subjects that you're interviewing, must be either ignorant or stupid. For you, as I understand what you're saying, there are obviously structures that constrain people's lives, but the people on the ground that you talk to recognize their own moral autonomy in the structures within which they act.

OP: Absolutely. In an essay I did in *Daedalus* I try to work out a kind of framework by which one can assess *responsibility* – given that so many outcomes in life can be partly attributed to circumstances and some to choices that people make.[7] So I developed this framework in which I try to separate the kinds of things which are basically or almost completely within the power of individuals to change or resolve, choices they make that they could have made otherwise, as opposed to occasions in which circumstances were so overwhelming that they are not to be held responsible. But, also, the complication is that some individual outcomes are the result of structural factors, and some structural factors emerge from the kind of *lifestyles* that people have adopted. It got quite complicated, but, basically, I tried to see what kind of actions you can say people are primarily responsible for, and what kind of actions you could say that they're primarily *not* responsible for. And, therefore, the state or society has a moral need to assist, and those who run it have a duty to help with it. I tried to work that out; I began thinking about that in *Ordeal*.

DS: Unexpectedly for me, one of the figures who appears toward the very end of *The Ordeal of Integration* is Martin Luther King Jr. And I wondered whether, for you, King embodied or represented a resolution of the relationship between moral autonomy of the individual and the commitment to moral community.

OP: Yes, King was a great figure. And I think he saw that, too, in his more philosophical writings. I think he was fully aware of that question. What could be a greater assertion of moral autonomy than to start a movement to change a society, rather than sitting back and demanding that society provides the solution. I believe in a just state that removes all restraints that are beyond one's control, that provides an income floor beneath which no one will fall, and that compensates for iniquities that led to both external and internal injuries, but leaves room for the individual to define their own goals, shape their own future and empower themselves – in other words, makes possible the

THE PARADOX OF FREEDOM

positive freedom of what Amartya Sen calls personal capability and what I call simply self-determination, both real and imagined.

DS: Thinking again about Orlando Patterson and method, I wonder how you think about the relationship in your work (and one sees this in *The Ordeal of Integration* quite starkly), the melding, if you like, of existentialism, rationalism, and empiricism. Your commitments to existentialism appear more strongly in some works than in others, but it is a consistent thread. At the same time there is also a strong streak of rationalism. You say, at a certain point in *The Ordeal of Integration*, that with "clear thinking" we can get beyond the errors of race thinking, and in other parts of the book you will assert that the "data" will indicate clearly that such and such a thinker is wrong. How do you navigate the different methodological claims on you as you work?

OP: You know, I don't know if I self-consciously think about this, but I do think that some kinds of issues are best settled empirically, and some kinds of issues are essentially moral and can only be resolved, ultimately, in moral terms. What most academics try to do is to claim that they can separate the two completely. I don't think that that's possible. I think it's important to bear in mind the differences and to use arguments that are appropriate to the issues. My general strategy is that, where certain issues are unambiguously empirical, you use the appropriate data. But there are many issues where it's very hard to do that and you just have to, as skillfully as you can, shift from one orientation to the other. On this I have been influenced, or should I say reinforced, by the philosopher Hilary Putnam, a colleague I greatly admire.[8]

Rituals of Blood

DS: Now we turn to *Rituals of Blood*. The task of *The Ordeal of Integration*, you said, was to take stock, with guarded optimism (even if, as you now say, that optimism has waned a bit). By contrast, the task of *Rituals of Blood* is to explore the persisting problems of interethnic relations. And, again, there is to my mind a provocative methodological gesture. You are self-conscious that *The Ordeal of Integration* is written in a mood of optimism, while the second volume, *Rituals of Blood*, is characterized by a certain soberness. This is how you put it (I'm glossing a little bit): "If the patient has been sick and is being treated, it is appropriate that an

208

RITUALS OF BLOOD

assessment should isolate and emphasize the indicators of progress. Here optimism is justified, even called for. But when it comes to diagnosing the persistent ailments, responsibility demands a cautious, wary eye, anticipating the worst."[1] Now, to my mind, this is a very interesting methodological dictum, and I am again quite taken by the self-consciousness with which each of your texts is constructed. Can you elaborate this particular methodological gesture?

OP: Well, you will note that *Ordeal* was written in a context of a great deal of general pessimism, which had become almost the politically correct norm among sociologists and analysts. And, to an extent, it still is. There've been a large number of works after Obama that are explicitly denying that there's been any real progress. There's a dictum that I got from David Riesman about scholarship (he's one of my mentors in this respect) that you should always go against the grain as an *intellectual* and as a *methodological* stance. That was his strategy, actually, and I've always found it a useful one: *to go against the grain*. I hate conforming, and I always loathe to go with the intellectual flow. So, it was natural that, since I was exploring, in a context of pessimism, victimization, and assertive identity, which emphasized no progress, to show in fact where progress had been made. But then, not to be misunderstood, it doesn't mean that you don't recognize what the persistent problems are. And for me the biggest persistent internal problem, which loomed large and still does, is the problem of gender relations (as I prefer to call it) – relations between persons both outside and within the family and its consequences for young people for the future. And if you look at that – and there you're moving also from broader, more macro issues, toward the more individual level, you see problems that in a way are more *internally* related. *Ordeal* focused on *externally* related problems. This touched on a question we've already discussed, namely: What are the sources of problems and hence the sources of solutions? Things like integration and the degree of political participation are external, in the sense that they are due to racist laws and patterns of discrimination with causes outside the Black community. When you move down to look at the issue of gender relations, you're talking about internal problems, problems that laws and politics are not going to solve. You can do things in terms of early childhood education, some of which I mentioned. But, in the final analysis, the breakdown or, to use the current acceptable term, the "fragility" of the Black family and relationships are the critical internal problems that only the group itself can solve. No amount of laws can ever solve that.

THE PARADOX OF FREEDOM

DS: It's interesting that you are focusing here on what you think of as the internal factors generating the crisis in African American life because it connects to your philosophic view of the crucial role of the moral autonomy of individual practice.

OP: Right. In the end, they have to change – as they *did*. The civil rights movement, for me, was a great example of moral activism generating a social movement. It didn't come from outside. There's no way that liberals and liberal policymakers could have generated those changes. The changes could only have come from an *internal* struggle and change and reform. And it's interesting that they came from the Black church, which involved a quite radical shift on its part. Langston Hughes has an incredible poem in which, almost mockingly, he says, effectively, "Goodbye, Jesus. I've had it. This isn't working. All you're doing is telling us how we should accept our lot prayerfully and pray for the next world."[2] He was mocking the preachers. The Black church was viewed almost with contempt among intellectual elites in the Black community of the Harlem Renaissance period. Understandably so. The church was, in classic Marxian fashion (and it's significant that Hughes wrote that poem after he became a communist), opium for the Black masses. So, it's remarkable that it's that same church that led the revolution. And where did that come from? That didn't come from outside. That came from a real fundamental change in attitudes, a Camus-type situation where those Southern Baptists simply said, "Enough." And at that point they went through this incredible transition, one that was consistent with their theology of non-violent resistance. Something like that will have to happen internally in terms of whatever transformation is going to take place in the dynamics of African American gender relations. The problem right now is really terrible.

DS: In that story of the civil rights movement, what is your appraisal of the Black Power movement? Because whenever you refer to that period you almost invariably *don't* mention the Black Power movement.

OP: The Black Power movement is simply a more radical version of what the church was doing. Although it had some effect, it was far less effective than what the church did. But it was the same sort of thing. In fact, that movement was a deliberate choice to reject King's "beloved" society, non-violent movement for a more activist, politically muscular approach. How much good it did is open to question.

210

RITUALS OF BLOOD

DS: The first chapter of *Rituals of Blood* is concerned precisely with the way the contemporary crisis manifests itself in gender relations. You detail the various empirical dimensions along which this problem exists. Historically, though, the problem goes back to slavery and Jim Crow. *Here* is the catastrophic argument with which your name is very much associated. But, for several decades since the 1970s, this argument was rejected. I was wondering whether the rise of feminism in the 1980s and 1990s helped to shape a rethinking of the family.

OP: Yes, it was significant. If you go back, that change, along with a counter-revisionist position among historians, was saying, "Wait a minute. The Black family in slavery was really not this suburban harmony." This was coming from Black scholars. Deborah White was one of the earlier ones, but several others who were looking at the data said, "This isn't adding up."[3] And then there were several important quantitative studies that also began to question the cliometric claims. The census data were made available somewhere in the 1980s in which the confidentiality rule was removed, so you now had detailed data at the individual level from the late nineteenth century. And there it was possible to show that, in fact, the situation was far more problematic than people had made out. There's Steven Ruggles, an historical sociologist at the University of Minnesota, who was very important in this. His work showed clearly that the cliometricians had gotten it wrong.[4] So during all this time it was quite clear to me that these people were mistaken. But the simple point I've always made to these people is, yes, the data show that, but you were confusing a "demographic unit" with a "family." The fact that you have a man, a woman, and children doesn't mean that you have *stable* gender relations, or even a real family. That Herbert Gutman had counted within his families what's called "away" families, where a lot of the men were living away in other plantations, was weird.[5] Why are you calling *that* a family? To see your wife, you must get permission and walk sixteen miles – you call that a family or a marriage? What are you talking about? And the closer people looked at it, the more problematic it became. For example, the quantitative data were based on the large plantations, which kept records. But most American slaves were not on the large plantations. They were on the small ones, which showed a much higher proportion of problems. Anyway, without getting into details, people began to reconsider and came back around to the position that I never veered from, that a central component of the social, cultural holocaust of slavery was the destruction of the family and the poisoning of gender relations.

211

THE PARADOX OF FREEDOM

DS: Now, your view of the role of gender relations, or the family and the crisis of African American social life, is, of course, *not* uncontroversial. When you speak of the importance of stable unions (call them what you like and constitute them how you may) as a context for raising new generations of social actors, you are taken to be advancing a *conservative* or *normative* view of the family, and especially of partnering. Why is that? Why are you misunderstood, since you make clear in the work that you're talking about "stable" unions? You don't have a view that stable unions should take some particular *normative* shape.
OP: Because people don't *read* carefully.

DS: I'm thinking expressly about that seminar on *Ordeal* and *Rituals* at Skidmore College, organized by Robert Boyers and published in *Salmagundi* in 2002, in which I can hear you continuously trying to reject the interpretations that have been attributed to you.[6]
OP: Exactly. People do not read carefully, especially people who don't know the literature in sociology. They pigeonhole you. As I keep pointing out to people, I'm making no presumption about what *form* the family should take; there are many different ways of skinning a cat and bringing up a kid.

DS: But *partnering* and *union* are crucial. And that's what's absent.
OP: That's right. And that's why the title of that chapter is not "The Breakdown of the Family" but "Gender Relations." I emphasize that, if they had taken the trouble to read it. And, by the way, it's interesting the number of people making this point now. The so-called family, you use that term to cover a complex field of interactions that ought to be broken down: there's the obvious one between husband and wife, but there's also the one between not just parent and child but mother and daughter, mother and son, father and daughter, father and son. You have to go down to that *micro* level. There's an old saying in the Black American community that Black parents, Black mothers in particular, raise their daughters and spoil their sons. Which points to the fact that, even in the mother–child relationship, you have to distinguish between the mother–son relationship and the mother–daughter relationship. There's a lot of truth in that old saying, reflected in the fact that Black women are doing better now than Black men, especially among the disadvantaged. *Nobody* reads that. It's just intellectual laziness. But people are coming around to recognizing it. Because my own position was that the state has a very important role in supporting Black families, whether it's a

single mother trying to bring up her son with huge expenditures for child support, or education, or daycare, and so on. The few people who bothered to read what I said clearly came away realizing that I supported affirmative action. So, they scratched their heads and didn't know what to make of me. Occasionally people would describe my position as a "maverick" one. But I think people have come around, women in particular, to seeing that my position cannot be described as conservative. That's just a simplistic caricature.

DS: But there's something also in what appears to many as the somewhat *counterintuitive* view that it's not poverty itself that leads to the crisis in Afro-American gender relations, but it is gender relations that constitute a trigger for poverty.
OP: One of my favorite economists is the Nobel laureate George Akerlof, who has a great paper on male unemployment and childrearing in which he takes on William Julius Wilson and says the sociologists have all got it wrong.[7] The sociologists claim that men are not marrying because they don't have jobs; but Akerlof thinks it's the other way around – that they're not having jobs because they're not married. It's a wonderful paper, in which he's using very complicated instrumental variables to try to tease out the cause and the *direction* of the problem. In a way, my own position is a little more complicated because I see a *feedback* on how it's happening. The point is, work disappears in a lot of other contexts in which people do not have the same gender response or familial response, as Black people. And, indeed, when work disappears, what happens in a lot of other cultures is that people *turn* to the family. Because two people on welfare living separately (I think I made that point in the book) are under constraints. But if you pool your resources, you're a little better off. Your *household* income is doubled. In a way, what's always puzzled me is why people would ever think this was not problematic. Because the norm for human beings, the default position for human beings, is to have some kind of stable union. It makes so much sense economically and socially. It's obvious that poverty couldn't explain the gender problems in the Black family, since most people the world over are poor but nevertheless don't have these gender problems. I just sat down on my own on this one and never wavered, and they're all coming back now.

DS: Staying with this theme of Black life in America, Black youth, the Black family, the Black middle class, and so on, do you think that the Obama years were transformative for Black America? If so, in what ways?

THE PARADOX OF FREEDOM

OP: It was transformative in the political and public culture of America and of one important aspect of the Black condition. One lingering consequence of the culture of slavery that persisted after the juridical abolition of slavery was the natal alienation of Black Americans, the persistent assumption on the part of the White majority that they somehow did not belong to the body politic, to what defines America as America. The election of Obama was the final triumph over that negation. Black Americans, with his election, became an unquestioned, integral part of America's body politic. And I think that that also marked – coincided with rather than caused – and symbolically proclaimed another public achievement, namely, the fact that Black Americans and their cultural creations were now seen as integral to any American definition of itself. But the disalienation was not complete. The great paradox that America now presents is the near complete public integration of Black Americans with the persistence of their private segregation. They are still socially alienated, still segregated, still, by and large, people "we" (meaning White people) don't live with, people "we" don't go to church with – as Martin Luther King said, 11 o'clock on a Sunday morning is still the most segregated moment in America – people "we" don't network with, with whom "we" share few strong ties, and even fewer weak ones. I discuss this in several recent articles.[8]

DS: Perhaps the first of the killings of young Blacks that begins to dramatically alter America's sense that there is a deepening problem about the value of Black life, the 2012 killing of young Trayvon Martin in Sanford, Florida, took place during the Obama administration. As did the police killing of Michael Brown in Ferguson, Missouri, in 2014. Is this coincidental?

OP: My take on this is that what has changed is the increased value placed on Black life, especially Black youth. For most of American history, cops and others having been killing Black youth with impunity, not to mention lynchings by civilians. However, although the rate at which cops kill Blacks remains over four times the rate for other ethno-somatic groups, the rate itself has declined by 70 percent over the past half century, according to the Center on Juvenile and Criminal Justice. With the public integration of Blacks, reflected in Obama's election and presidency, the killing of Black youth began to elicit far more outrage. This has been reinforced by the Black Lives Matter movement. It is all part of the process that I called the outrage of liberation in *The Ordeal of Integration*.

214

DS: Do you think there has been a White backlash against perceived gains by Blacks in America? There has certainly been a rise of the White ultra-right, and arguably the presidency of Donald Trump was partly enabled by, and partly promoted, this ultra-right. Is White supremacy once again a threat in America?

OP: I have no doubt that Trump's unexpected victory and continued hold on the Republican party was in good part due to White backlash against Obama's presidency and to the wish and hope for a restoration of White privilege and supremacy perceived to have been lost to Blacks and other non-Whites. However, a good part of the populist upsurge is also attributable to the economic decline in the fortunes of the White working class, which is also blamed on immigrants and on globalization. I was always convinced that, in spite of the demonstrable decline in White personal racism since the civil rights movement, there remained a hard core of about 20 to 25 percent of Whites who are White supremacists. Trumpian populism has tapped into both sets of grievances, and the two overlap, but we need to understand the differences. Otherwise we cannot explain the substantial number of Whites who voted twice for Obama, then became die-hard Trumpites and who still insist that they aren't racists. We must also bear in mind that over 30 percent of Latinos voted for Trump and that a non-trivial number of Blacks also did. America is terribly complicated in ethno-racial terms right now and we have to be careful how we interpret what's happening.

DS: In light of what you've said about Martin Luther King Jr, what is your assessment of Black Lives Matter? Does Black Lives Matter embody some of the new values you perceive in Black American youth?

OP: I think the Black Lives Matter movement is extremely important in pushing forward the agenda of Black equality, in making it clear to White Americans that Black Americans are not prepared to settle for half or three-quarters or even four-fifths of the respect and dignity claimed by Whites. It's all equality or outrage.

The Confounding Island

DS: *The Confounding Island*, published in 2019, brings together essays many of which have their sources in your policy relationship to Michael Manley's government in the 1970s. Before we get to

THE PARADOX OF FREEDOM

the essays themselves, what prompted this return to thinking in historical-sociological and public policy terms about Jamaica?

OP: I have long wanted to return and refocus on Jamaica. Of course, I never really left intellectually. I have always taught a course on the Caribbean here at Harvard which kept me up to date with developments there. However, the focus of my research has been on comparative work as well as American ethno-racial issues. My previous book, as you know, was *The Cultural Matrix*: *Understanding Black Youth*, which is an edited volume, about a third of which was written by me, including a long chapter on my view of culture and one that summarizes my understanding of the Black American condition, especially its youth. After producing that work I felt that I came near to the end of my full engagement with scholarship on Black America. I have a slight feeling of resignation, sometimes bordering on melancholy, about my work on American ethno-racial problems, and more specifically about sociological studies on Black America. The failure, the refusal, to see how culture matters interactively with structural factors in accounting for the persisting gaps and problems of Black American life is disheartening to me. As a life-long left-leaning social democrat, I strongly believe in the role of the state in overcoming the many inequalities and social problems that Black Americans face. But I am convinced that some of the most chronic problems, such as violence in the Black communities, educational failures, and fraught gender relations leading to unfavorable conditions for childrearing, require deep self-examination and radical, inner-directed social movements of the sort that inspired the civil rights revolution. And I don't see any of this happening. Indeed, the exclusive and totalizing emphasis on structural factors and systemic racism strikes me as misguided, however well meaning. In more academic terms, I am at odds with the prevailing theories of culture in sociology. I made my position clear in the *Annual Review* chapter on culture, which was the opening, prefatory chapter in that volume.[1] That, I see, as my swan song on the subject. More generally, I am unhappy with two major problems in contemporary American sociology: the parochialism of the discipline and its presentism. Read the leading journals, starting with the *ASR* [*American Sociological Review*], and you will be struck by how obsessively American the articles are, and also by the ignorance of the role of history in understanding contemporary issues.

This is a long detour in answer to your question, but what I'm basically saying is that I think that I have said and thought all I have to say and think about America and its ethno-racial problems.

216

Because I take culture and history seriously, I am grotesquely maligned as a conservative, and I've given up arguing with fellow sociologists, especially White ones desperately hailing their allegiance to racial justice. So, it was clearly time to return to where I started, and where I am least likely to be misunderstood – the Caribbean and especially Jamaica. Don't forget that I began with a deep commitment to an understanding of Jamaica and its problems, and my long departure was motivated by the intellectual desire to better understand Jamaica by journeying to other places and periods. It's been a long odyssey. Indeed, the odyssey almost became the goal, but I'm back. *The Confounding Island* was the announcement of my return, so to speak. It deliberately looked back to the point where I left but also looks at the present and looks forward.

DS: The first essay, "Why Has Jamaica Trailed Barbados on the Path to Sustained Growth?," has at its core a thesis you've argued for some time, namely, the distinctive nature of the Jamaican colonial – and in particular colonial slave – experience. Though superficially similar, Jamaica's historical experience is markedly different from that of Barbados. And not merely in its raw brutality, but specifically in the inability or unwillingness of its slave-owning regime to commit itself to building the institutional forms of a sustainable society. Slave-owners in Barbados, more of a "settler" colonial society than Jamaica, were more committed to these forms; and, consequently, Barbados has a deeper, more successful history of the institutional frameworks needed for social and economic development. Do I have this correctly?

OP: Yes, correct. What I said above is relevant here also. My interpretation was historical, cultural, and institutional. It's taking history very seriously, something my American colleagues are not willing to do, especially when talking about ethno-racial issues. They are dead scared of saying the wrong thing, of being accused of blaming the victim. Here is an example of how studying the Caribbean differs from studying ethno-racial issues in America. If I wrote something similar in America I would have been immediately blasted for blaming the Jamaican victims and for seeming to say positive things about the White colonialists, not to mention for just taking culture seriously. I received none of that from Jamaicans. No one has suggested that I did not fully recognize the racism and slave-mongering oppression of Barbadian Whites. I made it clear that Barbadian Whites were and remain quite racist, ironically more so than those remaining in Jamaica, and that I personally would not want to live in Barbados

THE PARADOX OF FREEDOM

because it's segregated and culturally somewhat dreary. Nonetheless, this should not prevent one from recognizing the consequences of their settler colonialist system and the fact that they ran not only a more efficient system but one that employed and used the Black population in ways that allowed them to acquire the procedural knowledge of the creolized British and local institutions. As for my theory of subaltern cultural appropriation, I think that would elicit howls of outrage from the typical American scholar working on Black Americans. Nonetheless, I could cite many cases of Black American subaltern appropriation, starting with the Black church, the very Christian Black church, which inspired its most important radical movement, the civil rights movement.

DS: A central thread in your argument about Jamaica's failure is the distinction between different kinds of knowledge of institutions – between "declarative" and "procedural" kinds of knowledge of institutions. Jamaicans have declarative knowledge but lack sound procedural knowledge of institutions. Barbadians have both. Can you sketch the nature of this distinction and say something about how these kinds of knowledge are socially acquired?

OP: The theoretical basis of this distinction was worked out in my paper on culture which I mentioned earlier. It is taken from cognitive psychology as well as one important thinker in cognitive anthropology, Edwin Hutchins, whose masterpiece, *Cognition in the Wild*, was very influential.[2] Declarative knowledge is factual knowledge, knowing what a thing or a process is – book knowledge, if you like. Procedural knowledge is knowing how to do things, how to make things work. The favorite analogy is the bicycle. Someone may know everything there is to know about a bicycle, as well as all there is to know about the mechanics of how to ride a bicycle, but with all this knowledge could never ride a bicycle. Not until you get on the thing and practice riding it will you know how to do it. It's how-to knowledge, as distinct from simply being knowledgeable. Hutchins's account of how each member of the crew of a navy ship contextually learned the distributed, procedural knowledge of how to work with fellow crew members to bring these great vessels to shore is an even better example, especially when talking about a group phenomenon such as institutions, because he emphasized the fact that there is a critical distributed aspect of acquiring procedural knowledge. Jamaicans were as knowledgeable as Barbadians about the creolized British institutions on their islands, but Barbadians acquired how-to and distributed knowledge, in how to run an education system, a

218

THE CONFOUNDING ISLAND

bureaucracy, a legal system, a sugar plantation, and of course how to play cricket. Jamaicans know all about cricket and even produced a few good cricketers, and it's not by accident that it was a Jamaican prime minister who found time to write a history of cricket in his retirement (Michael Manley), which no Barbadian politician has ever bothered to do. But Barbadians, with one-tenth of the Jamaican population, has produced far more great cricketers and repeatedly whips the Jamaicans in cricket, not to mention beating the British themselves at their own most quintessentially British game. By the way, the book I am now writing is a short biography of C. L. R James, who has a lot to say about this, and it is part of my intellectual return to the West Indies, in addition to my current work on the reform of Jamaica's education system.

DS: Connected to this distinction is the relative importance of "institutions" and "policies" for sustained development. Your argument is that, whereas obviously both are crucial, good institutions (and procedural knowledge of sound institutional practice) are more important than good policies. Jamaica has had no shortage of good policies but a dearth of certain kinds of institutional learning. Do you think it is unfair to say that you treat the distinction here as though it was merely a technical one concerning certain kinds of practices or behaviors, rather than partly an ideological one concerning the politics of policy or institutions?

OP: It's both. Jamaicans got badly misled by empty ideology. I remember being really bothered by Manley's love of the whole New World Order idea. It sounded good, and he got a lot of praise for it, but this was a highfalutin notion which was best left to politicians and policy types in the First World who were in a position to do something about it, assuming that they wanted to. Also Michael and the Jamaican left got heavily into dependency theory and held on to it long after it was clear that it was of limited explanatory power and was increasingly being contradicted by the experience of developing countries, especially the East Asian Tigers, Singapore in particular, which has often been compared to Jamaica to highlight our failures in development.

DS: It's interesting that one process of institutionalization that you say has been successful in Jamaica concerns athletics – specifically, the institutionalization of the learning process that produces sprinting excellence (Champs is a central part of that institutionalization). Why has this kind of institutionalization not taken hold

219

THE PARADOX OF FREEDOM

where other sports are concerned, in say football, for example? There is a primary school football competition, and the Manning Cup is a crucial part of secondary school life. And why are the institutionalization processes that shaped the reproduction of cricket learning failing now to produce those older forms of excellence of the 1950s and 1960s when West Indians were so dominant? Do you think the decline of West Indies cricket is connected to the decline of the very idea of the West Indies?

OP: Good questions. Regarding the first, about our failure to replicate athletic success in football, it's interesting that, when the Brazilian coach René Simões, who famously took the Jamaican Reggae Boys to the World Cup finals in France in 1998, quit his post, he complained about the failure to develop an adequate infrastructure such as a professional league and the inadequate playing infrastructure such as well-prepared football fields. The success in 1998, he said, was something of a fluke in that the national team had "erected a roof without preparing a foundation," another way of saying there was no institutional support. But that begs the question. You will recall that there is a psychocultural part of my explanation of Jamaican athletic success, what I call our combative individualism, which is found in many areas of our social behaviors – in dancehall sound clashes, in endless arguments at rum bars – the social psychologist Madeline Kerr documented it well in her 1950s book *Personality and Conflict in Jamaica*. The world got a glance of it when Usain Bolt, on the point of breaking the world and Olympic record in Beijing, turned to look at the other runners panting behind him and pounded his chest in triumph. Now my argument is that this extreme combative individualism works well with track athletics, which is a highly individualistic sport, but it is a hindrance in group sports, where players have to harmonize with each other, as in soccer. There is also a very dark side to Jamaica's combative individualism, which undoubtedly plays a part in our high rate of violence. Your other question on the decline of West Indian cricket is a complex matter. From what I gather, the rise of the T20 format in cricket, the understandable insistence by the players that they earn more for their talent and effort, the decline of West Indian collective nationalism, and a lot of individual bickering and tensions, as well the ending of the careers of an amazing collection of talented players who came together between the mid-1970s and mid-1990s, are all factors. It's a fact that many of the most talented West Indian players, such as Chris Gayle, Evin Lewis and Keiron Pollard, prefer to play franchise cricket than for their national or West Indian teams. Can you blame them?

220

THE CONFOUNDING ISLAND

It's sad to recall how relatively little the great players of the past were paid. The great George Hedley lived modestly in retirement. When he retired from English club cricket in 1954 his fare back home had to be paid by public subscription, for God's sake! There is also a view that US sports, especially basketball, pulled away a lot of players who might have been great cricketers. Patrick Ewing comes to mind. He is a local lad who came to Cambridge, Massachusetts, from Jamaica when he was twelve and actually attended our local high school, Cambridge Rindge and Latin, not long before my own daughter, then went on to become a great basketball player. Whenever I saw him play I thought what a great fast bowler he might have made. He always reminded me of the great Wes Hall. Who knows?

DS: Let me step back a minute and ask you a wider question about the character of the essays in *The Confounding Island*. They have a certain form, I think. Each problem you tackle invariably has a historical source – and this source is to be found in the singularly brutal and chaotic character of Jamaica's slave history. Does this make you a kind of historicist? Do you reject that characterization – someone who invariably finds historical sources for contemporary problems?

OP: I don't like the term "historicist," especially since it reminds me of Karl Popper's famous definition of it in his book *The Poverty of Historicism*. One shouldn't confuse historicism with the view that history matters. Historicism, as Popper criticized it, entails the view that there are laws of history, which, like Popper, I don't believe in. However, if you mean that I firmly believe that no social problem can be understood, no social question fully answered, without a knowledge of its origin and development, then, yes, I stand guilty as charged. Indeed, as I mentioned earlier, I am waging a quiet, and losing, war right now against my discipline, sociology, for its chronic presentism, which I think is theoretically and methodologically impoverishing.

DS: On the question of violence and Jamaica's democracy, you emphasize that there is a commitment on the part of Jamaicans to democracy and political freedom. Jamaica's democracy is genuine and thoroughly ingrained, you hold. But, notably, your emphasis is on the *procedural* character of democracy, the regularity of elections, and the continuous rhythm of regime change. But is there a commitment among Jamaicans to a democratic ethos, a commitment, say, to a participatory and deliberative idea of democratic practice?

221

THE PARADOX OF FREEDOM

If we shift our perspective in this direction, what does the problem of violence look like?

OP: It looks damn awful. We are a violent nation, and the problem seems to get worse each day. I dread reading *The Gleaner*. It's all about every imaginable kind of violence, including violence against women and children. However, I'm not sure I fully agree that the democratic ethos entails peace – participation, yes, and I think Jamaicans are all for that. But deliberation, no. And that's true of democracy generally, I'm afraid. That's one of the points I was making in the chapter on democracy in Jamaica. That it engenders violence, especially in changing societies that have stalled or in slowly growing economies. Look at India, the world's largest democracy. And look at what's happening in America. Trumpism has taken over the Republican party. They believe that Democrats traffic and eat infants! And the American left is becoming more and more intolerant of dissent.

DS: I am intrigued by your return to the world of public policy in Jamaica. And I am intrigued especially by your return to policy in the form of advising the prime minister of a Jamaica Labour Party regime, Andrew Holness. I've always thought of you as an old PNP man. What brought you back to policy in Jamaica? How would you characterize the differences between your involvement in policy in the 1970s and your involvement in policy now?

OP: I don't think there is much difference between the parties anymore. I still feel a sentimental attachment to the PNP, but there really is no difference between the policies of the two parties. I still have friends in the PNP and I've been in touch with P. J. Patterson. In fact, he invited me to meet for drinks when I next travel to Jamaica, and I plan to. I've also agreed, at his invitation, to be part of his P. J. Patterson Center for Africa–Caribbean Advocacy, which was launched in 2020.

DS: You have praised Nigel Clarke, the present [2022] minister of finance, and Peter Henry, the former dean of the Stern School of Business at New York University (and author of a book on Third World development, *Turnaround*). What is it about this younger generation of Jamaican intellectuals and public servants that you so admire? Suppose one were to suggest that part at least of the difference between the 1970s leadership and the present is the (seeming) post-ideological character of the latter – they are not driven by the old warring post-independence ideological divisiveness

222

THE CONFOUNDING ISLAND

(whether Black Power or Marxism). I wonder whether you believe that part of the problem with the 1970s is the loud-mouthed ideology that made responsible policymaking difficult. Clarke and Henry are deeply committed, highly gifted, and educated technical people who have answers to real but procedural problems. The issue for them is not ideologies of growth, but results.

OP: Yes. Most definitely. I've become good friends with Nigel and his family. And I greatly admire Prime Minister Holness. They are really smart and deeply committed to the development of the island. And they are men of integrity. Nigel is very special to me partly because of a personal factor that forges a link with my Jamaican past. His father was a very good friend throughout my schooldays at Kingston College. We entered KC the same year, in the same form, and remained in the same forms throughout our schooldays. We lost touch with each other after high school. But decades later, after he had passed, I met his son at a conference, before he went into politics, and we hit it off very well. When we are together I feel a connection with my past, remembering his father, and also a connection with the present and future of Jamaica. I also feel more optimistic about the country, since they are doing such a great job and are still so young.

DS: Jamaica confounds. It has always done so. This is its virtue and this is its curse. This is what fascinates and what repels. This is its source of failure and its resource of hope. Is this your view?

OP: Yes. Completely. It's one of the most perplexing countries on earth. There is so much to love and admire there – the resilience and survival of its people, their ambition and striving, their ironic sense of humor, the earthy wisdom of its country people reflected in their proverbs and folk music, the haunting beauty of its hills and valleys, the passion for freedom and deep if rowdy embrace of democracy, the world-class triumph of its athletes and musicians, the dignity and defiant calm of the Rastafarians, the vitality of its transnational communities. But there is also so much to dislike – the violence, the recklessness on and off the road, the "boastiness" and chaotic individualism, the paternal abandonment, the sexism and killing of women, the corporal abuse of children, the homophobia, the creeping corruption of public servants, the noisiness and disorder, the chronic praedial larceny in the countryside, the grudgefulness of the peasants, which they even sing about – Sammy Dead, Oh! – and the outrageous level of inequality and craveness of the elites, their lack of shame at living so well in the midst of so much poverty and misery, the lingering color bias still there in the marriage patterns and use

THE PARADOX OF FREEDOM

of skin whiteners, the failure of our institutions – these all make me sad, despair, but I still love the place, compelled to it, a home you must leave but are bound to return to, if only to wake up early in the morning when it's still cool and quiet, smell the jasmine and moist greenery, hear the voices of the early risers and the mourning doves.

I've also learned from my own experience that Jamaicans are a welcoming and forgiving people. My intellectual life has been a long odyssey probing the challenges of other lands, though, as you have remarked repeatedly, with Jamaica always at the back of my mind. *The Confounding Island* was my intellectual journey back home, and I've been deeply moved by the reception. Prime Minister Holness welcomed me back with an invitation to his home, where we talked about the book and my earlier work for Manley and the government. Then he asked me to chair the Jamaica Education Transformation Commission, which is the opportunity of a lifetime for a public intellectual. And, to top it all, I've been honored with one of the nation's highest awards, the Order of Merit, which was conferred in 2020. In the expression of thanks that I was asked to make on behalf of all the other honorees that year, I spoke of our nation as a "strong-willed people, fearless, feisty, rebellious, never to be underestimated, small in number but forever *tallawah*," and I expressed the conviction that, in spite of the hand that history dealt us, we will prevail.[3]

The Perspective of an Historical Sociologist

DS: Having been taught by M. G. Smith and R. T. Smith, two anthropologists (indeed, two rival anthropologists), it's interesting that you decide on sociology rather than anthropology at the LSE. Certainly, you have the precedent of Edith Clarke (1926–31). And the LSE had a distinguished Anthropology Department at the time you went there. Given also your inclination to "fieldwork" in urban Kingston (however informal), why did you opt for sociology rather than anthropology?

OP: Perhaps if MG and RT hadn't argued so much and expressed such public disdain for each other, I might have decided differently. But I felt sociology, at LSE anyway, struck just the right balance between history, the social present, and economics for me to make sense of Jamaica and the problems of development, which were my primary intellectual goals. I also wasn't given much choice, since the demographer David Glass, a powerful figure in British academia,

224

THE PERSPECTIVE OF AN HISTORICAL SOCIOLOGIST

decided that he would be my supervisor after one of my other teachers, the demographer George Roberts, wrote him about me.

DS: There are many differences and similarities between you and M. G. Smith, and some of these we've already touched on. But one of the fascinating convergences where approach is concerned is that, for both of you, while history is centrally important, it is not the *final* point of the matter. You and Smith are social *theorists* more so than historians. The point is to understand the relation between the historical past and the social present. Do you agree?
OP: Yes. I think that's a fair assessment. My historical work on slavery moved naturally toward a theory of slavery; so did my work on freedom and my work on culture. Even with my aborted literary career, I was leaning toward a theory of literature. Remember that first formal meeting of the Caribbean Artists Movement in which I theorized about the nature of the novel and where Caribbean literature should be headed, to the horror of John Hearne.

DS: As a sociology, *The Sociology of Slavery* could not have resembled very many other texts existing at the time it was published, 1967, in British or American sociology. At its conceptual heart, *The Sociology of Slavery* is a critique of sociology – not just Parsonian sociology, specifically, but normative sociology altogether, inasmuch as it is a critique of the founding sociological assumption that takes as its starting point the idea of a "society." One could not make this assumption in the case of slave plantation Jamaica, certainly not in the eighteenth century. Is there a sense in which the very stark unnaturalness of Jamaica as a social formation, its patent artificialness, drew your attention to a problem that was at once a problem of history and of social theory?
OP: Indeed. I made that clear in the preface to the first edition of *The Sociology of Slavery* and elaborated on it in the introduction to the recent second edition. The theorist who most inspired me was Thomas Hobbes. Ironically, I was drawn to Hobbes by Parsons, who used Hobbes to pose what he considered the central problem of sociology, indeed of all social sciences, including anthropology, namely, the problem of order. How is society possible? That was a good starting point. But Parsons's solution, culture, begs the questions. Where did culture come from? How were institutions possible? Why did they persist? Jamaican slave society, especially in its heyday during the eighteenth century, posed the question in real, stark terms. It was the perfect case study of a society that started

225

THE PARADOX OF FREEDOM

from scratch in 1655 after expelling the Spaniards, who had earlier exterminated the indigenous Arawaks in the island's first genocide, then proceeded to create a genocidal slave system, the island's second protracted genocide, which existed constantly on the verge of Hobbesian disorder. So, studying eighteenth-century Jamaica was like doing fieldwork on the originating social state that Hobbes could only imagine, although he did point, inaccurately, to a few cases such as the English civil war and, patronizingly, the Indians of North America. He did, more accurately, point to ancient slavery, and did surmise that the slave relation came close to a state of nature. But the ancient slave systems never posed the problem of order that seventeenth- and eighteenth-century Jamaica did. Apart from the one great slave revolt of Spartacus during the early first century BC, they never faced any kind of major disruption, and certainly nothing like the sustained threats to the system which the large number of slave revolts posed, from the beginning in 1655 right down to the last years of slavery with Daddy Sharpe's Baptist revolt in 1832. Jamaica was a society of constant warring, of all against all, in individual day-to-day resistance as well as collective resistance, a society in which rape and violence and degradation were the norm, between Whites and Blacks, slave and free, privileged Blacks against less privileged ones, creoles against what they disdainfully call "salt water Naygahs," and between men and women, which soft-minded modern historians searching for a usable past don't want to talk about, turn their eyes away from. That's historical wokism. *The Sociology of Slavery* has faced a lot of that presentist denial of historical realities from bourgeois historians who are more concerned with their own historical needs than with telling truth to the present and in doing justice to the suffering of our ancestors by telling their experience accurately. Of course, in distorting the past, they distort their understanding of the present. The tragic truth of Jamaican slave society is that the war of all against all ran right through, right down, the entire system. Where the only forms of persuasion and discipline from the ruling and overseer classes were the whip, the noose, the treadmill, and the gibbet, and being chopped to pieces while still alive by the Maroons, it was inevitable that violence permeated relations between slave men and men, and between slave men and women, and even between parents and children.

DS: The idea of a comparative sociology of slavery is not the self-evident next move looking out from *The Sociology of Slavery*. You've said that you signed a book contract around 1973 for what became

THE PERSPECTIVE OF AN HISTORICAL SOCIOLOGIST

Slavery and Social Death. I wonder what your proposal looked like, since you've also said somewhere that the final shape of that book only emerged toward the end of writing it. At what point are you convinced that what slavery needs is a general theory, not just a particular or local one, and a general theory undergirded by comparative methodology?

OP: Look. This was a natural development from the great theorists who influenced me and all other up-and-coming young thinkers of the day. Marxism and Marxist historical writings were dominant. I was a member of the early *New Left Review* group, and when they talked about slavery all they discussed was the slave mode of production. Indeed, I found myself almost on the defensive in my archival study of a single, real slave society, while people like Perry Anderson were being praised for their work on the slave mode of production. I finally got fed up after reading that wildly theoretical work on the slave mode of production by Barry Hindess and Paul Hirst in their *Pre-Capitalist Mode of Production* and wrote a sharp critique of it, which I published in what was my parting publication in *New Left Review*.[1] In addition to Marx, all the other early theorists I read in sociology were comparativists who drew on history for their theoretical works – Weber, most notably, who was to become my greatest influence, Durkheim, Westermark, and, among more contemporary writers, Moses Finley, E. P. Thompson, and Eric Hobsbawm, who by the way, wrote a very favorable review of *The Sociology of Slavery* for the *Manchester Guardian*. I was also greatly influenced by the comparative anthropologists and historians of slavery – especially Lévy-Bruhl and Herman Nieboer, as well as the more contemporary work of David Brion Davis.

My initial intention for what became *Slavery and Social Death* was to write a comparative study more in the mold of Nieboer's *Slavery as an Industrial System*. It was to be more on comparative slave societies at the macro level rather than on the micro-level slave relation, and the plan was to use a combination of comparative statistical studies buttressed by selected case studies. I was very taken by newly developed statistical techniques of contingency table analysis, what became known as log-linear modeling, and that is what drew me to cross-cultural studies in anthropology, especially the work of G. P. Murdock. My proposal to Harvard University Press clearly indicated all this. My first publication in comparative slavery also shows this. It's called "The Structural Origins of Slavery: A Critique of the Nieboer–Domar Hypothesis from a Comparative Perspective" and was published in the 1977 volume of the *Annals of the New*

THE PARADOX OF FREEDOM

York Academy of Sciences on comparative slavery. The subtitle is significant. It was very critical of Nieboer's comparative thesis and marked not only my critique of Nieboer but a turn from the direction I was moving in. Right after that I shifted intellectual gears. I moved down from the macro level of writing a comparative study of slave societies to the micro level of writing about the relation of slavery and the meso level of writing about the institutions within which the relation was embedded. And my model shifted also from Nieboer and Lévy-Bruhl, and even Davis, to the kind of work that Finley was doing, but also at a higher level, to what Marx and, before him, Hegel theorized about in their writings on slavery.

DS: When did you discover George Murdock's sample of world societies? I see from reading the "Note on Statistical Method" that constitutes Appendix A that you are already coding data culled from it in 1974, 1975. So how did you happen upon this resource? Did you come upon it before you started to formulate a global comparative problem? Or was it the other way around: that it was your inchoate formulation of comparative questions that led you to the Murdock survey?

OP: It was, as I indicated above, the latter. I sought out Murdock after getting involved with Nieboer, because what Murdock was doing was largely an extension of the kind of work that Nieboer had done. There was another scholar I should mention, the cross-cultural anthropologist John W. Whiting, who had studied and worked at the Institute of Human Relations at Yale and had collaborated with G. P. Murdock. He joined the Harvard Social Anthropology Department in 1963, coming over from the School of Education, and was a leading figure in the Six Cultures Study of Socialization. I came to know him because I brought over my LSE and UWI assumption of a natural relationship between sociology and social anthropology to Harvard when I joined the department in 1971, not realizing – and later, when I found it out, not caring – that anthropologists and sociologists hardly spoke to each other. I thought that was absurd. The Social Anthropology Department was right under us, on the fourth floor of William James Hall, and we all used the same cafeteria on the second floor, but it soon dawned on me that I was the only sociologist who became involved with the anthropologists. Actually, one of my earliest friends at Harvard was David Maybury-Lewis, who invited me to co-found Cultural Survival in 1972 (along with Evon Vogt and Irven DeVore), a major advocacy organization for indigenous peoples. Through David I became friendly with several

228

THE PERSPECTIVE OF AN HISTORICAL SOCIOLOGIST

other anthropologists such as DeVore and Vogt, whose New Year's Eve parties were a blast. However, none of them had much to do with Whiting. Indeed, the tide had turned against cross-cultural studies in anthropology by the early seventies, especially after the serious critiques of the methods and findings of the Six Cultures childrearing work done by Whiting and his wife. Whiting, who was in his sixties at that time and nearing retirement, was a lonely figure in William James Hall, and I thought that was just silly. I introduced myself and we had regular coffee meetings after that. He was very happy to have a young scholar show interest in his work, and he very generously brought me up to date on everything worth knowing about cross-cultural research and also gave me and discussed tons of materials from the Yale research group – the Ethnographic Atlas, the Outline of Cultural Materials, and most of all the Standard Cross-Cultural Sample, which I used in developing my cross-cultural sample of slave societies. I really liked him and thought the slighting of his life's work by his colleagues was just plain academic bigotry, which I made clear to David, who, as you know, worked in the classic tradition of kinship studies in a tribe he came to own academically, in his case the South American Xavante. David and I just agreed to disagree on this one. His attitude was one of avuncular tolerance for a younger colleague who would eventually come to see the light. I never gave up on the standard cross-cultural sample. I think it's a powerful comparative tool, and it turns out that I was right. There has been a revival of interest in this work among economic historians, and just last year Joe Henrich, the chair of Human Evolutionary Biology at Harvard, published a remarkable study which tested the validity of the Ethnographic Atlas by comparing it with representative data from descendants of the sampled societies – and, lo and behold, the validity of the accounts was confirmed. I was so happy to read that.[2]

DS: One is reminded again and again how important data is for you, the evidential record, and therefore the methodological technologies that help you to organize the data of the historical record. So, you value empirical work enormously, but you would never think of yourself as an empiricist, right? You think of yourself, rather, as an interpretive scholar in the mode of Weber's *verstehen*. How would you describe the relation between data and interpretation that has guided your work?

OP: Right again. Of all my many influences, I'd say that Weber was the most powerful. Like Weber, I search for and use all available and relevant data for the task at hand, with the historical always

229

THE PARADOX OF FREEDOM

foundational. And, yes, an empiricist I am not, by which I mean someone who begins with a body of data or a data set, because it is there and conveniently ready for analysis, then finds a problem to address with it. There is a lot of that in sociology. My way is to begin with puzzles and problems that fascinate me, or that I think need understanding and deeper exploration, and then find the way to solve it.

DS: You've objected to the suggestion that "social death" is an abstract concept rather than an idea that belongs to first-order experience.[3] But even if you disagree with that formulation and the critical edge it assumes, surely "social death" is a kind of *generalizing* abstraction, in that it is seeking to capture, in a *synthesizing* manner, a vast swathe of descriptive world history? At the level at which you want it to operate, it would be hard for it to touch actual expressed experience (however that might have been recorded for the enslaved). You seem to want to hold on to the view that the legitimacy of the idea of social death must derive from its conformity to the authentic experience of the enslaved. But why can't its conceptual usefulness derive (as certainly I think it does) from the interpretive work it does (partly creative, partly analytical, partly descriptive) in drawing our hermeneutic attention to *plausible* rather than authentic dimensions of the lives of the enslaved? By insisting on its experiential character, aren't you allowing yourself to be drawn into the methodological trap of a dead-end discussion? I think one can argue that social death is *good to think with* (as Claude Lévi-Strauss might have said) without assuming that the enslaved themselves told us it was so.

OP: The idea of "social death" has, indeed, evolved as a generalizing concept used in many ways by scholars and to understand experiences somewhat removed from actual slavery and more related to slave-like conditions. As you say, people have found it useful to think with, one of my favorite examples being the distinguished feminist philosopher Judith Butler, who repeatedly draws on it in works such as *Antigone's Claim* and her theorization of precarity, livability, gender violence, and norms.[4] I have no problem with that, since from my twenties I was thoroughly persuaded by Sartre's view of writing, especially prose writing, as a joint enactment between writer and reader. The writer discloses his experiences and understandings of a particular aspect of the world, but it remains half-finished and is only completed by the reader, hopefully a discerning reader. Reading, in this sense, is the enactment of the existential possibilities imagined by the author. Butler has done things with social death that I had

230

THE PERSPECTIVE OF AN HISTORICAL SOCIOLOGIST

barely imagined or not imagined at all. Of course, as the author, I am still free to argue with one or other of these enactments and to say outright that, no, this is clearly not what I imagined and, more definitively, that this was not the way the idea was birthed, and on this I remain the unquestioned authority. As Sartre said, the reader cannot see the words I wrote as I did, since I know and knew my words before they became words, before writing them down. I alone can say how the words and thoughts and things the reader attempts to complete were brought into the world. When misinformed people say that social death is an abstract concept that does not belong to what you call, correctly, the first order of experience, they are presumptuously making claims about the existential origins and nature of the concept. The question here is: How did social death originate? What was its existential origin, what was it like before it was written down, before its birth, which is the same as saying its conception – and language beautifully identifies the origin of ideas with the first moment of creation in the womb – and what motivated the contemplation of its conception?

Okay. Here again then is how [the idea of] social death came into the world. It's going to be a mouthful, but you asked for it. Not long after completing *The Sociology of Slavery*, I began to have serious misgivings about the word "slavery" and its referent, the thing it described. These misgivings were undoubtedly prompted by my first assignment as assistant lecturer at LSE, which began right after I had completed my thesis, and this was to assist the social philosopher and anthropologist Ernest Gellner in the teaching of his course on social philosophy, as I think I may have mentioned earlier. Gellner's book *Words and Things*, which famously attacked the prevailing Oxford school of ordinary language philosophy, was a central part of the course, so I became immersed in the subject overnight, or rather over the summer before my lectureship began. I liked Gellner very much. He was a warm, kind man and I was in sympathy with much of his Enlightenment rationalism, his study of nationalism, and his critique of chauvinism, although I remained fascinated by Wittgenstein, whom Gellner truly thought was writing nonsense. However, what teaching with him alerted me to was the meaning, context, and use of words, on which I gained as much from the linguistic philosophers being criticized as from Gellner's own acerbic criticisms. I immediately began to think of the word "slavery" and the thing to which it referred, which I had just spent the previous three years studying. Very soon the penny dropped. "Slavery." What is this word? What does it really mean? Why have I been studying the thing slavery for

THE PARADOX OF FREEDOM

years without ever once questioning the idea behind it and, of course, the concept, the thought, the history loaded in it? I had unquestionably accepted the word and its meaning in English, but where did it come from and what was it doing to the thing, the referent? The referent? How stable, anyway, was the relation between word and referent? Was my acceptance of a stable and seemingly obvious word–thing relation a kind of linguistic colonialism on my part? The dictionary definition of slavery, which I had uncritically accepted, was the ownership of one person by another. I held on to that definition during the writing and transformation of my thesis into book form, but doubt was planted from my teaching of those tutorials in Gellner's course. Reading Finley and getting involved with ancient slavery, which was widely discussed at LSE because of the presence of my colleague and fellow lecturer in sociology Keith Hopkins (who had studied classics and was to take up the chair in classics at Cambridge, later publishing a definitive study on Roman slavery, *Conquerors and Slaves*), made me increasingly conscious of the deeply Western nature of the word and meaning of slavery, the fact that its meaning originated in the Roman legal notion of the ownership of one person by another.[5] I studied German and brushed up on my French during my first year of teaching at LSE, and I soon became aware of something very odd about the word "slavery." First, the word itself had no linguistic connection with the thing it referred to; the Roman object, slave, was the Latin *servus*, which from the early Middle Ages became assigned to another thing, serf. Digging deeper, I discovered another peculiar thing about the word "slave" – it originated in *sclavus*, the medieval Latin word for slave, which came about because of the large-scale enslavement of Slavic peoples during the Middle Ages. I was fascinated to learn that Africans were not the first peoples to be associated with enslavement by the West. This is what first led me to explore what was going on in the rest of Europe, especially during the Middle Ages, which led me to a third peculiarity of the word "slave." The fact that it is one – perhaps the only – word with the same root throughout the West European languages. All this led me to think that, if I were to get at the meaning of the word, beyond what the slaveholding Europeans have imposed on me, I had to go out of Europe and its orbit. That's when I began reading everything I could find on comparative slavery, of which there were a surprising number of studies. All the late nineteenth- and early twentieth-century comparativists, including Marx and Weber, had been deeply involved with the subject. This included Nieboer, whose work, as I mentioned earlier, I studied in depth. As

232

THE PERSPECTIVE OF AN HISTORICAL SOCIOLOGIST

I also mentioned, my first attempt at studying the subject comparatively was to do so at the macro level, a comparative study of slave societies. I mentioned that I later shifted to the micro level but didn't get into the deeper reasons for the change. This was connected to the linguistic and conceptual problems that had begun to bother me from my period teaching with Gellner. It is easy to get into linguistic and semantic tangles when you pursue a problem comparatively. It's the simple question: How do you know you are talking about the same thing? Is the thing described by the English word "slavery" or the German word "Sklaverei" the same thing described by the Igbo word "igba ohu" or the thing the Korean word is claimed to be associated with that Westerners call slavery? Even if there is a word for slave in the language of the people you want to investigate, how do you know that its meaning has not already been contaminated by the Western dictionary writers and colonialists, not to mention anthropologists, who have gone before you and on whom you are relying in studying the problem? I struggled with this problem even after signing my contract with Harvard University Press to write a book on comparative slavery. As I mentioned earlier, after initially pursuing the comparative study of slave societies, I changed course after publishing the paper on Nieboer, which turned out to be not just a critique of Nieboer, but of the very problem of the comparative study of slave societies. What I did was to down-shift to the study of slavery at the micro level, to the relations of slavery. Why this move? Because the macro-level idea of slave society was too conceptually loaded to study comparatively as a starting project. Later perhaps, but not for my first big comparative work. The construct of slave society refers to a complex social order which I doubted existed in the many small-scale, non-Western, especially African, societies I wanted to examine, drawn largely from the Murdock cross-cultural sample. On the other hand, the micro-level study of slavery as a relation of domination was clearly more feasible, as well as the meso-level study of the institutions within which it was embedded. The embeddedness of relations within institutions is universal. No one will argue with that. My task then was to read all I could on these relations of domination and decide for myself what they really were, and what they had in common if they approached the thing I knew to be slavery from my study of Jamaica.

Now, after this long detour, I can go back to your question. My approach to comparative study is always inductive and grounded. I never begin with a hypothesis and then go searching for data to test it; I'm just not into that hypothetico-deductive methodology stuff

233

and am skeptical of its use in sociology, especially since almost every paper ever published in the *ASR* finds its hypothesis confirmed. Isn't that odd? My approach begins with one or both of two questions: What is it? Why is it? My study of slavery comparatively was motivated by the question: What is it? Are there universal qualities? If not a crisp category, is there a Wittgensteinian family resemblance that I can unearth? In searching for the answer, I soon came upon the understanding of social death, the belief held by slaveholders and often slaves themselves that slaves are the embodiment of three inter-locked qualities that define them as living dead persons, as a nearly universal recurring social phenomenon: the understandings that they did not belong and had no claims of birth in the society (natal alien-ation, I call it) that they were utterly degraded, and that they were under the absolute power of the slaveholder who had the power of life and death over them – which amounted to a living death. This I found at the start of my research into the Western notion of slavery itself. Hobbes and Locke went straight to the point: slavery origi-nated as a substitute for threatened death in war; in Locke, the great lover of liberty, it was justified as a reprieve from deserved death. This sounds at first like an embarrassing rationalization, except that one finds it repeated ad nauseam, by the best and the lowest minds of Europe, to the point where one begins to think they really believed it. In non-Western societies we find it expressed in one way or another; among pre-literate peoples it is often powerfully expressed symboli-cally, such as the Calinago's requirement of slaves that they cut their hair in the style of persons mourning the dead – in the slaves' case, their own living death. So, no, social death is not an abstraction imposed on my findings but the product of what we call grounded theory in sociology: an idea, a meaning, a construct that emerged from the data. Of course, once it emerged from the ground, one begins to think with it, starting with my own reflections. My thinking with social death led me to thinking about the nature and origins of freedom. I found that it was also good to think with in my reflections on Christianity. Others have done so. That, as I said, is fine with me. Sartre had it right. Just don't be simple-minded about how the idea originated and the ways it can be used, including its original use as a way of understanding what slavery is all about.

DS: You've made the distinction between "dominion" and "doulotic" studies of slavery, the former being studies from the perspective of dominant power, the latter, studies from the perspective of the enslaved. I imagine, from your discussion in "Life and Scholarship in the Shadow of Slavery," that you'd think of your work as being concerned with a doulotic perspective. But I might offer a mild challenge to that. It seems to me that what characterizes your work is less whether it is the perspective of the enslaver or the enslaved that you capture and more the character of power you describe – specifically, relations of domination, as you call it (following Marx) in *Slavery and Social Death*. I read your work on slavery as principally asking about the nature of the relations of power that characterized the institution: the almost total power wielded by the enslavers and the almost total powerlessness experienced by the enslaved. But it's the *relation* that matters. How would you respond to that?

OP: I completely agree. But I don't see the problem. Relations of domination can, of course, exist at different levels, but I was mainly concerned with such relations at the micro level of master and slave in *Slavery and Social Death*, and also at the institutional or meso level, especially in my long discussion of manumission. And, of course, it is the meso level that links micro to macro. By the way, don't get me wrong, I do not denigrate the macro level, which is what I meant by dominion studies. I have written a lot at that level in my work on ethno-racial issues in America and in my most recent book on Jamaica, which explores the institutional basis of Jamaica's development problems.

DS: In that sad and telling opinion piece of yours in the *New York Times* of 19 May 2002, "The Last Sociologist," you write of David Riesman, and not only his passing earlier that month but the passing of a whole tradition of American sociology. You link this tradition to others like Erving Goffman, William Whyte, C. Wright Mills, Daniel Bell, Nathan Glazer, and Peter Berger. (Incidentally, most of these were crucial to Stuart Hall and the early New Left in Britain.) These sociologists engaged with subjects of common significance (the contradictions of capitalism, the nature of civil society, the virtues and dangers of individualism, and so on), and they did so in a style that spoke out of who they were as participants in a common world. This sociology has been replaced, you say, by one that aims to mimic the methodology of the natural sciences. When does this shift begin? What precipitated it? Are there trends that make you hopeful for a new sociology of the things that matter, a sociology with that "nerve" of which Riesman spoke?

OP: The trend toward hypothetico-deductive reasoning and the mimicking of the normal-science approach began somewhere in the mid- to late seventies and picked up speed during the 1980s.

THE PARADOX OF FREEDOM

Don't get me wrong. I'm not talking about the rigorous use of data or of statistics, both of which, as you pointed out earlier, I'm very committed to – in the case of statistics, I should qualify to say, when appropriate. I should mention that my closest colleague in the Sociology Department is Chris Winship, the leading statistical and methodological theorist in sociology, with whom I have co-authored several pieces in public sociology. Obviously, statistics doesn't work if you are going after what is subjectively meaningful, Weberian *verstehen*, which requires interpretation. What I'm skeptical about is the normal-science approach that now dominates the major journals. By the way, several major quantitative people are also skeptical of the blind embrace of hypothetical-deductive reasoning. For example, my late colleague Stanley Lieberson, who was as quantitative as you could get, felt very strongly that sociology made a big mistake when it adopted the normal-science approach instead of the strategies used in biology, which more naturally fits with a quantitative approach to the social world. We didn't of course, because of the very bad name that earlier uses of biology had in sociology, social Darwinism in particular. But, as you know, social Darwinism was a travesty of Darwinian thought. Anyway, that's a largely lost battle, although several very smart people have been probing in that direction. The work of my good friend Nicholas Christakis, especially his wonderful book *Blueprint: The Evolutionary Origins of a Good Society*, is an example of the kind of network-based neo-evolutionary theory I admire.[6] I also greatly admire the work of John F. Padgett, whose book *The Emergence of Organization and Markets* I liked so much that Chris Winship and I organized a conference around it, hoping to promote its adoption as the new way to go in sociology. However, sociology is too enamored with the inappropriate model of physics, with normal science, to change course anytime soon. It's a dead end; but who is listening?

DS: I have spoken of you (in the chapter on your work in the book I am completing, *Irreparable Evil*) as a "moral sociologist" and a "public moralist." I think that's what you're admiring in David Riesman. *The Lonely Crowd*, after all, is a work not of narrow academic significance but of public moral import. More than this, it is a call to public moral self-examination. Might this be one way to describe your work on the historical experience of Black folk? Here I am thinking not only of that 1973 essay "The Moral Crisis of the Black American" but, more broadly, of books like *Freedom* and, more recently, *The Confounding Island*. So: What do you want

236

THE PERSPECTIVE OF AN HISTORICAL SOCIOLOGIST

your work to do? What is the challenge you seek to provoke in your readers?

OP: In addition to David, you could mention several of my other heroes and models. Begin, of course, with the early Marx, Papa Weber, Georg Simmel; then, from the Caribbean, C. L. R James, Eric Williams, M. G. Smith; later, from Europe, Moses Finley, E. P. Thompson, Eric Hobsbawm, and Ernest Gellner; and, from America, W. E. B. Du Bois, St Claire Drake, C. Wright Mills, and my former colleagues Dan Bell, Nat Glazer, Marty Lipsett (with whom I taught a course at Harvard before he left for Stanford), from Yale, David Brion Davis and Edmund S. Morgan. It's fair to say that nearly all these models were public moralists and public intellectuals. They were, of course, all scholars first, but their scholarship drove them to reflect on public life and, in many cases, public action.

I want my work to enlighten some of the big issues of our time, such as freedom, democracy, and equality; I want to help my readers come to terms with the great evils of human history, such as genocide, slavery, colonialism, racism, classism, and colorism. I want people to be honest about how the past works in accounting for present outcomes, especially the tragic ways in which the historically oppressed become entrapped in their own oppression. In broader terms, I want people, especially in my discipline, and related ones like anthropology, to take history and culture seriously again. I am as puzzled by persistence as I am by change, and I strongly believe that we cannot come to terms with the latter, cannot bend change to our will, until we understand how the mechanisms of persistence prevent the change we want, and this is a problem I have repeatedly addressed.[7] I want to promote understanding of development and to engage with change. And in regard to my own little part of the world, Jamaica, I want so badly to see the burden of its horrendous past lifted, to relieve the still shocking levels of poverty, to see a reduction of the ghastly scourge of violence, to see the education system work, since it is the main path toward any kind of real progress.

DS: Earlier in our conversation you distinguished between your work on slavery and David Brion Davis's work in terms of the distinction between historical sociology and intellectual history. You have also (perhaps more fleetingly) distinguished your work on freedom from Quentin Skinner's on these grounds. I'd like to hear more about the nature of this distinction, how you see the differences in these contrasting approaches to the past. In some sense, like Davis, you are interested in the meaning of slavery; and, like Skinner, the

237

THE PARADOX OF FREEDOM

meaning of freedom. Is the difference between you and them to be sought in the different understandings or locations of "meaning"? Is there a difference in the way they treat meaning in context? Is there a difference in their assumptions about meaning and structures and institutions of power? Is there a difference in their conceptions of the relation between meaning and the material world? How should we get at the contrast between historical sociology and intellectual history?

OP: Yes. There are some major differences. In the first place, I am not a prescriptivist. I don't believe that freedom is a universal, that it either lies in the hearts of men or is a Platonic universal out there that we strive to understand. I think that both Skinner and Davis view freedom and other constructs in this way. I don't believe that freedom lies out there, because most cultures of the world, before coming in contact with the West, had no knowledge of, or interest in, freedom. Freedom for me is a value, a powerful value, but a value like other powerful values, which people may or may not prefer or may consider other values far more important. I think that freedom was invented, socially constructed, not discovered. So, my task is, first, to search for the social conditions under which it emerged, the forces that generated it. And inevitably it is from social struggles that freedom, like other great values, emerged. Once a value emerges, there is the further question of how it becomes institutionalized, how it acquires valency. The three big mysteries of freedom, once you assume that it is not hovering out there in the Platonic ether or inside the hearts of people, are how it was constructed and, then, how it became a supreme value, for there is nothing in the mere presence of freedom that guarantees that it will become supreme. It is a major mystery that freedom became so supreme in Western culture and politics. Finally, after its triumph, there is the third mystery: What were the forces that ensured its persistence – which is partly what led me to theorize about the nature and dynamics of continuity. We cannot take persistence for granted. Most things constructed in the social universe die away eventually. Freedom is the West's oldest value. How on earth did it persist for so long? Why does it continue to inspire and provoke us? These are questions that Skinner and Davis did not concern themselves with. However, I am not a pure social constructionist. My view is that, once values are socially created, if they capture the public imagination, they are immediately taken up by the student of ideas, who then idealizes them and creates a new tradition, that of discourse on the value. Once this happens we have two interacting traditions of the value, the ideational and the structural, and the two

238

THE PERSPECTIVE OF AN HISTORICAL SOCIOLOGIST

interact with each other, with the ideational sometimes acquiring ascendancy and influencing the underlying forces that are perpetuating it. We see this happening remarkably early in the history of freedom. First the Sophists take it up, begin the discourse on freedom, then Plato moves in and completely reinterprets it and, with aristocratic arrogance, declares that the socially constructed freedom out there in the world is not the real freedom, that real freedom lies inside. And so began the long millennia of discourse on freedom and the idea that the real thing is an essence, a universal, which one can contemplate and mold from the leisure of one's armchair, after which the history of freedom becomes the history of what former wise men, and sometimes women, thought about freedom. This is the history that Skinner draws on and writes about. It is also the freedom that Isaiah Berlin draws on and writes about. For me that's a one-sided, socially disembodied history and theory of freedom. The real history of freedom has to take account of both traditions of development of the value.

It may come as a surprise, but I should point out that my approach to the study of values and beliefs, and of freedom in particular, is in part derived from the *endoxic* method of Aristotle (developed mainly in the "Topics," one of the six works of the *Organon*). Aristotle's method of understanding things, *phainomenon*, was first to find the *endoxa*, which are the different conceptions of it, ranging from the common consensus of ordinary people to the views of the reputable, the mighty, and the expertise of the wise. Aristotle, however, never asked how or by what means the common view, the view of the many, came about. The historical sociology of beliefs, of values, that become not only the common view but reconceived by the wise, attempts to step back and do just that. My view is that all important beliefs and values are socially constructed in the first place by people struggling to make sense of some problematic phenomenon about which they disagree but which all consider important. What emerges first is the common *endoxon*, and only after it becomes entrenched is it taken up by the wise, who then establish their own tradition of discourse on it and in the end may well exercise their intellectual power and authority and influence over the politically and economically powerful, to refashion the *endoxon* in their own terms so that their interpretation becomes the only "true" and "real" one. Sometimes this works and sometimes it doesn't, in which case the ordinary folk reclaim the value or have it reclaimed for them by renegade members of the intellectual elite; or, as in the Middle Ages, by renegade priests who revealed to the serfs the "real" original freedom buried in the

THE PARADOX OF FREEDOM

Christian doctrine of redemption hidden from them; or, in the last years of slavery in Jamaica, in which the Baptist slave deacon turned revolutionary, Samuel Sharpe, anticipated by over a century the liberation theology of Latin America and led his people in the last, greatest, and most momentous of Jamaican slave revolts.[8] And so on. Skinner, Davis, Berlin are experts on the *endoxa* of the wise and powerful. My historical sociology of freedom is the story of both the wise and the ordinary, the powerful and the downtrodden, and the struggles over time to define and reclaim the value in terms that are meaningful to them and their own social status and condition. I consider myself one of a long tradition of intellectual renegades attempting to reclaim the history and meaning of freedom that best resonates with the *endoxon* of the common man and woman.

DS: Well, one final question then, Orlando, a *big* question. You mentioned that part of the reason you are sometimes read as a conservative has to do with your interest in Western civilization. I might say that this interest in Western civilization is a very Caribbean preoccupation. You are in the company of C. L. R. James, for example, and Eric Williams. In James's case, the story of Toussaint Louverture in *The Black Jacobins* is not merely the story of an obscure slave in an obscure colony but the story of a slave who produces *world-historical* action. And so is, as I keep saying, your story of the creole slave Quasheba who revolts – hers too is for you a story of *vast* consequences, not just for a slave in a slave colony but for our very idea of Western civilization. Is that a fair assessment?
OP: Absolutely, yes. So, first of all, the *style* of intellectualizing comes from James, who I told you had a strong influence, as did Williams. It was part of the kind of education I got even before university. I was clearing out my study and I saw this book that I had never returned to the library at KC, Jacob Burckhardt's book *The Civilization of the Renaissance in Italy*. It was all marked up. This was what I was reading when I was *seventeen*. I'm not quite sure why. It was in the library, but why I should be reading it in such detail, with margin notes – at seventeen? Clearly it was a result of the kind of education I was getting there. I was studying British history for my Senior Cambridge (A-level) final exams. Then, later, James and Williams came into my worldview. So, there's no doubt that there was that interest in civilization and how it influenced us. My focus has always been on not only how Western civilization and slavery influenced the Caribbean but also how they influenced the working and lower classes – as opposed to how they influenced, say, capitalism and the

240

THE PERSPECTIVE OF AN HISTORICAL SOCIOLOGIST

elites. You will notice that *Freedom in the Making of Western Culture* is still focused on the slaves and the serfs, the subalterns in all their forms: the structures of their oppression, the counterhegemonic modes of their reactions – politically, culturally, and ideologically.

DS: In a Jamesian tradition. Orlando, thank you very, very much.

NOTES

Introduction

1 See Orlando Patterson, *The Confounding Island: Jamaica and the Postcolonial Predicament* (Cambridge, MA: Belknap Press, 2019), in which, returning to Jamaica after a long detour, he explicitly develops this theme.

2 Orlando Patterson, *Freedom in the Making of Western Culture* (New York: Basic Books, 1991), p. xiii.

3 See David Brion Davis, *Slavery and Human Progress* (New York: Oxford University Press, 1984). For an account of the implications of this for the story of liberalism, see Domenico Losurdo, *Liberalism: A Counter-History*, trans. Gregory Elliott (London: Verso, 2011).

4 For more on the contextualization of Patterson's work, see David Scott, *Irreparable Evil: An Essay in Moral and Reparatory History* (forthcoming), chapter 4, "Fictions of Slavery's Evil."

5 It is interesting that the two significant engagements with Patterson's work are principally in response to *Slavery and Social Death: A Comparative Study* (Cambridge, MA: Harvard University Press, 1982). John Bodel and Walter Scheidel, eds, *On Human Bondage: After "Slavery and Social Death"* (Oxford: Blackwell, 2017), especially the response essay by Orlando Patterson, "Revisiting Slavery, Property, and Social Death" (pp. 265–96); and *Theory and Society*, 48/6 (2019), "Orlando Patterson, his Work and his Legacy: A Special Issue in Celebration of the Republication of *Slavery and Social Death*." Again, Patterson's closing essay, "The Denial of Slavery in Contemporary American Sociology" (pp. 903–14), is of special interest for the way he positions his work.

6 Orlando Patterson, *The Children of Sisyphus* (London: New Authors, 1964). For further reflections on this novel, see David Scott, "The Tragic Vision in Postcolonial Time," *PMLA* 129/4, Special Topic: Tragedy (October 2014): 799–808.

7 Albert Camus, *The Myth of Sisyphus*, trans. Justin O'Brian (London: Penguin, [1942] 1975), in particular, the section "An Absurd Reasoning."

242

NOTES TO PP. 5–11

8 Orlando Patterson, *An Absence of Ruins* (London: New Authors, 1967). Albert Camus, *The Stranger*, trans. Matthew Ward (London: Knopf, [1942] 1988). Another clear influence is Jean-Paul Sartre's *Nausea*, trans. Lloyd Alexander (New York: New Directions, [1938] 1964).

9 Albert Camus, *The Rebel*, trans. Anthony Bower (London: Penguin, [1951] 1971). For a discussion of the relation between *The Myth of Sisyphus* and *The Rebel*, see John Foley, *Albert Camus: From the Absurd to Revolt* (Stocksfield: Acumen, 2008).

10 See Orlando Patterson, "Slavery and Slave Revolts: A Socio-Historical Analysis of the First Maroon War, Jamaica 1655–1740," *Social and Economic Studies*, 19/3 (1970): 289–325.

11 Camus, *The Rebel*, p. 19.

12 Ibid.

13 Ibid.

14 One is reminded here of Frantz Fanon's formulation of decolonization in the famous first chapter of *The Wretched of the Earth*, trans. Constance Farrington (New York: Grove, [1961] 1963).

15 Camus, *The Rebel*, pp. 20–1. For a helpful discussion of Camus in this respect, see Jeffrey C. Isaac, *Arendt, Camus, and Modern Rebellion* (New Haven, CT: Yale University Press, 1992).

16 Orlando Patterson, *The Sociology of Slavery: An Analysis of the Origins, Development and Structure of Negro Slave Society in Jamaica* (London: MacGibbon & Kee, 1967), recently reissued with a new introduction as *The Sociology of Slavery: Black Society in Jamaica, 1655–1838* (Cambridge: Polity, 2022); and *Die the Long Day* (New York: William Morrow, 1972).

17 Patterson, *The Sociology of Slavery*, p. 282.

18 Ibid., p. 283.

19 See also the discussion of "existential rebellion" in Orlando Patterson, "The Moral Crisis of the Black American," *The Public Interest* (Summer 1973): 63–6.

20 Patterson, *Die the Long Day*, p. 30. Scott, *Irreparable Evil*, chapter 4, "Fictions of Slavery's Evil," is principally a reading of this novel.

21 Indeed, in a brilliant episode in the novel, having seduced Benjamin in order both to humiliate him and to extract money from him for her daughter, Quasheba berates him in the most withering and colorful language that illuminates the prejudiced prison house in which he lives – as well as the self-willed and cynical way she exploits every dimension of her condition. See, Patterson, *Die the Long Day*, pp. 56–9. On some of the complexities of the racial order of eighteenth-century Jamaica, see Brooke Newman, *A Dark Inheritance: Blood, Race, and Sex in Colonial Jamaica* (New Haven, CT: Yale University Press, 2018).

22 The character Jason also has allusive significance, in this instance to the Greek myth of Jason and the Golden Fleece. Patterson has been fascinated with Greek and Roman mythology since his secondary school days. I am grateful to Orlando for sharing this with me.

23 Patterson, *Die the Long Day*, p. 198.

243

NOTES TO PP. 11–17

24 Ibid., p. 203.
25 Ibid., pp. 206, 207.
26 Ibid., p. 207.
27 Ibid., p. 211.
28 Among reviews, see especially Martin Bernal's discussion in the *American Journal of Sociology*, 97/5 (1992): 1471–3. With an air of his own kind of expertise, Bernal writes that, while a work of admirable "synthetic" accomplishment, it is nevertheless "fatally flawed ... because the author has failed to transcend the secondary literature on which it is based." Patterson, he says, is a condescending Eurocentric inasmuch as he has "accepted the 'Western' monopoly of freedom and of the 'Greek miracle' in both the spirit and the letter" (p. 1471). But practicing his own version of condescension, Bernal closes the review in the following way: "I am sad to say this about such a distinguished sociologist and authority on modern slavery, but, in this work, I see him as a man fallen among the narrow scholars he thanks in his preface" (p. 1473). In many respects, this is a very sad assessment to read, especially given the trespasses he committed, and was accused of committing, in his daring and controversial work *Black Athena: The Afroasiatic Roots of Classical Civilization* (New Brunswick, NJ: Rutgers University Press, 1987). I myself have written about Patterson's book in this mistaken way. See David Scott, "The Government of Freedom," in *Refashioning Futures: Criticism after Postcoloniality* (Princeton, NJ: Princeton University Press, 1999), pp. 73–7.
29 Patterson, *Freedom in the Making of Western Culture*, p. x.
30 Ibid., p. xi.
31 ibid.
32 Ibid., p. xiii.
33 Ibid., pp. 41–2.
34 Ibid., p. 203.
35 Ibid., p. 363.
36 Ibid., p. 402.
37 Martha Nussbaum, *The Fragility of Goodness: Luck and Ethics in Greek Tragedy and Philosophy* (Cambridge: Cambridge University Press, 1986).
38 See, John Kekes, *Facing Evil* (Princeton, NJ: Princeton University Press, 1990), pp. 196–200. In Scott, *Irreparable Evil*, chapter 3, I offer a disagreement with Kekes on this point.
39 Patterson, *Freedom in the Making of Western Culture*, p. 405.
40 Martin Bernal, as I have mentioned (see note 28 above), would be chief among the doubters. But, for contrast, see the fascinating review by Karl Morrison in *American Historical Review* 97/2 (1992): 512–14, encompassing suggestively a discussion of Patterson's book alongside Donald Treadgold's more conventional *Freedom: A History* (New York: New York University Press, 1990), which appeared a year before. In the end, Morrison too demurs, but his doubts are framed by a recognition of Patterson's interpretive objective. There is reason to wonder, he writes,

244

NOTES TO PP. 17–25

"whether artistic license of brilliant darting eclecticism tends to deny evidence its own voice" (p. 513). Of course, one may well reply that the facts never speak for themselves, that what is called "evidence" is always already a frame of the real. In any case, thinking about Treadgold and Patterson together, Morrison closes insightfully: "Patterson's inventory of the house of freedom includes more unfamiliar entries than Treadgold's. There is reason to ask that some of the more surprising ones be verified. There is no question, however, that Patterson's lens has also refracted more obviously than Treadgold's the sufferings that the ideology of freedom has brought with it through war, persecution, enslavement, and oppression" (p. 514).

41 David Scott, "The Paradox of Freedom: An Interview with Orlando Patterson," *Small Axe* no. 40 (March 2013): 96–242. Besides the interview with Patterson, there are now ten interviews with Caribbean intellectuals published in *Small Axe*, as follows: "The Vocation of a Caribbean Intellectual: An Interview with Lloyd Best," no. 1 (1997): 119–39; "Strategy, Contingency, Politics: An Interview with Stuart Hall," no. 1 (1997): 141–59; "Memories of the Left: An Interview with Richard Hart," no. 3 (1998): 65–114; "The Archaeology of Black Memory: An Interview with Robert A. Hill," no. 5 (1999): 81–151; "The Re-enchantment of Humanism: An Interview with Sylvia Wynter," no. 8 (2000): 119–208; "The Dialectic of Defeat: An Interview with Rupert Lewis," no. 10 (2001): 85–177; "The Sovereignty of the Imagination: An Interview with George Lamming," no. 12 (2002): 72–201; "Counting Women's Caring Work: An Interview with Andaiye," no. 15 (2004): 123–217; "'To Be Liberated from the Obscurity Themselves': An Interview with Rex Nettleford," no. 20 (2006): 97–246; and "The Fragility of Memory: An Interview with Merle Collins," no. 31 (2010): 79–163.

42 David Scott, "The Temporality of Generations: Dialogue, Tradition, Criticism," *New Literary History* 45/2 (2014): 157–81.

43 On the practice of receptive listening I have in mind here, see David Scott, *Stuart Hall's Voice: Intimations of an Ethics of Receptive Generosity* (Durham, NC: Duke University Press, 2017).

44 I am thinking of course of the famous passage in *Beyond a Boundary* (London: Hutchinson, 1963), pp. 116–17, in which James says that what counts is the arc of a life's *movement* – "not where you are or what you have, but where you have come from, where you are going and the rate at which you are getting there."

A Mother's Project

1 *The Gleaner* is Jamaica's oldest daily newspaper. It was founded in Kingston in 1834 by two brothers, Jacob and Joshua de Cordova, and called the *Daily Gleaner*. In December 1992 its name was formally changed to *The Gleaner*, which reflected the way it was known in everyday parlance by Jamaicans. For one of the many references to Charles Patterson's detective work, see the *Kingston Daily Gleaner*, 18 May 1933, p. 21.

245

NOTES TO PP. 25–35

2 One of Orlando Patterson's early short stories is based on an unexpected visit by his father when he was about eight years old. See Patterson, "The Visitor," *Caribbean Stories*, ed. Michael Marland (London: Longmans, 1978), pp. 69–72. The story was written in the early 1960s.

3 On McKay (1890–1948), see Winston James, *A Fierce Hatred for Injustice: Claude McKay's Jamaica and His Poetry of Rebellion* (London: Verso, 2000), p. 44.

4 On Patterson's work on Garvey, see Colin Grant, *Negro with a Hat: The Rise and Fall of Marcus Garvey* (London: Oxford University Press, 2008), pp. 415, 417. I am grateful to Robert Hill, editor-in-chief of the Marcus Garvey Papers Project, for sharing some of the existing archival material on Patterson.

5 The Jamaica Police Federation came into existence in the wake of the labor unrest in 1938 as part of the making of the modern trade union movement in Jamaica. In 1944 the federation was duly constituted as part of the Jamaica Constabulary Force Act to enable subofficers and constables to make representations regarding their interests. See https:// jcf.gov.jm/about-us/history/.

6 Marcus Garvey, *The Philosophy and Opinions of Marcus Garvey; or, Africa for the Africans*, comp. Amy Jacques Garvey (Dover, MA: Majority Press, [1923] 1986); and St Clair Drake and Horace A. Cayton, *Black Metropolis: A Study of Negro Life in a Northern City* (Chicago: University of Chicago Press, [1945] 1993).

7 The Monymusk Estate in Clarendon is one of the oldest sugar plantations in Jamaica and still functions as a rum distillery today.

8 Kingston College was started in 1925. The Right Reverend Percival Gibson was its first headmaster, in which position he continued during his years as suffragan bishop of Kingston from 1947 to 1955. When he became the first Black bishop of Jamaica in 1955, he relinquished that position. He remained bishop until 1967. In 1958, the bishop founded the co-educational Glenmuir High School in May Pen, Clarendon parish, which *The Report of the Jamaica Education Transformation Commission* (2021), chaired by Orlando Patterson, recently ranked as the nation's best performing high school, with Kingston College ranked as no. 15 of the nation's forty-two traditional, largely church-founded secondary schools. In 1962 the great educator and churchman also founded another secondary school, this one for girls, the Bishop Gibson High School, in Mandeville.

9 Alpha Boys School, established in Kingston in the late nineteenth century as a school run by Roman Catholic nuns for wayward boys, became well known for its musical tuition and vocational training.

10 Mico Teachers' College was founded in 1835, through the Lady Mico Charity, as one of four such colleges in the British colonies in the West Indies, Mauritius, and the Seychelles, aimed at the education of the children of former slaves. In 2006 the government of Jamaica upgraded Mico to a university college.

11 Established in 1937 by Norman Manley, Jamaica Welfare Limited built

246

NOTES TO PP. 36–48

community councils in order to support local economies, education, leadership training, and more. Manley negotiated with the United Fruit Company and Standard Fruit Company to initially fund Jamaica Welfare, and the institution operated through the work of volunteers. Jamaica Welfare later became the Social Welfare Commission and then the Social Development Commission, but was replaced by the Hundred Villages Scheme in 1962.

Years of Decolonization

1 Alexander Bustamante (1884–1977) was the founder of the Bustamante Industrial Trade Union and, subsequently, the Jamaica Labour Party. He became the first prime minister of Jamaica in 1962. See George Eaton, *Alexander Bustamante and Modern Jamaica* (Kingston: Kingston Publishers, 1975).

2 See Trevor Munroe, *The Politics of Constitutional Decolonization: Jamaica, 1944–62* (Kingston: ISER, 1972).

3 Frank Hill (1910–80), Ken Hill (1909–79), Richard Hart (1917–2013) and Arthur Henry (1913–2012), known as "the Four H's," were part of the Marxist left of the People's National Party between 1938 and their expulsion from the party in 1952.

4 Aldwyn Roberts (1922–2000), known by his stage name Lord Kitchener, was a celebrated Trinidadian calypsonian. He was part of the first wave of migrants to England, traveling on the SS *Empire Windrush* in 1948. Patterson refers to the song "Victory Test Match" by Lord Beginner, which features the lyrics "Cricket, lovely cricket" and was composed by Lord Kitchener.

5 Hugh Foot (1907–90) served as colonial secretary (1945–7) and governor (1951–7) of Jamaica. He is the author of *A Start in Freedom* (London: Hodder & Stoughton, 1964).

6 On Claudius Henry, see Barry Chevannes, "The Repairer of the Breach: Reverend Claudius Henry and Jamaican Society," in Frances Henry, ed., *Ethnicity in the Americas* (The Hague: Mouton, 1976), pp. 263–89.

7 Aston Jolly, also known as Whoppy King, was a notorious criminal in the late 1940s and early 1950s who gained a reputation for raping women, especially in those spots along the Palisadoes Road favored by couples. On 11 June 1951, Whoppy King came upon Sidney Garel and Bernadette Hugh, two high school students, on the Palisadoes Road. He killed Garel and raped Hugh. King was subsequently arrested, tried, and convicted for the crimes. He was hanged at Saint Catherine District Prison on Friday 4 April 1952. See the front page of the *Daily Gleaner* of 14 June 1951 for the story of his arrest.

Kingston College

1 Douglas Forrest (1908–95) became the second headmaster of Kingston College in 1955.

2 Joseph Vere Everette Johns, known as Vere Johns (1893–1966), was a Jamaican journalist, impresario, radio personality, and actor. His radio

247

NOTES TO PP. 48–57

show "Vere Johns' Opportunity Knocks Talent Show" helped to launch the careers of many Jamaican musicians.

University College of the West Indies

1 It seems to me that there is a book waiting to be written about Aston Wesley Powell (1909–97) and Excelsior Community College. The school was founded in 1931. See www.ecc.edu.jm/.

2 Noel Austin White has belatedly been recognized as a pioneering teacher of West Indian history across many secondary schools in Jamaica, including Jamaica College, Kingston College, and Calabar High School, before he moved to Camperdown High School and later Mico Teachers' Training College.

3 Norman P. Girvan (1941–2014) was a distinguished intellectual, a member of the New World group, and author of many important monographs, including *Foreign Capital and Economic Underdevelopment in Jamaica* (Kingston: ISER, 1971).

4 Hector Wynter (1926–2002) was a Jamaican educator, editor, diplomat, and politician for the JLP. He was born in Cuba and went to the University of Havana. In 1948 he won a Rhodes Scholarship and attended Oxford University between 1949 and 1952 and the University of London in 1952–3. After returning to Jamaica, he taught Spanish at Calabar High School and the University of the West Indies and soon joined the JLP, serving as a senator in the independence Parliament. Wynter became the editor-in-chief of *The Gleaner* in 1976 and used this platform to attack the PNP administration of Michael Manley.

5 The West Indies Federation (1958–62) was an attempt to create a political union between various Caribbean islands that were a part of the British Empire with a view to their becoming independent as a single integrated unit. N. W. Manley and Eric Williams were strong protagonists. The capital was in Port of Spain. In 1961, the Bustamante-led JLP, which was against federation, forced a referendum on the issue, and the majority of the Jamaican electorate voted against it. Jamaica, the largest of the territories, was forced to withdraw from the union. Subsequently Trinidad withdrew, and this marked the end of the federal political experiment, which many progressive scholars and politicians saw as the only viable direction for West Indian sovereignty. See John Mordecai, *Federation of the West Indies* (Evanston, IL: Northwestern University Press, 1968).

6 Allan Isaacs was a stalwart of the early PNP of N. W. Manley.

The Repairer of the Breach

1 M. G. Smith, Roy Augier, and Rex Nettleford, *The Ras Tafari Movement in Kingston, Jamaica* (Kingston: ISER, 1960).

2 See David Scott, "'To Be Liberated from the Obscurity of Themselves': An Interview with Rex Nettleford," *Small Axe* no. 20 (2006): 164–5.

3 In August 1999, the institute was renamed the Sir Arthur Lewis Institute for Social and Economic Studies (SALISES).

248

NOTES TO PP. 57–59

4 A history is waiting to be written on the development of ISER. In the meantime, see Charles Carnegie's important study "The Fate of Ethnography: Native Social Science in the English-Speaking Caribbean," *New West Indian Guide* 66/1–2 (1992): 5–25. Michael Garfield Smith (1921–93), MG affectionately, was a poet and anthropologist. He conducted research in Nigeria, Jamaica, and Grenada. His various conceptualizations of pluralism are embodied in *The Plural Society in the West Indies* (Berkeley: University of California Press, 1965). His great rival was Raymond T. Smith (1925–2015), an English anthropologist who conducted fieldwork in British Guiana and Jamaica. He was the author of many books, but none more famous than the early study *The Negro Family in British Guiana* (London: Routledge & Kegan Paul, 1956). Lloyd Braithwaite (1919–95) was a Trinidadian sociologist and the author of the very important study "Social Stratification in Trinidad: A Preliminary Analysis," *Social and Economic Studies* 2/2–3 (1953): 5–175. Sir Alister McIntyre (1932–2019) was a Grenadian economist of large distinction regionally and internationally. Educated at the London School of Economics, he was director of the ISER between 1967 and 1974, when he was appointed secretary-general of CARICOM. McIntyre subsequently served as the vice-chancellor of the University of the West Indies between 1988 and 1998. George W. Roberts (b. 1918) was a Grenadian demographer who is recognized for his contribution to the development of censuses in the West Indies. He coordinated the 1970 census that was conducted in fifteen Caribbean countries. Roberts is perhaps best known for his book *The Population of Jamaica* (Cambridge: Cambridge University Press, 1957).

5 Archibald Wickeramaraja Singham (1932–91), known to most as Archie Singham or A. W. Singham, was a political scientist. He was born in Burma to Sri Lankan parents and educated in Sri Lanka and the US, gaining his PhD from the University of Michigan. He was one of the founding members of the Department of Government at the University of the West Indies, Mona, where he taught from 1960 until 1970. His best-known book is his study of Grenada's Eric Gairy, *The Hero and the Crowd in a Colonial Polity* (New Haven, CT: Yale University Press, 1968). After his departure from Jamaica, Singham became a scholar of the non-aligned movement. See, in particular, his book with Shirley Hune, *Non-Alignment in an Age of Alignments* (London: Zed Press, 1986).

6 David Edwards, *An Economic Study of Small Farming in Jamaica* (Kingston: ISER, 1961).

The Rise of the Social Sciences

1 Madeline Kerr, *Personality and Conflict in Jamaica* (Liverpool: Liverpool University Press, 1952); Edith Clarke, *My Mother Who Fathered Me: A Study of the Family in Three Selected Communities in Jamaica* (London: Allen & Unwin, 1957).

2 William Macmillan, *Warning from the West Indies: A Tract for Africa and the Empire* (London: Faber & Faber, 1936). *The Report of West*

249

NOTES TO PP. 59–69

India Royal Commission, also known as the Moyne Report, was commissioned by the British government to investigate the underlying reasons for labor protests and rebellions in the colonial Caribbean between 1934 and 1938. The commission was led by Lord Moyne and, though completed in 1938, not published until 1945, after the war, because it was feared that its exposure of the poor living conditions of Caribbean people would be damaging to Britain's reputation.

3 T. S. Simey, *Welfare and Planning in the West Indies* (Oxford: Oxford University Press, 1946).

4 Douglas Hall (1920–99) was an economic historian best known for his books *Free Jamaica, 1838–1865: An Economic History* (New Haven, CT: Yale University Press, 1959) and *In Miserable Slavery: Thomas Thistlewood in Jamaica, 1750–1786* (Kingston: University of the West Indies Press, 1998).

5 See Douglas Hall, *A Man Divided: Michael Garfield Smith, Jamaican Poet and Anthropologist, 1921–1993* (Kingston: University of the West Indies Press, 1997).

6 Vera Rubin (1911–85) received her PhD from Columbia University in 1952. She founded the Research Institute for the Study of Man in 1955. For biographical details, see Lucie Wood Saunders, "Vera Dourmashkin Rubin," in Ute Gacs, Aisha Khan, Jerrie McIntyre, and Ruth Weinberg, eds, *Women Anthropologists: A Biographical Dictionary* (New York: Greenwood Press, 1988), pp. 316–21.

7 See David Scott, "The Vocation of an Intellectual: An Interview with Lloyd Best," *Small Axe* no. 1 (1997): 119–39, at p. 123.

8 Carlyle Dunkley (1939–2017) was a distinguished trade unionist who led the PNP's National Workers Union in the 1970s. In the second Michael Manley administration, he served as minister of public utilities and transport (1979–80) and subsequently, minister of national security (1980).

The London School of Economics

1 Eric Anthony Abrahams (1940–2011) was a public servant and broadcaster. He was director of tourism (1970–5), a member of the Senate (1977) and House of Representatives (1980–9), and minister of tourism (1980–4). He is perhaps best known as one of the founders in 1992 of "The Breakfast Club," a popular morning current affairs radio broadcast.

2 Stuart Hall was also a Rhodes Scholar, and he was not White.

3 Michael Manley (1924–97) was a student at the LSE between 1945 and 1949. Famously he was much influenced there by Harold Laski.

4 On the West Indian Student Union, see Lloyd Braithwaite, *Colonial West Indian Students in Britain* (Kingston: University of the West Indies Press, 2001).

5 Elsa Goveia (1925–80) completed her PhD at the University of London; Douglas Hall (1920–99) completed a masters in economics at the University of Toronto and his PhD at the LSE, working with F. J. Fisher.

250

NOTES TO PP. 69–91

6 See Stuart Hall, "The First New Left: Life and Times," in Oxford University Socialist Discussion Group, ed., *Out of Apathy: Voices of the New Left, Thirty Years On* (London: Verso, 1989).
7 Orlando Patterson, "Ras Tafari: Cult of Outcasts," *New Society*, 12 November 1964, pp. 15–17.
8 Orlando Patterson, "On Slavery and Slave Formations," *New Left Review*, no. 117 (1979): 31–67.
9 See Orlando Patterson, "The Alien," *New Left Review*, no. 33 (1965): 82–92.
10 For another account of the James study group, see Walter Rodney, *Walter Rodney Speaks: The Making of an African Intellectual* (Trenton, NJ: Africa World Press, 1990), 28–9. Patterson is presently under contract with Penguin for a short biography of C. L. R. James.

The Children of Sisyphus
1 Leon Festinger, Henry W. Riecken, and Stanley Schachter, *When Prophecy Fails: A Social and Psychological Study of a Modern Group that Predicted the Destruction of the World* (New York: Harper, 1964).
2 Rex Nettleford, "African Redemption: The Rastafari and the Wider Society, 1959–1969," in *Mirror, Mirror: Identity, Race, and Protest in Jamaica* (Kingston: Sangster & Collins, 1970), pp. 42–3.
3 Orlando Patterson, "Ras Tafari: Cult of Outcasts," *New Society*, 12 November 1964, p. 17.
4 Mortimo Planno (1925–2006) was a Rastafarian leader of renown and large influence. He is perhaps best remembered for his role in quieting the massive crowds that swarmed onto the tarmac to greet the visiting Emperor Haile Selassie when the latter visited Jamaica in April 1966.
5 Famously, Haile Selassie granted land at Shashamane, a town in the Oromo region of Ethiopia, for members of the Ethiopian World Federation (EWF). The EWF was started by the Ethiopian government to mobilize the African diaspora to support Ethiopia against the Italian invasion of 1935–41. Caribbean EWF members began to settle in Shashamane in the 1950s, and the first Rastafarian migration to the area dates back to 1964. Rastafarians continued to use the land grants to repatriate to Shashamane after Selassie's visit to Jamaica in 1966.
6 For the review of *The Children of Sisyphus*, see the *Observer*, 15 March 1964, p. 27. The Longman 1982 reissue of the novel was reviewed by the British novelist and poet Robert Nye in the *Guardian*, 3 February 1983.
7 See Ferdinand de Saussure, *Course in General Linguistics*, trans. Wade Baskin (New York: Columbia University Press, 2011).
8 C. L. R. James, "Rastafari at Home and Abroad," *New Left Review*, no. 25 (1964): 74–6.

The Sociology of Slavery
1 Eric Williams, *Capitalism and Slavery* (Chapel Hill: University of North Carolina Press, 1944); Elsa Goveia, *Slave Society in the British Leeward*

251

NOTES TO PP. 91–98

Islands at the End of the Eighteenth Century (New Haven, CT: Yale University Press, 1965).

2 C. L. R. James, *The Black Jacobins: Toussaint L'Ouverture and the San Domingo Revolution* (London: Secker & Warburg, 1938).

3 Philip D. Curtin, *Two Jamaicas: The Role of Ideas in a Tropical Colony, 1830–1865* (Cambridge, MA: Harvard University Press, 1955).

4 See Edward Brathwaite, "Jamaican Slave Society: A Review," *Race* 9/3 (1968): 331–42.

5 Edward Kamau Brathwaite, *The Development of Creole Society in Jamaica, 1770–1820* (Oxford: Oxford University Press, 1971).

6 See Archie Singham, "C. L. R. James on the Black Jacobin Revolution in San Domingo – Notes Toward a Theory of Black Politics," *Savacou* 1 (June 1970): 82–96.

7 Orlando Patterson, "Frantz Fanon: My Hope and Hero," *New World Quarterly* 2/3–4, Guyana Independence Issue (1966): 93–5.

8 Orlando Patterson, "Slavery and Slave Revolts," *Social and Economic Studies* 19/3 (1970): 289–325; repr. in Richard Price, ed., *Maroon Societies: Rebel Slave Communities in the Americas* (New York: Anchor Books, 1973), pp. 246–92.

9 In this respect, see the story Patterson tells about his encounter with R. D. Laing in the introduction, "Life and Scholarship in the Shadow of Slavery," in *The Sociology of Slavery: Black Society in Jamaica, 1655–1838* (Cambridge: Polity, 2022), p. x.

10 Stanley Elkins, *Slavery: A Problem in American Institutional and Intellectual Life* (Chicago: University of Chicago Press, 1959). And, for the debate, see Ann Lane, *The Debate over "Slavery": Stanley Elkins and His Critics* (Urbana: University of Illinois Press, 1971). For more on Elkins, see Richard King, "Domination and Fabrication: Re-thinking Stanley Elkins' *Slavery*," *Slavery & Abolition* 22/2 (2001): 1–28.

11 Ulrich Bonnell Phillips, *American Negro Slavery* (Boston: D. Appleton, 1918); and Kenneth Stampp, *The Peculiar Institution: Slavery in the Ante-Bellum South* (New York: Knopf, 1956).

12 Orlando Patterson, preface (pp. ix–xiii) and "John Hope Franklin: The Man and His Works," (pp. 118–30), both in Kenneth Mack and Guy-Uriel Charles, eds, *The New Black: What Has Changed – and What Has Not – with Race in America* (New York: New Press, 2013).

13 Phillips wrote a well-known essay on slavery in Jamaica: "A Jamaica Slave Plantation," *American Historical Review* 19/3 (1914): 543–58.

14 This view of Jamaica as a distinctively brutal and destructive slave formation is echoed in Trevor Burnard, *Mastery, Tyranny, and Desire: Thomas Thistlewood and his Slaves in the Anglo-Jamaican World* (Chapel Hill: University of North Carolina Press, 2004) and, more recently, a volume of collected essays, *Jamaica in the Age of Revolution* (Philadelphia: University of Pennsylvania Press, 2020).

15 Orlando Patterson, "Context and Choice in Ethnic Allegiance: A Theoretical Framework and Caribbean Case Study," in Nathan Glazer

252

NOTES TO PP. 98–109

and Daniel P. Moynihan, eds, *Ethnicity: Theory and Experience* (Cambridge, MA: Harvard University Press, 1975), pp. 305–49.

16 Abram Kardiner and Lionel Ovesey, *The Mark of Oppression: Explorations in the Personality of the American Negro* (New York: W. W. Norton, 1951).

17 See Tim Barringer and Gillian Forester, eds, *Art and Emancipation in Jamaica: Isaac Mendes Belisario and His Worlds* (New Haven, CT: Yale Center for British Art, 2007).

18 See Philip Wright, ed., *Lady Nugent's Journal of Her Residence in Jamaica from 1801 to 1805* (Kingston: University of the West Indies Press, 2002).

19 James C. Scott, *Domination and the Arts of Resistance: Hidden Transcripts* (New Haven, CT: Yale University Press, 1990), p. 24.

20 Orlando Patterson, "Slavery and Slave Revolts: A Socio-Historical Analysis of the First Maroon War, Jamaica 1655–1740," *Social and Economic Studies* 19/3 (1970): 289–325; repr. in Richard Price, ed., *Maroon Societies: Rebel Slave Communities in the Americas* (New York: Anchor Books, 1973).

21 See Eugene Genovese, *From Rebellion to Revolution: Afro-American Slave Revolts in the Making of the Modern World* (Baton Rouge: Louisiana University Press, 1979), p. 160.

22 For a recent vivid study, see Tom Zoellner, *Island on Fire: The Revolt that Ended Slavery in the British Empire* (Cambridge, MA: Harvard University Press, 2020).

23 See Douglas Hall, *In Miserable Slavery: Thomas Thistlewood in Jamaica, 1750–1786* (Kingston: University of the West Indies Press, 1998).

24 Patterson is referring to Trevor Burnard, *Mastery, Tyranny, and Desire.*

25 M. G. Smith, Introduction to Clarke, *My Mother Who Fathered Me: A Study of the Family in Three Selected Communities in Jamaica* (2nd edn, London: Allen & Unwin, 1966).

26 Orlando Patterson, "Why Has Jamaica Trailed Barbados on the Path to Sustained Growth?" in *The Confounding Island: Jamaica and the Postcolonial Predicament* (Cambridge, MA: Belknap Press, 2019), pp. 21–119.

The Caribbean Artists Movement

1 See Anne Walmsley, *The Caribbean Artists Movement, 1966–1972: A Documentary History* (London: New Beacon Books, 1992). This is the definitive history of CAM.

2 On Ronald Moody (1900–84), John La Rose (1927–2006), and Aubrey Williams (1926–90), see ibid.

3 Andrew Salkey, *A Quality of Violence* (London: New Authors, 1959).

4 Dennis Scott (1939–91) was a Jamaican poet, playwright, actor, and dancer, best remembered perhaps for his prize-winning volume *Uncle Time* (Pittsburgh: University of Pittsburgh Press, 1973). He was head of the directing program at the Yale School of Drama from 1986 until his death.

253

NOTES TO PP. 109–119

5 Edward Brathwaite, "The Caribbean Artists Movement," *Caribbean Quarterly* 14/1–2 (1968): 57–9.
6 See Andrew Salkey, *Escape to an Autumn Pavement* (London: Hutchinson, 1960); and Salkey, ed., *Island Voices: Stories from the West Indies* (New York: Liveright, 1970), containing Patterson's stories "The Very Funny Man: A Tale in Two Moods" (pp. 133–8) and "One for a Penny" (pp. 139–45).
7 Orlando Patterson, "Twilight of a Dark Myth: Assessment of the Social Philosophy and Poetry of Negritude," *Times Literary Supplement* (special Commonwealth edition), no. 3316 (16 September 1965): 805–6.
8 See Walmsley, *The Caribbean Artists Movement*, pp. 49–50.
9 Louis James, ed., *The Islands in Between* (Oxford: Oxford University Press, 1968).
10 See Gordon Rohlehr, "A Literary Friendship: Selected Notes on the Correspondence with Kamau Brathwaite," *Small Axe* no. 67 (2022): 124–44.
11 John Hearne (1926–94) was a Jamaican novelist, journalist, and teacher. His first novel, *Voices Under the Window* (London: Faber & Faber, 1955), won the John Llewellyn Rhys Prize in 1956, making him the first Caribbean author to win a major British literary prize. See Shivaun Hearne, *John Hearne's Life and Fiction: A Critical Biographical Study* (Kingston: University of the West Indies Press, 2013).
12 See Gordon Rohlehr's memoir, *Musings, Mazes, Muses, Margins* (Leeds: Peepal Tree Press, 2020).
13 Kamau Brathwaite, "Jazz and the West Indian Novel," in *Roots* (Ann Arbor: University of Michigan Press, 1993), pp. 55–110. The essay first appeared over three issues of the journal *Bim*, 44 (1967), 45 (1967), and 46 (1968).

An Absence of Ruins
1 Derek Walcott, "The Royal Palms ... an Absence of Ruins," *London Magazine* 1/11 (1962): 12–13.
2 Orlando Patterson, *An Absence of Ruins* (London: Hutchinson, 1967), p. 159.
3 Orlando Patterson, "Toward a Future That Has No Past," *The Public Interest* no. 27 (1972): 25–62. *The Public Interest* (1965–2005) was a quarterly public policy journal founded by Daniel Bell and Irving Kristol. It became a leading neoconservative journal on political economy and culture, aimed at a readership of journalists, scholars, and policymakers.
4 See Anne Walmsley, *The Caribbean Artists Movement, 1966–1972: A Documentary History* (London: New Beacon Books, 1992), p. 75.
5 Ibid., p. 123.
6 Lucille Mathurin Mair (1924–2009) was a Jamaican historian and diplomat who pioneered the study of women and slavery. Her PhD dissertation, written under the supervision of Elsa Goveia and defended in 1974, was finally published as *A Historical Study of Women in Jamaica,*

NOTES TO PP. 119–128

1655–1844 (Kingston: University of the West Indies Press, 2006). For details, see Verene Shepherd, *Lucille Mathurin Mair* (Kingston: University of the West Indies Press, 2020).
7 Morris Cargill (1914–2000) was a Jamaican lawyer, businessman, planter, journalist, and novelist of controversial and largely conservative cultural, and right-wing political, views. An associate of John Hearne's, he was for many years a columnist for *The Gleaner*. See his memoir, *Jamaica Farewell* (New York: Barricade Books, 1995).
8 Jan Carew, *Moscow Is Not My Mecca* (London: Secker & Warburg, 1964). Carew died on 6 December 2012.

Returning Home
1 In 1962, with independence, UCWI ceased being a college of the University of London and became its own independent entity, the University of the West Indies (UWI). On the history of the university, see Philip Sherlock and Rex Nettleford, *The University of the West Indies: A Caribbean Response to the Challenge of Change* (Kingston: Macmillan Caribbean, 1990).
2 Perry Anderson, *Lineages of the Absolutist State* (London: New Left Books, 1974) and *Passages from Antiquity* (London: New Left Books, 1974).
3 Donald Sangster (1911–67) was a Jamaican solicitor and JLP politician. He became acting prime minister in February 1964 when Alexander Bustamante fell ill and, subsequently, prime minister in February 1967. However, he was soon stricken with illness and died in April that same year. Hugh Lawson Shearer, ON OJ PC (1923–2004), was a Jamaican trade unionist and JLP politician who served as the third prime minister of Jamaica. His portrait appears on the J$5000 banknote.
4 Edward Seaga (1930–2019) was a Jamaican politician who served as the leader of the JLP (1974–2005) and fifth prime minister of Jamaica (1980–9). He is the author of a two-volume memoir, *Edward Seaga: My Life and Leadership*, vol. I: *Clash and Ideologies, 1930–1980* (Oxford: Macmillan, 2009); and vol. II: *Hard Road to Travel, 1980–2008* (Oxford: Macmillan, 2010). See also Patrick Bryan's biography, *Edward Seaga and the Challenges of Modern Jamaica* (Kingston: University of the West Indies Press, 2009).
5 Sir Philip Sherlock (1902–2000) was a Jamaican educator, historian, social worker, and poet. He was a part of the Irvine Commission that set up the University College of the West Indies and became vice-chancellor of its successor, the University of the West Indies, in 1964, following the retirement of Sir Arthur Lewis.
6 Gladstone Mills (1920–2004) was a Jamaican scholar, cricketer, and public servant. See Mills, *Grist for the Mills: Reflections on a Life* (Kingston: Ian Randle, 1994).
7 The conference, "Slave Studies: Directions in Current Scholarship," was held in Waterloo, Ontario, in March 1979. See Michael Craton,

255

NOTES TO PP. 128–143

ed., "Roots and Branches: Current Directions in Slave Studies," *Historical Reflections/Réflexions Historiques* 6/1 (1979), special issue. Patterson's essay was not published, but see his commentary (pp. 287–92) on Walter Rodney's essay "Slavery and Underdevelopment" (pp. 275–86).

8 Rodney was assassinated on 13 June 1980 in Georgetown, Guyana. He was thirty-eight years old. For an account of his life and work, see Rupert Lewis, *Walter Rodney's Intellectual and Political Thought* (Detroit: Wayne State University Press, 1998).

Not Much of a Joiner

1 George Beckford (1934–90) was a Jamaican political economist best remembered for his book *Persistent Poverty: Underdevelopment in Plantation Economies of the Third World* (New York: Oxford University Press, 1972). See Robert A. Hill, "From New World to Abeng: George Beckford and the Horn of Black Power in Jamaica, 1968–1970," *Small Axe* no. 24 (2007): 1–15.

2 See Obika Gray, *Radicalism and Social Change in Jamaica, 1960–1972* (Knoxville: University of Tennessee Press, 1991), chap. 5.

3 See Orlando Patterson, foreword to Rachel Manley, *Slipstream: A Daughter Remembers* (Toronto: Key Porter, 2000), pp. 11–17.

4 Sir Robert Kirkwood (1904–84) was an English businessman who was the managing director of the West Indies Sugar Company and the chairman of the Jamaica Sugar Manufacturers. He was the nephew of Lord Lyle of Tate and Lyle, the British sugar company.

5 D. K. Duncan (1940–2020) was a prominent member of the left of the PNP in the 1970s. He was appointed national organizer in 1972 and general secretary in 1974. He is often thought of as the mastermind of the PNP landslide election victory in 1976. He was appointed minister of national mobilization in January 1977.

6 See Orlando Patterson, "Into the Dark," *Jamaica Journal* 2/1 (1968): 62–8.

Die the Long Day

1 Orlando Patterson, *Die the Long Day* (New York: William Morrow, 1972), p. 30.

2 Albert Camus, *The Rebel*, trans. Anthony Bower (London: Penguin, [1951] 1971), pp. 13–22.

3 H. G. de Lisser, *The White Witch of Rosehall* (London: Ernest Benn, 1929).

Arrival at Harvard

1 Ewart Guinier (1911–90), born in Panama of Jamaican parents, was the first chairman of the Department of Afro-American Studies at Harvard University, assuming the position in 1969.

2 On the making of Black studies in the United States, see Fabio Rojas, *From Black Power to Black Studies: How a Radical Social Movement*

NOTES TO PP. 143–156

Became an Academic Discipline (Baltimore: Johns Hopkins University Press, 2007).

3 Melville J. Herskovits, "Method and Theory in Afroamerican Studies," *Phylon* 7/4 (1946): 337–54.

4 Orlando Patterson, "Toward a Future That Has No Past," *The Public Interest* no. 27 (1972): 25–62, and "Rethinking Black History," *Harvard Educational Review* 41/3 (1971): 229–304.

5 Orlando Patterson, "Twilight of a Dark Myth: Assessment of the Social Philosophy and Poetry of Negritude," *Times Literary Supplement* (special Commonwealth edition), no. 3316 (16 September 1965): 805–6. See Orlando Patterson, "Ras Tafari: Cult of Outcasts," *New Society*, 12 November 1964, pp. 15–17.

6 Ernest Gellner, *Thought and Change* (London: Weidenfeld & Nicolson, 1965).

7 See Perry Anderson, "Science, Politics, Enchantment," in John Hall and I. C. Jarvie, eds, *Essays on Power, Wealth, and Belief* (Cambridge: Cambridge University Press, 1992), pp. 187–212.

Engaging Black America

1 Orlando Patterson, "The Moral Crisis of the Black American," *The Public Interest*, no. 32 (1973): 43–69.

2 See Nathan Glazer and Daniel Patrick Moynihan, *Beyond the Melting Pot: The Negroes, Puerto Ricans, Jews, Italians, and Irish of New York City* (Cambridge, MA: MIT Press, 1963), and Orlando Patterson, "Context and Choice in Ethnic Allegiance: A Theoretical Framework and Caribbean Case Study," in Glazer and Moynihan, eds, *Ethnicity: Theory and Experience* (Cambridge, MA: Harvard University Press, 1975), pp. 305–49.

3 William Ryan, *Blaming the Victim* (New York: Pantheon, 1971).

4 Daniel Bell, *The End of Ideology* (Glencoe, IL: Free Press, 1960).

5 Orlando Patterson, *Ethnic Chauvinism: The Reactionary Impulse* (New York: Stein & Day, 1977).

6 See Orlando Patterson, "On Guilt, Relativism, and Black–White Relations," *American Scholar* 43/1 (1973): 122–32.

7 Tommie Shelby, *We Who Are Dark: The Philosophical Foundations of Black Solidarity* (Cambridge, MA: Belknap Press, 2005). Also see Orlando Patterson, "Being and Blackness," *New York Times Book Review*, 8 January 2006: 10 (www.nytimes.com/2006/01/08/books/review/being-and-blackness.html).

8 See Paul Gilroy, *Against Race: Imagining Political Culture beyond the Color Line* (Cambridge, MA: Belknap Press, 2002).

9 See Henry Louis Gates Jr, *Thirteen Ways of Looking at a Black Man* (New York: Vintage, 1998), p. 75.

10 Colin Powell, *My American Journey*, with Joseph E. Persico (New York: Ballantine Books, 1995).

11 The term "cultural capital" was coined and defined by Pierre Bourdieu and Jean-Claude Passeron in their essay "Cultural Reproduction and Social

257

NOTES TO PP. 156–165

Reproduction," in Jerome Karabel and A. H. Halsey, eds, *Power and Ideology in Education* (New York: Oxford University Press, 1977), pp. 487–511, and further developed by Bourdieu in "The Forms of Capital," *Handbook of Theory and Research for the Sociology of Education*, ed. J. Richardson (Westport, CT: Greenwood Press, 1986), pp. 15–29.

12 Stokely Carmichael and Charles V. Hamilton, *Black Power: The Politics of Liberation in America* (New York: Vintage, 1967).

13 John Skrentny, *The Ironies of Affirmative Action: Politics, Culture, and Justice in America* (Chicago: University of Chicago Press, 1996).

14 Michael Novak, *The Rise of the Unmeltable Ethnics: The New Political Force of the Seventies* (New York: Macmillan, 1972).

15 David Riesman appears to have initiated the use of the term *ethnicity* in its current meaning in his essay "Some Observations on Intellectual Freedom," *American Scholar* 23/1 (1953–4): 9–25.

16 David Riesman, with Nathan Glazer and Reuel Denny, *The Lonely Crowd* (New Haven, CT: Yale University Press, 1950), and *Individualism Reconsidered* (New York: Free Press, 1954). See Orlando Patterson, "The Last Sociologist," *New York Times*, 19 May 2002: 15 (www.nytimes.com/2002/05/19/opinion/the-last-sociologist.html).

17 Patterson, *Ethnic Chauvinism*, p. 11.

18 See ibid., p. 32.

19 The image actually comes from James Joyce's 1916 classic *A Portrait of the Artist as a Young Man* (New York: Penguin, 1964), p. 220. Davin is telling Stephen Dedalus that a man's country comes first. "'Do you know what Ireland is?' asked Stephen with cold violence. 'Ireland is the old sow that eats her farrow.'" A "farrow" is a litter of newborn piglets. Joyce is suggesting that Ireland's history is one in which it destroyed everything worth saving.

20 See Anthony Smith, *The Ethnic Origins of Nations* (Oxford: Blackwell, 1986).

21 Hannah Arendt makes the same point in a famous remark: "If one is attacked as a Jew, one must defend oneself as a Jew. Not as a German, not as a world-citizen, not as an upholder of the Rights of Man." Arendt, "'What Remains? The Language Remains': A Conversation with Günter Gaus," in *Essays in Understanding, 1930–1954: Formation, Exile, and Totalitarianism* (New York: Schocken Books, 1994), p. 12.

22 See Andrew Greeley, "Who's a Chauvinist?" *Contemporary Sociologist* 8/4 (1979): 517–19.

23 Orlando Patterson, *The Ordeal of Integration: Progress and Resentment in America's "Racial" Crisis* (New York: Civitas, 1997).

24 Orlando Patterson, "Four Modes of Ethno-Somatic Stratification: The Experience of Blacks in Europe and the Americas," in Glenn C. Loury, Tariq Modood, and Steven M. Teles, eds, *Ethnicity, Social Mobility, and Public Policy: Comparing the US and UK* (Cambridge: Cambridge University Press, 2005), pp. 67–122.

25 Patterson is referring to the influential work of the anthropologist Fredrik Barth.

258

NOTES TO PP. 168–182

Making Public Policy in Socialist Jamaica

1 See Orlando Patterson, "Why Do Policies to Help the Poor so often Fail?" in *The Confounding Island: Jamaica and the Postcolonial Predicament* (Cambridge, MA: Belknap Press, 2019), pp. 281–313. Anthony Spaulding was a Jamaican politician and the PNP minister of housing under Michael Manley from 1972 to 1980.

2 Michael Manley, *A History of West Indies Cricket* (London: Andre Deutsch, 1988).

3 Orlando Patterson, Foreword, in Rachel Manley, *Slipstream: A Daughter Remembers* (Toronto: Key Porter, 2000), pp. 11–17; repr. as "Sad about Manley: Portrait of a Flawed Charisma," in *The Confounding Island*, pp. 314–20.

4 For an interesting view, see Beverly Manley, *The Manley Memoirs* (Kingston: Ian Randle, 2008).

5 For a portrait of Edna Manley, see Wayne Brown, *Edna Manley: The Private Years, 1900–1938* (London: Andre Deutsch, 1975).

6 On the Jamaican left, see David Scott, "The Dialectic of Defeat: An Interview with Rupert Lewis," *Small Axe* no. 10 (2001): 85–177.

7 See Rosie Stone, *No Stone Unturned: The Carl and Rosie Story* (Kingston: Ian Randle, 2007).

8 Carl Stone, *Democracy and Clientelism in Jamaica* (New Brunswick, NJ: Transaction Books, 1980). On the significance of Stone's work, see David Scott, "Political Rationalities of the Jamaican Modern," *Small Axe* no. 14 (2003): 1–22.

9 Michael Manley, *The Politics of Change: A Jamaican Testament* (London: Andre Deutsch, 1973), and *A Voice at the Workplace: Reflections on Colonialism and the Jamaican Worker* (London: Andre Deutsch, 1975). For some discussion of these texts, see David Scott, "'The Word is Love': Michael Manley's Style of Radical Political Will," *Small Axe* no. 58 (2019): 169–86.

Slavery and Social Death

1 Frank Tannenbaum, *Slave and Citizen: The Negro in the Americas* (New York: Random House, 1946).

2 Orlando Patterson, "Slavery," *Annual Review of Sociology* 3 (1977): 407–49.

3 See the important discussion of *Slavery and Social Death* by classicists in John Bodel and Walter Scheidel, eds, *On Human Bondage: After "Slavery and Social Death"* (Malden, MA: Wiley, 2017), especially the introduction (pp. 1–14) and Patterson's response (pp. 265–96).

4 Moses Finley, *The World of Odysseus* (New York: New York Review Books, [1954] 2002) and "Was Greek Civilization Based on Slave Labor?" *Historia: Zeitschrift für alte Geschichte* 8/2 (1959): 145–64.

5 In September 1951, testifying before the House Un-American Activities Committee, Wittfogel stated that Finley was a communist. In March 1952 Finley himself appeared before the committee and invoked the Fifth Amendment regarding his connections with communism. Later

259

NOTES TO PP. 182–190

that year Finley was fired from his position at Rutgers University. See M. I. Finley, "Un-American Activities," *New Statesman*, 28 February 1969, p. 77; and Wilfried Nippel, "Finley's Impact on the Continent," in Daniel Jew, Robin Osborne, and Michael Scott, eds, *M. I. Finley: An Ancient Historian and His Impact* (Cambridge: Cambridge University Press, 2016), p. 276.

6 See John Bodel, "Ancient Slavery and Modern Ideologies: Orlando Patterson and M. I. Finley among the Dons," *Theory and Society* 48 (2019): 823–33.

7 David Brion Davis, *The Problem of Slavery in Western Culture* (Oxford: Oxford University Press, 1966), and *The Problem of Slavery in the Age of Revolution, 1770–1823* (Ithaca, NY: Cornell University Press, 1975).

8 David Brion Davis, *Slavery and Human Progress* (New York: Oxford University Press, 1986), pp. 10–11.

9 See Victor Turner, *The Forest of Symbols: Aspects of Ndembu Ritual* (Ithaca, NY: Cornell University Press, 1967), and *The Ritual Process: Structure and Anti-Structure* (New Brunswick, NJ: Transaction Books, 1969). Clifford Geertz's landmark book *The Interpretation of Cultures* (New York: Basic Books, 1973), with its famous essay "Thick Description," had only just been published.

10 Henri Lévy-Bruhl, "Théorie de l'esclavage," in *Quelques problèmes du très ancien droit romain* (Paris: Éditions Domat-Montchrestien, 1934); **repr.** in Moses Finley, ed., *Slavery in Classical Antiquity: Views and Controversies* (Cambridge: Cambridge University Press, 1960), pp. 151–69.

11 See Claude Meillassoux, *The Anthropology of Slavery: The Womb of Iron and Gold*, trans. Alide Dasnois (Chicago: University of Chicago Press, 1991).

12 Kenneth Stampp, *The Peculiar Institution: Slavery in the Ante-bellum South* (New York: Knopf, 1956).

13 Robert Fogel and Stanley Engerman, *Time on the Cross: The Economics of American Negro Slavery* (New York: Little, Brown, 1974); and John Blassingame, *The Slave Community: Plantation Life in the Antebellum South* (New York: Oxford University Press, 1972).

14 Malcolm X, "The Ballot or the Bullet," in Archie Epps, ed., *The Speeches of Malcolm X at Harvard* (New York: William Morrow, 1969).

15 On the analogy between the Jewish Holocaust and New World slavery, see Orlando Patterson, "Life and Scholarship in the Shadow of Slavery," in *The Sociology of Slavery: Black Society in Jamaica, 1655–1838* (Cambridge: Polity, 2022).

The Paradox of Freedom

1 The first verse of "Rule Britannia" goes as follows: "When Britain first, at heaven's command /Arose from out the azure main, / This was the charter, the charter of the land, / And guardian angels sang this strain: Rule, Britannia! Britannia, rule the waves! / Britons never, never, never shall be slaves."

260

NOTES TO PP. 192–209

2 Isaiah Berlin, *Two Concepts of Liberty* (Oxford: Clarendon Press, 1963).
3 See Bernard Semmel, *Jamaican Blood and Victorian Conscience: The Governor Eyre Controversy* (Boston: Houghton Mifflin, 1963).
4 It is perhaps not surprising that Beckles would not agree with Patterson's perspective. A selection of the Goveia lectures are published in Hilary Beckles, ed., *Inside Slavery: Process and Legacy in the Caribbean Experience* (Kingston: University of the West Indies Press, 2002).
5 See Orlando Patterson, "Slavery: The Underside of Freedom," *Slavery and Abolition* 5 (September 1984): 87–104.
6 Karl Popper, *The Open Society and its Enemies*, 2 vols (London: Routledge, 1945).
7 See Quentin Skinner, *Liberty before Liberalism* (Cambridge: Cambridge University Press, 1998).
8 Orlando Patterson, "The Ancient and Medieval Origins of Modern Freedom," in Steven Mintz and John Stauffer, eds, *The Problem of Evil: Slavery, Freedom, and the Ambiguities of American Reform* (Amherst: University of Massachusetts Press, 2007).

The Ordeal of Integration
1 See Orlando Patterson, "Black Americans," in Peter Schuck and James Q. Wilson, eds, *Understanding America: The Anatomy of an Exceptional Nation* (New York: Public Affairs, 2008), pp. 375–410.
2 See Orlando Patterson, "Four Modes of Ethno-Somatic Stratification: The Experience of Blacks in Europe and the Americas," in Glenn C. Loury, Tariq Modood, and Steven M. Teles, eds, *Ethnicity, Social Mobility, and Public Policy: Comparing the US and UK* (Cambridge: Cambridge University Press, 2005), pp. 67–122.
3 Orlando Patterson, "Ecumenical America: Global Culture and the American Cosmos," *World Policy Journal* 11/2 (1994): 103–17.
4 Lawrence Bobo, James R. Kluegel, and Ryan A. Smith, "Laissez-Faire Racism: The Crystallization of a Kinder, Gentler Antiblack Ideology," in Steven A. Tuch and Jack K. Martin, eds, *Racial Attitudes in the 1990s: Continuity and Change* (Westport, CT: Praeger, 1997), pp. 15–44.
5 Touré, *Who's Afraid of Post-Blackness? What it Means to be Black Now* (New York: Free Press, 2011); and Orlando Patterson, "The Post-Black Condition," *New York Times Book Review*, 22 September 2011.
6 C. L. R. James, *American Civilization* (Oxford: Blackwell, 1993).
7 Orlando Patterson, "Beyond Compassion: Selfish Reasons for Being Unselfish," *Daedalus* 131/1 (2002): 26–38.
8 See, in particular, Hilary Putnam, *The Collapse of the Fact/Value Dichotomy and Other Essays* (Cambridge, MA: Harvard University Press, 2004).

Rituals of Blood
1 See Orlando Patterson, *Rituals of Blood: The Consequences of Slavery in Two American Centuries* (New York: Civitas, 1999), p. viii.

NOTES TO PP. 210–230

2 Langston Hughes, "Goodbye Christ," *Negro Worker* no. 2 (November–December 1932): 32.
3 See Deborah Gray White, *Ar'n't I a Woman? Female Slaves in the Plantation South* (New York: W. W. Norton, 1985).
4 Steven Ruggles, *Prolonged Connections: The Rise of the Extended Family in Nineteenth-Century England and America* (Madison: University of Wisconsin Press, 1987).
5 See Herbert Gutman, *The Black Family in Slavery and Freedom, 1750–1925* (New York: Pantheon, 1976).
6 See "Afro-America at the Start of a New Century," *Salmagundi* nos. 133–4, special issue (winter–spring 2002): 81–238.
7 George A. Akerlof, "Men Without Children," *Economic Journal* 108/447 (1998): 287–309; George Akerlof and Rachal Kranton, "Gender and Work," in *Identity Economics: How Our Identities Shape Our Work, Wages, and Well-Being* (Princeton, NJ: Princeton University Press, 2010).
8 See Orlando Patterson, "Affirmative Action: Opening up Workplace Networks to Afro-Americans," *Brookings*, March 1, 1998. Also "Equality," *Democracy: A Journal of Ideas* no. 11 (winter 2009), https://democracyjournal.org/magazine/11/equality/.

The Confounding Island

1 Orlando Patterson, "Making Sense of Culture," *Annual Review of Sociology* 40 (2014): 1–30.
2 Edwin Hutchins, *Cognition in the Wild* (Cambridge, MA: MIT Press, 1995).
3 The investiture and presentation of national honors and awards ceremony was made on Monday, October 19, 2020. Patterson's peroration, upon receipt of the Order of Merit, the nation's third highest honor, concluded his remarks on behalf of all recipients of awards: "To this island, this cane-clad rock of struggles and survival that soars above a sea of history's vilest inhumanities. To this strong-willed people, fearless, feisty, rebellious, never to be underestimated, small in number but forever *tallawah*, punching beyond our weight for better, and for worse, among the peoples of the world. To this still young nation, full of hope and love and troubles from its first search for the light of progress in the dark, in the dark that history left us, yet in no doubt whatsoever that we will find our way forward, that we will prevail. To this place that we call home, this big little land of haunting beauty, lush from our tears and our dreams, we say, thank you Jamaica, thank you." I am grateful to Patterson for sharing this with me.

The Perspective of an Historical Sociologist

1 Orlando Patterson, "On Slavery and Slave Formations," *New Left Review*, no. 117 (1979): 31–67.
2 Duman Bahrami-Rad, Anke Becker, and Joseph Henrich, "Tabulated Nonsense? Testing the Validity of the Ethnographic Atlas," *Economics*

NOTES TO PP. 230–240

Letters, 204 (2021), www.sciencedirect.com/science/article/pii/S016517 6521001579?via%3Dihub.

3 See, for example, Vincent Brown, "Social Death and Political Life in the Study of Slavery," *American Historical Review* 114/5 (2009): 1231–49.

4 Judith Butler, *Antigone's Claim* (New York: Columbia University Press, 2002).

5 Keith Hopkins, *Conquerors and Slaves* (Cambridge: Cambridge University Press, 1981).

6 Nicholas Christakis, *Blueprint: The Evolutionary Origins of a Good Society* (Boston: Little, Brown, 2019).

7 See Orlando Patterson, "Culture and Continuity: Causal Structures in Socio-Cultural Persistence," in Roger Friedland and John Mohr, eds, *Matters of Culture: Cultural Sociology in Practice* (Cambridge: Cambridge University Press, 2004), pp. 71–109; and "The Mechanisms of Cultural Reproduction: Explaining the Puzzle of Persistence," in Laura Grindstaff, Ming-Cheng M. Lo, and John R. Hall, eds, *The Routledge Handbook of Cultural Sociology* (2nd edn, New York: Routledge, 2019), pp. 122–32.

8 On Sharpe's anticipation of liberation theology and how it inspired his revolution, one that was a critical factor in the British decision to pass the Act of 1833 abolishing slavery, see Tom Zoellner, *Island on Fire: The Revolt that Ended Slavery in the British Empire* (Cambridge, MA: Harvard University Press, 2020). Patterson explored the medieval serfs' secret rediscovery of the freedom buried in Christian doctrine with the help of renegade priests in "The Ancient and Medieval Origins of Modern Freedom," in Steven Mintz and John Stouffer, eds, *The Problem of Evil: Slavery, Freedom and the Ambiguities of American Reform* (Amherst: University of Massachusetts Press, 2007), pp. 31–66.

INDEX

Abeng 128–9, 130
Abrahams, Anthony 64, 251n1
An Absence of Ruins (Patterson) 5, 6, 62, 73, 111, 115–22
  Alexander Blackman (book character) 115, 116, 117, 255n3
  CAM public session 118–20
  existentialism 117–18
  literary-philosophic preoccupation 115
absurdity
  feeling of 5, 6
  of slavery 7
act of defiance 135–6
affirmation 7, 8
African American studies 89, 140, 141, 143
"African Redemption" (Nettleford) 81
African slaves, creole slaves and 102–3, 104–5
Afro-Jamaican creole 106
Afro-Jamaican culture 104
Afro-Jamaicans 165
AIDS 177
Akan slaves 103
Akerlof, George 213
Alley 190–1
Alley Infant School 27–8, 29

Alpha Boys School 32, 247n9
Ambassador Cinema 42
American Journal of Sociology 196
American Negro Slavery (Phillips) 95–6
American Scholar 150
American slavery 180, 186, 189
American Sociological Association (ASA) 164
American Sociological Review (ASR) 164, 216
American sociology 216
American studies 185
  parochialism of 186
Amiel, Jean 66–7, 75, 76
Amiel, Keith 66
Anancy 105
ancient Greeks 13
  city-states 15
  fate and meaninglessness 87
  freedom as power 192, 195, 195–6
  freedom to enslave 192
  slave labour 181, 182, 185, 192, 199
ancient slavery 232
  revolts 180
  systems 226
Ancient Slavery and Modern Ideology (Finley) 181
ancient world 183

INDEX

Anderson, Perry 69, 70, 123, 145, 227
Anglican Church 31–2, 36, 76
anglophone Caribbean intellectual tradition 18
Annals of the New York Academy of Sciences 227–8
Annual Review of Sociology 181, 216
anomie 8
anthropology 56, 121, 145, 183, 224, 229
  cross-cultural studies in 229
anticipation 82, 83–4
anticolonialism 162
Aptheker, Herbert 96
Arawaks 226
Arendt, Hannah 259n21
Aristotle 192, 239
  endoxic method of 239–40
Augier, Roy 54, 55
authority 34
autonomy 205–8

Back-o-Wall 42–3, 53
bagasse industry 167
Bales, Robert F. 146
Balzac, Honoré de 74
Baptist War (1831–2) 194, 226
Barbados 52, 107
  disciplined society 107
  education of Black people 107
  knowledge of institutions 218–19
  settler colonialist system 217–18
  violence, low rate of 107
  White racism 217–18
BBC 109
Beckford, George ("G-Beck") 129, 131, 132, 141, 256n1
Beckles, Hilary 194–5
Becoming (Allport) 95
Belisario, Isaac Mendes 100
Bell, Daniel 144, 146, 148–9, 235
Beloved (Morrison) 136
Berger, Peter 235

Berlin, Isaiah 192, 239
Bernal, Martin 196, 244n28
Bertram, Arnold 174
Best, Lloyd 61, 62, 69
Beyond a Boundary (James) 72
Beyond the Melting Pot (Glazer and Moynihan) 147
BITU (Bustamante Industrial Trade Union) 37
Black America/Americans 147–66
  American body politic 214
  aspirations of individual autonomy 153
  Black solidarity 153
  Black youth
    autonomy 206
    decision-making 206
    increased value placed on 214
    race and 206
  culture and 216–17
  dilemma for OP 153–4
  election of Obama 214
  future unburdened by tradition 151
  hemispheric Black experience 150–1
  hustling 154
  incommensurable moral systems 153
  "The Moral Crisis of the Black American" (Patterson) 147
  natal alienation 214
  neofascism, danger of 149–50
  OP coming to terms with 150
  paradoxical situation 153
  parochialism 150
  preoccupation with history 151
  private segregation 203, 214
  public integration 203, 214
  self-determination 153
  thick and thin identity 151–2
  "Toward a Future That Has No Past" (Patterson) 147, 150, 152, 180
  US liberalism 149
  White backlash against 215

265

INDEX

Black American culture 205
Black arts movement 139
Black Athena (Bernal) 196
Black Atlantic idea 150
Black church 210
Black cosmopolitanism 152
Black family 187, 211
  state support for 212–13
Black family life 147–8, 187
Black identity movement 148, 149
  fundamental assumption of 155
  liberal guilt and 149–50
Black identity politics 187
The Black Jacobins (James) 91, 92, 93, 94, 240
Black Jamaican culture 104
Black Jamaicans 92, 98
Black Lives Matter (BLM) 214, 215
Black Metropolis (Drake) 26
Black middle class 203
Black movement 143
Black particularism 152
Black Power movement 143, 156, 210
Black pride 148
Black racial advocacy 205
Black scholars 211
Black studies 143, 144
Blackburn, Robin 69–70, 89, 123
Blackness 165–6
Blake, Vivian 130, 178, 179
Blaming the Victim (Ryan) 148
Blassingame, John 187
Bobo, Lawrence (Larry) 203
Bolt, Usain 220
Bourdieu, Pierre 155
Boyers, Robert 212
Boyne, Ian 164
Braithwaite, Lloyd 57–8, 59, 62, 70, 95
Brathwaite, Doris 110, 133
Brathwaite, Edward (Eddie) Kamau 91–2, 95, 103, 132
  The Development of Creole

    Society in Jamaica 92, 97, 103–4
  research for 92
  differences with OP 105–7
  folk culture 187
  meetings with OP 132–3
  radicalization of 103
  research on missionaries 91–2, 103, 104
  Rights of Passage 113, 132
  slave society 103
  see also CAM (Caribbean Artists Movement)
Brother Man (Mais) 47, 87–8, 113
Brown, Michael 214
Burckhardt, Jacob 240
Bushas 60
Bustamante, Alexander 36, 37, 39–40, 51, 52–3, 54, 247n1
Butler, Judith 230–1

CAM (Caribbean Artists Movement) 92, 108–15, 132, 225
  Brathwaite and OP's views
    differences between/shared 113–14
  early meetings 108
  launching of 110
  presentations
    "Jazz and the West Indian Novel" 113, 119–20
    West Indian aesthetic 111–12
  significance of 121
  women contributors, lack of 120
Camus, Albert 5–8, 12, 73–5, 82, 160
  act of defiance 135
  existentialism of 75–6
  OP's rejection of 86
  works
    The Myth of Sisyphus 5, 6, 73–4, 85–6
    The Rebel 6–7, 86, 117, 193
    The Stranger 5–6
Carew, Jan 121, 134

INDEX

Cargill, Morris 120
Caribbean society 111
Caribbean Studies: A Symposium
(Rubin) 60–1
Carmichael, Stokely 89
Carter, Jimmy 158
Carter, Martin 72
Castro, Fidel 174, 179
catastrophic theory of slavery 187,
188, 211
censorship 125
Césaire, Aimé 152
The Children of Sisyphus
(Patterson) 5, 56, 71, 73,
77–90
characters in book
Brother Solomon 5, 81, 82,
84–5, 86, 86–7, 116
Dinah 5, 80, 86–7
Daily Telegraph review 111–12
millenarianism 80–1
Pocomania music 79
publication of 88
Rastafari 79–81
anticipation 82, 83–4
failure of 86
psychology of withdrawal 81–2
struggling women 77–8
suicide 86
Christakis, Nicholas 236
Christianity 16, 194, 197, 198
absurd beliefs 83
anticipation in 84
missionaries 102, 103–4
OP's loss of faith in 76, 80
radical version of 102
tripartite notion of freedom 198
uniqueness of 16
Churchill, Sir Winston 40
Cicero 4
citizenship 162
civic freedom 15, 195
civil rights movement 143, 156, 210
Clarendon 29
Clarendon College 31, 32

Clark, Kenneth 147
Clarke, Edith 65, 66, 106, 224
Clarke, Nigel 222–3
Clarke, Oliver 110
classicists 181, 182
cliometrics 87, 188, 211
coalition politics 156
Cognition in the Wild (Hutchins)
218
colonialism 107
Comitas, Lambros 61
Commonwealth Scholarship 65
community councils 167–8
comparative anthropology 183
The Confounding Island (Patterson)
215–24
character of essays 221
Jamaican colonial experience
contrast to Barbados 217–18
distinctive nature of 217–18
Conrad, Joseph 112
Contemporary Sociology 164
"Context and Choice in Ethnic
Allegiance" (Patterson) 98
contextualization 19
contingency table analysis 227
Coopers Hill 138–9
cotton revolution 189
Craton, Michael 128
Creative Arts Centre 119, 120
creole slave(s) 8, 102
African slaves and 102–3, 104–5
phenomenological picture of 8–9
revolts 8, 103
self-recognition 9
creole society
chaos 104, 105, 106
Hobbesian society 105
reproduction, lack of 105
social order 105
*see also The Development of
Creole Society in Jamaica*
(Brathwaite)
creolization 95, 97
Cudjoe (Maroon leader) 101

267

INDEX

cultural capital 155–6
cultural deficit 156
cultural identity 155
The Cultural Matrix (Patterson) 206, 216
Cultural Survival 228
culture 225–6

Daedalus 207
Daily Telegraph 111–12
data 229
Davis, David Brion 14, 183, 184, 227, 237–8
de Freitas, Michael (Michael X) 89, 90
de Lisser, H. G. 73, 138
decolonization 35–6
deep identity 152
democracy 221–2
Democracy and Clientelism in Jamaica (Stone) 177
Denham Town 42
dependency theory 219
determinism 153, 154
The Development of Creole Society in Jamaica (Brathwaite) 92, 97, 103–4
DeVore, Irven 229
dialogical generations 19–20
Die the Long Day (Patterson) 8, 9–12, 116–17, 132, 133–8
  characters in book
    Africanus 136, 137
    Cicero 135, 136
    Quasheba 133, 134–5, 136, 137
  plantation life 11–12, 137
  reconstruction of slave life 138
The Do-Good Woman (Patterson) 56, 77–8
domination 133–4
  freedom and 1–2
  moment of refusal 6, 7, 134
Dore, Ron 145
Drake, St Clair 139, 140
Du Bois, W. E. B. 96, 147, 187

Duncan, D. K. 132, 142–3, 174, 175, 257n5
Dungle 53, 79, 80
Dunkley, Carlyle 63, 64, 67, 139, 250n8
Durkheim, Emile 227

Economics Society 61, 67
Ecumenical America (Patterson) 201, 202
Edwards, David 58, 62
Elkins, Stanley 94, 99, 100, 180
  Sambo thesis 94, 100, 101, 185
Empire Day 40, 190
empiricism 208, 230
empowerment 192
The End of Ideology (Bell) 149
Engerman, Stanley 187, 188
enslavement *see* slavery
Epps, Archie 187
Ermine (half-sister to OP) 78–9
Escape to an Autumn Pavement (Salkey) 109
ethnic allegiance 161
Ethnic Chauvinism: The Reactionary Impulse (Patterson) 146, 148, 149–50, 153, 156–7, 158–62
  critique of Jamaican left 179
  ideology 163
  methodological stance 159
  nationalism 161
  race, avoidance of 164–5
  responses to 164
  sorcerer 160
  Western civilization 162
ethnic cleansing 161
ethnic politics 161
ethnic revival 149
ethnicity 157, 158, 163, 165–6
Ethnicity: Theory and Experience (Glazer and Moynihan) 147
Ethnographic Atlas 229
ethno-somatic 164–5, 165
Ewart, Barclay 167

268

INDEX

Ewing, Patrick 221
Excelsior school 48–50, 77
  teaching role for OP 48–9, 57
existential philosophy 156
existentialism 75–6, 117–18, 208

family
  away families 211
  cliometrics 211
  conservative/normative view of
    212
  at the micro level 212
  stable unions 212, 213
  as a unit 211
  see also Black family
Fanon, Frantz 93–4, 99
feminism 211
Festinger, Leon 80, 85
fideism 84, 85
Finley, Moses 14, 178, 181–3, 184,
    227, 228, 260n5
Firth, Raymond 65, 121
Fletcher, Peter 67, 177
Fogel, Bob 187, 188
Foot, Sir Hugh 40
Foot, Michael 40
Ford, Gerald 157, 158
Forrest, Douglas 45, 49, 74
The Fragility of Goodness
    (Nussbaum) 16–17
Frankfurt School 182
Franklin, John Hope 96
Frazier, E. Franklin 147, 187
Free Jamaica (Hall) 91
freedom
  as capability 192
  contradictory value 191
  cultural construct 191
  emergence of 238
  freedom from 191
  freedom to 191
    empower yourself 192
    enslave 191–2
    exercise power 191
    overpower others 192

freedom with 191
  sharing power 191
hope and dream of 11
idea of 15, 191, 197, 199
as an institution 191
institutionalization of 197, 199
in Jamaica 193–4
in medieval society 16
mystery of 238
Nazi Germany 200–1
as power 191, 195, 195–6
as a social value 14, 15
as socially reconstructed 191
as a tragedy 13, 200
as a triadic concept-value 14–15,
    16, 195
as a value 197, 199, 238
Western 14
worthlessness of 11
freedom and slavery
  defamiliarizing assumptions
    about 2
  dialectic of 1, 13, 14
  domination and 1
  generation of freedom 14
  historical story of 1
  internal relation between 193
  paradox of 1–5, 12, 14, 16
  portrayal in Western history 2–3
  sociohistorical roots of 3
  tragic pair 200
freedom from slavery
  existential birth of 5–12
  historical birth of 12–18
Freedom in the Making of Western
    Culture (Patterson) 15–16,
    17, 189–201
  Bernal's review 196
  critique of the West 197, 200
  genealogy 13–14
  historical sociology 14
  key to understanding OP's body
    of work 13
  paradoxical relationship between
    slavery and freedom 2–3

269

INDEX

Freedom in the Making of Western Culture (Patterson) *(cont.)*
value of freedom from slavery 12
West's misunderstanding of itself 198–9
French Revolution (1789) 162
Freud, Sigmund 95
From Slavery to Freedom (Franklin) 96

Garvey, Marcus 25–6
Gates, Henry Louis Jr ("Skip") 155
Gayle, Chris 220
Geertz, Clifford 183–4
Gellner, Ernest 145–6, 231, 232
gender relations 209, 211–13
poverty and 213
genealogical isolates 187
Genovese, Eugene 101
Gibson, Bishop Percival 31, 34–5, 36, 246n8
Gilroy, Paul 152
Ginsberg, Morris 65
Giovanni, Nikki 139
Girvan, Norman 50, 64, 67, 69, 88, 132
National Planning Agency 175
planning office 142
returning to Jamaica 122
Glass, David 64, 65, 72, 101, 224–5, 229
Glass, Ruth 89–90
Glazer, Nathan 147, 158, 235
The Gleaner 25, 27, 45, 53, 120, 246n1
coverage of violence 222
review of *Ethnic Chauvinism: The Reactionary Impulse* 164
Goffman, Erving 99, 235
Gomes, Peter 146
good and evil 16–17
Gordon, Derek 176
Gordon, George William 173
Goveia, Elsa 69, 91

Graeculus 185
Graham, Billy 76
Graham, Russell 171
Grand Rapids 157
Grange Hill 23
Greeks *see* ancient Greeks
Greeley, Andrew 164, 165
Guinier, Ewart 140, 257n1
Gurkhas 107
Gutman, Herbert 211

Hall, Douglas 59, 60, 64, 69, 91
Hall, Stuart 69, 70, 114, 235
Hamilton, Charles 156
Harris, Wilson 108, 109, 114
Hart, Richard 39
Harvard Educational Review 144
Harvard University 89, 138–47
invitation to OP from Talcott Parsons 140
office space for OP 140
OP's European perspective 144
Social Anthropology Department 228
Sociology Department 140, 141, 146
tenured position for OP 141
Hearne, John 72, 73, 88, 109, 111, 254n11, 254n12
disagreement with OP 119–20
unpopularity 120
Heartman, Ras Daniel 126
Hedley, George 221
Hegel, G. W. F. 7, 9, 200, 228
Henrich, Joe 229
Henry, Arthur 39
Henry, Revd Claudius 43–4, 53–4, 56, 79
Henry, Peter 222–3
Herskovits, Melville 96, 97, 143, 187
Hibbert, Mavis 27, 29
Hibbert, Toots 30
Hibbert, Trevor 48
Higham, John 158

270

INDEX

Higman, Barry 104, 105, 188
Hill, Frank 39
Hill, Ken 39
The Hills Were Joyful Together
(Mais) 47
Hindess, Barry 227
Hirst, Paul 227
historical fiction 133
historical sociology 8, 13, 14, 16,
91, 145–6
of beliefs and values 239–40
intellectual history and 237
perspective of 224–6
historicism 221
History of West Indies Cricket
(Manley) 171
History Teachers' Association 193
HIV/AIDS 177
Hobbes, Thomas 225, 226, 234
Hobsbawm, Eric 181, 227
Holness, Andrew 222, 223, 224
Homans, George 140, 141, 144
Hopkins, Keith 232
housing schemes 168, 169, 170
Hughes, Langston 210
Huie, Albert 46
Hutchins, Edwin 218
hypothetico-deductive reasoning
235–6

ideational values 238–9
identity movement 144
ideology 163
IMF (International Monetary Fund)
175
immiseration 95
independence 39–40, 54, 143
JLP 39–40, 54
PNP 39–40, 54
see also West Indies Federation
India 222
Individualism Reconsidered
(Riesman) 159
Indo-Jamaicans 165
Inkeles, Alex 146–7

Institute for Advanced Studies 157,
183
institutions 218
intellectual biographies 18
intellectual history 237
Isaacs, Allan 51–2
ISER (Institute for Social and
Economic Research) 57, 59,
60
as a policy-orientated institution
68

Jackson, Jesse 155
Jamaica
athletics 219–20
Black movement 143
combative individualism 220
constitution 63
cricket 219
decolonization 35–6
democracy 221–2
empty ideology 219
football 220
freedom-loving people 190, 196
freedom-loving Whites 193–4
genocide 226
independence 39–40, 54, 143
Indian immigration 29
knowledge of institutions 218–20
modernization 52
national identity 40–1
polarization of 178
positives and negatives of 223–4
public policy *see* public policy
(Jamaica)
slavery 2, 91, 96, 99, 105, 186,
188
brutality of 193
New World 2
rebellions 191
revolts 8
slave society 225–6
transformation of cultural-
political consciousness
128–9

271

INDEX

Jamaica (*cont.*)
  violence 53–4, 107, 176, 178, 221, 222, 226
Jamaica Education Transformation Commission 224
Jamaica House of Assembly 194
Jamaica Labour Party (JLP) 36, 37
  accuses PNP of political violence 53–4
  anti-independence 39–40, 54
  convergence with the PNP 38
  indistinguishable policies from the PNP 222
  opposition to federation 51–3
Jamaica Library Service 35
Jamaica National Archives 56
Jamaica Police Federation 26, 246n5
Jamaica Teachers' Union 47
Jamaica Welfare 35, 247n11
Jamaican Blood and Victorian Conscience: The Governor Eyre Controversy (Semmel) 193
Jamaican creole slaves 8
Jamaican intellectuals 21
Jamaican people
  Afro-Jamaicans 165
  Black Jamaicans 92, 98
  character of 224
  freedom-loving people 190, 196
  Indo-Jamaicans 165
  White Jamaicans 59–60, 62, 65
  see also Rastafari (Rastafarianism)
Jamaican Reggae Boys 220
James, C. L. R. 22, 71–2, 88–9, 240, 245n44
  The Black Jacobins 91, 92, 93, 94, 240
James, Louis 110
James, Selma 72
Jane and Louisa (Patterson) 132, 133
jazz music 118, 151

Jefferson, Thomas 4
Jim Crow 156, 211
Johns, Vere 48
Johnson, Lyndon B. 157
Jones, Claudia 89
Jones, Evan 110
Jones Town 42
Joyce, James 160, 161, 161–2, 259n19

Kant, Immanuel 82, 85
Kardiner, Abram 95, 99, 147, 148
Kenya 163
Kenyatta, Jomo 162, 163
Kerr, Madeline 99, 220
Kierkegaard, Søren 84
Kilson, Martin 146
King, Martin Luther, Jr. 89, 149, 207
King, Whoppy (Aston Jolly) 43, 247–8n7
Kingston, Jamaica 23
  demographic changes 41
  safety 41
  standard of living 41
Kingston College 27, 31–5, 44–8, 246n8
  fees 27, 33
  OP attends
    cultural transition 44
    exam results 46, 50
    physics 46–7
    reads local novels 47–8
    scholarship 27, 33
    underachievement of 45
    wins competition for best essay 47
  reputation of 31–2
  scholarship 27, 33
  teachers 34–5, 44–5
Kingston Technical High School 32
kinship 187
Kirkwood, Sir Robert 131, 257n4
Kitchener, Lord 40, 247n4
Kluckhohn, Clyde 146

INDEX

Krystol, Irving 148, 149
Kumina 98

La Rose, John 108, 110, 114
Lady Nugent's Journal 100
Lamming, George 72, 93, 114–15
Laski, Harold 65
Latin America 186
Levy-Bruhl, Henri 184, 227
Lewars, Barbara 130
Lewis, Sir Arthur 55
Lewis, Evin 220
Lewis, Oscar 148
Lewis, Rupert 172
liberalism 149
liberty 4, 192
Liberty before Liberalism (Skinner)
    197
Lieberson, Stanley 236
life
    meaning of 6, 75, 85, 87
    value of 5
Lightbourne, Robert 38
Lilith (Patterson) 78
liminality 184
Lionel Town 27, 29, 190
Lipset, Marty 140, 141, 144, 146
Literary Society 61, 67
Little Dorrit (Dickens) 78
Locke, John 4, 234
London 68
London School of Economics (LSE)
    see LSE (London School of
    Economics)
The Lonely Crowd (Riesman) 159,
    236
Loury, Glenn 202
Lowenthal, David 61
LSE (London School of Economics)
    interdisciplinary seminars 145
    OP attends 64–72, 121–2, 197,
        204
    lectureship 90, 114, 122, 145
    meets Nerys 121
    opts for sociology 66, 224–5

PhD thesis *see The Sociology
    of Slavery* (Patterson)
    reputation 65
"Sociology of Development"
    seminar 145
Lyon, Noel and Max 48

Mair, Lucy 65, 121–2, 145
Mais, Roger 41, 47, 72, 73, 87–8,
    113
Malcolm X 89, 187
Manley, Beverly 171–2, 173
Manley, Edna 57, 73, 173
Manley, Glynne 167
Manley, Michael 67, 120, 122,
    123–4, 129–30
    Anglo-Jamaican tastes 172
    elected MP 124
    elected prime minister 166–7,
        175
    election victory (1972) 141–2
    embracing Fidel Castro 174, 179
    friends and acquaintances 171–2
    global limelight 174
    intellectualism of 171, 179
    model of British Labour Party
        174
    mother's British influence on 173
    New World Order idea 219
    and the PNP left 142–3, 174, 179
    as a political animal 170, 178–9
    presidency 130
    private life 171–2
    relationship with women 171
Manley, Norman 35, 36, 51, 54,
    67, 122, 124
    Anglo-Jamaican culture 173
    character of 172
    as a classic Brown man 172–3
    loyalty of the people 39
    "The man with the plan" 38
    middle-class background 172
    role model 37
    rural background 172–3
Manley, Rachel 130, 171, 172

273

INDEX

manumission 10, 186, 189
  US hostility to 186
Marcel, Gabriel 100
The Mark of Oppression (Kardiner)
  95, 99
Marley, Bob 42
Maroons 101, 137
Marsden family 28–9
Martin, Trayvon 214
Marx, Karl 71, 86, 227, 228
Marxism 72, 131, 227
Mathurin, Lucille 119
Maupassant, Guy de 73–4
May Pen 29–30, 60, 190
May Pen Elementary School 29, 30,
  33–4
Maybury-Lewis, David 228–9
McCarthy, Joseph 182
McIntyre, Alister 57, 249n4
McKay, Claude 25, 47, 73
meaninglessness 80, 87
Meillassoux, Claude 184
Melhado, O. K. 172
mento tradition 40
Mico Teachers' College 32–3,
  247n10
Middle Ages 16, 198
middle-class integration 202
Mifflin, Art 113
migration 41–2, 43
Mill, John Stuart 193
millenarianism 80–1
Mills, C. Wright 235
Mills, Gladstone 128
Mintz, Sidney 138
Miss Lou (Louise Bennett) 56
missionaries 102, 103–4
Mittelholzer, Edgar 72
Monymusk sugar estate 28–9
Moody, Ronald 108
Moore, Gerald 119
moral autonomy 205–8, 210
moral community 207
Morant Bay Rebellion (1865) 47,
  193

Morgan, Edmund 14
Morris, Myra 27, 29
Morrison, Karl 244–5n40
Morrison, Toni 134, 136
mother–daughter relationships
  134–5, 188, 212
mother–son relationships 212
Moyne Report (1945) 59, 250n2
Moynihan, Daniel Patrick 147, 148,
  149, 158
Muir Park 35
Munroe, Trevor 176
Murdock, G. P. 227, 228
My Mother Who Fathered Me
  (Clarke) 59
Myers Street 42, 56
The Myth of Sisyphus (Camus) 5, 6,
  73–4, 85–6
The Myth of the Negro Past
  (Herskovits) 97

Naipaul, V. S. 72
natal alienation 184, 214
nationalism 161, 162
  in Africa 162
nation-state 162
  Anglo-American concept 162–3
  legitimacy of 163
The Nature of Prejudice (Allport)
  95
Naygah (Neager) 135
Nazi Germany 200–1
negative freedom 192, 195
Negritude literature 110, 111
The Negro American Family (Du
  Bois) 147
Nettleford, Rex 54, 55–6, 62, 65,
  81, 142
New Day (Reid) 47
New Left group 69, 123
New Left Review 69, 71, 122–3,
  227
New Society 70
New Statesman 70, 73
New World Black studies 143

274

INDEX

New World group 131
New World intellectual movement
    61
New World Quarterly 93, 128–9
Newsweek 113
Nieboer, Herman 227–8, 233
Nigeria 163
Nixon, Richard 156
normal-science approach 235–6
*Notebook of a Return to My
    Native Land* (Césaire) 152
Notting Hill 69
  riots (1958) 68
Novak, Michael 157, 158, 165
Nussbaum, Martha 16–17

Obama, Barack 154, 213–14
The Observer 85
*The Open Society and its Enemies:
    The Spell of Plato* (Popper)
    197
oppression 99, 100, 196
The Ordeal of Integration
    (Patterson) 155, 201–8
  externally related problems 209
  interventions 202
  moral autonomy of the individual
    205–8
  OP's intellectual orientation
    203–5
order, problem of 225–6
Outline of Cultural Materials 229

Padgett, John F. 236
Palmer, Miss 33, 34
Paris protests (1968) 123
Parsons, Talcott 58, 70, 140, 146,
    225
Patterson, Almena "Mina" (née
    Morris) (mother of OP) 23–5
  Anglicanism 31–2, 76
  barter arrangement with Miss
    Palmer 33
  devotion to OP 24
  dressmaking skills 27

financing OP's education 27–8,
    30–1
middle-class values 44
OP as project 24, 30
opposes OP's marriage to Jean
    66–7
PNP's leadership struggle 38
political activism 36, 37
radical views 36, 37
reciprocal relationship with OP
    30–1
reconciliation with Charles 25, 27
relationship with OP 28
separation from Charles 24
strong-willed character 27
threatens OP with trade school
    31, 32
Patterson, Charles (father of OP)
    23–5
  authoritarian manner 26, 27, 32
  denial of pension 38
  detective in colonial police 24–5
  political beliefs 36, 38–9
  radicalization of 26
  reconciliation with Mina 25, 27
  relationship with OP 26–7
  separation from Mina 24
  shorthand skills 25
  tailing Marcus Garvey 25–6
Patterson, Nerys (wife of OP) 133,
    141
  marriage to OP 65, 110, 122
  meeting at the LSE 121–2
  politics of 123
Patterson, Orlando
  articles, essays and short stories
    "Context and Choice in Ethnic
      Allegiance" 98
    "Four Modes of Ethno-Somatic
      Stratification" 165
    The Gleaner 45, 97–8
    "Life and Scholarship in the
      Shadow of Slavery" 234–5
    "The Moral Crisis of the Black
      American" 147, 153

275

INDEX

Patterson, Orlando, articles, essays and short stories (*cont.*)
  New Left Review 70–1
  New Society 70
  "Rethinking Black History" 144
  The Star 45–6, 77
  "The Structural Origins of Slavery" 227–8
  Times Literary Supplement (*TLS*) 109, 111
  "Toward a Future That Has No Past" 147, 150, 152, 180
  "A Tragedy of Youth" 45–6
  "Twilight of a Dark Myth" 109, 111, 145
Black culture 92
childhood 23–5, 25–6, 27–9, 31, 35
class differences, experiences of 60
cricket 64–5
differences with Kamau Brathwaite 105–7
dualism theory 98
editorial and reviews
  "Frantz Fanon: My Hope and Hero" 93–4
  The Guardian 109
  New Statesman 70, 73
  New World Quarterly 93–4
  New York Times Book Review 151, 204
  The Pelican 61, 63, 67
  TLS (*Times Literary Supplement*) 70, 73, 109
  Who's Afraid of Post-Blackness? (Touré) 204
education
  Alley Infant School 27, 28, 29
  Kingston College 27, 31–5, 44–8
  London School of Economics (LSE) 64–72

  May Pen Elementary School 29, 30, 33–4
  University College of the West Indies (UCWI) 46, 48–53
family home 23–5
film and projections 46–7
friendships
  David Riesman 159
  Gordon Rohlehr 112–13
  Leroy Taylor 129
  Norman Girvan 122
  Robin Blackburn 69, 70
  Victor Turner 183
  Walter Rodney 63–4
heroes and models 237
intellectual life of 21–2
living conditions in London 123
marriage to Nerys 65, 110, 122
  meeting at the LSE 121–2
music 48
Order of Merit 224, 263n3
philosophy, interest in 75
plays
  The Do-Good Woman 56, 77–8
relationship with C. L. R. James 88–9
relationship with Jean 66–7, 75, 76
  calls off marriage to 66–7
religion
  attending church 76
  giving up on 76
  growing up with 75, 76
returning to Jamaica 122–8
solitude 30
special advisor role 167–78
teaching 57
  Excelsior 48–9, 57
  Harvard University 138–47
  LSE (London School of Economics) 90, 114, 122, 145
  University of the West Indies (UWI) 127–8
White House visit 158

276

INDEX

works (books)
  An Absence of Ruins 5, 6, 62, 73, 111, 115–22
  The Children of Sisyphus 5, 56, 71, 73, 77–90, 111–12
  The Confounding Island 215–24
  Die the Long Day 8, 9–12, 116–17, 132, 133–8
  Ethnic Chauvinism: The Reactionary Impulse 146, 148, 149–50, 153, 156–7, 158–62, 163–5, 179
  Freedom in the Making of Western Culture 2–3, 12–13, 14, 15–16, 17, 189–201
  Jane and Louisa 132, 133
  Lilith 78
  The Ordeal of Integration 155, 201–8
  Rituals of Blood 201, 208–15
  Slavery and Social Death 9, 12, 13, 149, 179–89, 227
  The Sociology of Slavery 8, 13, 22, 91–107, 225, 226
Patterson, P. J. 222
Patterson, Victor (half-brother of OP) 68, 139
Paul the Apostle 16, 198
peasant revolts 198
peasantry 106, 107
The Peculiar Institution (Stampp) 96, 185
The Pelican 61, 63, 67
People's National Party (PNP) 25, 26, 36
  accused of political violence by JLP 53–4
  Claudius Henry affair 53–4
  convergence with the JLP 38
  disarray 67
  election victory (1972) 141–2
  expulsions 39
  indistinguishable policies from the JLP 222
  leadership struggle 38–9

OP and
  commitment to 129
  disillusionment with 131
  party of education and progress 36, 37
  policies 36
  pro-independence 39–40, 54
  radicalism 37, 38
  radicalization of 173–4
  rhetorical left 179
  slogan 38
  socialism 175
  songs 36
  support for federation 51–3
    mobilization of students 51–2
  supporter base 53
People's Plan 175–6
personal freedom 15, 195
Personality and Conflict in Jamaica (Kerr) 59, 99, 220
phenomenology 8–9
Philadelphia Negro (Du Bois) 147
Phillips, U. B. 95–6
The Philosophy and Opinions of Marcus Garvey (Garvey) 26
Planno, Mortimo 81, 126
plantations 8, 131, 134
  in Barbados 107
  chaos 106
  as a concentration camp 99
  Die the Long Day 11–12, 135, 137
  Mediterranean 200
  New World 200
  practical purposes in 11
Plato 239
Plumb, Jack 178, 181
Pocomania 56, 98, 104
  music 79, 104
  resignation 83
  spirituality 83
Pohlenz, Max 14
political violence 53–4
Pollard, Kieron 220
Popper, Karl 197, 221

277

INDEX

positive freedom 192
post-Blackness 204
poverty 156, 213
Powell, Colin 154–5
Powell, Wesley 48, 49–50
power, freedom and 191
Pre-Capitalist Mode of Production
    (Hindess & Hirst) 227
prejudice 95
Présence Africaine 109–10
Princeton University 102, 140–1
The Problem of Evil 198
The Problem of Slavery in Western
    Culture (Davis) 183, 184
problem-spaces 19, 21
The Public Interest 118, 144, 147,
    148–9, 153, 255n3
public moral self-examination
    236–7
public policy (Jamaica) 166–79
  bagasse industry 167
  "The Condition of the
    Low-Income Population in
    the Kingston Metropolitan
    Area" report 168
  housing schemes 168, 169, 170
  OP's office 169–70
  urban upgrading project 168–70
Putnam, Hilary 208

Raaflaub, Kurt 14
race 164–5
racism 95–6, 206
  justification for 192
  origins of 185
  subtler forms of 203
racist ideology 163
Radcliffe-Brown, A. R. 65
Ramchand, Kenneth 119
Rastafari (Rastafarianism) 41, 43
  anticipation 82, 83–4
  criticism of society 82–3
  demand on society 83
  dreadlocks 43
  fear of 53

  ideology 83
  OP's interest in 56, 79–80
  OP's involvement with 126
  paradox of 81
  request for help 55
  sociologists' approach to 83
  see also Brother Man (Mais);
    The Children of Sisyphus
    (Patterson): Rastafari
Rastafari Report 126
rationalism 208
rationality 15
The Rebel (Camus) 6–7, 86, 117,
    193
rebellion 7–8, 37, 136, 154
  Morant Bay Rebellion (1865) 47,
    193
reggae 40, 113
Reid, V. S. (Vic) 71, 72, 73
revisionist theory 187, 188
revolt
  Akan slaves 103
  creole slaves 8, 103
  distinctions between eighteenth
    and nineteenth centuries
    102
  in the moment of 101, 137
  The Sociology of Slavery
    (Patterson) 100–1, 102
Rhodes Scholarship 64, 65
Riesman, David 140, 141, 144,
    146, 157, 235, 236
  Individualism Reconsidered 159
  influence of 158–9
  The Lonely Crowd 159, 236
  scholarship 209
Riesman, Evey 146
Rights of Passage (Brathwaite) 113,
    132
Rituals of Blood (Patterson) 201,
    208–15
  gender relations 209, 211–13
  interethnic relations 208
  internal problems 209
  soberness 208–9

INDEX

Roberts, George 57, 58, 65, 225
Robinson, Joyce 35
Rocky Point 29
Rodney, Walter 61, 62, 63, 63–4, 67, 68, 71, 88
  Black nationalism 127
  expulsion 128, 138, 139
  "A History of the Upper Guinea Coast" 127
  Nerys Patterson and chauvinism towards 127
  disapproves of OP's marriage to 126
  objects to speaking engagement 126–7
  Rastas
    involvement with 124, 125–6
    little interest in 126, 127
  Rodney riots 124–5, 125–6, 138, 139
  Waterloo conference 128
Rohlehr, Gordon 110–11, 112–13
Roman Empire 15–16
Romans 185
  freedom as power 196
Roosevelt University 139, 140
Robotham, Don 176
Rubin, Vera 60–1
Ruggles, Steven 211
"Rule Britannia" 190, 261n1
Ryan, William 148

Salkey, Andrew 72, 73, 108–9, 114
Sangster, Donald 124, 125, 256n3
Sartre, Jean-Paul 73, 74, 75–6, 205, 230, 231, 234
Savacou 133
Savanna-la-Mar, Westmoreland 23
Schapera, Isaac 65, 121, 122, 127
Schuck, Peter 202
Scott, Dennis 109, 254n4
Scott, James 100
Seaga, Edward 38, 125, 256n4
segregation 155

Selassie, Emperor Haile 79, 82, 85, 251–2n5
self-awareness 7–8
self-determination 9, 205, 208
Selvon, Samuel 72
Semmel, Bernard 193
Sen, Amartya 191, 192, 208
serfdom 200
shadow concept 160
Sharpe, Sam "Daddy" 102, 104, 194, 198, 226, 240, 264n8
Shearer, Hugh 124, 125, 126, 256n3
Shelby, Tommie 151–2
Sherlock, Philip 127
short stories 45, 74, 77
Simey, T. S. 59
Simões, René 220
Singapore 219
Singham, Archie 58, 62, 93, 249–50n5
Sisyphean idea 87
Six Cultures Study of Socialization 228, 229
Skinner, Quentin 197, 237–8, 239
Skrentny, John 156
The Slave Community (Blassingame) 187
slave community argument 187
slave-learning societies 3–4
slavery
  in Carolingian France 200
  catastrophic theory of 187
  classicists on 181, 182
  comparative study of 232–4
  concept of 231–2
  dominion studies of 234–5
  doulotic studies of 234–5
  freedom and *see* freedom and slavery; freedom from slavery
  general theory of 227
  internal trade in the US 188
  large-scale agricultural estates 15
  manumission 10, 186, 189
  nature of 13

279

INDEX

slavery (*cont.*)
  psychology of 94
  in Renaissance Italy 200
  Romans 185
  structure of natal alienation 184
  see also *The Sociology of Slavery*
    (Patterson)
Slavery (Elkins) 94
Slavery and Abolition 195
Slavery and Social Death
    (Patterson) 9, 12, 13, 70,
    149, 179–89, 227
  comparative slave study 180,
    183
  contract with Harvard Press 180
  slavery as an anomaly 185
slave(s)
  absence of custodial claims on
    children 188
  African 102–3, 104–5
  Akan 103
  American 180, 186, 189
  as a Black person 185
  claiming humanity 135
  creole *see* creole slave(s)
  cutting hair 185
  desire for independence 153–4
  disappearance of 188
  discovering humanity and
    rebellion 136
  folk culture 187
  French 200
  Greek 181, 182, 185, 192, 199
  Italian 200
  Jamaican *see* Jamaica: slavery
  kinlessness 185
  lives of 91–2
  male children sold 188
  origin of term 232
  as an outsider 184
  as revolutionaries 91, 94
  Roman 185
  as symbolically and socially dead
    184–5
Small, Hugh 129, 132

Small Axe 18
Smelser, Neil 181
Smith, Anthony 161
Smith, M. G. "MG" 54, 57, 60, 62,
    99, 172, 249n4
  anthropology 55–6, 58, 224
  differences and similarities with
    OP 225
  special advisor role 167
  split with left 178
  Technical Advisory Council 142
  tripartite view 98
Smith, R. T. 57, 58, 106, 224
Social and Economic Studies 101,
    180
social Darwinism 236
social death 9, 184, 186–7, 230–1,
    234
social integration 202
social policy 60
social psychology 95, 99
social realism 112
social relations 146
social sciences 58–64
social segregation 203
social theory 225
socialism 174, 175
sociology 58, 70, 96, 121, 146,
    202, 224–6
  American 70, 216, 225, 235
  critique of 225
  hypothetico-deductive reasoning
    235–6
  normal-science approach 235–6
  presentism 216, 221
  redefining of 144
  in the US and the UK 144
  see also historical sociology
The Sociology of Slavery (Patterson)
    8, 13, 22, 91–107, 226
  Brathwaite's review of 92, 114
  catastrophic view 98
  critique of sociology 225
  destructive experience of slavery
    95–6, 97

280

INDEX

dualistic societies 98–9
fragmented social order 98
lives of slaves 91–2
revolt 100–1, 102
Sam "Daddy" Sharpe 102, 104, 194
slave personality debate 99
social psychology of slavery 94
syncretisms 97
solidarity 156
Sophists 239
sovereignal freedom 15, 195
Spaulding, Anthony 168, 169–70
spiritual liberation 16
Stampp, Kenneth 96
Standard Cross-Cultural Sample 229
The Star 45–6, 77
state of nature 226
statistics 236
Stone, Carl 176–8
Stone, Rosie 177, 178
The Stranger (Camus) 5–6
strong woman–weaker man relationships 135
structural values 238–9
symbolic anthropology 183
symbolic interactionism 197–8
syncretic creole 106
syncretic creolization 104
systemic analysis 206–7
systemic reductionism 207
systemic violence 8

Tannenbaum, Frank 180, 186
Taylor, Leroy 129, 132
Technical Advisory Committee 142, 167
Tertullian 83–4
thick/thin identity 151–2
Thirteen Ways of Looking at a Black Man (Gates) 155
Thistlewood, Thomas 104, 105, 188
Thompson, E. P. 227

Thought and Change (Gellner) 145, 146
Time on the Cross (Fogel & Engerman) 187
Tiro, Marcus Tullius 4
Tivoli Gardens 168
TLS (*Times Literary Supplement*) 70, 73, 109, 111
Touareg people 184–5
Touré 204
Trench Town 43
Trump, Donald 215
Turner, Victor 183–4
Two Jamaicas (Curtin) 91

United States of America (USA)
  Black middle class 203
  police killings of Black people 214
  private segregation 203
  public integration 203
  White middle class 203
  see also Black America/Americans; White Americans
universality 7, 8, 9, 135
University College Hospital 51
University College of the West Indies (UCWI) 46, 48–53
  as a federal institution 52
  OP and
    history course, denied 50
    Jamaica Government Exhibition Scholarship 48
    reading economics 50–1, 57–8
    social sciences 58–64
  West Indian identity 52
University of the West Indies (UWI) 122, 127–8
  sabbatical 139, 141
  salary and atmosphere 123
  soldiers with guns 124–5, 125–6, 138, 139
  Walter Rodney affair 124–5, 125–6, 138, 139

281

INDEX

urban slums 106
USAID (United States Agency for International Development) 169

values 238–9
violence
in Jamaica 53–4, 107, 176, 178, 221, 222, 226
political justifications for 6
Virginia Assembly 189
Vogt, Evon Z. 229

Walcott, Derek 72
Walford, Leroy 48
Warning from the West Indies (Macmillan) 59
"Was Greek Civilization Based on Slave Labor?" (Finley) 181
Weber, Max 227, 229–30
Welfare and Planning in the West Indies (Simey) 59
West India Commission 59
West Indian fiction 72–6, 109
West Indian Social Survey (1947–9) 59, 65
West Indian Society for the Study of Social Issues 61, 63
West Indian Student Union 68, 69
West Indies 220
West Indies cricket team 40, 220–1
West Indies Federation 51–3, 248–9n5
collapse of 51
independence and 54
Westermark, Edward 227
Western civilization 13, 14, 17, 117, 162, 194, 240
White, Deborah 211

White, Noel "Sleptoe" 44–5, 46, 50, 248n2
White American liberalism 205
White Americans
attitudes on race 203
White as a category 165
White ethnic movement 149
White Jamaicans 59–60, 62, 65
White middle class 203
White supremacists 215
White ultra-right 215
The White Witch of Rosehall (de Lisser) 47, 138
White working class 215
Whiteman, Edgar 29, 44
Whiteness 165–6
Whiting, John W. 228, 229
Whiting, Roy 229
Who's Afraid of Post-Blackness? (Touré) 204, 205
Whyte, William 235
Williams, Aubrey 108, 109, 110
Williams, Eric 71, 72, 89, 91, 92, 240
Wilson, William Julius 213
Winship, Chris 236
Wittfogel, Karl 182
Wittgenstein, Ludwig 231
WLL (Worker's Liberation League) 175, 176
Woodson, Carter 96
Words and Things (Gellner) 231
The World of Odysseus (Finley) 181
Wynter, Hector 50, 248n4
Wynter, Sylvia 72, 120–1

Young Socialist League 129, 130
Young Socialists 129

Zola, Émile 74, 111

282